The Stewart Dynasty

The Stewart Dynasty

Stewart Ross

Thomas & Lochar

The bad end unhappily, the good unluckily.
That is what tragedy means.
– Tom Stoppard, *Rosencrantz and Guildenstern are Dead*.

British Library Cataloguing in Publication Data

Ross, Stewart.
  Stewart Dynasty
  I. Title II. Beer, Julie
  941.06

  ISBN 0 946537 92 5

Printed in Great Britain
by Redwood Books, Trowbridge
for Thomas & Lochar
PO Box 4, Nairn, IV12 4HU

Contents

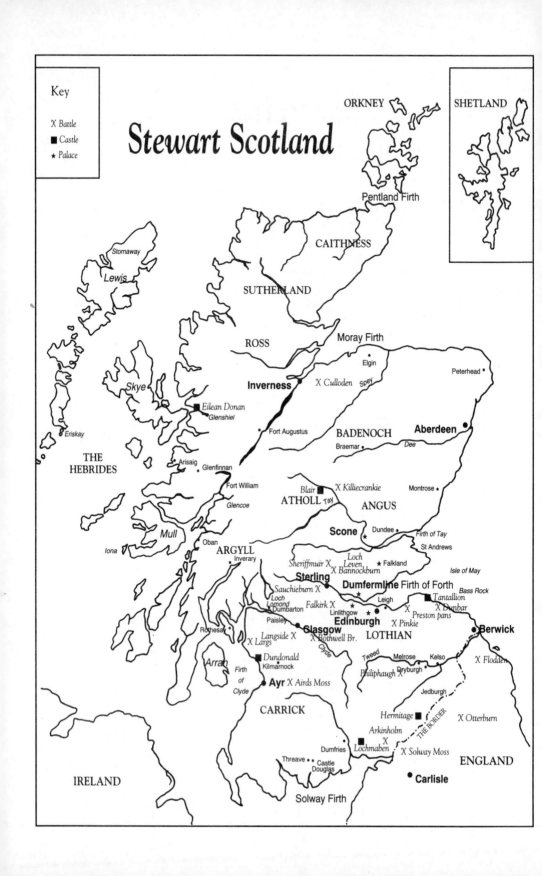

Preface and
Acknowledgements

As far as I am aware, it is now more than a century since anyone has published a complete history of the Stewarts. Since the appearance of Percy Thornton's *Stuart Dynasty* in 1890 the family has lost none of its fascination, but scholarly research has altered considerably our understanding of the drama's principal characters as well as the stages upon which they appeared. Like most history, therefore, this work is a fresh telling of a traditional tale.

Compiling a comprehensive yet readable new account of Britain's most influential family involves walking a number of tightropes. Firstly, this is no 'life and times' book – for the Stewarts that would be virtually a complete history of the British Isles from the twelfth to the nineteenth centuries. On the other hand, the Stewarts did not somehow float in socio-political space: their lives make sense only in the context of the world in which they lived. And since they were a major political family, much of their importance and interest lies in the influence they had on contemporary events. So this is neither a sonata nor a symphony, but a concerto in which the line of the principal instrument is enhanced by what is going on around it – life *within* times, rather than life *and* times.

The book's second aim is to present the history of a family rather than a string of self-contained biographies. For obvious reasons, we are obliged to follow the main stem of the family tree rather than pursue each branch to its tip, necessitating a chronological and biographical approach. Yet personal and historical continuity are patently evident within this framework: each member of the family was to a greater or lesser extent influenced by previous generations, and one of the more interesting discoveries made in the course of researching this book was the extent to which certain of the Stewarts' physical and psychological traits passed from generation to generation.

Finally, the text is intended to be both academically respectable and accessible to the general reader. The two qualities are by no means mutually exclusive, although sometimes they are believed to be so. Where practicable, particularly early on, original sources are the book's foundation. Where time and money (in practical terms indistinguishable) have rendered this impossible, the most reliable secondary material has been used. On four occasions, deliberately and quite obviously, I have indulged in a little 'faction'. The overall result, I hope, is a volume which will entertain as well as inform.

I am indebted to the work of countless scholars who have written on various aspects of Stewart history. The best thanks that can be offered them is to suggest that if the reader finds what follows in any way interesting, they should regard it merely as an *hors d'oeuvre* to the fuller works listed in the bibliography.

On a more personal note, I should like to thank Tabby Winnifrith for advice on aspects of the Stewarts' medical history, and all who read and corrected the manuscript at various stages of its preparation. I am particularly indebted to hawk-eyed Anne Roscorla and to my cousin Graeme, the perfect general reader, who ploughed through the jungle of an early draft with estimable equanimity. Numerous librarians have given me generous help, particularly those at the Kent County Library, Springfield, and at the University of Kent's Templeman Library. My thanks are also due to the Royal Bank of Scotland for allowing me the wherewithal to keep my family clothed, fed and housed during the writing of this book, and to David St John Thomas for rescuing the work after the unhappy collapse of its original publisher.

Without doubt, for her perceptive comment, tolerance and invaluable assistance, my deepest debt is to my wife Lucy, to whom this book is most affectionately dedicated.

Note: Stewart/Stuart

The descendants of Walter Fitz Alan acquired the family name 'Stewart' from their position as hereditary stewards of Scotland. Mary Queen of Scots and her cousin-husband Henry, Lord Darnley, frequently employed the French variation of their surname – 'Stuart' – and from the time of their son this is the name by which the family is generally recognised, particularly outside Scotland. To avoid confusion, however, throughout the book the dynasty in general is referred to as Stewart, while individual members of the family are given the surname by which they were normally known to their contemporaries. Thus, for example, Robert III is Robert Stewart and Charles II is Charles Stuart, although both belong to the Stewart dynasty.

Part I

Dapifers
and
Stewards

CHAPTER 1

Full Circle

In the late morning of 29 September 1746 two warships quietly dropped anchor in the sheltered reaches off Roscoff in northern Brittany.

L'Heureux and *Le Prince de Conti* were privateers based at St Malo. There was nothing unusual about the presence of such vessels in Breton ports at this time. Many local captains had taken advantage of the Anglo-French hostilities of the past six years to hoist the colours of the House of Bourbon and plunder the rich merchant shipping of the north Atlantic.

In normal circumstances the appearance of privateers would have interested only businessmen keen to bargain for the booty in the ships' holds, or to chandlers and victuallers seeking profitable contracts to repair, refit and resupply the craft for further voyages. But from the behaviour of Roscoff's citizens it was clear that there was something different about *L'Heureux* and *Le Prince de Conti*.

Within minutes of the ships being sighted a lively crowd had collected on the quay. People were talking loudly, staring out to sea and pointing. Seafaring men scanning the vessels' decks with their telescopes were soon surrounded by knots of agitated listeners. Eager to be the first with any news, they urged the watchers to sharpen their focus and look more closely. Garbled snatches of information were shouted back to friends marooned on the edges of the crowd.

The warships riding at anchor about five hundred metres from the shore were well known to the townspeople jostling together on the cobbled jetty. They were aware, for example, that *L'Heureux* was not commanded by a French captain but by an Irishman, Colonel Warren. And it was rumoured that the ship's mission had been the most important she had ever undertaken. Local sages told anyone prepared to listen that upon its success hung the fate of one of the leading families in Europe. And, conceivably, even of the war itself.

The narrow eyes of the telescopes revealed the crew of *L'Heureux* going about the routine tasks following a long sea voyage. Men were rolling and stowing the sails, tidying thick brown sheets and heaving barrels of rubbish over the side. They then made ready to lower a small rowing boat.

Of greater interest to the people of Roscoff was the presence of a tall, dark figure plainly visible pacing about the deck amid all the activity. Now and again he paused to talk to the sailors. They stood to attention as he addressed them. When all was ready, he was seen to bid a warm farewell to Colonel Warren and his crew, and climb nimbly down a ladder into the cockboat bobbing alongside.

A thrill of expectation ran through the onlookers.

As the tender eased away from the steep barnacled side of *L'Heureux*, the sound of cheering drifted across the waters from the men lining the rails of both warships. The distinguished-looking stranger, now seated in the stern of the cockboat, turned and waved heartily back. The acknowledgement drew forth even louder acclamations.

The spectators were impressed. Exchanging encouraging glances with each other, they bade their lookouts redouble their efforts.

Suddenly the stillness was rent by the noise of gunfire. All around the harbour gulls rose screaming into the autumn air. Twenty-one times the ships' cannon fired in honour of the departing passenger, clearly a man of consequence.

The salute produced an instant reaction among the men and women gathered on the quay. Some took up the cheering of the sailors. Others broke into excited, rapid conversation about the meaning of the news. Their suspicions had been confirmed. *L'Heureux* had accomplished her mission successfully and the town must be made ready. Tonight they would be entertaining royalty.

Prince Charles Edward Stuart had been saved.

* * *

The twenty-five year old prince who stepped ashore at Roscoff that dank morning was the last of the Stewarts to feature prominently in European affairs. In fact, although he was unaware of it at the time, the adventure from which he had just returned was his family's final political act of any significance. He had escaped with his life, but little else. He had no crown, no kingdom, no money, and precious few supporters prepared to back him with more than sympathetic rhetoric. In short, it was soon apparent that the cause of the exiled Stewarts was lost for ever.

From Roscoff Charles made his way swiftly to Versailles, where he was well received by his patron, Louis XV. We do not know the exact route taken by the prince, but he is likely to have travelled to Morlaix then due east through Guingamp and St Brieuc to Lamballe. Here the road divides. The southern route, most probably followed by Charles, passes through Rennes and Le Mans before turning north-east towards Chartres and the capital.

Had Charles borne right at Lamballe, however, shortly after Dinan he would have passed through the ancient Breton town of Dol. If this was the road he followed, then the man responsible for the final extinction of Stewart ambitions would have passed through the very spot where, some six centuries previously, those ambitions had first been kindled. From Dark-Age anonymity, through majesty and power, and back now almost to oblivion, the cruel wheel of Stewart fortunes had turned full circle.

Riding through the green countryside of Brittany, Bonnie Prince Charlie had come home.

THE CATHEDRAL OF ST SAMSON, DOL-DE-BRETAGNE

CHAPTER 2

The Dapifers of Dol

I

The picturesque town of Dol-de-Bretagne is a proudly independent marsh capital lying about seven kilometres inland between Mont St Michel and St Malo. To the north the land falls away steeply into the Marais de Dol, a broad sweep of low-lying land reclaimed from the sea in the Middle Ages. The only relief amid the monotonous lattice of dykes and boulders is Mont Dol, a great volcanic blister standing a short distance to the north of Dol, upon whose summit in a more credulous age Satan is said to have battled with St Michael.

Today, as at the time of the Bonnie Prince, Dol is dominated by a huge granite cathedral. Dedicated to St Samson and more like a fortress than a house of God, it was begun in the thirteenth century to replace the building destroyed by English troops. However, this ancient and imposing building was not even a master-builder's dream when the first Stewart ancestors emerged from their obscure Celtic past. We need to turn instead to broad avenue some 100 metres south of the cathederal – the Grande Rue-des-Stuarts.

House number 17 in this busy street, appropriately named the Maison des Plaids, is probably the oldest building in Dol. Erected during the eleventh century and still boasting some fine Romanesque arcades, so grand a secular building must have been constructed by a local dignitary of wealth and standing. There is no way of telling who that person was, although we do have the names of several magnates who might have commissioned these graceful arches. One of those neo-Celtic lords, though by no means the greatest, was 'Fledaldi senescali', or Flaald the Seneschal, the earliest known member of the Stewart dynasty.

* * *

Eleventh-century Brittany was a turbulent region. In pre-Roman times it had been settled by Brythons, a Celtic tribe whose name endures in the British Isles as well as the rugged peninsular of north-western France. In the succeeding centuries the Celts faced a series of invaders – Roman, Frankish,

Viking and Norman – as well as a fresh wave of Celtic immigrants from Britain at the time of the Anglo-Saxon incursions. Once an independent kingdom, by about 1050 the Duchy (or County) of Brittany had become a dependency of the dukes of neighbouring Normandy, and many Bretons accompanied William the Conqueror on his invasion of England in 1066.

Along with numerous other ancient families of north-western Europe, the Dukes of Brittany claimed descent from the legendary King Arthur. In about 1000 AD a cadet branch of the ducal family was headed by Hamon, Vicomte de Dinan, a town some twenty-five kilometres south-west of Dol. Hamon had at least four sons. The most successful was Junkeneus, Archbishop of Dol and a powerful influence at the Breton court. Showing a laudable sense of fraternal solidarity, he used his wealth and contacts to further the careers of his brothers, Hamon, Rhiwallon (Lord of Dol and Combourg) and Josselin (Vicomte de Dinan). For Rhiwallon he built a substantial castle at Comburg, seventeen kilometres south of Dol. The building still stands, the heavy masonry of the original fortress clearly visible against the lighter and more sophisticated work of later additions. The florist's shop in Dol may be another of Junkeneus' monuments.

* * *

Where Flaald the seneschal fits into the picture we are not quite sure. He crops up as witnessing one of Rhiwallon's charters some time between 1032 and 1064, and he had a younger brother named Haton, who himself was witness to a charter dated between 1065 and 1070. Flaald may have been Rhiwallon's brother or nephew, in which case he would have been well-born. But this is conjecture. Unless new evidence comes to light it is probably safer to assume that the obscure founder of the Stewart dynasty was the lord of Dol's trusted follower rather than his relation.

The only insight we have into Flaald's character comes from his position. The Germanic word 'seneschal' means literally 'old servant' – the most trusted and experienced of his lord's retainers – and is interchangeable with 'dapifer', the title given to Flaald's son and his successors. 'Dapifer' derives from the Latin 'daps' (food) and 'fer-' (bearing), meaning 'the one who brings food to the table'.

Flaald was no humble waiter. The formal meal was at the heart of the strict ritual of a medieval household, and only the most valued retainer was entrusted with laying comestibles before his lord. After all, standing behind his master's undefended back he had a fine opportunity for eavesdropping, and even for assassination or the administration of poison. In a Christian society there was also an obvious parallel between his task and that of the priest who brought the Bread of Life to worshippers at mass. Furthermore, the dapifer had to see that all food was of good quality, well prepared and presented in a punctual and becoming manner. In other words, if he was to do his job properly he had to have control over most of the other branches of the household, including the finances.

By Flaald's time the dapifership had become hereditary and partly honorary in some households. This had happened at Dol, which is why the title would have been suitable for Flaald even if he were related to his over-lord. Whatever his background, Flaald would have received what was still principally an administrative position in a relatively small household only if he had at least some of the right qualities: trustworthiness, loyalty, efficiency and authority. He was almost certainly literate, too, with a good head for figures.

Flaald's character was the rock on which his family fortunes were raised. It was his invaluable bequest to future generations, worth far more than land or title, and the principal reason for the dynasty's rise to prominence. Like an hereditary birthmark, the seneschal's staunch personality was repeated in most of his immediate descendants; only in his grandson and, three genera-tions later, in Alan the Steward does one catch a glimpse of the attractive yet fatal irresponsibility which distinguished some of the later Stewarts.

II

By 1080 Flaald had been succeeded in his post at Dol by his son Alan ('Alanus filius Flaadi'), who in turn passed on the title to another Alan, the eldest of his three sons. First mentioned in Brittany in about 1095, Alan II did not enjoy his dapifership for long. At Clermont in November 1095 Pope Urban II called for a crusade to drive the infidel from the Holy Land. Bishop Baudri of Dol was present when the appeal was made, so it is not surprising that his Breton neighbour Alan, 'dapifer Dolensis', was among the first to volunteer. Like many ambitious young men who took the cross, he died on foreign soil.

The fact that Alan fought as a knight and not as a common footsoldier suggests wealth and social standing. The knight was the lynch pin of a mili-taristic society, a costly piece of military equipment which only well-to-do families could provide. To have gone on crusade, the dapifer must have had estates capable of furnishing him with enough cash to fit him out, as well as pay for retainers, transport and supplies.

Alan had two younger brothers, Rhiwallon and Flaald. Since Rhiwallon was a monk at the abbey of St Florent de Samur near Dol, Flaald inherited the dead crusader's title and estates. Flaald II is scarcely more distinct than the other faceless dapifers, yet he played a crucial role in Stewart fortunes. Having attached himself to the rising star of Henry, third son of William the Conqueror, he made the auspicious move from Dol to Britain, where the future of the Stewart dynasty lay.

King William the Conqueror had died in 1087, leaving the Duchy of Normandy to Robert, his easy-going eldest son. William Rufus, who inherited more of his father's toughness of purpose, had taken over the English crown as William II. Henry, the youngest, ablest and least scrupulous of the three brothers, had received no land but 5000 pounds of silver. This he had used to buy Cotentin and Avranchin, immediately to the north-east of Brittany, from his brother Robert.

There was bitter feuding between the three brothers throughout the 1090s. Unable to challenge Duke Robert and King William openly, Henry bided his time, acquiring a reputation as a competent if somewhat unrelenting administrator and building up a loyal following among the lords of north-west France. Eventually, in 1100 he saw his chance to bid for real power. Duke Robert was still making his way back from the Holy Land when on 2 August William II was killed in mysterious circumstances while hunting in the New Forest. Henry immediately seized the royal treasury at Winchester. On 3 August he had himself proclaimed king, and he was crowned at Westminster two days later.

The coup did not go unchallenged. In 1101 the tyrannical Robert of Belleme, seeking a more amenable overlord, led a revolt of English barons against the new king. In return for considerable annual payments, Henry persuaded Duke Robert to let him keep the English crown, thereby freeing himself to tackle the rebels. In 1102 he cornered the Lord of Belleme in his castle at Shrewsbury, compelled him to surrender and then banished him to Normandy. The earldom of Shrewsbury was abolished and Robert's property, including the lordship of Arundel and extensive lands on the Welsh marches, was handed out among Henry's loyal supporters.

Henry's Breton allies were among the chief beneficiaries of the redistribution of lands which followed his accession. If we believe the prejudiced comments of William of Malmesbury, the Bretons were far from popular. 'Regardless of right and affinity', he complained, 'they decline not even civil war, provided they are paid for it…'. The testy chronicler goes on to note that Henry I had been quick to recognise this mercenary trait and turn it to his own advantage. He 'used to lavish money on these Bretons, thereby hiring the faith of a faithless nation'. Perhaps successful immigrants are not popular in any generation. But there was no way that Henry's Breton friends, the dapifers of Dol included, were going to allow native prejudice to stand in the way of their rocketing upward mobility.

Henry certainly knew Flaald II, who crossed the Channel on at least one occasion. In 1101-2 he was present with William, Lord of Monmouth (and grandson of Rhiwallon, Count of Dol), at the dedication of Monmouth Priory. Flaald probably died shortly after this and it was his son Alan III who benefited most from Henry's patronage. By about 1116 he was a substantial English landholder. Sometime sheriff of Shropshire and possessing 70 manors in the county, he was known locally as Lord of Clun and Oswestry. It was crucial for the king that the strategically important Welsh marches were in the hands of competent servants he could trust implicitly. Alan Fitz Flaald was clearly such a man.

At some stage in his career Alan married Avelina de Hesdin, a wealthy heiress whose father had been a previous sheriff of Shropshire and master of widespread property in England and France. To the Fitz Flaald lands along the Welsh border the union added estates in ten English counties, particularly in Norfolk and around Arundel and Chichester in Sussex. So powerful a marriage could have been made only with the king's consent, and is another indication of the high esteem in which Alan was held. As a gesture of thanksgiving for his remarkable good fortune and showing a touching loyalty to the family's religious traditions, Alan founded a cell of St Florent at Sporle in Norfolk.

III

The remote village of Clun, now the refuge of hill farmers and retired schoolmasters, is chiefly remembered for the reference in A.E. Houseman's 'A Shropshire Lad':

> 'Clunton and Clunbury,
> Clungunford and Clun
> Are the quietest places
> Under the sun.'

According to legend the rhyme dates from long before Houseman's time, and the adjective originally applied to the settlement was not 'quietest' but 'drunkenest' or 'wickedest'. Either of these would have been a more appropriate epithet when Alan Fitz Flaald was lord of those parts.

At both Clun and Oswestry the remains of huge Norman motte and bailey castles remind us that in the early Middle Ages the frontier between England and Wales witnessed an almost continual dialectic of raid and counter-raid, which threatened to gather without warning into full-scale military operations. Built by Robert de Say shortly after the Norman Conquest, by the twelfth century the Clun stronghold had become the first known British base of the Fitz Flaalds.

* * *

Alan Fitz Flaald, Lord of Oswestry, had three sons. Upon his death some time before 1121 the family titles and properties were divided between them. Jordan, the eldest, inherited the dapifership of Dol and estates in Brittany. William Fitz Alan, the second son, became the new lord of Oswestry; following his father's example of advancement through marriage, he proceeded to establish the powerful Fitz Alan dynasty of the Earls and Dukes of Arundel. Walter, the third son, came off worst. He was left with only

CLUN CASTLE

Manhood in the vicinity of Chichester, Cound in Shropshire, and North Stoke near Arundel, which he held from his eldest brother.

When Walter came of age in about 1130 and took stock of his position, he was faced with a number of difficult decisions. To judge by his subsequent behaviour he was both ambitious and able. But since he had no power base of his own, those qualities were not enough. To one of his social standing, commerce was out of the question. That left three possible courses of advancement open to him. Like Junkeneus, he could join the church and try to work his way up the ecclesiastical hierarchy. If that path did not suit him, which obviously it did not, then, as his brother William was to do, he might seek out a well-endowed widow or heiress prepared to merge her family fortunes with his. Either Walter failed to encounter such a bride or, more likely, no woman of substance was prepared to join him in what would have been a rather one-sided union. That left him with only one viable option. He had to attach himself to a feudal superior who was prepared to recognise and reward his talents.

The situation in England was looking ominous. Having taken all the precautions he could to ensure his daughter Matilda's unchallenged accession, Henry I died in 1135. But when his nephew, Stephen of Blois, outmanoeuvred Matilda and seized the crown for himself, conflict between the two parties was certain.

Political instability might have been turned to advantage by a poorly endowed knight prepared to play fast and loose with his allegiance. But this sort of behaviour did not appeal to the Fitz Alans, whose hallmark was loyalty. Besides, as William Fitz Alan's career demonstrated, participation in the feuding between Stephen and Matilda was a dangerous game. When after a year or two's vacillation William joined King Stephen, he came close to losing all that his family had gained in England over the last fifty years. Besieged in Shrewsbury Castle by the king, he made a daring escape and fled abroad, forfeiting all his lands. His uncle, Arnulf of Hesdin, chose to fight on and was hanged when the castle eventually fell. Only several years later, after Stephen and Matilda had agreed to settle their differences, did William get his inheritance back.

Long before all this Walter had been compelled to make up his mind about what he was going to do. During the winter of 1135-6 he had spent many long hours beside the fire with his brother, discussing the uncertain political situation and what bearing it had on his future. By January he could delay no longer. He had received an offer from one of the most successful monarchs of his generation. David, the perspicacious King of Scotland, had invited Walter to join him.

David's proposal was an attractive opportunity for a young and little-known knight without fortune or estate. Yet in southern eyes twelfth-century Scotland was a poor and barbaric country, not an obvious place in which to seek one's fortune. The youngest of the Fitz Alans was a cautious man too, loath to take unnecessary risks. For once, however, Walter chose to gamble. During the spring of 1136, as life was returning to the rolling Shropshire countryside, he too was preparing for a fresh start. He had decided to make Scotland his home.

History was to justify Walter's move unequivocally. Neither he nor King David ever had cause to regret their decisions. Almost at once they struck up a relationship beneficial to them both and to their successors. The northern kingdom gained a line of loyal and extremely capable stewards, and Walter set his family on a course which was to carry it higher and further than he could ever have imagined possible.

IV

In the fullness of time the truth about the Stewarts' obscure Celtic origins was lost and replaced by a more glamorous descent. The rise of the hard-headed but somewhat prosaic dapifers of Dol was superseded by an improved family history, at the heart of which lay the plausible but wholly inaccurate 'Banquo myth'.

Shakespeare's *Macbeth*, written in 1606, contains references clearly intended to flatter Scotland's James VI, who in 1603 had ascended the English throne as James I. James was the most recent in a long line of Stewarts to wear the crown of Scotland. In the later middle ages a number of stories had been concocted to demonstrate that the Scottish royal house boasted a pedigree second to none. Such invention was the product of the budding nationalism spawned by the wars with England rather than any attempt at cosmetic genealogy on the part of the Stewarts, whose surname made no mystery of their humble origins.

Shakespeare has his witches revealing to Banquo:

'Thou shalt get kings, though thou be none.'

The prophesy persuades Macbeth to have Banquo and his son Fleance murdered. But Fleance escapes, causing Macbeth to visit the witches once more to ask:

'Shall Banquo's issue ever

Reign in this kingdom?'

The answer is given in a procession of eight kings (the Stewart monarchs of Scotland before James VI), headed by Banquo. The last spectre holds a mirror in his hand, presumably so that James VI, sitting in the audience, could see himself as the latest in the long line of Banquo's illustrious descendants.

When we mention that Flaald's name was subject to a variety of spellings, including Flahault, it soon becomes obvious what had happened. Unsure of the Stewarts' true origins, through guile or ignorance Scottish chroniclers had confused Flaald with Fleance, son of Banquo and Thane of Lochquhaber. The story came to Shakespeare via Holinshed, Boece and John Barbour. The latter's *Stewartis Original*, which probably first set out the Fleance story, is unfortunately now lost. Barbour believed that Banquo's family, and hence the Stewarts, could be traced back to Ninus, the supposed founder of Nineveh. (Another even more far-fetched genealogy was offered to Pope Bonniface VIII by Baldred Bisset when pleading Scotland's case for papal support against England: the Scots could trace their ancestry back to Scota, the daughter of the Pharaoh ruling Egypt at the time of Moses, who had been responsible for bringing the Stone of Scone – Jacob's pillow – to Scotland!)

It took quite some time for hard fact to be revealed beneath these layers of fanciful yet harmless supposition. Even Sir Walter Scott was not quite sure where the truth lay:

'It is said, that the Stewarts were descended from Fleance, the son of Bancho, whose posterity the witches declared were to be kings of Scotland, and who was murdered by Macbeth. But this seems a very doubtful tradition.' (*Tales of a Grandfather*)

Any remaining confusion about the origin of the Stewarts was removed at the beginning of the twentieth century. Step by step the thin and twisting thread of family history was followed back over the border to the Welsh March and thence to Brittany and Dol itself. Superstition and mysterious Biblical references were stripped away. What remains, though not so alluring, at least has the benefit of being true. The earliest Stewarts owed their success not to witchcraft but to a potent mix of diligence and reliability, spiced with a pinch of good fortune. Happily for them, the recipe remained in the family for many generations to come.

CHAPTER 3

'At the Very Edge of the Inhabited World'

I

In 1320 a number of influential Scots (including Walter Fitz Alan's great-great-great grandson) wrote to Pope John XXII describing their homeland as 'the tiny country of Scotia lying at the very edge of the inhabited world'. It was a deliberately pathetic piece of propaganda, designed to pluck at the papal heartstrings. Nevertheless, there was an element of truth beneath the litotes.

In the Dark Ages Iona and Whithorn had ranked among the more important religious and cultural centres in north-west Europe. Subsequent Norse invasion destroyed much of this achievement, but still left Scotland linked to the wider Viking world. It was only when the Scandinavian tide began to withdraw in the eleventh century that Scotland found herself marooned on the fringe of European affairs.

Beset by continual and debilitating internal wrangling, the kingdom emerged as a viable political entity when it acquired Lothian from the Northumbrians after the Scots' decisive victory at Carham-on-Tweed in 1018. Following the troubled reigns of Duncan (1034-40) and Macbeth (1040-57), the throne passed to Malcolm Canmore. Malcolm, whose sobriquet means 'Big Head' or, more politely, 'Great Chief', survived until he was killed by the English in 1093.

Canmore's relations with the new Norman power to the south were rarely cordial. He infuriated the Conqueror by marrying Margaret, sister of the exiled Saxon heir to the English throne, Edward Atheling. On five separate occasions Malcolm raided northern England, provoking savage reprisals. Indeed, his cross-border foray of 1091 achieved what might have been thought impossible: unity between the three sons of William I. They swept north, overwhelmed Malcolm and forced him to do homage to the English king.

Although the Scottish military threat was never particularly serious, it was a constant irritant to Norman monarchs preoccupied with continental ambitions. In 1100, therefore, only three months after his coronation, Henry I played a card absent from Rufus' homosexual hand: he married one of Canmore's daughters, Matilda. The young queen lived at the court of Henry I with her youngest brother David, then aged about sixteen.

The children of Malcolm Canmore and Queen Margaret had lived in exile in England since their father's death. Prince David spent at least twenty years soaking up the cosmopolitan, feudal atmosphere of his brother-in-law's Anglo-Norman household, where he 'grew up, trained among the boys of the household'. An intelligent and able young man, whose reserved personality contrasted sharply with that of his rapacious overlord, he probably accompanied Henry I during his campaign to conquer Normandy, concluded successfully at the battle of Tinchbrai in 1106. It was about this time that David first became acquainted with the baronial families from Brittany who later featured so strongly in his plans for Scotland.

Malcolm Canmore's death had led, almost inevitably, to bitter squabbling over the succession. The dead king's sexagenarian brother Donald III seized the crown in 1093. Deposed briefly by his nephew Duncan II, the old man managed to claw his way back to power for a further three years before he was finally deposed, blinded and imprisoned for what was left of his life. Three of Canmore's sons by Queen Margaret then ruled in succession. The first two – Edgar (1097-1107) and Alexander I (1107-24) – left no legitimate offspring, so upon Alexander's death the crown passed to the forty-four-year-old David.

Like his patron Henry I, David had been virtually landless during the early part of his life. The situation had changed nominally in 1107 when for some reason his brother King Edgar had bequeathed him much of the southern part of his kingdom, including lower Lothian, Strathclyde and Teviotdale. Alexander I had been understandably reluctant to share his inheritance and had clung on to David's estates until threats of military action forced him to release them in about 1113.

Within a year of this, David's fortunes had taken another turn for the better when Henry I had given him the hand of Matilda, a well-connected and extremely well-endowed English heiress. The lady was a daughter of Earl Waltheof of Northumbria and had been previously married to the powerful Simon de Senlis. Through union with her David acquired an English earldom, wide estates in the east Midlands and a claim on Northumberland. He also had access to a pool of ambitious and land-hungry Anglo-Norman knights. The arrangement had only one drawback: David held his English fiefs directly from King Henry, whose feudal subordinate for those lands he now became.

II

The kingdom which David inherited in 1124 was still relatively isolated from the mainstream of Western European developments. This is not necessarily a qualitative judgement, but to David's way of thinking, after what he had seen and heard further south, Scotland was quaintly old-fashioned. In striving to bring church and state more into line with Continental practice, he believed he was not only making his own lot easier but also doing what was right by his subjects. Walter Fitz Alan was patronised in the knowledge that he would help in the enterprise.

David's subjects numbered around 500,000, mostly dwelling in tiny, widely scattered agricultural or pastoral communities. All but the wealthy lived in rough huts of wood or stone which they shared with their livestock. The life of the ordinary countryman, particularly the landless serf, was dreich, painful and brief. Nevertheless, apart from the obvious climatic hardships, the average peasant in medieval Scotland probably had to endure no tougher lot than that of his counterpart in Shropshire or the Cotentin. In fact, given the late and imperfect nature of Scottish feudalism and the traditional rugged independence of upland folk, many of David's more lowly subjects probably led less restricted lives than people of the south.

Large tracts of the Scottish countryside – not necessarily heavily wooded – were termed forest, meaning they were set aside for hunting and grazing. One of the broadest of these regions, known simply as The Forest, embraced the vales of Yarrow and Ettrick. The kingdom had no fixed capital, and such towns as there were would today scarcely rate as more than villages. The resources available to the king were a good deal less than those of his English counterpart. Until David's reign the country did not even mint its own coinage.

As far as David was concerned, more worrying than Scotland's comparative poverty was the strength of the centrifugal forces continually threatening to pull the kingdom apart. Nationalism was a sentiment unknown before the thirteenth century, and the diversity of Scotland's population is suggested in the number of languages then in current use: English and Cumbric in the south, Gaelic and Old Norse in the north and west, with French advancing as the fashionable tongue of court and aristocracy. The people of Lothian had more in common with Northumbrians than with Highlanders, and until the middle of the thirteenth century the isles of the north and west belonged to the Kingdom of Norway.

The presence of the universal Roman Catholic church helped foster unity. But much still depended upon the person of the king, whose task resembled that of the driver of an unwieldy chariot harnessed to an ill-assorted team of powerful, headstrong horses. Each animal was just as liable to make off in its own direction as to pull with the others. Too gentle a hand on the reins or an over zealous application of the whip, and the whole operation could get completely out of control.

It was not essential for the king to be a warrior, but he needed good health and immense physical stamina. The court was peripatetic, which allowed the crown's more influential subjects once in a while to see the king in person to seek justice or beg a favour. Constant travelling also enabled him to keep in contact with the more remote regions, such as Galloway and the Highlands, where his authority was constantly being undermined by local chiefs.

A monarch who took the Scottish throne in the hope of leading a life of luxurious ease did not last long. The price of survival was eternal vigilance, tact and accessibility.

III

No country, least of all Scotland, was ever embraced by a uniform feudal 'system'. Geography, tradition and sheer human bloody-mindedness saw to that. But the feudal idea served for a while to bring a degree of order and stability to the principalities of medieval Europe. It bound men one to another with webs of allegiance and duty, helped to clarify precisely who held what land, and kept in check the anarchic tendencies always present in a society whose leaders were permanently on a war footing.

Drawing on his extensive experience in Normandy, England and southern Scotland, David initiated what became a feudal revolution in the Scottish state. Displaying a wise sensitivity, he began cautiously and tactfully. Many Scots considered their new king an alien and treated him with suspicion or even hostility. For David to have swept north and announced to his bemused Scottish subjects that henceforward they were to accept feudal customs and law would have been to court inevitable disaster. Even in the next century the Barnwell chronicler wryly observed: 'Scotland's more recent kings regard themselves as French in race, speech and customs, and only people of similar background are welcome in their households'.

What David performed was a neat balancing act. However distasteful it might have been to him personally, he began on the right foot by accepting the semi-pagan ceremony by which Scottish kings had traditionally been inaugurated. He did not make a clean sweep of the household but retained the Gaelic-speaking Aelfwine Mac Archil in the sensitive post of 'divider of food' ('rannaire') and another man of Celtic stock as door-keeper (or doorward, whence the Durward family). As long as they were loyal, he respected the titles and estates of established landholders, particularly the earls of the north. By and large these measures were sufficient to calm the fears of traditionalists, leaving the king free to get on with more important matters.

Because he was an outsider, David needed support. He achieved this by welcoming to Scotland a number of barons, knights, freemen and merchants who shared his outlook, rewarding them with privileges and land. Foremost among these immigrants were representatives of three powerful Anglo-French families. Like the dapifers of Dol, the de Brus family from Brix on the Cotentin peninsular had sided with Henry I before his accession to the English throne. Shortly after 1100 they were rewarded with land in Yorkshire. Less than a quarter of a century later some of family moved still further north when Robert de Brus received Annandale from David King of Scots.

At about the same time another of David's Anglo-Norman cronies, Hugh de Moreville, one of the king's Midland barons, was given estates in the border country around Lauderdale and the Tweed valley. The third loyal follower from south of the border to benefit greatly from David's Scottish patronage was Walter Fitz Alan.

* * *

David's astute kingship drew fulsome praise from both Scots and Englishmen alike. To a culture steeped in Old Testament mythology his very name was believed auspicious. Writing after the king's death, the English prior John of Hexham was no doubt influenced by his Christian education when he generously admitted of David: 'In our time there has been no prince like him'. Prior John's admiration was all the greater because of his traditional anti-Scottish prejudice, which is evident in the highest compliment he was able to pay his subject: 'His wisdom enabled him to temper the ferocity even of his barbarous kingdom'. Dr Johnson was by no means the first Englishman to believe that the breeze of civilisation failed to clear the barren peaks of the Southern Uplands.

We know precious little personal detail about King David. He was morally scrupulous, more than conventionally pious, unusually conscientious in his approach to the task of governing his realm, and generous to all he thought deserving. In his youth he learned the art of soldiering and showed sufficient intelligence to be appointed a justice by Henry I. In later life he was a keen gardener. The only known pictorial representation of him is within the initial capital M of the charter granted to Kelso Abbey. Encircled by weird serpent-like creatures which twist and stretch to form the letter itself, the grey-haired and spindly-legged king sits on some sort of plain throne, staring earnestly before him. In his hands he holds a sword and what looks like a small orb – marks of his authority – while on his head rests a heavy jewelled crown.

To support this conventional vignette we have a complementary literary description of a king who was prepared to give up the exhilarating relaxation of a day's hunting to see that justice was maintained:

'Wherever he happened to be…, David made it his custom to sit for some time at the entrance to the royal hall. Here the poor and elderly who sought redress of their grievances were summoned before him… to state their case. The king was at great pains… to ensure that each case was concluded to the satisfaction of all parties.'

This flattering passage, like another which relates how the Christ-like David 'often washed the feet of the poor', cannot be taken at face value. But the good sense in much that the king did, the numerous references to his worthiness and the memorable image in the Kelso charter produce an imposing testimony to an outstanding man.

It is worth speculating briefly on David's character because of the light it throws on his future steward. Walter owed everything to David, which guaranteed his loyalty. He had just the right background, too: his Celtic ancestry facilitated his acceptance in western Scotland, and during his years in the unstable Welsh marches he had gained experience in policing frontier territory. David was quick to make use of this knowledge. The problems associated with Walter's fiefs around Strathgryfe, at the heart of the old Kingdom of Strathclyde and crucial to Scotland's western defences, were similar to those of the Fitz Alan lands in Shropshire.

We have no way of telling what passed between the two men before Walter decided to move to Scotland. It is unlikely that someone as cautious as Walter would have gone north without a guarantee that it would be worth his while. Presumably, too, he made at least one reconnaissance trip into Scotland before taking the irretrievable step of translating his household there.

Respect between knight and king was mutual. Walter was drawn not just by the offer of Scottish titles and lands, but by his new lord's wisdom and sense of justice. David was a good judge of character, too. He would not have rewarded a desperado, a restless younger son with little to offer but the physical stamina and attractive braggadocio of youth. The exceptional King of Scots wanted by his side exceptional councillors.

CHAPTER 4

'Our Intimate Friend'

I

Walter Fitz Alan was in his mid-twenties when he accepted the lordship of King David and moved to Scotland. It is alluring to imagine him wending his lonely way northward through the grey-green scrub of the border hills, like a legendary young knight from the court of King Arthur on a quest for fame and fortune in a foreign land. The reality, unfortunately, was rather more prosaic.

As a member of an established and respected baronial family, Walter would have been accompanied by members of his household as well as wagonloads of what the insurance business would term 'personal effects' – armour, weapons, clothing, bedding, furniture, tapestries, papers and the like. He probably travelled at least some of the way by sea, at that time by far the quickest and most convenient way to transport heavy goods. Furthermore, Walter would not have thought of Scotland as a 'foreign country' in the modern sense. The twelfth-century political frontier between Northumberland and Lothian was as ill-defined as the geographical one, and Walter belonged to a French-speaking Anglo-Norman aristocracy loyal to their feudal superior, not to a particular state.

The first record of Walter in Scotland was witnessing a royal charter granted to Melrose Abbey in 1136. Already in the king's trust, shortly afterwards he began to accumulate the widespread estates which became the foundation of Stewart power. David took care not to give any individual a consolidated territorial power base which might develop into a petty kingdom of its own, and he bestowed on Walter three scattered clusters of fiefs in Renfrewshire, territory further south and west, and Lanarkshire.

Walter's headquarters were at Renfrew, where he was given the royal castle, an ungainly wooden structure raised on a huge inverted flowerpot of earth known as a motte. In an unusual mark of royal favour, he was also granted the borough of Renfrew. As a general rule the king kept all such towns for himself, for they were virtually his sole source of monetary income. Walter's other holdings in that part of the country included Paisley, Pollok and Prestwick.

Fiefs to the south and west of Renfrew, in what had been the old Kingdom of Strathclyde, were entrusted to Walter for strategic reasons. They formed part of a chain of loyal estates around the rebellious Galloway region, and were an important bulwark against seaborne attack on the rich agricultural country in the centre of the kingdom. The area around the mouth of the Clyde, guarding a vulnerable fissure in the realm's natural armour, was reserved for barons of unimpeachable reliability.

The rest of Walter's estates were divided between East Lothian and Berwickshire. In the former group lay Stenton and the prosperous Innerwick. The property further south, of greater military significance, included Birkenside and Legerwood, beside the Leaderwater. David was not obliged to part with land on realistic terms. We learn from the reign of his successor, for example, that for most of Walter's holdings he was obliged to provide the service of only five knights, way below what might be termed its 'market value' and a special privilege for an esteemed royal servant.

* * *

Walter's household did not attend to the daily supervision or husbandry of their fiefs. Retaining a small amount for personal needs, the Lords of Renfrew enfeoffed a dependent clientele of their own, furthering David's feudalisation of the realm. Among their vassals were men from Shropshire, Kent and France, some of whom are remembered in current place names. The French knight Robert le Croc, a vassal of both Walter and his son Alan, is remembered in Crookston. Ralston recalls either Walter's chaplain, Ralph, or one of his knights, Ralph of Kent. One name stands out immediately among Walter's Shropshire connection: Richard Walensis, or 'of Wales', a title which in time became the surname 'Wallace'. Richard began with a garrison-sergeant's fee in Shropshire, held from Walter's nephew, William II Fitz Alan. When Richard came north as a vassal of Walter he was rewarded with land known as Riccardes-tun, or Riccarton, south of Kilmarnock, where the family thrived. Like many other twelfth-century immigrants, including their lords, over the next century and a half the Wallaces developed such a deep and lasting attachment to their new homeland that they were prepared to lose all they had, even their lives, to preserve its independence.

As was customary, Walter used his new-found wealth to patronise the church. He gave generously to David's Cistercian foundation at Melrose, and in 1163, as his thoughts turned increasingly towards his demise, he endowed a foundation of his own: an independent settlement of Cluniac monks at Renfrew, staffed by brothers from the order's house at Much Wenlock in Shropshire. Shortly after its foundation the monastery was moved to a more suitable site (Monkton) on the Paisley estate, where Walter was buried in 1177. Much Wenlock itself was given land in Renfrew, which it later exchanged for the distant Fitz Alan holding at Manhood near Chichester.

Walter did not favour St Florent, the traditional family darling. He preferred instead the more popular St James the Great, to whom his foundation at Paisley was dedicated along with a couple of less cosmopolitan worthies: St Milburga of West Mercia, the guardian of the Much Wenlock house, and a local lass, St Mirren. As part of their sustenance Walter granted the monks one tenth of all the venison and skins killed in the forest at Paisley during the open season, and the skins of all hinds slain during the close season for stag hunting. Walter clearly enjoyed his hunting. His house at Blackhall, with easy access to the forest, was one of his most regularly used residences.

King David may have provided Walter with a wife as well as land. We do not know when Walter married Eschina, but it was almost certainly before his patron's death in 1153, when Walter was in his mid-forties. An even more shadowy figure than her husband, Eschina may have been related to Thomas 'de Londres', a courtier in possession of lands near St Boswells in Roxburghshire; or (as Eschina 'of Mow' in the parish of Morebattle) she could have been a member of an influential native family.

* * *

David's third gift to Walter was the post and title of steward, which in time became the family's famous surname. To maintain law and order David relied at the highest level upon two groups of immigrants. One comprised those best described as his friends: the Lindsays, de Bruses, de Somervilles, Avenels and the family of Freskin 'the Fleming', who erected the great motte at Duffus near Elgin and founded the Murray ('de Moravia') family. The other group had more specific responsibilities: de Moreville, the constable; Richard Cumin (Comyn), the chancellor; and de Soules, the honorary butler. After 1147 the name of Walter Fitz Alan, the steward, needs to be added to the list.

'Steward' is used to translate two different Latin words, 'dapiferus' and the slightly more grand 'senescallus', the former being the head of the family's official title until the time of Walter Fitz Alan's grandson, Walter II. Was there something in the Fitz Alan blood which suited them to this post? 'Worthy but dull' is perhaps a bit harsh, but there was an element of stolidity in the way each generation of stewards (with the exception of Walter's son Alan) efficiently got on with their business, rarely putting a foot wrong and never attracting undue attention to themselves. Reliable and hard-headed, they seem almost to have been taken for granted by their royal masters. Only much later, when they found themselves at the top of the tree which they had assiduously cultivated, did the Stewarts (as they had become) begin to display the flamboyant characteristics for which they are now chiefly remembered.

Walter is not specifically referred to as steward in any document from David's reign, but an impressive charter of Malcolm IV's, signed at Roxburgh on 24 June 1161, makes it clear that by then Walter had held the position for some time. The Roxburgh document confirmed Walter in all the lands granted to him by David, added to them and acknowledged his stewardship as hereditary. It went on to give him a residence (called a 'toft'), with sufficient land to support it, in every royal borough and near every lodging used by the king. In other words, wherever the king went, Walter would be there to assist and advise him.

Malcolm IV was only eleven when he had succeeded his grandfather David in 1153. During the first part of his reign much of the burden of administration was handled by experienced personnel left over from the previous reign. Of the eighteen who figured prominently in this unofficial minority, only four (the earls of Fife and Dunbar, and the Bishops of Dunkeld and Caithness) were native Scots. Of the remaining fourteen, Walter was the most assiduous in handling day-to-day matters, his name appearing far more frequently than any other as a key witness to charters. The admirable steward had made himself indispensable.

Until his death in 1162, the senior councillor in the royal household was Constable Hugh de Moreville. Thereafter, for the next fifteen years, the privilege was held by Walter. His stewardship did not become purely honorary until the time of Malcolm's brother, William I (1165-1214), and during his first years in Scotland Walter was probably involved quite closely with running the household (counterbalancing a testy 'rannaire'?), as well as advising the monarch on matters of state. But by the end of the twelfth century routine administration had devolved to clerks, enabling the steward to play a more general, advisory role. Thus when Walter came to hand on his position to his son Alan in 1177, the trusted retainer's many years of successful service to three monarchs had elevated the stewardship to one of the most respected titles in the kingdom.

II

Perhaps we have too static or clerkly a picture of Steward Walter? Administration was clearly his forte, and by helping to extend feudal tenures, increase the royal revenue and expand the network of sheriffdoms he had played a key role in the crown's attempts to bring Scotland into line with other western European states. But military service, not paperwork, was the foundation of society, and no fit man in Walter's position ever ceased to be a soldier. As one of the realm's principal barons, the steward had to be prepared at all times to answer the king's call to arms.

Walter had been in Scotland less than two years when he first rode with the king into battle. The occasion was David's renewal of his claim to England's northern counties. Demonstrating a somewhat surprising cynicism for one of his hallowed reputation, in 1135 the King of Scots had conveniently forgotten the oath sworn to Henry I to uphold Matilda's accession and occupied large tracts of northern England. Stephen had marched north to confront David at Durham, where a peace was agreed in February 1136, probably at about the time when Walter was preparing to leave Shropshire.

After a further year of half-hearted fighting, early in 1138 Scottish forces, now including Walter, again entered Northumberland. Here they engaged in a lamentable orgy of wanton destruction under the pretext of securing the earldom of Northumberland for David's elder son, Henry. At the end of a period of inconclusive small-scale raiding, a detachment of Scottish knights under William Fitz Duncan was victorious in an engagement at Clitheroe. This may well have been the first time that Walter experienced the full horrors of medieval warfare, and he is unlikely to have been impressed by what he saw. But what followed was worse.

Richard, the English prior of Hexham, reported the campaign with unashamed subjectivity. He explained that 'the sins of the [local] people' had been the cause of Scottish success – to his mind an event so catastrophic as a visitation by hoards of barbaric 'Picts' (as he called the enemy footsoldiers) could only have been divine punishment for breaking God's commandments. He had every justification for regarding the Scot as a sort of latter-day Philistine, for the bulk of David's troops were little more than land pirates, wild warriors from Galloway, the Borders and the remote north and west. War to them meant plunder and booty, human as well as material, and after the fight they began collecting all they could lay their hands on. With journalistic hyperbole worthy of a modern broadsheet (and subsequently enhanced in a romantic translation by the Victorian vicar of Leighton Buzzard), Prior Richard offered his account of their behaviour:

> '...sparing no rank, no age, no sex, no condition, they first massacred, in the most barbarous manner possible, children and kindred in the sight of their relatives, masters in the sight of their servants, and servants in the sight of their masters, and husbands before the eyes of their wives; and then (horrible to relate) they carried off, like so much booty, the noble matrons and chaste virgins, together with other women... Afterwards they were distributed with other booty...
>
> And finally, these brutal men, making no account of adultery, incest or such crimes, when tired of abusing these poor wretches... made them their slaves, or sold them like cattle to other barbarians.'

David's terrifying levies were useless when it came to a pitched battle. Rallied by Archbishop Thurstan of York, the barons of northern England confronted the Scots on Cowton Moor in Yorkshire's North Riding on 22 August 1138. Unusually, the battle is not known by its location but by a strange device employed by the English to enable their men to get their bearings during the inevitable chaos of hand-to-hand conflict. The Battle of the Standard was named after a tall mast, somehow fixed upright on a cart, to which were affixed the banners of St Peter, St John of Beverley and St Wilfrid of Ripon, and a silver pix containing the consecrated host.

Before the two armies met there was some argument among the Scots over who was to take the front rank, the regular soldiers or the Galwegians. According to Ailred of Rievaulx, the 'naked and almost unarmed Picts' scoffed at the apprehension shown by David's mailed knights – 'Why dost thou so greatly dread those iron tunics which thou seest afar off?' – and demanded to lead the assault. The king acceded to their wish, and the ill-disciplined tribesmen were swiftly overrun, suffering terrible losses. The English chronicler gleefully reported that some were so stuck with arrows that they rolled about in agony like huge screaming hedgehogs.

After an hour or so of this slaughter it was clear to the Scottish commanders that there was no point in continuing the battle.

'The chiefs, therefore, induced the king to call in the horses [the battle had been fought on foot], and march off with his ranks unbroken, lest he, too, should perish with his men.'

David wisely did as he was advised and retired from the fray with the majority of his professional soldiers unharmed. Can one detect the cautious voice of Walter among those of the anonymous 'chiefs' who urged the king to cut his losses and leave the field? It was certainly the sort of wise counsel that would have appealed to him. One also wonders whether he had advised against the knights bearing the brunt of the English attack; had they done so, on that fateful summer's morning Walter's career might well have come to a premature, abrupt and bloody halt.

The Battle of the Standard had taught David a salutary lesson. A few months later he gained through negotiation almost all he had failed to win by force of arms. Walter, too, had learned much from the battle. In particular he had been shown just how useless traditional Scottish soldiers were when confronted by a modern enemy. He did not forget what he had seen.

* * *

A curtain of obscurity covers much of Walter's remaining activity as a soldier and advisor in foreign affairs. It is quite likely that he became involved in the English civil wars when David descended into England in support of Matilda, and he may have joined his brother in the queen's army at Oxford and fought beside him at Winchester. Sixteen years later Walter sat behind the young Malcolm IV when he was forced to concede to Henry II the Solway-Tweed frontier between the northern and southern British kingdoms. He was with Malcolm again in 1159 when they accompanied Henry on an unwise foray against Toulouse. But as far as we know, the sternest test of Walter's military prowess came in 1164, when he was well into his fifties and probably no longer keen to appear on the battlefield in person.

The occasion was an attack on the Scottish kingdom by Somerled Macgillebrigte, Lord of Argyll, known in some quarters as 'King of the Isles'. Although no one can be quite sure of the family origins of this daunting, part-Norse, part-Celtic adventurer, his deeds were real enough. He was well-connected, too, for his sister had married Malcolm Mac Heth, Earl of Moray, a probable descendant of Macbeth and a serious threat to the Anglo-Norman policies of David and his successors.

After the defeat and imprisonment of Earl Malcolm in 1134, for a while Somerled was content to live as a loyal subject of King David, paying him a nominal tribute for his lands in Argyll and Kintyre and providing at least some of the scantily clad and ill disciplined soldiers who had been so easily routed at the Battle of the Standard. Somerled was a restless and ambitious fellow, however, and in 1154 he joined with Mac Heth's son Donald in rebellion against the young Malcolm IV. When this venture failed and Donald was securely incarcerated with his father in the gloomy depths of Roxburgh Castle, Somerled began a long campaign to make himself master of the Western Isles, at that time held by the King of Man from his overlord the King of Norway.

Seaborne commando-style raids were much more to Somerled's liking than pitched battles. In a series of daring actions he won control of the Isles, sending the King of Man to Norway, via Malcolm's court, bleating of how he had been mistreated. Meanwhile, Malcolm Mac Heth had been released and given the earldom of Ross, encouraging Somerled to seek the reconciliation with the king which was effected in 1160.

That Christmas, Somerled was given pride of place at Malcolm's court, where he acquired the nickname 'Sit-by-the-king'. Quite what the sophisticated French-speaking barons made of this intrusion we do not know. But it is not hard to imagine the tension between men such as Walter, who had devoted their lives to serving the crown, and the rebel who now sat so easily in their midst. The sight of the hoary old western warrior, full of boasting and drink, holding the young king enthralled with his stories of raid and plunder must have filled the steward with apprehension and anger. This was not the sort of court he had worked for.

Somerled was quite aware of Walter's resentment. He had no love for these upstart foreigners who now dominated the household and marred the countryside with their towering, ugly mottes. A burning mutual hatred arose between the two men.

It was not in Walter's nature to let his feelings get the better of him. But this was not true of the flamboyant 'King of the Isles', and before long Somerled decided it was high time to cleanse the kingdom by driving the rapacious Anglo-Norman barons back over the border. He knew exactly where he would strike first – at the lands of the man who epitomised all he despised: Walter Fitz Alan, the parvenu steward of Scotland.

Somerled returned to the west. Here, far from the scornful gaze of the courtiers, he was revered and respected. His summons drew just the sort of untamed freebooters who had served the king so unsuccessfully at the Battle of the Standard. From Ireland came ferocious adventurers, eager to plunder the prosperous farms and homesteads of central Scotland. They were joined by warriors from the Hebrides and Argyll, loyal to their new lord and fired by lurid stories of the sycophancy, luxury and exploitation at court. A fleet of 160 ships was assembled to transport this great army, and in 1164 it sailed proudly up the Clyde to Renfrew, at the very heart of the steward's territory. Here the men disembarked and prepared to move overland to the east.

If Somerled had expected Walter's tenants to share his dislike of the Breton overlord, he was disastrously mistaken. The western warriors were not greeted by friendly crowds hailing them as liberators, but by a small, skilled and determined phalanx of mounted knights; 'a few locals' one commentator modestly called them. The invaders were seafarers and scavengers, many of whom had probably never seen iron-clad cavalry before. They lacked any idea how to cope with these new-fangled and technologically superior soldiers. It was like the Battle of the Standard over again, except that this time Walter was on the winning side.

The fighting was over very swiftly. The intruders were scattered by a single charge from the mailed knights, allowing footsoldiers to move in and complete the slaughter. Before long Somerled's men were fleeing back to their boats, leaving many colleagues lifeless upon the grass. When the pursuit was finally called off and the enemy bodies examined to see who had fallen, the 'King of the Isles' and one of his sons were found lying among them.

We are not told what part Walter had played in the remarkable victory. However, although the monks of Glasgow were quick to credit the success to the watchful eye of St Mungo, we may safely assume that even if Walter had not been present on the field in person, he had masterminded the operation. It was the crowning vindication of his organisation and reliability, confirming that on the battlefield as in the council chamber the crown of Scotland had no more illustrious servant than Walter Fitz Alan.

As the great steward would surely have wished, the last word may be left to the anonymous chronicler of Melrose Abbey, who when he came to write up the events of 1177 included an epitaph as poignant as it was brief:

'Walter Fitz Alan, the steward of the king of Scotland, our intimate friend, died. May his blessed soul live in glory!'

CHAPTER 5

Stewardship

I

Born into a position of power and influence, the second steward, Alan Fitz Walter, displayed a confidence wholly lacking in his cautious father. Like his lord, King William the Lion, Alan was a military man. What little we know of him suggests that he was prepared to take positive steps to further the family fortunes rather than work diligently and wait for reward. He was a crusader, a patron of the fashionable shrine of Thomas Becket at Canterbury and, on one celebrated occasion, was arrogant enough to defy the wishes of the king himself. We are left with the impression of a rather dashing, attractive yet irresponsible man, who perhaps took after his great-grandfather Alan, also a crusader. In the very different templates of the first two stewards we have the outlines of many of their more celebrated descendants.

The date of Alan's birth is not recorded. If, as suggested, Walter had married in about 1150, Alan was born probably some two years later, for he attended court during his father's lifetime. This would have made him about twenty-five (ten years younger than King William) when he came into the stewardship and fifty-two at the time of his death in 1204. We cannot ascribe his impetuosity to lack of years.

King William I, the second grandson of David I, had succeeded his brother Malcolm to the Scottish throne in 1165. High-handed, energetic and warlike, William differed sharply from his two predecessors. His long reign was dominated by overlapping struggles to extend royal authority and to preserve Scottish independence in the face of Angevin expansion. For a while, following his capture by the English at Alnwick in 1174, William was obliged to do homage to Henry II for the Scottish crown, which meant that his barons – including Steward Alan – owed their primary allegiance to the King of England. But in 1189 Richard the Lion Heart's obsession with crusades allowed William to break free from Angevin overlordship; and although relations with his successor, King John, were never easy, when William died in 1214 he was still master of an independent principality.

Steward Alan's title was purely honorary. His name crops up quite regularly as one of the important figures at court, but he did not have his father's administrative interest or capacity. Preferring the lance to the pen, he fought beside

William in various domestic and cross-border campaigns and accompanied him on the Third Crusade, where he learned something of the latest developments in military engineering. A few years later he incorporated these into his new castle at Rothesay on the Isle of Bute, the earliest surviving Stewart monument in Scotland.

Lying like a watchdog at the entrance to the Firth of Clyde, Bute had been given to the stewards after its capture from the King of Man in the second half of the twelfth century, perhaps after the defeat of Somerled's rebellion in 1164. The Lord of the Isles' invasion had brought home to the king Bute's strategic significance, leading to the construction of Rothesay Castle as a bastion against further attack from the west. One of Scotland's first stone castles, Rothesay initially comprised a simple yet massive round keep of neatly cut blocks. This was later reinforced with four towers after a Norwegian assault in 1230 had revealed that the original design did not allow for adequate defensive cross fire. Having failed to take the fortress by scaling or battering down the walls, the Scandinavians had simply sheltered beneath an umbrella of shields and hacked through the soft stone curtain with axes. The castle steward (one of Alan's relations?) had been killed in the final assault.

In time the beautiful castle at Rothesay acquired a reputation for tranquillity as well as robustness, and the first two Stewart monarchs, Robert II and III, frequently used it as a sort of Scottish Camp David. The energetic Alan would have been delighted to know that his moated masterpiece remained of service to the family so long after his death, although he would no doubt have reserved a soldier's scorn for the purpose to which it was put by his enervated ancestors.

* * *

Alan married twice, on both occasions taking a wife from a native Scottish family. His first wife was Eva, daughter of Swain, son of the first recorded sheriff of Lothian. The arrangement has all the hallmarks of Walter's handiwork. A wise rather than an ambitious liaison, it linked the stewards to an established Anglian dynasty and to an office which the king was seeking to extend around the kingdom. Unfortunately Eva died young, leaving no children.

The steward's second marriage was an altogether more ambitious business. His partner this time was Alesta, daughter of Morgrund, the Celtic Earl of Mar. The union of a leading Anglo-Norman family with one of the ancient earldoms, possibly put forward jointly by the king and Alan, was a step up the social ladder for the stewards; it also fitted in with William's efforts to extend his personal authority northwards and promote harmony between the new and old aristocracies. The Scottish kings were well aware of the dangers of creating a governing class isolated from the country's traditional leaders.

There was definitely no royal approval for the third marriage with which Alan was concerned. In 1200, while William was at Lincoln doing homage to King John, 'Duncan, son of Gilbert Fergus' son carried off Avelina, daughter of

Alan Fitz Walter, Lord of Renfrew' without bothering to obtain royal consent for the match. The 'carrying off' had clearly been executed with parental approval, for when he heard what had happened King William 'was exceeding wroth' with both Alan and Duncan. The ferocity of the king's reaction stemmed from the turbulent history of south-west Scotland over the previous half century or so.

When Walter Fitz Alan had settled at the court of King David, the master of remote Galloway had been Fergus, a Norse-Celtic lord of ancient lineage. He was the sort of independent-minded chieftain who regarded his annual tribute of 1,000 beasts to the King of Scots more as the price he had to pay for being left to his own devices than as a recognition of David's overlordship.

Matters came to a head in 1160, when Fergus rebelled against Malcolm IV. Three times Walter the steward and other loyal barons descended on Galloway, harrying and slaughtering until Fergus was finally brought to heel. Exhausted and dispirited, he took holy orders and spent the remaining years of his life as a canon of Holyrood. His possessions were divided between his sons, Gilbert (a cousin of England's Henry II) and Uhtred. Thereafter Anglo-Norman settlement of the region continued apace, led by the de Berkeleys, de Morevilles and de Bruses; even Uhtred participated in the process of feudalisation, constructing the huge Motte of Urr, the largest fortification of its kind in Scotland.

The spirit of the Galwegians was far from broken, however, and after King William's capture at Alnwick in 1174 they rose in revolt once again. Seizing the royal castle at Dumfries, they slew all English and French officials they could lay their hands on. Then Gilbert, the prime mover in all this, engineered the murder of Uhtred and slyly offered his allegiance to England's Henry II.

The approach put Henry in a difficult position. He had no liking for rebels, but Gilbert was his relative as well as a proven enemy of William the Lion. Pilate-like, Henry passed the problem over to the King of Scots. Only too delighted to give practical vent to his loathing for Gilbert and his kin, William moved into Galloway, seized the traitor and delivered him to Henry in 1177. Some sort of compromise followed by which the unreliable Gilbert was allowed to remain in possession of his lands until his death, which came in 1185.

Galloway was then claimed by Gilbert's son Duncan. But King William was not a forgiving man, and he plotted for Uhtred's son Roland to succeed to the troublesome fief. Once again Henry II intervened, cobbling together another compromise the following year. Roland Fitz Uhtred kept the estates he had seized and Duncan Fitz Gilbert, without doubt a 'persona non grata' in William's eyes, was fobbed off with the earldom of Carrick in northern Galloway, bordering the steward's Kyle lands.

By this time it was obvious that William would regard any approach towards Duncan with extreme suspicion. Like his father, the new Earl of Carrick was loath to accept Scottish overlordship and was prepared to accept English help to preserve his independence. In 1197 William had built a new castle at Ayr, north of Carrick, to keep him in check.

With this background in mind, how are we to interpret Alan's decision to marry his daughter Avelina to Duncan of Carrick during the king's absence in 1200? Perhaps it was simply naivity on Alan's part. But if that was the case, then why did he wait until William was out of the country before going ahead with the marriage? And was it not doubly suspicious that the union should have been arranged when Roland, Lord of Galloway, lay dying – precisely when Duncan might have been preparing to restate his claim to the whole of the province? Romantics may believe that the steward thought Duncan and Avelina so in love that he took pity on them and agreed to their union when there was least chance that it would attract attention. But almost certainly that would be to overlay the past with the psychology of a later age.

The other possibility is that by allowing Avelina to marry Duncan, Alan was backing his new son-in-law's claim to Galloway and dreaming of establishing a formidable family power bloc in the south-west, possibly under English protection. If this was Alan's game, then it was a very dangerous one indeed and could have jeopardised all his father's achievements.

When news of the Stewart marriage reached him, William had his hands full trying to cope with the demands of King John. The last thing he wanted to hear was that his own barons were making dangerous dynastic arrangements behind his back. Moreover, judging by the ferocity of his reaction, this was not the first time that Alan had annoyed him. Determined to bring him to heel once and for all, William demanded 'from Alan Fitz Walter twenty-four pledges that he would preserve peace with him and with his land'. Alan duly obliged, realising that he had overstepped the mark rather seriously.

The steward's loyalty was never again called into question. If, as is generally agreed, Rothesay Castle was built shortly after 1200, then it was a concrete sign that William had forgiven him. Alan survived the unhappy Carrick affair by only four years. The king probably received the news of his death with mixed feelings, sadness at the passing of a fellow soldier mingling with relief that so turbulent a baron was now safely out of the way. The tight-lipped monks of Melrose, who had recorded Walter's death so poignantly, could find no such kind words for his son. Their bald notice of the second steward's passing – 'Alan Fitz Walter died' – was probably all that the king would have wished them to say.

* * *

The Carrick-Stewart partnership initiated by Steward Alan and Earl Duncan was not killed stone dead in 1200. It was revived a generation later and persisted into the next century, with surprising results.

Alan's granddaughter married Earl Duncan's son and heir, by whom she had a daughter, Marjory. Marjory then gave the Carrick estate and title to her second husband, Robert Bruce, a descendant of William the Lion. In 1306

Robert Bruce's son was crowned Robert I of Scotland. Robert I's daughter, another Marjory, then re-established links with the Stewarts by marrying Steward Alan's great-great-grandson, Walter III. In 1371 Walter and Marjory's only son, Robert Stewart, became King Robert II of Scotland, from whom are descended the royal Stewarts and, incidentally, the present House of Windsor. To this day one of the Prince of Wales' many official titles is Earl of Carrick.

II

Alan's son, Walter II, was the first steward whose title was used as a surname, now customarily written with a 't' in place of the 'd': Stewart. The third steward was a minor when his father died, but when he started to act independently it was clear that in character he resembled his careful grandfather, Walter I, rather than the more irresponsible Alan. Having skipped a generation, Stewart dependability had calmly reasserted itself.

Scotland now had a new king. Alexander II, who had come to the throne in 1214, was very much in the mould of David I, and his reign witnessed a renewal of the fruitful partnership between monarch and steward which had begun during the middle years of the previous century. In common with his predecessors, Alexander II faced four principal tasks: maintaining the independence of his inheritance, extending his sway into the northern and western parts of Scotland, securing obedience to the royal will, and providing for an undisputed succession at his death. In all these matters Walter offered unflagging loyalty and support. The two men were about the same age; they got on well and grew wise together in the art of government.

* * *

It is not possible to chart the precise influence Walter had on Alexander's relations with England. Like the king, he was young and inexperienced when first he entered government. But he was quick to learn, and in the increasing pragmatism and sophistication of Scottish diplomacy it is tempting to see the steward's cautious influence. Walter did not make policy; his was one of the quiet voices of reason which helped guide Alexander towards his eventual prudent settlement of his disputes with England.

The reign began inauspiciously. When the Scots sided with the disaffected English barons who forced King John to come to terms at Runnymede in 1215, they were placed under a papal interdict and subjected to a devastating attack from John's bloodthirsty mercenaries in the winter of 1215-6. Alexander replied in like manner with a raid on northern England the following spring. Although the death of King John that autumn brought some easing of the tension, Alexander was still no nearer his original goal of being acknowledged master of England's northern counties.

Relations with England improved during the 1220s, when Alexander married Henry III's sister Joan and had the Honour of Huntingdon restored to him. Decades of Anglo-Scottish hostility were finally brought to a close by the Treaty of York in 1237. The terms of the agreement were eminently sensible. A number of long standing disagreements between the two countries, most notably the Scots' claim to Northumberland, Cumberland and Westmorland, were settled, almost entirely in favour of Henry III. Alexander's principal gain was implicit in the nature of the treaty, a pact made between equals. For the time being, at least, the English king dropped his claims to overlordship and Scotland was internationally accepted as an independent kingdom. It comes as no surprise to find the name of Walter Fitz Alan third in the list of Scottish witnesses to the agreement.

Some eight years after his accession, Alexander moved against Argyll, intending to bring it into closer union with the rest of the kingdom. The loch-torn western seaboard was difficult terrain in which to operate, unsuitable for mounted knights and requiring complicated liaison between land and sea forces. The royal army included a number of Galwegians, whose skill in operations of this sort made up for their lack of discipline. The young Walter sailed with the king and obviously conducted himself well, for after the men of Argyll had been beaten into submission, Cowal was added to the extensive Stewart holdings in the west. The king paid for the construction of a castle at Dunoon in southern Cowal, providing Walter with a secure base in his new territories within easy reach of the Clyde.

Walter was closely concerned with a second of Alexander's internal military ventures, the campaign against Galloway in 1235. Since the death of Roland of Galloway in December 1200, the region had been under the sway of his son Alan, another of those piratical heroes of the west who appeared from time to time to disrupt the orderly designs of the Scottish kings. Alan was held to be

> '...the greatest warrior of his age. He had a mighty army and numerous ships with which he plundered about the Hebrides for a long time.'

Not only that, but he was also the king's constable (a position which Alexander had innocently confirmed in 1214) and kinsman – Alan's second wife was William the Lion's sister Margaret. Keen to preserve Alan of Galloway as an ally rather than a foe, the king used Galwegian troops in his expedition against Argyll and was prepared to turn a blind eye to Alan's troublesome activities, as long as they did not openly endanger royal authority.

When Alan died in 1234, he left three daughters and a bastard son, Thomas. To the extreme annoyance of the Galwegians, who wished their lord-ship to remain intact, Alexander divided it equally between the heiresses. Rebellion inevitably followed, and in July 1235 Alexander gathered together an army and entered Galloway. Once again, Walter Stewart and his men were prominent among those riding with the king.

Recalling previous royal invasions, the Galwegians wisely refused to meet

Alexander's troops in open battle and remained instead 'lurking among the mountains', shadowing the enemy. The tactic almost succeeded. Just as the king's forces were setting up camp one evening, the guerrillas launched a surprise attack. For a few minutes it looked as if Alexander might receive a serious setback. Then, before the assailants could press home their advantage, Earl Farquhar of Ross fell upon them from behind.

Dawdling towards the camp site in the late afternoon sunshine, the earl's contingent had fallen some way behind the main body of the army. When the embarrassed earl finally caught up and saw what was going on, he made up for his inefficiency by leading a devastating charge into the Galwegians' rear. Beset on both sides, those rebels who were able to extricate themselves from the fray fled into the hills. After this the rebellion quickly petered out and Alexander returned home, leaving Walter Comyn to restore law and order in the region.

Comyn was a hard and tactless man. It did not take him long to drive the Galwegians into revolt again, allowing Thomas the Bastard to come over from Ireland with a band of mercenaries to reclaim his lordship. In the end, however, the insurrection proved no more successful than the previous one, and Thomas was captured and incarcerated for life. (Surprisingly, he was still alive in 1296, when the English took a more favourable view of his claim and released him.) Unexpectedly deprived of a leader, paymaster and cause, the miserable Irish soldiers drifted north into Stewart territory, where they were even less popular than they had been in Galloway. Upon entering Glasgow, they were ambushed by the citizens and chopped to pieces in the streets.

The lordship of Galloway was divided between the king and several baronial families, notably the Balliols and Comyns. John Balliol married Dervorguilla, one of Lord Alan's daughters. The child of this marriage became King John of Scotland, whose brief and ill-fated reign (1292-6) formed a prologue to the Wars of Independence and the eventual accession of the Stewarts.

* * *

Walter II was known formally as 'Steward of Scotland', implying that his responsibilities were to the kingdom as a whole, and not just to the king and his household. (The distinction was more theoretical than real, for at least until the next century it was the king who defined the kingdom.) This enabled Alexander to employ Walter's talents as he saw fit.

The post of justiciar was the highest office in the crown's gift. Those who held the position were charged with acting for the king in legal affairs and keeping a general eye on all aspects of government. Since, for geographical and political reasons, it would have been unwise for one man to attempt the task single handed, it was customary to appoint two or even three justiciars. After the subjugation of Galloway, for example, the region was given its own justiciar

to partner those already operating in Lothian and Scotia, the southern and
northern parts of the kingdom. The justiciarship of Scotia was a demanding job
and gave its incumbent such power that it too was sometimes sub-divided. A
justiciar's legal brief was to travel round his territory, keeping in close contact
with the sheriffs and hearing on the crown's behalf all relevant cases, both
appeals and suits in the first instance.

In 1231, when the court was at St Andrews, 'Walter Alanson, Steward of
Scotland, came to the king and was made his justice.' Walter took over as justiciar of Scotia from Earl William Comyn and held the post until his death in
1241, when it was divided between two lesser men. The appointment was a
singular mark of Alexander's trust and respect, and confirmed Walter as one of
the most influential men in the kingdom. It suggests that he was blessed with a
fortunate combination of intelligence, firmness and tact; and although he had
clerks to assist him in all decisions, he must also have possessed a sound
grounding in law and custom.

As land was the principal key to wealth and power, the majority of cases
brought before the justiciars involved disputed titles or boundaries. If justice
was not seen to be done and one party left the justiciar's presence disaffected,
civil disorder might easily follow. At that time men were quick to take up arms
to defend territory they believed to be theirs by right. This is precisely what
happened under Walter's successors, whose failure to settle a dispute between
the Comyns and the Bissets led to a nasty feud and the dismissal of the justiciars in 1244.

One example illustrates the sort of steps Walter took to ensure that matters
did not get so out of hand under his justiciarship. In 1236, the year after the
Galloway uprising, Walter was called upon to hear a dispute over land in
Aberdeenshire between Arbroath Abbey and Countess Marjory, the widow of
the previous justiciar, Earl William Comyn. The Comyns, fast becoming the
most powerful baronial family in the land, were not to be treated lightly. But
the king also understood the need to protect the church, which was unable,
literally, to fight its own battles and whose support was essential to the crown.
Having heard what both sides had to say, the court determined to ascertain the
truth by visiting the land in question and examining it physically. By walking
or riding round the boundaries of the estate with representatives of both parties
(quite a common practice), it reached a decision acceptable to both the abbey
and the Countess. Then, in order to prevent either party from reneging on the
agreement, the judgement was set down in writing. Through actions such as
this, repeated time and again during his justiciarship, Walter helped put in
place that cornerstone of all civilized society – the rule of law.

* * *

For much of his life Alexander II was tormented by a gnawing anxiety: if he
should fail to provide a male heir, years of careful diplomacy and administra-

tion might disappear in the maelstrom of civil war. The chilling example of what had happened in England during the dispute between Matilda and Stephen gave vivid credence to the king's fears.

Alexander's only male nephew, Prince John, died in 1237. When the following year the unhappy Queen Joan followed him childless to the grave the situation became critical. The Bruce family later claimed that Alexander had stipulated that, should he die heirless, the crown should pass to Robert Bruce, the son of John's sister Isabel. But there is no concrete evidence for this. Besides, Alexander remarried in 1239. His second bride was Marie de Coucy, daughter of a powerful French baron and 'a lady fair and pleasant'. The honour of escorting her to Scotland was given to the man whom the king trusted above all others, his lifelong friend and companion Walter Fitz Alan, justicia of Scotia and steward of Scotland. It was one of the last major services Walter rendered his lord. Knowing that the queen was with child but probably before the birth of the future Alexander III, the third steward died in 1241.

Walter himself had married with the same family as his father, and his wife Beatrice, daughter of Gilchrist Earl of Mar, linked the Stewarts to the upwardly mobile Durward family. The couple had three sons and a daughter who survived into adulthood. The latter, as we have seen, married Earl Neil of Carrick. The eldest son, named Alexander after the king, followed his father into the stewardship and married into the ancient family of the Lord of the Isles. Sir John, the second son, died in 1249 while crusading beneath the banner of St Louis of France. The ambitious youngest son, Walter, was unwed at the time of his father's death. But he too married well, thus playing his part in spreading the seeds of Stewart power across the soil of Scotland.

III

Alexander Stewart inherited the stewardship at the age of twenty-seven. He did not take on his father's role of justiciar, and he is chiefly remembered for his achievements as a soldier. To contemporaries he was known as Alexander of Dundonald, a title adopted from the stronghold he built on the rugged outcrop which rises above the farmland south-west of Kilmarnock. Dundonald Castle was laid out according to the most up-to-date defensive principles, with all its strength focused around a massive twin-towered gatehouse-keep. Unfortunately the original building was badly damaged during the Wars of Independence as part of Robert Bruce's scorched earth policy, and the present rather stark tower house was erected by Robert II. Like Rothesay, it was a favourite residence of the first two Stewart kings, Robert II dying there in 1390.

The new Steward served the ageing Alexander II for eight years. The period marked the beginning of an important phase in the expansion of royal power into the Western Isles and undoubtedly provided the Lord of Dundonald with valuable military experience. While much of the mainland was now part of the Scottish kingdom, most of the isles were still under the crown of Norway.

Several local magnates, such as the Lord of Argyll, owed allegiance to two kings. Given the remoteness of their possessions, it was not difficult for them to exploit their position by playing off one overlord against another; on occasion they were not above involving a fourth party, the King of England, in their bid to remain free spirits. By these means they had managed to maintain a largely independent jurisdiction over their territories until the middle years of the thirteenth century.

Alexander II regarded the situation as highly unsatisfactory. From 1244 onwards, when he offered to buy the Western Isles from King Haakon IV of Norway, he determined to solve the problem by gathering all mainland Scotland and its offshore islands under the direct control of the Scottish crown. Apart from King Haakon, the man who most resented such a plan was Ewen, Lord of Argyll since 1237.

In 1248 two events persuaded Alexander II that it was time to act. First, Haakon gave Ewen the title of 'king' – a direct insult to the reigning House of Canmore. Secondly, after the death of the King of Man, Haakon provisionally granted Ewen control over all the Western Isles, from Man to Lewis. At this, Alexander's fury finally boiled over. He assembled a large army, transported it to Argyll and relieved Ewen of his lordship, whereupon the recalcitrant magnate made a hasty retreat to Lewis. For the next few years he earned a precarious living as a mercenary, before being restored to his title at the insistence of Henry III six years after Alexander II's death.

Alexander Stewart was present on the Argyll campaign, noting closely all that he saw. The tips he picked up, especially on how to deploy knights against a less heavily-armed foe, were one day to prove invaluable. For the moment, however, it was his political rather than military skills which he needed to draw on.

The campaign came to an abrupt halt on 8 July 1249 when Alexander II died of fever on the small island of Kerrera, off the coast of Lorn near Oban. The heir to the Scottish throne, Prince Alexander, was a young lad of eight. However well organised a medieval kingdom might be, the accession of a minor inevitably meant a tangled power struggle. In this case it was waged between two factions, one headed by Alan Durward, the other by the Comyns. The situation was further complicated by Henry III of England, who from time to time backed whichever side appeared most likely to further his interests. It says a good deal for the stability of Scottish government, and for the common sense of some of the more influential figures involved in the squabbling (particularly Steward Alexander) that the country did not deteriorate into outright civil war.

Alexander Stewart may have been happier supervising the construction of a castle than scheming across the council table, but he was no political rabbit, and we do him a grave disservice if we put him in the same category as Alan the crusader. His behaviour during the minority showed him to be a survivor, shrewdly adept at walking the tactical tightrope between hostile parties. Had this not been so, he would never have been in a position to earn his reputation as a military commander in later life.

Alan Durward and Alexander Stewart were together in Argyll when Alexander II died, and their subsequent behaviour illustrates sharply the contrast between the careerist and the crown servant. Since his position was under no immediate threat, Alexander could afford to take a reasonably relaxed attitude to the situation, sitting back, watching and holding his weighty influence in reserve. Alan, on the other hand, was the ambitious man on the make. Lest the Comyns steal a march on him and seize control of the government in his absence, he dreaded being away from the centre of affairs for a single day.

On the king's death the political spotlight swung instantly from west to east, from remote Kerrera to Scone, where Prince Alexander was staying with his mother. Without wasting a minute, Alan took to the saddle and rode pell mell across the country to be with the prince. (Before 1329 no man was regarded as king until he had been through an elaborate inauguration ceremony.) The steward remained behind in Argyll to supervise the winding up of Alexander II's expedition. He recognised Durward's competence, and probably offered him some words of encouragement before he set off on his frantic journey back to the Scone. But despite family ties between the two men, any support Alexander tendered was strictly provisional. He wanted to see how Alan behaved.

Over the next year or so Alan Durward engineered a spectacular coup. The Comyns were removed from office and replaced by Durward supporters, Alan himself becoming justiciar for the whole country. Marie de Coucy, who might have opposed this behaviour, chose instead to return to her native France, and for a brief while Durward was the most powerful man in the kingdom. But, tempted by the possibility of prizes still more glittering, no sooner had he grasped power than he began to overreach himself. He alienated the church. Far more serious, as far as his fellow magnates were concerned, was his attempt to legitimise his wife, a bastard daughter of Alexander II. Should he have succeeded, then only the life of the young Alexander III would have stood between the Durwards and the throne. Who knows what deeds Alan was planning to further his vaulting ambition? The steward was growing increasingly anxious.

Durward's downfall was prompted by the marriage in 1251 of the young king to Henry III's daughter, Margaret. The union gave Henry, who was genuinely solicitous of his daughter's welfare but also keen to exploit her husband's weakness, an excuse to interfere in Scottish affairs. What followed was an ominous foretaste of the tribulation which beset Scotland at the end of the century. Durward was overthrown and an English-backed coalition based around the Comyn faction returned to power. The new government was headed by Walter Comyn, Earl of Menteith, and contained two representatives of Henry III, Robert de Ros and John Balliol. Behind them stood Alexander Stewart. He was no kingmaker, but fearful of Durward's designs and sensing a change in the political wind, he had thought it wise to drop his former comrade in arms and switch his allegiance to the Comyns. For the time being, too, he welcomed the support of Henry III, although he was well aware of its dangers. The last thing he wished was to encourage England in her ancient claims to Scottish over-lordship.

The Comyn ascendancy lasted for about four and a half years. By September 1255 Durward was back in another coalition, led this time by Patrick, Earl of Dunbar, and again backed by Henry III. With impeccable timing, the steward switched his allegiance for the third time in six years. While no doubt announcing publicly that he was the honest broker, eager for a balanced and representative government free from factional bias, in private he must have congratulated himself on his uncanny knack of identifying his own fortunes with those of the kingdom at large.

Durward's second period of power ended when the Comyns seized the person of the king in October 1257. Yet again Durward had used his position to increase his wealth and status. His backers – particularly the steward – had also become concerned at the increasing influence of Henry III. It was at Henry's insistence, for example, that Ewen of Argyll had been reinstated. (The move proved a wise one: Ewen's loyalty to the Scottish crown remained stead-fast from this time onwards, and he refused to side with the Norwegians when they launched a massive assault on the west in 1263.)

For a few months after Durward's fall civil war seemed a real possibility. But Alexander III was now old enough to act on his own behalf, and in 1258 a compromise was reached. A new council was set up, including both Durward and the Comyn Earl of Menteith. Needless to say, a place was also found for Alexander Stewart. Some powerful groups were excluded, including influen-tial families such as the Bruces, but it was probably the best that could be done in the circumstances.

King Alexander took over full control of the government in 1260, when amicable relations with England were also restored. The Kingdom of Scotland had come unharmed though a most trying period. So had Alexander Stewart. His skill in changing sides at just the right moment no doubt saved his political skin; but his judicious balancing act had also helped prevent any single group overreaching itself, and the middle way had eventually prevailed. Stable and reasonably united, the country was now free to turn its attention once more to the problem of the west.

* * *

Eager to busy his barons' giddy minds with quarrels outside the realm, as soon as he was personally in charge of Scottish affairs Alexander renewed his father's offer to buy the Western Isles from Norway. King Haakon was not interested. Having failed in his appeal to Norse avarice, Alexander determined to provoke his rival into military action. One of the first to benefit from this change of policy was the steward's brother, Walter 'the freckled'.

Walter Comyn, Earl of Menteith, who had played such a prominent part in the troubles of Alexander III's minority, had survived the compromise of 1258 by only a few days. With his death the Menteith earldom reverted to his wife Isabel, the countess in her own right. A year later she married an English knight, Sir John Russell, who thereby acquired the Menteith title and estates. But Sir John was not allowed to keep his wife's lavish wedding gift for long.

It was soon rumoured, with some plausibility, that in order that they might enjoy the Menteith estate and each other, Isabel and Sir John had arranged to have Walter Comyn murdered. The couple were arrested, forced to resign the earldom and grant away lands and pensions, then driven from the kingdom. The original plan was for the Menteith title to revert to Sir John Comyn, Earl Walter's heir, but not his wife's. Since, strictly speaking, the earldom had always been Isabel's and not Walter's, the decision was open to question. At this point Walter Stewart appeared on the scene.

Walter was married to Mary, one of Countess Isabel's cousins, and he now put forward a claim to the disputed earldom on his wife's behalf. The king decided the matter early in 1261. He did not wish to increase Comyn power, particularly in the light of what had gone on during his minority, and the Stewarts were very much a family in favour; so judgement was made in favour of Walter, who became Earl of Menteith. The Comyns did not let the issue rest, however, and it rumbled on for another quarter of a century until the king was finally persuaded to divide the disputed Menteith inheritance in two, letting the Comyns have half and leaving the title and the other half with Earl Walter. The acquisition of an earldom, although not by the head of the family, was a significant honour for the Stewarts, putting them firmly among the country's leading aristocratic families. The line of the Stewart Earls of Menteith remains unbroken to this day.

Menteith was not the king's only gift to Walter Stewart. At about the same time he was also given the Macsween lands in Knapdale and Arran. This westward expansion of a major baronial family was a deliberate provocation of Haakon, as was the devastation of Skye perpetrated by the Earl of Ross in 1262. Unable to let such behaviour pass unchallenged, in 1263 Haakon set about assembling a massive expeditionary force with which, he boasted, he would teach the young King of Scots a lesson in warfare.

Sadly for Haakon, it was he who needed a course at staff college. The story of his ill-fated armada is a catalogue of errors and misjudgements. To begin with, he missed the operational window available to him for a seabourne attack on Scotland. By delaying his departure until 11 July, he left insufficient time to achieve his goals before the autumn gales set in, a mistake which had grievous consequences.

Having made a safe passage to Lerwick (Shetland), the Norwegians wasted further precious weeks trying to persuade the locals to join them; it was mid-

August before they finally rounded Cape Wrath and joined up with the King
of Man, the Lord of Garmoran and smaller bands of Islesmen. Ewen of Argyll,
who surrendered his lands but retained his allegiance to Alexander III, was
placed under house arrest. It was reported that Haakon now commanded about
4000 men and 150 ships – the mightiest overseas force ever assembled by a
Norwegian king. Although formidable, it was hardly sufficient to bring the
Scots to their knees, particularly as they had time very much on their side.

Accompanied by his steward, Alexander III entered into negotiations with
Haakon at Ayr in late August. The Scottish king dragged the talks out for as
long as he could, knowing that the Norwegians' chances of success diminished
with each day that passed. Eventually Haakon lost patience. Returning to his
fleet, he sailed north to the Cumbraes in the Firth of Clyde: Stewart territory.
Like Somerled, he was bent on breaking the family's hold over the region; but
Steward Alexander showed himself as equal to the challenge as Steward
Walter had been two centuries before. While scouts and lightly-armed
bowmen kept watch from the shore, the steward and his knights positioned
themselves inland, prepared to move forward the moment a Norwegian
landing was reported. At this point Haakon made another critical error. He
split his forces.

A raiding party of Islesmen was sent up Loch Long and thence overland
into Loch Lomond, where they tried to compel the Scots to return to the negotiating table by ravaging the countryside round about. While they were away
the weather suddenly took a turn for the worse.

On the evening of Sunday 30 September a great gale blew up from the west,
rising to a fury of intensity during the night. Several of Haakon's ships were
forced to cut their masts, and many including a valuable cargo vessel, dragged
their anchors and were cast upon the Scottish shore at Largs. When morning
broke and the Scottish lookouts saw what had happened, they sent messengers
riding urgently inland to tell their commander the news. They then set about
picking off the stranded crews with their bows and arrows. As there was still
quite a gale blowing, many arrows fell onto the sandy beach, harmlessly short
of their target.

That morning Haakon and his commanders met on board their flagship to
assess what had happened and plan the next move. The situation was tricky,
but by no means disastrous. With careful planning they could easily extricate
themselves from their difficult position and resume offensive operations. After
further discussion, they dispatched a landing party to salvage what it could
from the wrecked vessels and rescue their crews. The light Scottish forces were
unable to do more than harry the new arrivals, 'attacking them sometimes, but
always from a distance'. This desultory fighting continued for much of the
tempestuous day.

By Tuesday the storm had blown itself out. Taking advantage of the calmer
conditions, at first light Haakon ordered a much larger body of men to the
beach. They were soon joined by the king himself, who supervised the

unloading of the stranded merchantman. The Scots on the hills to the east watched their movements, from time to time casting urgent glances over their shoulders. Where was the steward and his force of knights and men-at-arms? If they did not arrive shortly, the enemy would have finished their work and returned safely to their ships.

It had taken several hours for the news of the Norwegians' enforced landing to reach Alexander on Monday morning, and by the time his warband had assembled it was too late to advance on Largs. The steward had no wish to confront Haakon until he had a sizeable force under his command. Well aware of the enemy's strength, he knew that if he failed to rebuff the assault the Norwegians would be able to establish a dangerous bridgehead on Scottish soil.

Soldiers continued to gather at Alexander's camp throughout the night of 1-2 October. At daybreak, confident that he now had sufficient men for the task ahead, the steward ordered the advance. He rode in the vanguard with about 100 mounted knights, better armed and trained than anything under Haakon's command. The rest of his host comprised a few hundred professional foot soldiers, drawn from castles in the vicinity, and hundreds, perhaps thousands of locals who had been called up at short notice and equipped with whatever weapons they could lay their hands on.

The Scots reached Largs at about midday. Leaving his men in the village, Alexander moved forward to see for himself what was going on. He walked a few hundred yards to the crest of a hill overlooking the sea, then lay down and gazed on the busy scene before him.

The bulk of the Norwegian fleet was anchored some distance from the shore. In the foreground the wrecks of the merchant vessel and three longships rested on their sides, stranded like whales in the sand. Small boats were splashing rapidly backwards and forwards between the ships riding at anchor and the beach, ferrying men to help with the work on land and returning with cargo salvaged from the supply craft's hold.

Up to a thousand enemy troops had come ashore. Some were lined up in human chains, carrying goods from the disabled vessels to the rowing boats wallowing in the shallows. Others were digging and shoving at the warships, trying to refloat them. Further up the beach warriors stood guard, peering up at the slopes where Alexander was watching, hidden from view.

What fears and hopes went through the mind of the forty-nine-year-old steward as he lay there in the wet grass that fateful morning? Careful and canny, he disliked having to make decisions on the spur of the moment. From a military point of view, it was quite clear what he had to do: he should order an immediate attack, taking the enemy while they were divided and unprepared. Yet his own forces were no larger than those of Haakon and many of them were simple farmers, untrained and unused to warfare. Was it wise to risk them against the Norwegian's hardened and desperate warriors? Besides, Alexander mused, once battle had been joined anything could happen. His men could be ignominiously routed. He might even lose his own life, leaving only a baby son to succeed him. What then might become of the honour and estates which his family had so carefully built up over the last hundred years? It was not just the pride of Scotland which was at stake: the fate of the Stewarts probably hung in the balance, too.

Alexander shuddered. Such thinking led nowhere. A single principle had guided his family this far; and now, in this moment of extreme peril, it had to suffice once more. The steward would do his duty.

Crawling backwards until he was out of sight of the beach, Alexander rose and strode purposefully back to his troops. Those who knew him well could tell by his bearing that his mind was made up. As soon as he was within earshot of his soldiers, he gave his orders: the Scots might never be given so favourable an opportunity again – they would attack at once. A few minutes later Alexander's troops were pouring down the slopes towards the enemy. The fight had begun.

The conflict which followed was more a series of skirmishes than a full-scale battle. The elderly Haakon, keen to get beyond the range of Scottish archers and stone throwers, returned to his ship as soon as the assault began. For some time, finding his army assailed by so numerous an enemy, he had 'imag-ined...the Scottish king himself to be there'.

Following their leader's example, Haakon's men took up defensive positions and began to re-embark. The move was precisely what Alexander had hoped for, and he was quite prepared to see them go. Careful in battle as in politics, he commanded his soldiers to harass the retreating foe, but not to risk losing their position by over-extending themselves. The Norwegians had only a quarter of their army on the beach. If the remainder saw the Scots falling back, they might well come ashore and turn the withdrawal into a rout.

Despite the cautious tactics adopted by either side, it was a bloody fight. Alexander's knights acquitted themselves well, time and again charging the defensive line held by the terrifying Ogmund 'Crow-dance'. The spears, slings and axes of the steward's foot soldiers also accounted for dozens of Norwegian lives. The battle was at its most ferocious around a low mound, which the Scots captured, lost and then re-took. When late in the afternoon the last of Haakon's men scrambled into their overloaded boats and pulled for the safety of the vessels offshore, the beach was littered with dead and dying men. Among them lay the body of the knight Peter de Curry, a young tenant of the steward whose gorgeous armour and military prowess so impressed his enemies that they generously found a place for him in their *Saga of Haakon*.

The Norse saga claimed the Battle of Largs as a victory. It tells how, outnumbered ten to one by the enemy, the warriors of the north and west had put the enemy to flight and retired in good order to their fleet. But the account was drawn up long after the event, when time and vanity had blurred the memory. Men on both sides had indeed shown great valour. But from a strategic point of view the engagement was a devastating Norwegian defeat.

It was now too late in the year for the campaigning to continue. Battered by the autumn gales and discomfited whenever it came ashore, Haakon's depleted army slowly made its way back along the course it had sailed so proudly a few months before. Reaching Orkney in late October, the Norwegians decided to spend the winter there before launching a fresh assault the following year. But Haakon did not survive to see the spring. On 16 December 1263, after an illness lasting several weeks, he died in the bishop's palace at Kirkwall. With his death Norse hopes of rebuilding an empire in the west vanished for ever.

The rest of the story is easily told. The next year Scottish forces conquered Man and extended their sway over almost all the Western Isles, so that by 1265 only a few remote strongholds in the Outer Hebrides still adhered to their Norwegian overlord. Haakon's successor, King Magnus, accepted the inevitable. By the Treaty of Perth, signed in 1266, he ceded Man and the Western Isles to the King of Scots for the sum of 4000 merks, payable over four years. A struggle which had lasted for almost five hundred years was thus finally concluded in favour of Scotland.

From Barra to the Borders Alexander III now reigned supreme. Although it seems obvious to us that Scottish rule should embrace all the country's offshore islands, there was nothing inevitable about Alexander's achievement. Had his steward failed to take advantage of the enemy's weakness at Largs on that still October morning, Haakon and his formidable army might have survived to fight on. Worse, had the Norwegians won a swift victory and marched directly inland, then it might have been the Scots who were forced to sign away their rights in the west.

Largs had not been a spectacular battle, and it had not been won by spectacular generalship. But it had been decisive. At the time it was the greatest single contribution a Stewart had made to his country's fortunes. For this, if for nothing else, Alexander of Dundonald deserves to be remembered as long as a Scottish state survives.

CHAPTER 6

The Reluctant Patriot

I

By the late thirteenth century the Stewarts were one of the most important families in Scotland. Their landed power had expanded from their original estates into the western Highlands, where they now held fiefs in Kintyre, Cowal, Bute and Arran. Six stone castles – Renfrew, Rothesay, Dunoon, Dundonald, Glassary and Eilean Dearg – stood as impressive, tangible manifestations of the family's status. No royal council was complete without a steward, whose invariably wise advice had been sought by the crown for over a century and a half. The family served at local level too, Walter II as a respected justiciar, and his grandson James as sheriff of both Ayr and Dumbarton. Above all, the Stewarts were sure of that most conspicuous sign of royal favour, immediate access to the person of the king himself.

Dol and its obscure dapifership now belonged to a different world. The Stewarts were no longer outsiders, immigrant barons whose behaviour and thinking jarred the sensibilities of the indigenous population. In the west, where they commanded galley fleets and were the hereditary lords of scattered settlements of Gaelic-speaking clansmen, they were the proud heirs to loyalties which stretched back deep into Scotland's Celtic past. Alexander, the fourth steward, had married into the family of Angus, Lord of Bute, a descendant of the mighty Somerled. This union between the ancestors of the protagonists of 1164 symbolised a burgeoning unity within the realm. Slowly and at times painfully a Scottish nation was being born, with the Stewarts near its heart.

* * *

If the House of Stewart faced the future with a degree of optimism, the same was not true of the House of Canmore. Since 1058 the dynasty had provided a succession of capable kings, and during the reigns of Alexander II and III Scotland is said to have occupied a more prominent European position than at any other time in her history. When James the fifth steward came into his inheritance in 1283, however, the luck of the Canmores was running out.

Alexander III's minority had offered an unhappy foretaste of what lay in store. Over the last quarter of his reign, as if prearranged by some vengeful god, events in Scotland took on a tragic downward momentum of their own. Queen Margaret died in 1275, aged only thirty-five. Six years later her second son David followed her to the grave, leaving no offspring. 1283 saw the death not just of Steward Alexander but also of Margaret, the king's only daughter, who had married the King of Norway in 1281 and had died shortly after giving birth to another Margaret, the 'Maid of Norway'. Finally, in January 1284 Alexander III's only surviving son, the Lord Alexander, passed away after a long illness. Once again the divisive question of the succession rose to the top of the political agenda. If the Scottish crown could be worn by a woman, then one day it might adorn the Maid of Norway; if, on the other hand, the female line was barred, the prize was open to a number of claimants.

Alexander III was only too aware of the seriousness of the situation, and in November 1285 he married again, choosing a young and attractive French bride, Yolande de Dreux. But Fate had not yet completed her cruel round of woe. On a stormy night in the following March, attempting to return late at night to the comfort of Yolande's bed, Alexander was thrown from his horse and killed. When his widow's pregnancy turned out to be wishful thinking, and four years later the infant Margaret of Norway perished while crossing to the kingdom she had never known, the line of Canmore was at an end.

Trouble had descended on Scotland long before it was decided to send for Princess Margaret. The great baronial families divided against each other, law and order began to break down and England's ambitious Edward I exploited the mounting turmoil by pressing his claim as lord superior of Scotland. Ere long the country's very existence as an independent state was being called into question. If ever the country had needed a trusty steward, this was surely the moment.

* * *

James Stewart was born in about 1260. He may have been named after St James the Great, whose shrine at Compostella his father had visited in 1252. The name must also have pleased the Stewart foundation at Paisley. Even so, the rejection of a traditional family name was unusual, and it has been suggested that James may have had an elder brother, a Walter or an Alan, who had died young. At the time of his father's death the fifth steward was in his early twenties; he was therefore at the height of his powers when the sudden death of Alexander III forced him to the very centre of the political stage.

James's personality remains strangely elusive, despite the major role he played in the crucial events of the next quarter of a century. Beside giants like Robert Bruce and William Wallace he appears very ordinary, almost a political pigmy. He was an unheroic figure born into an heroic age, a chief engineer called from below decks to assist the bridge officers with navigation during a violent storm. As his father and grandfather before him, James was essentially a royal servant, a facilitator and negotiator with no pretensions to national leadership. Predisposed to seek the middle way, only when this was blocked would he commit himself, and even then not necessarily openly, and certainly never recklessly.

And yet, for all his prevarication and lack of charisma, James's contribution to Scotland's struggle for independence was not insignificant. His attachment to the national cause lent it prestige and credibility. On a more practical level, for years he worked carefully and unobtrusively to reconcile opposing factions and assist the more positive actions of others. It is true that when under pressure he openly pledged his support to the English on a number of occasions; but he was by no means the only Scottish aristocrat to do so, and it was only his rather timorous way of coping with near-impossible situations. It represented what was temporarily expedient rather than a fundamental change of allegiance. James was by nature a survivor, a pragmatist content to leave dramatic gestures to others while he plotted his own more cautious course.

In all his actions James was assisted by that most convenient of life-saving qualities, a nimble conscience. When necessary, this enabled him to accept the convenient aphorism that the needs of the Stewarts and the common good of the realm were one and the same. To some extent the belief was justified. The Scottish cause was not short of martyrs, but it often lacked the sort of respectable backing which James had to offer. He saw no point in risking his own life and inheritance when they could be preserved by a formula of words. What would have been gained, he might have reasoned, had he been killed or his estates placed permanently in English hands?

No ballad-maker sung James's praises when he was gone. Some of his actions appear downright cowardly, and self-interest and duty were too tightly intertwined in his slippery personality for anyone to find him particularly attractive. Yet in his peculiar way he was true to his family tradition; and at a time when many wore their loyalties as lightly as their cloaks, in his heart if not always in his actions James remained steadfast in his stewardship.

II

The ability of the Stewarts to provide a line of capable royal councillors probably meant that each steward attended carefully to the political education of his successor. This certainly seems to have been the case with Steward Alexander and his son James. At the age of sixteen the boy was already shadowing his father's business, witnessing charters, turning up at court and probably eavesdropping on policy discussions. In this manner he was introduced to the right people and given a chance to see at first hand how Alexander operated. The lessons in cautious statecraft were not lost on him.

James did not figure prominently during the three years between the deaths of his father and Alexander III, when the ageing king relied on more experienced advisors. Nevertheless, the young steward attended council meetings and was among those who in 1284 put forward an entail giving the succession to Margaret of Norway if the king should fail to produce a male heir.

The events of 1286 brought James's political apprenticeship to an abrupt end. Meeting in April shortly after the king's death, parliament sidestepped the succession issue and called on all magnates to swear to keep the peace. It then appointed six guardians to govern on behalf of the 'community of the realm'. Two were earls (Comyn of Buchan and Duncan of Fife), two were bishops (Fraser of St Andrews and Wishart of Glasgow) and two were representatives of the most puissant baronial families: John Comyn of Badenoch and James Stewart.

James's title and family history obviously played a part in his selection. He was also chosen because he helped maintain a careful balance among the guardians between north and south, young and old. But he was put forward because of who he was, as well as what he was. Still in his twenties, he already showed unusual maturity and responsibility – when the Norwegians complained to the provisional government about the seizure of one of their ships, it was to James that they directed their plea, not one of his more senior colleagues.

No one could be sure that the Maid of Norway was entitled to the Scottish throne. Two prominent Scottish families, the Bruces and the Balliols, both descended from the younger brother of William the Lion and consequently not included among the guardians, announced for obvious reasons that her sex debarred her from the succession. This put James in a tricky position. He was related to the Bruces by marriage, and his strong family links were reinforced in September 1286 with the signing of a controversial piece of evidence known as the 'Turnberry Bond'.

The public purpose of the agreement was to pledge support for some venture in Ireland for two Irish magnates, Richard de Burgh, Earl of Ulster, and Thomas de Clare. In a match which may have been first mooted at Turnberry, a few years later James married de Burgh's sister Egida, thereby acquiring estates near Coleraine. This suggests that the meeting had been called for no more sinister purpose than to discuss matters of common local interest.

But the bond may be interpreted otherwise. It made ambiguous references to the feudal overlordship of the king of England, and its illustrious cabal of signatories included Robert Bruce, Lord of Annandale, who had a claim to the throne, and his son, another Robert Bruce, Earl of Carrick. Alongside were the names of two guardians, the Earl of Dunbar and James Stewart. Also present were two of James's kinsmen: his uncle Walter, Earl of Menteith, and his brother John of Jedburgh. Might the Bruce faction have gathered their supporters at Turnberry to discuss the Lord of Annandale's right to the throne?

If this was the purpose of the bond, nothing came of it. At least, not for the time being. Certainly it would have been out of keeping with James's later actions if so early on he had plotted to get the crown for his relatives. For sure, along with Bishop Wishart and Earl Duncan he was prepared to back the Bruces against the Balliols, but it was not in his nature to countenance grossly irregular behaviour. Besides, the guardians (who by 1289 were down to four following the murder of the unsavoury Earl of Fife and the death by natural causes of the Earl of Buchan) made a point of identifying themselves only with those who had the true interests of the community at heart. James, probably more than any of them, had been responsible for quelling the civil disturbances which followed Alexander III's fatal accident.

Until the death of Margaret of Norway, James believed that the safest way forward was to prepare the nation to accept a queen. He had no particular objection when Edward I proposed that Margaret marry his son Edward, provided that Scotland's independence was carefully set out in writing. This was duly done in the Treaty of Birgham (June 1290). Although the steward understood that if the plan came to fruition Margaret would spend much of her time in England, he probably looked rather favourably on the idea. If he played his cards right, his guardianship might last indefinitely.

But early that autumn news came from Kirkwall of the death of the delicate queen elect, invalidating at a stroke every move already made in the succession game. As they picked up the counters and prepared to start all over again, the original players were filled with a depressing sense of ominous foreboding. There was a new presence at the board. Powerful enough to load the dice and write the rules as he went along, Edward I had joined in determined to win.

The English king was helped considerably by the situation within Scotland, where bitter divisions among the aristocracy were giving credence to the call for an impartial outsider to settle the succession dispute amicably. The steward was in a tricky position. He was torn between his wish to back Robert Bruce, who had already acknowledged Edward I's overlordship and asked for his support, and his duty to the kingdom, whose best long-term interests were probably not best served by outside interference. In August 1291 he made a small gesture of independence by rejecting an English bribe. But James was no hero, and after a token show of resistance he and the rest of the guardians paid homage to Edward, allowed themselves to be reappointed by him, and accepted his offer to mediate over the succession. This done, and having surrendered to English officers the royal castles in his care, James traipsed over to the west and started hearing oaths of loyalty on Edward's behalf.

The steward was not happy with what he had been asked to do. Yet as he gazed down at the succession of heads bowed in humiliating submission before him, he took comfort from two thoughts. Firstly, the Scots had managed to shake off English overlordship in the past; and, secondly, it was quite likely that his ally Bruce would get the throne. That, at least, would be better than a Balliol triumph.

It was not to be. Edward's special Court of Claims declared in favour of John Balliol, on the grounds that he had the most direct descent from William the Lion. Distressed but loath to appear disloyal, James stated publicly that although he did not like the decision, he would abide by it. He then retired to his estates to wait on events. On one count he need not have worried. Rather than victimise his steward, King John chose instead to involve him closely in a proposed administrative reorganisation in the west by appointing him to the new and strategically important sheriffdom of Kintyre. Had the reform been put into effect, it would have enhanced Stewart power considerably.

Other developments were less propitious. While James's influence waxed, that of the new king waned, painfully. Acknowledging Edward's general overlordship, within that broad parameter John considered himself free to manage his own affairs. Edward thought otherwise, and encouraged by his success in 1290-2 he insisted that his puppet king dance to an English tune. His aim was simple, straightforward, cynical: to reduce Scotland from an independent kingdom to a mere English barony, whose lord was graciously permitted to retain his ancient, if rather fanciful title. To this end he heaped humiliation after humiliation upon his unfortunate vassal. John's laudable attempts at good government were hamstrung by lack of English approval, and he was even required to attend the English parliament in person to answer for his courts' actions.

If Edward believed he was driving home a lesson he had already taught, he made a serious miscalculation. If, on the other hand, he was hoping to provoke the armed uprising he needed as an excuse to occupy Scotland and establish his direct rule there by force, his policy was initially an unqualified success. Instead of being cowed by English goads, the Scots were merely pricked into action by them, and when in 1294 Edward demanded military service overseas from his Scottish subjects, they had had enough. The nation rose in revolt.

III

Steward James disliked making decisions, particularly major ones. Now that he had two to make, both critical, he paused for a while to take stock.

The Bruces had never reconciled themselves to the choice of John Balliol as king. The Lord of Annandale who had contested the succession in 1290-2 was dead. His son and grandson, both also Robert Bruces, refused to commit themselves to the Scottish cause in 1294 and later slipped south into England, where they were joined by the Earls of March and Angus. The

Bruce lands in Annandale were given to John Comyn, Earl of Buchan.

What should James do? He had little time for the Comyns, with whom his uncle Walter had been at loggerheads over the disputed earldom of Menteith, and the Bruces were family friends and allies, as the Turnberry Bond had shown. But to join with the knot of self-seeking Scots opposing King John would be to break a tradition of loyalty which had endured for well over two centuries. Conservative to his fingertips, James Stewart decided to remain in Scotland. He still retained his affection for the Bruces, and one day would renew his alliance with them; but only after they had decided where their true loyalties lay.

James's second decision was even more difficult. There was a move afoot to wrest the government from John's hands and pass it to a group of magnates acting in the king's name, and James had been invited to join this new exec-utive council. Whatever formula of fine words was used, to accept the invi-tation would mean breaking his oath to Edward I and imply that he esteemed the community of the realm above the person of the king. Fortunately, the former problem was solved in 1294 when Pope Celestine V formally released the Scots from their sworn obligations to the English king. Seven months later, still with some misgivings, James agreed to join the council. It was a momentous decision, as important for the Stewarts' future as when Walter Fitz Alan had chosen to enter the service of King David in 1136. The coun-cillors were now not just servants of the crown, but part of a small group claiming the crown's powers. It was their first taste of real power.

The council lost no time in making its independent position clear. In what was in effect a declaration of war, on 23 October Scottish envoys drew up a treaty with Edward's principal Continental protagonist, Philip IV of France, binding both sides in a defensive and offensive alliance against England. The move received widespread support from all sections of Scottish society. When it was ratified early the following year, Steward James's name appeared among the guarantors.

Although he was now unequivocally tied to the Scottish cause, James still harboured doubts about the wisdom of his countrymen's precipitous action. Was it really sensible to challenge Edward so openly? He was, after all, master of one of the most effective war machines in Western Europe. His ships controlled the narrow seas between Scotland and her ally, and the English army was larger, better equipped and more experienced than anything the Scots could hope to muster. Would the Scots not be crushed beneath the weight of English armour, just as the Welsh had been twenty-five years before? Haunted by these practical misgivings, James garrisoned the key border fortress at Roxburgh in readiness for an English attack. Here, secure for the moment behind the walls of one of the kingdom's most powerful castles, he settled down to see what would happen.

The campaigning of 1296 confirmed James's worst fears. Edward smashed his way into Berwick, the largest town in the country, slaughtering many of its inhabitants. Four weeks later the Earl of Surrey destroyed the main Scottish army near Dunbar. Edward swept north. Edinburgh held out for only a week. Stirling Castle was abandoned before the English arrived and the inhabitants of Perth surrendered as soon as enemy knights appeared before its flimsy defences. King John and his Comyn backers gave themselves up in July and were packed off to London, along with the precious Stone of Destiny and other time-honoured relics and regalia. Having pushed on as far as Elgin without meeting any substantial resistance, in August Edward returned south. Scotland was his.

* * *

Unwilling to admit that Scotland still existed as a separate kingdom, Edward declined to call himself King of Scots. Instead, he ruled the whole of Britain as King of England. What had begun as a brave attempt to maintain Scotland's independence seemed to have ended all too quickly in the kingdom's extinction. James Stewart saw no virtue in trying to remain upright in such a gale. On 5 May, eight days after the disaster at Dunbar, he had surrendered Roxburgh Castle to the invader without a fight, and a week later he had renewed his fealty to Edward. For the moment he was bent on survival, prepared to beguile the time by looking like it. From his later behaviour, however, it is clear that what he spoke with his mouth and what he believed in his heart were clean different things.

For a while James's English masters trusted him. He was charged with receiving Kirkintilloch and Dumbarton Castles on Edward's behalf and with seeing that his tenants swore fealty to the King of England. But by the autumn the steward's surface compliance was beginning to look a bit suspect. He was reluctant to take steps against tenants who refused the new oaths and made little effort to crush a revolt by Alexander Macdonald of Islay. Furthermore, he was again in contact with Robert Bruce the younger, Earl of Carrick, whose family ambitions had been deliberately and openly snubbed by Edward after Dunbar. As a precaution, therefore, the steward was ordered to surrender all castles and hostages in his charge, and to give up his position as Sheriff of Dumbarton.

James spent the next few months plotting. His fellow conspirators included his brother Sir John Stewart, Bishop Wishart (a fellow member of the 1295 executive council), the disaffected Earl of Carrick, Sir William Douglas and Sir Alexander Lindsay. The inspiration for this high-born conspiracy was mounting hostility to English efforts to control Scotland from their base at Berwick.

The country was more easily taken than held, and throughout the winter of 1296-7 local administration steadily reverted to Scottish hands. The occupying forces found that no sooner had they dispatched soldiers to deal with one show of resistance, than another broke out somewhere else. The most

successful rebel was the outlaw William Wallace, one of James' vassals from
Paisley whose family had moved to Scotland with Walter Fitz Alan. While
publicly condemning Wallace as a lawbreaker, the steward and Wishart were
almost certainly keeping him secretly supplied with weapons and information. Having thus built up his strength beneath his lord's shield, in May 1297
Wallace emerged as commander of a potent nationalist force. At this point
James, Wishart, Carrick ('aspiring to the kingdom', it was claimed) and
several of their cronies cast aside their disguises and joined the revolt.

Now that they could see their enemy plainly, the English collected a large
army and marched through Annandale to Irvine, on the west coast between
Largs and Ayr, where the Scots were gathering. Suddenly, several aristocratic
rebel leaders, including James, appeared to lose their nerve, and the two
armies met not in a major battle but in an extended parley.

We do not know why James backed down at this crucial juncture. The
most straightforward reason is that he was not, and never had been, a fighter.
But since some of his fellow negotiators – Sir William Douglas, for example
– were not so timorous, other explanations are more plausible. To begin with,
the nationalist commanders probably felt they did not yet have an effective
fighting force. Moreover, as was pointed out at the time, the Scots were not
truly united. They shared an icy antipathy towards the English; but while
Wallace and the majority of the leaders were fighting for the deposed King
John, Robert Bruce was standing beneath quite a different banner: that of his
father's claim to the throne. A charitable explanation of the steward's reluctance to fight would be that he saw the foolishness of taking on the English
under such circumstances, and so chose to play for time.

James used the negotiations, which dragged on for a month, to advertise
the nationalist cause, announcing that the rebels spoke for the whole
community of Scotland which was being destroyed by Edward's unreason-
able, high-handed demands. Eventually, having strung things out for as long
as he could, James accepted an undignified submission, pledging his future
good behaviour in return for a pardon. Wishart was imprisoned in Roxburgh
Castle and Sir William Douglas in Berwick Castle. But Wallace and Robert
Bruce, who had refused to be party to the surrender, were still at large.
Although James's apparently pusillanimous behaviour had discredited the
aristocratic leadership of the national revolt, his prevarication had at least
ensured that others were free to continue the struggle.

The 'Capitulation of Irvine' settled nothing. Indeed, for the great
majority of Scots it was no capitulation at all and they emerged more determined than ever to rid themselves of their hated alien overlords. During the
summer of 1297 the national revolt grew in might and momentum, feeding
on the military success of Wallace in the south-west and of Andrew Murray
north of the Tay. Misjudging the firmness of his grip at home, Edward I left
for Flanders on 22 August, leaving Scottish affairs in the hands of Treasurer
Cressingham and the Earl of Surrey. As the combined forces of Murray and

Wallace were by now posing a very real threat to their control over all but the very south of the country, Edward's deputies gathered an army of about 10,000 men and advanced towards Stirling. Embarrassed and plagued by doubts at what he was doing, James trailed along with them, accompanied by several other time-serving Scottish magnates.

When the two armies had gathered on opposite sides of the Forth, with Stirling Bridge between them, James was sent forward to ask Wallace to surrender. The steward was well suited to his mission. Recalling what had happened on previous occasions when the Scots had tackled the English in pitched battle, he was undoubtedly sincere when he pleaded with his countrymen to lay down their arms. But in their eyes James's credibility had been destroyed by the Irvine debacle, and they refused to heed his words. It was with a heavy heart, therefore, that James rode back to his men stationed at the rear of the English army and prepared for the worst.

For once the steward's prophesies of doom proved wholly unfounded. Unable to cross the narrow bridge in sufficient numbers, the English were first divided, then routed. When James was certain which way the tide was running, he ordered his men to join in the pursuit, slaying many of their former allies and seizing their baggage wagons. The incident might have helped restore James' reputation as a true Scot, but it was one of the less distinguished actions of his career. One cannot help wondering how he would have behaved if Wallace's men had been put to flight.

* * *

As Andrew Murray had died of wounds received at Stirling Bridge, Wallace was the hero of the hour. Knighted and appointed sole guardian of the realm, for ten glorious, gaudy months he was uncrowned King of Scotland, leaving the country's traditional leaders no choice but to walk in the giant's shadow. They did not all do so gracefully.

The brightest flames burn briefest, however, and so it was with Wallace. Edward I returned to Scotland in 1297 with yet another powerful army. At first the guardian played the part of Cunctator, avoiding battle but harrying the foe and laying waste the countryside. Then in late July for some reason he changed his strategy. Having established his forces in a strong defensive position near Falkirk, spear-carrying infantry in the vanguard and knights in reserve, he waited confidently for Edward to attack. As one might expect, James had placed himself safely towards the rear of the Scottish lines, the experience of Stirling Bridge not having whetted his appetite for battle one jot.

The fighting began early on 22 July, and lasted throughout the hot summer's day. Unprotected by their own high-born cavalry, who hung about uncommitted at the back of the field, man by man, rank by rank, the Scottish infantry were gradually worn down by the deadly fire of the enemy bowmen and the constant assaults of their armoured horsemen. James's brother, Sir John Stewart, the commander of the archers of the Forest, was slain in a charge of English knights. No such honourable fate befell the steward – together with most of the Scottish magnates, he fled the slaughter without so much as drawing his sword.

The Falkirk disaster destroyed Wallace's power. He resigned his guardianship and resumed his role as a guerrilla leader until captured by the English in 1305 and subjected to a terrible traitor's death in London. Craven though his behaviour had been, James was now clearly out of Edward's favour too, for he had changed sides once too often. At the end of August the English referred to him as the 'late steward of Scotland', and his estates were given to his erstwhile ally, Sir Alexander Lindsay.

IV

For the time being James was firmly and openly committed to re-establishing Scotland's independence, and over the next five years he devoted all his energies to that end. Avoiding the limelight, he took the part of elder statesman, working behind the scenes to persuade his more hot-headed companions to sink their differences and work for the common cause. It was a crucial, if somewhat unglamorous role.

Fortunately for the Scots, Edward had been unable to follow up his victory at Falkirk, and Scotland again came under a double administration. From their bases at Edinburgh, Berwick and Roxburgh, the English maintained their hold over the south-east, while the aristocratic guardians, united in the cause of the community of the realm, gradually re-established control elsewhere. But all was not harmony in the Scottish camp. Most nationalists, particularly King John's nephew, John Comyn the Red, remained loyal to the exiled Balliol, now in semi-retirement in France. The Earl of Carrick would have none of this. For him the struggle was, and always had been, part of the Bruces' campaign to win the inheritance denied them in 1292. The bitterness of the ongoing Balliol-Bruce quarrel, and the steward's role in preventing it from tearing the community apart, is well illustrated by an incident which took place during a council meeting at Peebles on 19 August 1299.

William Wallace had recently left the country on some undisclosed diplomatic mission. Sir David Graham, a Comyn supporter, claimed that as Wallace had departed without first obtaining the guardians' permission his lands were forfeit. William's brother, Sir Malcolm Wallace, took exception to this. The quarrel became heated, and both men draw their daggers.

At this point Robert of Carrick and the Red Comyn got involved. According to an English spy, 'John Comyn leaped at the Earl of Carrick and seized him by the throat'. Others quickly joined in and the gathering deteriorated into a dangerous brawl. Even Bishop Lamberton of St Andrews, a

Wallace protégé, was drawn into the fracas. Unless someone acted swiftly, there was a real possibility that the guardians would end up spilling each other's blood rather than their enemies'.

It was James Stewart who saved the day. Ever the pacifist, he put himself between his feuding colleagues and persuaded them to resume their seats. Gradually, the anger died down and an edgy harmony was restored to the meeting.

The Peebles incident was only one indication of the jealous hostility dividing the Scottish leadership. Bruce-Comyn antipathy simmered on, until seven years later it finally did draw blood; and different combinations of guardians, some more successful than others, all failed to provide the nationalists with the cohesion they desired. In truth, collective leadership was almost certain to fail. The nation in crisis could not unite behind a compromise committee or an ineffectual exile. As Wallace's meteoric career had shown, it yearned for a single, active, charismatic leader of military and political distinction. Several years were to pass before such a saviour figure emerged, however, and in that time the nationalist position deteriorated badly.

Edward re-occupied the south-west in 1300-1. The next year, faced with a possible restoration of King John, Carrick once again deserted to the English. Even worse, despite the efforts of a powerful Scottish diplomatic delegation headed by Guardian Sir John Soulis and including James Stewart, the Scots were excluded from an Anglo-French peace signed in Paris in May 1303. This freed Edward at last to concentrate all his efforts on his tiresome northern province, and once more he swept into Scotland, scattering all opposition. True to form, James came forward to ask for pardon.

The harsh terms the English imposed on James this time showed that they viewed him as a dangerous opponent, no longer a mere carpet-bagger. He was refused safe conduct until Wallace had been handed over, a task which James had neither the power nor inclination to perform. The outlaw was eventually seized in Glasgow on 3 August 1305 and passed on to the English by Sir John Stewart of Menteith, younger son of Earl Walter. And in November 1305, after a grovelling submission to Edward I, Steward James received his lands back from the Earl of Lincoln, who had held them since 1301. Neither deed did the Stewarts much credit.

* * *

The Bruces were not exactly endearing themselves to the nationalists, either, for during the two years following his volte-face in 1302 the Earl of Carrick served his new master with some distinction. Nevertheless, by 1304 it was dawning on Carrick that he was backing the wrong horse. Two things were becoming clear. It was highly unlikely that King John would ever return to Scotland, and it was equally unlikely that Edward I would allow John's position to be taken by a Bruce. When Carrick's father died in the same year, therefore, Robert Bruce was free to start putting his ambitious plans into operation.

Firstly, Robert won to his side Bishop Lamberton, the most powerful cleric in Scotland. Then he began sounding out other possible allies. We do not know whether he approached the steward directly, but James probably showed some approval for what was going on – as soon as Robert's bid for the throne became public in 1306, James's lands reverted once more to the Earl of Lincoln. The next stage in Robert's designs involved winning over the Red Comyn, the son of King John's sister and the man in whom the Balliol and Comyn claims to the throne were combined. Robert made him several offers, all of which were rejected.

On 10 February 1306 Robert decided on one final effort, agreeing to meet John at Greyfriars kirk in Dumfries. There was little love lost between these tough and ambitious young firebrands. Neither was prepared to back down an inch. As at Peebles seven years before, they began quarrelling. This time there was no wise steward to come between them. Tempers flared, and in his fury Robert stabbed the Red Comyn to death near the high altar.

Robert had no choice but to press his claim to the crown at once, and he persuaded Countess Isabel of Buchan to install him as King of Scotland on 25 March 1306. Whether he had a legal right to the crown or not, his chances of success seemed minimal. Not only was he a sacrilegious murderer and an outlaw, but his rash behaviour and previous tergiversations had raised serious doubts about his qualities as a leader. Understandably, at first he did not win widespread popular support, and he conducted his initial military campaigns against both English and Scottish opponents.

Whatever his innermost feelings, the loss of James's estates had been enough to bring about his most painful submission to date. In October 1306 he swore everlasting loyalty to Edward on an array of holy objects, including crosses, gospels and venerated relics. This done, he got his lands back. But not his elder son Andrew. The youth was taken to London as a hostage and never heard of again.

James had always believed his quarrel with the King of England to be just and lawful, a form of trial by combat fought according to the rules of war. Edward had never accepted this, and denounced his Scottish opponents as traitors. The difference in attitude caused James much pain. We know, for example, that he was deeply upset when the English raised his nephew's head on a spike above Lochmaben Castle, and his son's disappearance can hardly have toughened his resolve to abide by his new oath.

Sometime after the death of Edward on 7 August 1307, the weary steward changed sides for the last time, coming out firmly for Robert Bruce. Thereafter he played little part in national affairs. His last political act was to witness the momentous proceedings at St Andrews in March 1309, when parliament concluded three years of remarkable achievement by officially recognising Robert I as their king.

Scotland's fifth hereditary steward died on 16 July 1309. He was not an old man, but fifteen years of extraordinary vicissitudes had undoubtedly sapped his strength. He had changed sides so many times that it is difficult to decide just where his true loyalty lay. Probably with himself first, the Stewarts second and Scotland third. Although not an impressive hierarchy of priorities, it was no different from that of most of his contemporaries, including Robert Bruce. It is also worth mentioning that life might have been much easier for James if he had sided with the English from the outset. Had he done so the Scottish revolt might have run along a very different course.

At the last, therefore, James was able to look back on a career of some achievement. He had ridden the storm with his inheritance intact. And he had done what he could, in his unspectacular way, to bring about the birth of the Scottish nation. It was now up to his son Walter to help the infant survive into adulthood.

CHAPTER 7

'Good Sir Walter'

I

Walter Fitz James, son-in-law of the great Robert Bruce, was the Stewarts' first hero. His reportedly extrovert and charismatic personality probably owed more to his mother, Egida de Burgh, than to the vacillating James. Unfortunately, like most of her female contemporaries, Egida is little more than a name, so there is no way of estimating for certain the influence she had on her talented son.

Born in a time of turmoil, when his father was preoccupied with national affairs, and only sixteen when he became steward, Walter escaped the customary family indoctrination in civil service virtues. His elder brother Andrew would have been groomed for the stewardship, and when he tragically disappeared in about 1307 there was insufficient time to bridle the zest of the youthful Walter. Determined to cut a greater dash than his father, the sixth steward simply responded instinctively to the situation in which he found himself. In Robert I Scotland at last had a leader capable of healing the kingdom's self-inflicted wounds and driving back the invader. Walter's senior by twenty years, it was not advice that Robert needed from his young steward, but action. And that is precisely what Walter was best fitted to give.

Over the course of his short, valorous career, posthumously written up with uncritical approbation, Walter managed to change public perception of the Stewarts from cautious administrators to proud warriors worthy of marriage into the royal family. But prodigy though he might have been, the figure which emerges from the chronicles is a medieval version of the conventional Hollywood cowboy: a macho cardboard superstar, largely two-dimensional and lacking real personality. We might have a Stewart hero, but we do not yet have enough information to reconstruct the dynasty's first complete human being.

* * *

The demise of a great medieval family was usually the result of its failure to produce male heirs. Crude though it may seem, therefore, the Stewarts' unflagging sexual drive and fertility played a crucial part in their long-term success. However lacklustre the performances of some of them on the battlefield, they rarely failed when it came to their duties in bed. And thus the dynasty multiplied, its future secure.

Until the early fourteenth century the Stewarts had been a compact, manageable group, unencumbered by links with many other leading kin groups. But the fourth and fifth generations initiated a fecund Stewart spring. The bole of the family tree, hitherto straight and largely uncluttered by offshoots, suddenly sprouted a dozen branches, each in turn subdividing into yet more stems. And since every new household was eager to further its fortunes, principally through marriage, before long there was scarcely a major family in the country which was not in some way linked to the Lords of Renfrew.

The sons of Walter Stewart, Earl of Menteith, were progenitors of earls of Menteith, Ruthven and Mar. The other side of the family was even more prolific, thanks largely to the efforts of a younger son of Steward Alexander, the eponymously titled Sir John Stewart of Bonkyl who fathered seven sons and at least one daughter. Five of these sons founded dynasties of their own, and their sister Isabella married Robert Bruce's great commander Thomas Randolph, Earl of Moray. Sir John's aunt was mother of Robert I's other principal military officer, Sir James Douglas 'the Good', who assisted the inexperienced Walter III at Bannockburn. When Walter's heir Robert had sired a dozen legitimate sons and daughters, all of whom lived to produce children, Scotland was swept by a great Stewart wave, engulfing everything in its path. The Comyns and even the Bruces were overtaken in the rush, and in the end Robert Stewart was swept to the throne itself.

II

Robert I's reign could hardly have begun less auspiciously. His forces were defeated first by the English, then by the Comyns, keen to revenge the Greyfriars' murder. Shortly afterwards the king disappeared into the isles, lochs and mountains of the north-west.

Before slipping away, Robert the king had made provision for those he was leaving behind. He was most concerned for the safety of his second wife, Elizabeth de Burgh (Walter's cousin), and Marjory, his ten-year-old daughter by his first wife, Isabella of Mar. A posse headed by John of Strathbogie, Earl of Atholl, and the king's brother Neil was charged with escorting the queen, her step daughter and several other ladies to safety. The party travelled north to the Earl of Mar's stronghold at Kildrummy, which had been considerably strengthened over the last few years on the personal instruction of Edward I.

The houses of Bruce and Mar were linked by two marriages: Robert with Isabella, and his sister Christian with Isabella's brother Gratney, Earl of Mar. The Mars had been one of the first families to back the Bruce's bid for the throne. But Gratney had recently died, leaving Robert ward of his young son Donald and master of Kildrummy. The English soon heard of the flight, and when the ladies learned of the approach of Edward Prince of Wales they decided to fly further north rather than trust the castle's defences. According to John Barbour's *The Bruce*, written in 1375, they were accompanied on their retreat by the Earl of Atholl and a 'Walter Stewart of Scotland'.

We do not know who this Stewart was. It might not have been Walter but Andrew, at that time still alive and at liberty. This would tie in well with the known facts. Earlier in the year Andrew had been in the custody of Bishop Lamberton of St Andrews, a staunch Bruce supporter. When Robert made his move, the English had demanded that Lamberton hand over his hostages, which he refused to do, releasing them instead in June 1306 with instructions that they were to fight for King Robert. Thus the teenage Andrew may have been among those who fled Kildrummy and were subsequently captured in Ross. If this is what occurred, then it would explain how Andrew came to be taken to England, where he died.

On the other hand, would Barbour really have muddled the nondescript Andrew with Walter, his future hero? It is more likely that the Stewart who rode out of the gates of Kildrummy with the ladies and squires of the court was indeed the thirteen-year-old Walter, who may have been with the queen, his cousin, to avoid being taken hostage when his father was grovelling before Edward I. The boy's presence would also have been a tangible gesture of Stewart solidarity with Robert I.

As the refugees made their way swiftly over the hills towards Strathspey, Glen Rothes and the open, level coastline between Elgin and Inverness, the young Walter – if it was he – had plenty of opportunity to observe his fellow travellers. He must have shown a particular fascination for Marjory Bruce, his junior by some three years, and he probably guided his horse next to hers so that they could chat as they rode along.

Walter was interested in Marjory not just because he wanted a young person to talk to. Having heard rumours of a possible match between their two families, he knew that one day either he or his brother might find themselves married to the young girl cantering beside him. Understandably curious, he wished to get to know her better.

Many years later the couple did marry. By then Walter had grown into steely manhood, hardened by the grim experiences of war and the death of his first wife; and Marjory's youthful zest had been crushed by years of cruel incarceration in an English prison. During their brief married life the couple may have recalled with affection the embarrassed glances and halting conversation of their childhood adventure. But the happy innocence of that first ride together was lost for ever.

After heroic resistance led by Sir Neil Bruce, the Kildrummy garrison was forced to capitulate when a traitorous blacksmith named Orbourne fired the castle grain store. Sir Neil and many others were executed. Meanwhile, the ladies and their escort had taken sanctuary at St Duthac's in Tain on the Dornoch Firth. It was a vain gesture. Where matters of state were concerned,

Earl William of Ross believed that practicality outweighed principle. He forced his way into the sanctuary, arrested the entire company and handed them over to the English.

Walter Stewart now disappears from the record until he crops up again at Bannockburn. The fate of Marjory and others seized by the Earl of Ross is better known. The queen was kept under dreary house arrest in England, Marjory was shut up in the Tower of London and her sister Christian sent to a nunnery. Far worse punishments were reserved for another sister, Mary, and Isabella of Buchan, the lady who had crowned Robert I. They were taken to Roxburgh and Berwick castles respectively, and there locked into specially made iron cages suspended on chains from the vaulted ceilings. At one time the English planned to do the same with the child Marjory, but for some reason they relented and gave her less humiliating accommodation. All the women remained captive until after Bannockburn.

The terrible events of 1306 turned King Robert from an adventurer into a sincere patriot. Henceforward he regarded monarchical power as less an end in itself than as a means for liberating his country, and one by one the great families came round to support him. As we have seen, the steward finally made up his mind in about 1307. His nephew Sir Alexander Stewart of Bonkil changed sides at the same time as his brother-in-law Sir Thomas Randolph, following their capture by Sir James Douglas. Sir John Stewart of Menteith, the betrayer of William Wallace, also came over, although it took him quite a while to convince the king of his trustworthiness. At the 1309 parliament, where the ailing James Stewart made his final public appearance, we find even William, Earl of Ross, in attendance. It says a great deal for Robert I's self-control and political wisdom (or cold heartedness) that he tolerated the presence of the traitor who had betrayed his wife and daughter.

The clergy set out parliament's position most clearly, declaring that 'Lord Robert, the king who now is' had been chosen on account of his birth, deeds and inherent virtue 'with the concurrence and consent' of the people. They went on to say that these same 'faithful people of the kingdom will live and die…with one who…has by the sword restored the realm.' Armed with this endorsement, which was echoed by the other estates, Robert continued to roll back the carpet of English occupation.

Friendly relations were established with France in 1309 and Norway in 1312. A half-hearted English assault in 1310 was met with scorched earth tactics and retaliatory cross-border raids the following year. By the summer of 1313 only Lothian lay outside Robert's control, and within twelve months that too had fallen. In the spring of 1314 'the Good Sir James' Douglas and Thomas Randolph, now Earl of Moray, took the castles at Roxburgh and Edinburgh, leaving only five important strongholds still in English hands. The furthest north was Stirling, where the governor had announced that he would surrender unless relieved by Midsummer's Day. Edward II was drawn into the conflict at Bannockburn because he could not allow so important a castle to fall without at least making an effort to save it.

Bannockburn was Walter III's first reported experience of warfare. Barbour wrote that

> 'Walter Stewart of Scotland fine,
> Who then was but a beardless youth,
> Came with a group of noble men
> That might by countenance be known.'

In other words, although still young the steward turned up with a distinguished band of followers. He was in fact probably about twenty years old, and Barbour inserted the 'beardless' epithet for effect rather than because it was strictly true – it suited the poet's epic theme to show that Scots of all ages were lined up with the king, and he wanted to give the impression that Walter, a commander of the future, was given his first taste of battle in one of Scotland's greatest victories. The chances are, however, that Walter was already quite an experienced soldier. Since his early teens Scotland had been continuously at war. He obviously enjoyed matters military and showed considerable skill in them; he also got on well with Sir James Douglas, one of the country's foremost commanders. Furthermore, however lofty Walter's status, it is unlikely that the hard-headed king would have knighted a complete novice along with Sir James Douglas on the eve of Bannockburn; nor would he have allowed a mere apprentice to share the command of a key brigade in battle.

The story of Bannockburn has been often told and the steward's part in the victory, though impressive, was not distinctive enough to merit yet another account. Suffice it to say that Walter conducted himself with bravery and skill, and in so doing confirmed the popular opinion that he was a man to watch, the rising star of his generation.

III

Comparison between the stories of Bannockburn and David and Goliath is not limited to the obvious similarity of native pluck overcoming a huge foreign bully. Just as David's victory was only one event in a protracted war, so Robert I's triumph was a single episode in a conflict which had not yet run half its course. Bannockburn worked wonders for the Scots' morale, and gave them an initiative which lasted for the rest of Robert's reign. Its immediate practical results, however, were the surrender of Scottish strongholds remaining in English hands (apart from Berwick) and a long-awaited exchange of prisoners.

In return for the Earl of Hereford, Edward II released his five most important hostages: Bishop Wishart, Queen Elizabeth, Princess Marjory, the king's sister Christian and her son Donald of Mar. Except for Earl Donald, all returned home under the escort of the young steward. After eight years in England Mar had developed such a deep attachment to that country (and to her king in particular) that by the time he reached Newcastle he found that he missed his southern friends so much that he turned back, remaining at the English court until Edward II's death thirteen years later.

As Robert I had no legitimate male offspring, he welcomed the return of Queen Elizabeth for dynastic as well as personal reasons. In theory Marjory was his heir apparent; but this looked too much like the situation at the end of Alexander III's reign for the king's liking, so he determined to put matters on a more secure footing. While persevering with his own attempts to produce a son (efforts which went unrewarded until the birth of Prince David in 1324), he arranged for Marjory to marry, and drew up a formal rearrangement of the succession. At Ayr in April 1315 Robert's brother Edward was proclaimed heir apparent until such time as the king should, God willing, have a son. Marjory agreed that the succession should revert to her side of the family only if Edward and Robert died without leaving male issue.

Marjory Bruce was now nineteen. Her life thus far had been a long catalogue of misery. She had lost her mother when still a child, and she hardly ever saw her father. Eight of what should have been her most pleasurable years had been spent in English captivity. Now, as she prepared to marry Walter Stewart, the young man whom she might have first met under such romantic circumstances, perhaps for the first time ever she allowed her spirits to rise a little. Her material future was secure. For a fleeting moment she would be at the centre of the nation's attention, then she would have a household of her own and a husband who by all accounts was at least chivalrous. But marriage, even for a princess, was by no means all dalliance and delight. Over every wedding ceremony hung the dark and perilous cloud of childbirth.

Marjory Bruce and Walter Stewart, hero of Bannockburn and royal favourite, were married in May 1315. To mark the occasion the king furnished his steward with valuable gifts, pensions and lands, including the baronies of Bathgate and Ratho. The greatest honour yet paid to a Stewart was a reward not just for Walter but for his whole family, in recognition of two centuries' faithful service to the crown. Moreover, although the Ayr agreement reduced the chances of the couple or their children ever taking the throne, Marjory had not abandoned her rights entirely. If Fortune were to desert the House of Bruce, the Stewarts would be there, waiting their call. The dynasty was not simply expanding; it was upwardly mobile too.

On 2 March 1316 Marjory gave birth to a healthy baby boy, christened Robert in honour of his grandfather. The young mother's happiness was tragically short-lived. She died a little over a year later and was buried in the abbey church at Paisley, near where she had spent her two brief years of married life. The cause of her death is unclear. She did not break her neck as the result of a fall from her horse while riding from Paisley to Renfrew, as used to be thought; she is more likely to have perished from complications arising out of a difficult second labour.

As a glance at any genealogical table of the period testifies, the death of a young wife was an unexceptional event. Walter was no doubt saddened at having lost so illustrious and spirited a partner, but he was unlikely to have shed many tears when told of her passing. This does not make him a callous man but a realistic one who had braced himself to accept death at every turn. Wives, like soldiers, invariably died in the course of their duty, so to avoid getting hurt it was better not to attach oneself too closely to them. Besides, Walter had already lost one wife, Alice Erskine, by whom he had a daughter Jean. After Marjory's death he did not wait long before taking a third partner, Isabel Grahame, who bore him a second son, James.

As time went on, however, Walter may have found himself thinking of Marjory with increased affection. This was not a late-flowering love for the lady herself, but a growing regard for the son she had produced the year before she died. As the king's only direct male descendant, the infant Robert was precious the instant he was born. The events of the next two and a half years made him doubly so.

The Ayr declaration had stipulated that Marjory and her offspring came only third in the line to succeed, behind King Robert and his brother Edward. By late 1318 the king still had no legitimate son and prince Edward had been slain, leaving no issue. A document drawn up on 3 December revised the Ayr pronouncement in the light of recent events: if Robert I should have no son, the crown of Scotland was to pass to his grandson. Robert Stewart was heir to the throne.

* * *

After his marriage to Marjory Bruce, Walter matured in judgement and experience, gathering himself, as it were, for the trials ahead. He spent a good deal of time in his father-in-law's company, attending the king on his visit to Tarbert in 1315 when he received the homage of the Islesmen. By the following year, when Robert went to assist his brother in Ireland, he had sufficient faith in his young protégé to leave him joint warden of the realm with Sir James Douglas.

Walter crossed to Ireland himself later, but he was fortunate not to get too closely involved in what turned out to be Robert I's most serious military and political miscalculation. The purpose of the Irish enterprise was to open up a second front against Edward II, depriving him of a useful supply of soldiers and compelling him to withdraw forces from his northern frontier. Behind the scheme lay a somewhat vague idea of a Celtic coalition between the Irish, Welsh and Scots to take revenge on the English for years of exploitation and aggression.

Edward Bruce, Robert's brother, was given the responsibility of turning the dream into reality. He succeeded in conquering large parts of Ireland and was invested as the country's high king in 1316. But lacking his brother's judgement and strategic brilliance, Edward was unable by force of arms or personality to unite a fragmented and volatile island, and twice when Dublin lay at its mercy the Scottish army passed the city by. Finally, on 14 October 1318 he angrily rejected the prudent counsel of Sir John Stewart and risked battle with a numerically far superior foe. Edward Bruce and several other leading Scots were slain in the ensuing conflict, and Robert's second front collapsed. More important as far as the Stewarts were concerned, Edward's death led directly to the rearrangement of the succession in favour of the king's infant grandson.

The reversal in Ireland was to some extent counterbalanced by achievements nearer home. Spearheaded by 'the Good Sir James' Douglas, in the years following Bannockburn the Scots engaged successfully in large-scale cross-border raiding. Their motives were twofold. They maintained pressure on the north of England in the hope that Edward II would make peace and recognise Robert I as king of an independent Scotland, and the attacks brought in useful wealth in the form of booty, ransom and protection money. Many English border towns were prepared to pay handsomely to keep the rampaging Scots from their gates. Edward II was irritated by these tactics, but refused to come to terms or to sanction a large punitive expedition against Scotland. One nasty bite from the Scottish lion had made him doubly shy. He finally stirred into action in March 1318 only when he heard that the Scots, after years of intermittent siege, had succeeded in capturing the town and castle of Berwick. Barbour reported that Edward was 'annoyed greatly' at the news.

When faced with a major English cross-border incursion, Robert's customary defensive tactic was to retreat before the enemy, where possible harassing their flanks and laying waste the countryside to deny them sustenance. Although this scorched earth policy was effective, it involved untold suffering and material loss. Four years after Bannockburn, now that the English had been driven from every corner of the kingdom, Robert felt strong enough to halt a future invasion on the border. The problem was how best to do this. The Scots had little chance of winning a pitched battle against a large English army in the south; such set piece victories as they did achieve were against an enemy drawn deep into hostile territory. The alternative was to tie up the bulk of an invasion force in a protracted siege, then raid the unprotected countryside to its rear. It was this tactic which the capture of Berwick now allowed Robert to pursue.

To prevent the English from ever reusing them as bases of occupation, Robert normally destroyed all the castles he recaptured, including the Stewart stronghold at Dundonald. But with Berwick he made an exception. Since the Scots had taken the place by treachery, not assault, he reckoned it to be an ideal site on which to base his new, more positive defence policy. No English army would dare advance far into Scotland with Berwick holding out behind it. Therefore, instead of razing its walls and making preparations to evacuate the area in the event of a counter-attack, he took the calculated risk of strengthening the garrison and stuffing the town full of food and ordnance.

Once Robert had determined to hold Berwick at all costs, he had one further decision to make. Who should command the fortress? Now that Edward Bruce was dead, the leading Scottish commanders were Sir James Douglas and the king's nephew Thomas Randolph, Earl of Moray. Both would have done the job excellently.

Robert had other plans. If the English did lay siege to Berwick, as seemed increasingly likely by the beginning of 1319, then he did not want his most experienced field officers shut up in the town. So he had to entrust his new fold to a second-rate shepherd, or to one with potential but little experience. Opting for the latter, in January 1319 Robert appointed Walter Stewart, his twenty-six-year-old son-in-law, warden of Berwick. It was not a choice he ever had cause to regret.

John Barbour recorded the subsequent siege of Berwick in fascinating detail. His description of the formal military operation is also the first full and specific account of the deeds of a member of the Stewart family. Keen to take up his post, the 'young and valiant' Walter made his way quickly to Berwick and set about putting the place in readiness. He brought in food and other essentials sufficient for a year's siege and provided 500 of his own men to stand alongside the crown's bowmen and the local militia (from the king's point of view, another good reason for giving the wardenship to a wealthy aristocrat). The defenders were fortunate to have the services of a Flemish engineer named John Crabbe, an expert in the manufacture and operation of war machines 'of great subtlety'. When he was sure that the town was in good shape, Robert withdrew to the north,

> '*And Walter Stewart, that was stout,*
> *He left in Berwick with his rout* [company].'

Barbour makes it quite clear that Walter was not just a good strategist, but a natural leader of men. The English had occupied Berwick for many years and defended it against blockade and repeated attack at high cost to the citizens, so it cannot have been easy for the new commander to persuade the townsfolk to make further sacrifices on behalf of those who, less than a year ago, had been their enemy. But the steward apparently treated everyone in the town 'so lovingly' that he soon won their allegiance. There would be no repetition of the betrayal which had occasioned the town's surrender the previous spring.

About eighteen months elapsed between Edward II's hearing of the loss of Berwick and his appearance before its walls. In the meantime he had smoothed the ruffled feathers of baronial opposition and collected an army of some 8000 men, well armed and furnished with plenty of siege equipment (scaffolds, ladders, slings and so forth), but apparently without the massive catapults so beloved of Edward I. One explanation for this omission is that Edward II did not believe that the Scots would try to hold Berwick; alternatively, he may have been told that it was not worth going to the expense of manufacturing and shipping north huge war engines to puncture Berwick's low walls. Some idea of their inadequate elevation can be gathered from Barbour's remark that an assailant standing on the ground before the ramparts could stab a defender in the face with his spear.

Edward's army arrived in early September – not a good time to begin a siege. It then spent a week digging in and preparing for the assault. The Scots sat and watched with interest, no doubt relieved to find no sign of machines like Edward I's devastating 'War Wolf' which in 1304 had hurled missiles even up to Stirling's lofty battlements.

During the interlude Walter rode about the town checking the defences and preparing his men for the coming ordeal. Apparently the Scots were not unduly dismayed by the enemy's show of force, which suggests that the warden had worked successfully on their morale. Walter's thoughts at this critical juncture are not hard to imagine. A veteran of Bannockburn and other actions, he knew full well that in the brutal and chaotic lottery of war he might easily receive a ghastly wound or lose his life. But that probably worried him less than the responsibility he bore to king, country and family. Robert had entrusted his steward above all others to hold the very gate of Scotland. No Stewart, save perhaps Walter III's twelfth-century namesake, had ever been graced with royal favour as he had been. Now he was being put to the test. Should Berwick fall, or its governor acquit himself unworthily, the reputation of Walter and his dynasty would be deeply tarnished.

The English finished their preparations on about 7 September. At first light the next day trumpets sounded all around the town. Before the noise had faded away, archers leapt from their trenches or leaned round barricades to release a shower of arrows onto the battlements. Then, with much shouting and yelling, enemy infantry advanced as quickly as they could towards the walls, carrying ladders and arrow-proof hoardings through a hail of Scottish missiles. By about eight o' clock that morning Berwick was under attack along its entire landward front.

Although ferocious, the straightforward onslaught was countered relatively easily with conventional tactics: hurling objects onto the heads of the assailants and tipping up their ladders 'flat long to the ground'. All the while Walter rode along the line with a hand-picked reserve of experienced warriors, stopping to help wherever he found the enemy pressing hardest. Shouting encouragement one minute and orders the next, and never far from the centre of the action, the warden's doughty soldiering made a lasting impression on the whole garrison.

Lying at the broad but shallow mouth of the Tweed, at high water Berwick was easily approached from the seaward side. At about ten o' clock, when the tide was fully in, the English used their naval superiority to launch an unusual surprise attack. Further down the coast their engineers had fitted a large vessel with some sort of crane. Next they had placed a smaller boat, with a drawbridge cut into its side, onto the deck of the parent ship and filled it with soldiers. The whole contraption had then been hauled up to Berwick by rowing boats and manoeuvred towards the walls on the rising tide.

To begin with the Scots had no idea what was going on. As the floating assault platform drew near, however, and they saw the boatload of soldiers winched up the rigging of the larger vessel to the height of Berwick's seaward battlements, they suddenly realised the danger. If the English managed to get close enough to lower the smaller boat's drawbridge over the top of the walls, the men in the gigantic crow's nest would pour into the town.

Walter made a point of being 'where men pressed most', and when he heard of the extraordinary seaborne attack he rushed over to the ramparts overlooking the estuary to take personal charge of defensive operations. A quick glance told him that the obvious target for his archers and slingers was not the unwieldy but heavily armoured assault craft itself, but the smaller boats trying to steer it into position. On Walter's command, missiles were soon raining down on the unfortunate oarsmen. The effect was devastating. The tugs began pulling in different directions while their charge drifted away from the wall, its drawbridge flapping uselessly over the water and its thwarted warriors shouting furiously to be moved closer to the enemy. Seeing what was going on, the Scots broke into jeers of relief and derision.

At this point the vessel ran aground. So caught up were they with trying to line up their newfangled landing craft, the English had forgotten about the tide. Ten minutes later their clumsy ship was stuck fast, listing heavily. The raised boat swung against the mast, tipping some men into the sea and sending the others scrambling down to the deck. While all this was going on, archers on the battlements continued to take long range pot shots at them, wounding many and forcing the rest to keep their heads below the gunwales.

After another hour or so, the tide had ebbed sufficiently for a party of Scots to sally forth from the town and scramble over the muddy foreshore to the stricken vessel. A minute later and the ship was ablaze, the crew and soldiers fleeing like vermin from the conflagration. Some peeled off their armour and waded into the sea, hoping to swim to safety. Many were killed and even more captured, including the hapless engineer who had designed the ungainly contraption. By the time English reinforcements hove into view, alerted by the smoke from the burning ship, the Scots had withdrawn into the town with their prisoners.

Desultory fighting continued until evening. But having seen their master plan fail, and with so many killed and wounded 'full cruelly', the heart had gone out of the English. As night fell it was clear that the first day's fighting belonged unequivocally to the Scots and their doughty young warden. Having 'set good watches to their wall', the victors retired forthwith to celebrate their success in time-honoured fashion:

> 'Then to their inns went they all
> And eased themselves who weary were.'

* * *

Both sides had taken such a battering that the next morning they arranged a five-day truce so that the wounded could be collected and treated, and the dead buried. The pause gave Edward time to prepare his next piece of unusual military technology. This was a huge mobile shelter known as a 'sow', filled with armed men and mining equipment. The operations of the burrowing sow were to be supported by further frontal attacks and naval operations. The 'good steward' arranged his defences as before, keeping himself and his special band in reserve to plug gaps in the line as they occurred. Walter also worked on a number of surprise measures of his own.

Edward II launched his second attack at dawn on 13 September. As with the previous assault, it began with a salvo from the archers, followed by wave upon wave of charging footsoldiers who again placed ladders and scaffolding against the low walls and struggled to climb to the battlements. Many fell before they reached the top, but in several places the English were driven back only after fierce hand-to-hand fighting. So that his men did not run short of ammunition, Walter had arranged for women and children to move about the streets gathering arrows which fell harmlessly between the houses. These were then tied into bundles and hurried up to battlements by youths eager to play their part in the operation.

Half an hour after the first trumpet had sounded, the scene in Berwick was one of frenzied, chaotic activity: soldiers hacking, wrestling, stabbing on the walls, archers loosing shaft after shaft into the foe below, officers tearing about trying to keep control, messengers dashing from point to point with urgent requests or pieces of information, and boys sprinting up the steps of the ramparts with armfuls of arrows. All around men lay dead and dying, pierced or mutilated by the ghastly flesh-rending weapons of medieval conflict. Noises of war added to the hideous pandemonium, filling the morning air with the clash of steel on steel, the whizz of arrows, hoarse shouts of command, the screams of the injured and the low groans of the mortally wounded.

The Scots had resisted stoutly all morning when their lookouts raised a new cry: 'The sow! Look to the sow!' Before them, slowly and deliberately, the great machine was edging towards the town like a Juggernaut, impervious to the rain of arrows and small stones rattling down upon it. Walter was not dismayed. Fully prepared for this new eventuality, he ordered the engineer captured during the previous attack to fire a great catapult which he had been forced to construct under threat of death during the truce.

The first shot fell behind the sow, doing no damage. The machine ground forward, relentlessly. The second shot fell short, and still the wooden monster advanced. Now it was 'right by the wall', so the catapult cast a third stone of 'great weight' high into the air. Down it fell, and this time the aim was true. It 'hit the sow', smashing its main beam and causing a mighty cheer to go up from the walls of Berwick. Soldiers poured from the stricken engine and ran for their lives back to the trenches. On seeing this, the Scots burst into laughter, crying out 'The sow has farrowed'!

Fearing that the machine might be repaired, Walter ordered his resident engineer, John Crabbe, to wheel out a specially constructed mobile derrick. This raised into the air vast bundles of highly inflammable material – pitch, tar, lint, flax, sticks and brimstone – which were lit and lowered over the wall onto the broken sow. Within a few minutes the wreck was nothing but a heap of smouldering ashes.

But Edward was not done yet. As soon as the sow episode was over, a naval attack began, several ships approaching the walls and trying as before to get close enough for men in raised boats to leap onto the battlements. Simultaneously the attack was renewed on the landward side.

An hour later, when Walter's mobile reserve was down to one man, a messenger ran up with alarming news: the enemy had set fire to the drawbridge at the Mary Gate and were forcing their way into the town. Walter rushed over to the gate to see for himself what was going on.

The situation was indeed perilous. The gate and part of the gatehouse were burning, and the English were on the point of breaking through the exhausted defenders. The arrival of Walter transformed the situation. First he organised a group of men to 'put away' the fire; then he personally led a fierce counter-attack against the intruders who 'pressed on him with bare weapons'.

It was Walter's greatest triumph. His 'sturdy defending' of the Mary Gate lasted until nightfall, when the 'wounded and weary' English retreated back to their camp. Almost singlehanded, we are told, the steward had saved the town. That night the Berwick pub talk was all of Walter and how, like Horatio, he had held the gate against overwhelming odds.

* * *

To the Scots' surprise and undoubted relief, the action at the Mary Gate concluded Edward II's attempt to recapture Berwick. Before he could regroup and plan a third assault he heard of a serious reversal to the south. Sticking to his original strategy, Bruce had not tried to relieve Berwick directly, but had sent Thomas Randolph and James Douglas on a powerful raid into northern England. They had moved swiftly into Yorkshire, where they had hoped to capture the queen, and at Mitton on 20 September they confronted and routed a motley force assembled by the Archbishop of York. Owing to the number of priests whom the archbishop had pressed into arms, the Scots wryly referred to the battle as the 'Chapter of Mitton'.

The defeat divided Edward's commanders. The southerners were happy to proceed with the siege; but the northerners, led by Earl Thomas of Lancaster, wanted to move south to protect their lands from further Scottish ravages. Lancaster finally decided the matter by leading off his men without permission. (A few years later he showed his dislike of Edward even more positively by joining the Scots in battle against him. Although defeated and beheaded for treason, Thomas acquired a posthumous saintly reputation and miracles were reported at his shrine.)

No miracle came to save Edward. Depleted and dispirited, and having failed to intercept the Scottish raiding party on its way home, he returned south with nothing whatsoever to show for an expensive and humiliating campaign. The Scots, on the other hand, were overjoyed at their success and celebrated it with 'gaming and glee'. King Robert came down to Berwick to hear what had happened and congratulate the defenders, whom he 'loved...greatly'. He was particularly impressed when told of his son-in-law's 'great defence' of the gate, commending it as 'beyond the life' – more than could have been expected of anyone. Scotland had found a worthy successor to Randolph and Douglas, and the name of Stewart stood among the most respected in the kingdom.

It was a timely boost to the dynasty's reputation. After generations of laudable but rather mundane stewardship and James's equivocal patriotism, as the family neared the throne it stood in urgent need of the image enhancement which Walter's valour brought. He had been given command of a vital operation while still young, and had shown exceptional physical bravery and prowess, steadfastness under pressure, a capacity for organisation and the gift of inspiring devotion in those he led. In short, the young steward was as good a stock as any upon which to base the future of the Scottish monarchy. Although not everyone readily accepted the Stewarts' eventual occupation of the throne, without Walter's opportune contribution the hostility would undoubtedly have been greater.

IV

After the sharp spotlight of the Berwick siege, Walter's career returns to the shadows. He was very much preoccupied with political and military matters, and his name heads the list of barons signing the celebrated Declaration of Arbroath, a moving letter to Pope John XXII justifying Scotland's struggle for national independence and requesting papal recognition for Robert I. Such commitments probably left the steward little time for domesticity, and his elder son Robert, ten when Walter died, was unlikely to have seen much of the esteemed father whose reputation he was never able to live up to.

Walter fought his last campaign in 1322. Edward II overcame the baronial revolt which ended with Thomas of Lancaster's execution, and advanced into Scotland once more. This time Robert I reverted to scorched earth tactics and compelled the starving invader to withdraw southward. Walter and a number of Scots then pursued them with alacrity, surprising them near Rievaulx and driving the shaken and humiliated Edward back into York. Walter sat scornfully before the city gates, daring the English to come out and fight. When no one took up his challenge, he 'turned again' and withdrew. The next year a thirteen-year truce brought hostilities to a temporary close.

Barbour was sure that if Walter had lived to see middle age his 'renown should have stretched far'. But, as the poet whimsically put it, death had 'at his worship great envy' and carried him away 'in the flower of his youth'. He died on 9 April 1326, not falling in battle as he might have wished, but more prosaically to some unknown 'great sickness'.

Barbour devoted a whole section of *The Bruce* to 'The death of good Sir Walter'. Allowing for obvious poetic licence and customary rhetoric, his description of the obsequies afforded the first Stewart to win the hearts of the nation makes a fetching epitaph:

> 'Arose there then a doleful cry,
> When worthy knights and ladies high
> Gave public showing of their grief,
> With common folk who mourned their chief;
> The nation wept as one for he
> Who'd been the flower of chivalry.
> When last this grieving was forsook
> The corpse to Paisley kirk was took;
> Here psalms were sung, the coffin blessed,
> And young Sir Walter laid to rest.
> Almighty God, we thee emplore
> To bless his soul for evermore! Amen.'

Part II

Stewarts Royal

CHAPTER 8

Heir Presumptive

I

It is late in the afternoon of 24 April 1390. High above the roof of Dundonald Castle the lion of Scotland flutters from the masthead in a mild south-westerly breeze. The original Stewart stronghold has been rebuilt in the form of a fashionable yet secure tower house, elegantly crafted, compact and comfortable. The royal standard proudly announces that the fortress is no longer the property of crown servants, but of the king himself.

Little else suggests the royal presence.

New grass is pushing through the cobbles of the courtyard. The soldiers of the guard lean idly on their weapons, chatting to each other, their bawdy conversation thick with grumbling oaths. Every now and again they pause to spit like catapults or throw ribald comments at the servant girls who clatter hurriedly by on their way to the cookhouse.

Inside there is the same casual, almost unreal air about the place. Many windows are shuttered fast. The great hall, with its fine ribbed vault of clean stone, lies empty, like some vast and echoing tomb. Beneath the graceful hooded fireplace the hearth is cold and unswept. Dust lies on the long tables. Even the oak-backed chair standing at the centre of the dais has a dull, unused look to it.

A dreadful lethargy pervades the whole run down community. It lacks purpose, direction and, above all, leadership.

Only in a small private chamber, lit by a single narrow barred window, is the atmosphere different. Here the guards at the door are alert, their armour polished, their halberds honed to a gleaming sharpness. Inside, despite the clemency of the weather, half a dozen logs blaze in the grate, their flickering shadows dancing on the tapestried walls. The air is stuffy, the smell of spice and incense failing to mask the unmistakable pungent stench of human ordure.

At one end of the room liveried servants are quietly setting out a frugal meal on the heavy table. Besides muffled clatter and the crackling of the fire, there is only one other sound. It is a man's voice. He is reading from the scriptures, translating the Latin into English as he proceeds. His delivery is slow and careful, as if addressing a child.

Seated on a low stool beside the fire, it is clear from the reader's dress that he is a priest. He appears to be reading for his own amusement or for the edification of the servants, for there is no sign of any other person in the chamber. But when he has covered the better part of a chapter, the man pauses and glances enquiringly at the chair beside him.

Until this moment a visitor might be excused for taking little notice of this unremarkable feature. After all, it seems nothing but an ordinary wooden seat into which a variety of blankets, rugs and furs have been cast.

But now, as the prelate hesitates, unsure whether to continue his lesson, the ungainly pile of clothing moves.

A thin, wasted hand emerges from the sleeve of a fur-lined coat. With a feeble gesture it bids the reader continue. The movement reveals that within that shapeless bundle there is indeed a human form. He is a man of great age. Closer inspection reveals his head, brushed with a few strands of wispy hair and half covered by a huge woollen cap. The skin of his face is yellow-white, the texture of old paper. Particles of food rest in his discoloured cobweb beard, suggesting that those who care for him have grown slack in their duties.

For much of the time the old man's eyes remain closed beneath dry, flaky lids. And when they do open, it is only for bleared red eyes to gaze sightless towards the warmth of the fire.

Who is this pitiful figure, so frail and seemingly inconsequential? The answer lies in the narrow circlet of gold hanging carelessly on the back of his chair. The invalid is none other than the king himself. Exhausted, senile and blind, here sits Robert II, the only son of Walter the Steward and Marjorie Bruce, and the first Stewart monarch of Scotland.

Rarely can a ruling dynasty have been launched by so unprepossessing a figure.

II

The tragedy of Robert II is that he inherited the Scottish throne at the age of fifty-five, when his mental and physical powers were already in decline. He then lived a further nineteen years to become the oldest person ever to wear the Scottish crown. As a result, he has the unfortunate reputation of being little but a puppet figure, king in name only when the nation needed firm, unequivocal leadership. Ironically, implicit criticism is also levelled at him for the vigour of his private life in his younger days. Robert's matrimonial adventures and remarkable fecundity laid up a store of problems which plagued the family for several generations to come. In fact, simply to dismiss him as a profligate and self-seeking youth who deteriorated into useless senility when he came to the throne is to draw too simple and damning a sketch of the seventh hereditary steward.

Undoubtedly Robert Fitz Walter did not possess the drive or charisma of his father or his illustrious maternal grandfather, Robert Bruce. Instead, he seems to have been endowed with the qualities we have come to associate with generations of stewards: moderation, a reluctance to take up arms, caution and a willingness to compromise. Above all, though physically active, he lacked the ruthless singlemindedness which marked so many of medieval Scotland's national heroes. But such figures were rarely pleasant human beings, and whatever else was said about Robert – and unfortunately not much was said about him – he was never reported to be anything other than good-natured and generous.

* * *

Robert had lost both his parents by the time he was ten. Presumably thereafter he was raised at the court of Robert I, after whom he had been named. Although for five years following the birth of David Bruce on 5 March 1324 the young Stewart was not heir presumptive, his rights should Robert I father no more children or David die childless were confirmed at Cambuskenneth in 1326. Robert Bruce died three years later, having finally wrung from the English a grudging recognition of Scotland's independence in the Treaty of Edinburgh (1328).

The Edinburgh agreement did not mark the end of Scotland's long War of Independence, but merely the close of one phase of it. When the struggle was resumed in the 1330s it reverted to the form in which it had begun – a civil war between the Bruces and the Plantaganet-backed Balliols. This time the Balliol challenge was upheld by Edward, son of the unfortunate King John who had died on his French estates in 1313. With tacit English backing, Edward Balliol invaded Scotland in 1332, routing his opponents and killing the guardian Earl of Mar (the hostage who had refused to be parted from Edward II after Bannockburn). Edward Balliol the usurper was crowned at Scone on 24 September 1332.

That winter Balliol was driven out almost as quickly as he had arrived, forcing the young Edward III to reject the Treaty of Edinburgh and intervene personally in Scottish affairs. At this point, aged scarcely seventeen, Robert Stewart was thrown into the political arena.

* * *

Robert's prominence in the 1330s owed more to his blood than his behaviour. As steward and heir presumptive again, next to the young king he was the obvious figurehead of the Bruce faction. A whole generation of great national leaders was passing away. Thomas Earl of Moray, commander of the left wing at Bannockburn and guardian of 1329, died in 1332 when leading his forces against Edward Balliol. Two years earlier his fellow commander, the

'Good Sir James' Douglas, had perished in Spain where he had carried the heart of Robert I on crusade. The two soldiers who might have succeeded them, Walter Stewart and Andrew Murray, were out of the reckoning – the steward had died in 1326 and Andrew had been a prisoner in England since October 1332. And, as we have seen, Mar had been slain at Duppin. A year later yet another guardian died in battle. Archibald Douglas, a younger brother of Sir James, fell amid the slaughter on Halidon Hill, a rise overlooking the approaches to Berwick.

The battle was in many ways a mirror image of Bannockburn. The besieged garrison (which had to contend with the devices of John Crabbe, now in English pay) had threatened to surrender unless relieved before a certain date, forcing the Scots to commit themselves in the open. Such was the slaughter wrought in the ensuing fray by Edward III's archers and dismounted knights that the English believed the Scots no longer had anyone left capable of leading an army. Berwick's dejected defenders promptly surrendered the town.

The one-sided confrontation at Halidon Hill was probably the teenage Robert Stewart's first experience of war. Guided by Sir James Stewart of Rosyth, he had commanded one of the four Scottish companies. The disruption of civil turmoil, the futile butchery of battle and the subsequent loss of the fortress his renowned father had fought so valiantly to defend may all have affected the impressionable young man quite deeply. Like his grandfather, Robert I, he now saw the folly of challenging the English in pitched battle. As we shall see, his unwillingness to indulge in further gestures of futile bravery was later to earn him an unkind reputation for physical cowardice. Furthermore, the painful experience of his first command probably strengthened an innate distaste for conflict, both physical and political, and increased the appeal of compromise or appeasement, both of which became marked features of his later administrations.

For the time being, however, Robert's one concern was to make good his escape. Established as King of Scotland for a second time, Balliol gave the steward's lands and titles to David Hastings of Strathbogie. Robert went into hiding on Bute. From here he fled in a rowing boat to Dumbarton Castle, where he joined David II and the queen mother. With the help of loyal tenants, Robert then participated in a successful guerrilla campaign, the only time in his life when he showed any capacity as a soldier. He seized Dunoon Castle in Cowal, then returned to Bute and captured his ancient family stronghold at Rothesay. Finally he made his way to the mainland and rallied the people of his Renfrew estates to the Bruce cause.

By this time David II had been sent to France for his safety and Robert was acting as joint guardian with another teenager, John Randolph, 3rd Earl of Moray, the younger son of Robert Bruce's renowned lieutenant. The heir apparent's behaviour during the troubled years of David's first exile is difficult to fathom. Understandably, given the age and lack of political experience of the partners, the joint guardianship was not a success, and it ended when Randolph was captured by the English in 1335. Shortly afterwards Robert was obliged to come to terms with Edward III when his lands were attacked by Irish mercenaries. Although Robert did not remain in the English camp for long, for the next three years his activity on behalf of King David was at best perfunctory, and the leadership of the Bruce party passed to Sir Andrew Murray. Only after Murray's death in 1338 did Robert come to prominence again, this time as sole guardian and nominal commander of the Scottish forces.

With England increasingly preoccupied with what became known as the Hundred Years War with France, Robert 'summoned a general gathering of everyone who might bear arms' and oversaw the gradual recapture of almost all the major Scottish fortresses which had been in English hands. Perth, the invader's administrative headquarters, fell in 1339. John Randolph was ransomed the next year and inspired a final wave of counter-attacks. Edinburgh was taken in April 1341 and two months later the seventeen-year-old King David II and Queen Joan landed at Inverbervie. Robert Stewart promptly relinquished his guardianship. He was still only twenty-five, younger than his father had been when given his first command at Berwick.

* * *

As a soldier, although Walter Bower was to speak of his 'great deeds' against the English, Robert was largely a figurehead during this difficult period. It is true that he featured in the capture of Perth and put in formal appearances on other fronts from time to time, but the real heroes were Sir Andrew Murray and, after 1338, Sir William Douglas (the 'Knight of Liddesdale') and Sir Alexander Ramsay, whom the Douglas clan was later to starve to death in the dank vaults of Hermitage Castle. Moreover, Robert had neither the inclination, experience nor, probably, the skill to attend regularly to administrative matters, and he made no effort to begin reconstructing his grandfather's strong monarchy. He handed over to his young uncle a treasury in deficit and a government sorely lacking in direction.

If Robert was not often risking his life in battle against the Balliols and their English backers, and he was not spending hours attending to the governance of the realm, what was he doing at this period of his life? The answer, it seems, is that he was spending a good deal of time chasing women.

Robert was attractive, 'beautiful beyond the sons of men' Bower called him. To Fordun, who may well have seen the steward before age had impaired his good looks,

'he was a comely young man, tall and strong, modest, generous, high-spirited and well-mannered; and the innate sweetness of his personality ensured that he was loved by all true-hearted Scots.'

Particularly the ladies, one might add. Well-born and handsome, undoubtedly flattered from an early age and deprived of a father or mother's restraining discipline, who can be surprised that Robert was easily sidetracked from dull or dangerous duty into the bed of his latest paramour?

The best known example of Robert's amorous adventuring occurred in 1336. When Edward III was campaigning against the towns of north-east Scotland, the steward was preoccupied with a little siege of his own. His target was Elizabeth Mure, the daughter of Sir Adam Mure, one of his tenants from Rowallan, six miles from Dundonald.

Such dalliance with a neighbourhood beauty was all very well, but Robert was too smitten with the girl to be content with covert assignations and the possibility of having to meet the expenses of an illegitimate child. With Elizabeth almost certainly pregnant, the couple eloped. It is believed, particularly by those of a romantic disposition, that Robert brought his lover to Dundonald, which is why in his dotage he preferred that retreat to any other.

We are now told that

'Robert, Great Steward of Scotland, having taken away the said Elizabeth, drew to Sir Adam her father an instrument that he should take her to be his lawful wife'.

The couple were married shortly afterwards by a priest named Roger McAdam. Honourable though the twenty-year-old steward's behaviour might have been, from a political point of view it was extremely unwise, reinforcing the impression that at this stage of his life Robert could have done with sensible family advice and guidance. The union with Elizabeth Mure prevented Robert from using marriage as a means of strengthening his position among the Scottish aristocracy. Coming from a line no more distinguished than several other leading families, the heir apparent would have been better off with a Douglas or Randolph bride, thereby building an alliance which might later have been of service. As it turned out, however, the choice of a relatively lowly partner was the least unsatisfactory aspect of Robert's love match.

There was also the problem that at the age of eleven Elizabeth had been betrothed to Hugh de Giffard. This made it illegal for her to marry another and rendered illegitimate any children she might have by another partner. Even more serious was the fact that Robert and his bride were related in the fourth degree and therefore banned by canon law from marrying. It has usually been argued that the couple did not know of their consanguinity at the time of their wedding, and that as soon as they learned of it they had the barrier removed by papal dispensation (1347). This permitted them to marry and, according to canon law, legitimised their children.

In normal circumstances this would have been the end of the business. But it remained open to question whether subsequent marriage really could clear children of the stigma of their illegitimate origin. The argument would probably have been forgotten if Robert had not been heir presumptive. As it was, during their ten years of questionable marriage the steward and his wife had produced five daughters and three sons; the oldest of the latter, John Stewart, stood next in line to the throne after his father.

Two matters brought the legitimacy question to the very top of the Stewart family agenda. By the second half of the century it was becoming clear that David II was unlikely to father any children. Furthermore, following the death of the exhausted Elizabeth, in about 1355 Robert remarried. In political terms his second wife was an altogether wiser choice. And since she was also a distant relative of his, this time he took the sensible precaution of receiving prior papal dispensation for the union. Robert's second bride was the charmingly-named Euphemia, daughter of Hugh, Earl of Ross, and widow of the steward's old rival, John Randolph, 3rd Earl of Moray. Euphemia was not only well-connected, but fertile too, providing the unflagging Robert with a further three children: David, Earl of Strathearn, Walter, Earl of Atholl, and Isobel, who married James, 2nd Earl of Douglas. In the course of time these children and their families were to raise once again the issue of their half-brothers' legitimacy. This was no legal quibble. At stake was not simply the ancient Stewart inheritance, but, after 1371, the crown of Scotland.

Deeply though Robert may have loved Elizabeth Mure, his sexual thirst was never slaked for long by a single partner. Beside his thirteen offspring by his two wives, he fathered innumerable illegitimate children by several mistresses. Estimates of the eventual size of his family vary between twenty-one and at least twenty-three – it is probable that not all his bastards received official recognition, and we are certainly ignorant of casual liaisons which did not lead to the birth of a healthy child.

What does this explosion of Stewarts tell us of Robert and his career? Apart from confirming reports of his attractiveness and youthful high spirits, it also helps explain his uneasy relations with David II. Like Robert, King David also married twice, first to Princess Joan of England and second to Margaret Logie. But in striking contrast to his fruitful steward, the king had no children. Disliking a nephew who was older than himself and not wishing the succession to pass into Stewart hands, David desperately wanted a son of his own. Therefore each fresh report of Robert's success in a field where he was so glaringly deficient irked him considerably, fuelling the hostility between two very different men.

III

The first period of David Bruce's personal rule, 1341-1347, was probably the happiest in Robert's life. He was in his late twenties, healthy, popular and not weighed down with the responsibilities of government. He attended court, where he was given the recognition due to the heir apparent; but given his unspectacular performance during the king's minority and exile, he was not involved in his young uncle's energetic and quite successful attempts to restore royal authority.

David not only kept Robert at arm's length, but he made quite clear what he thought of his steward by showing favour to Robert's erstwhile rival, John Randolph. Robert's uncomfortable standing with the king is illustrated by the fact that when David gave Robert the earldom of Atholl in 1342, he rather pointedly refrained from granting him the title that accompanied the estates. Withholding such an honour from the heir to the throne was quite clearly intended as a deliberate snub.

* * *

Robert was more than happy to leave military matters to those who enjoyed them. David successfully raided northern England in 1342 and by the end of the year Berwick was the only major Scottish fortress still in English hands. These early successes may have given the king a false impression of his own competence as a commander, for four years later he launched a campaign which undid all his work of reconstruction and came close to costing him his life.

Following Edward III's remarkable victory over the French at Crecy on 26 August 1346, the Scots found themselves under some pressure to assist their Continental allies with a positive move into England. As the bulk of English forces were on the other side of the Channel, David duly summoned a size-able army and struck south. He proudly announced that he 'might right well travel all the way to London' – which, indeed, he did, though not in the manner he envisaged. Never keen on exchanging the domestic comforts for the hardships of camp life and still haunted by memories of Halidon Hill, Robert Stewart tagged along somewhat reluctantly as joint commander of the third and largest Scottish battalion.

The battle of Neville's Cross, fought outside Durham in wet and misty conditions on 17 October 1346, confirmed the worst of Robert's fears. Outnumbered and overconfident, the Scots experienced yet another painful and costly defeat at the hands of the English. With the benefit of hindsight, one cannot help but wonder why generation after generation of Scottish commanders insisted on risking the lives of thousands of their countrymen in pitched battles on the Borders. At least from the reign of Robert I the example of a successful alternative strategy was on hand, yet time and again it was rejected in favour of hot-headed and invariably disastrous confronta-tion.

Robert Stewart's part in the fray at Neville's Cross was, to say the least, ambiguous. Driven from their defensive position by a storm of stinging English arrows, the first two Scottish battalions, led by John Randolph and the king, stumbled forward in an ill-disciplined attack. They suffered heavy casualties and were driven back into the battalion led by Robert and the Earl of March. After some rather half-hearted resistance, the reserve was led from the field, leaving the others to fend for themselves as best they could. Wyntoun believed Robert 'escaped'; Fordun stated unequivocally that he fled. *The Lannercost Chronicle* pilloried those who led the retreat: 'if the one was worth little,' it mocked, 'the other was good for nothing'. This was followed by the famous remark that 'these two, turning tail...led off the dance, leaving David to caper as he wished.' Earl Randolph was killed and the king, weakened by a grievous wound in the face from an English arrow, was taken prisoner. Many other high-ranking Scots were either slain or led into captivity along with their young leader.

What are we to make of Robert's behaviour? Was it cowardice or a sensible withdrawal to avoid further bloodshed at a time when defeat was inevitable? The answer probably lies somewhere between the two. Never keen on the idea of battle in the first place and seeing what had happened to the first two battalions, Robert probably decided to get away with his men while there was still time. A more valiant commander might have organised a stand or a counter-attack; but such action could have led to the total annihilation of the Scottish army, something Robert was not prepared to risk.

As the Scots needed a scapegoat for their defeat, the steward's conduct made him an obvious target. Nevertheless, although mocked by the English and scorned by his king, Robert no doubt earned the undying thanks of those he took with him from that dismal field.

* * *

The capture of the king left Robert Stewart once more guardian (or strictly speaking 'the king's lieutenant') of Scotland. It was a well-nigh impossible task – he had to govern the nation like a monarch but without a monarch's authority. It is true that he could have behaved as if he were king and tried to exploit his position to build up his personal power. But even if he had wanted to do this, it was most unlikely that he would have been able to get away with it. The Stewarts were but one of a number of leading families, the rest of whom would certainly have resisted overbearing behaviour from a man who was not even an earl. The exiled David would also have resented Robert using his lieutenancy too broadly, and no doubt would have used what influence he had to undermine it. In short, if Robert had behaved in too positive a manner he might well have lost his privileged position – and his family's right to the succession to boot.

Given Robert's genial, easy-going nature, there was little chance of this happening. Not a man to select a rugged path when a smoother way lay open to him, he chose conciliation rather than confrontation. He took over the vacant earldom of Strathearn and probably that of Badenoch too, but he studiously avoided actions which might have been construed as using his position for divisive personal aggrandisement. Whenever possible he ruled by consent, keeping things ticking over, avoiding friction with any major power blocs and leaving the day to day matters of government to look after themselves. He made a point of keeping in with the potentially troublesome Douglases and with the powerful Patrick Dunbar, son-in-law of the 3rd Earl of Moray and head of the Randolph interest since 1346. It was hardly a glamorous way of going about things, and it has not won much approval from historians; but it is difficult to imagine a more dynamic lieutenant making much more of the tricky situation.

Robert's policy has been kindly described as an administrative failure but a political success. Power slipped from the centre to the localities. For example, when faced with a revival of the lordship of the Isles under John MacDonald, instead of trying to crush the potential troublemaker Robert tried to keep in with him by offering the hand of his daughter Margaret in marriage. Law and order inevitably declined. Without an army or police force, Robert was totally dependent upon the support of others to see his wishes carried out. When in 1348 Robert heard that the sheriff of Dumbarton was collecting exorbitant dues from Paisley Abbey, he wrote to the officer:

'For our own part we beseech you, and on the part of our lord the king we firmly command and direct you, that...you desist from exactions of this sort.'

It was not the sort of directive that demanded obedience.

Royal finance also suffered during the king's second absence. Revenue fell far into arrears and accounts went unaudited for years on end. Nevertheless, when in 1357 the lieutenant handed back the tiller to his king for a second time, he could at least claim to have kept his master's vessel afloat at a time when a more ambitious pilot, however well-intentioned, might have wrecked the craft altogether.

Robert had another, more personal reason to feel quietly pleased with his lieutenancy. In order to make the most of David's capture, Edward III soon dropped the cause of Edward Balliol: David was far more useful to the English as a king than as a pretender. David's childlessness, too, made a most useful bargaining counter. For much of David's captivity Edward included in the terms for his release a clause stating that if the Scottish king died childless the succession should pass to the King of England or one of his sons. David had no objection to the scheme, even presenting it in person to the Scottish parliament in 1352, for which express purpose he had been granted a provisional release from the Tower.

From a purely practical point of view the plan was quite attractive. The combination of the English and Scottish crowns within a single family might have prevented further debilitating warfare between the two countries. Rather than weaken Scotland, the proposal could have protected her independence. Furthermore, John of Gaunt, the man most likely to get the Scottish crown, was an intelligent and thoroughly competent administrator and commander. In David's eyes he contrasted most favourably with the flaccid steward, whose niddering behaviour at Neville's Cross he blamed for his capture and the disfiguring facial wound which did not heal until 1351. Just as their contrasting fortunes in paternity exacerbated David's dislike of his fertile nephew, so his scarred appearance also fuelled his enmity for the better-looking man.

If David's espousal of his captor's suggestion was based as much on emotional bias as on political wisdom, so was the general council's rejection of the scheme. It was inconceivable that any but a small minority of broad-minded observers would have agreed to a distortion of the succession which made a mockery of all that the country had been fighting for over half a century. Only a man of David's political insensitivity would have dared commend such terms for his release. His reward was a further five years of captivity and the threat, which fortunately for him came to nothing, that if he persisted with the English scheme he would be deposed.

Robert's reaction to the ill-considered proposal can easily be guessed at, and no doubt he used all his charm to see that it was rejected. In the end the unfortunate episode only helped the Stewarts, elevating them into a sort of totem of Scottish independence, a bastion against detested Anglicanisation. Robert had never been short of friends. Now, thanks to David's naive behaviour, he was becoming one of the most valued men in the land. With each day that passed, the Stewarts drew ever nearer to the throne.

IV

After his second sojourn abroad, the thirty-three-year-old King David arrived in Scotland on 7 October 1357. The terms of his release had been agreed at the Treaty of Berwick, and consisted chiefly in a Scottish promise to pay a ransom of 100,000 marks at the rate of 10,000 marks a year for ten years. Robert's eldest son John was sent to England along with a number of other hostages to ensure that the payments were maintained.

Unsure of his position and not wishing to provoke too much antagonism at a time when huge sums were being levied to pay his ransom, for a few months David followed a conciliatory policy. He rewarded Robert for his uninspiring lieutenancy with the title of Earl of Strathearn, and similarly elevated Robert's partners, Douglas and Dunbar, in 1358 affording the former the singular honour of creating a new earldom – Douglas – especially for him. But the honeymoon did not last long, and within a year or so Robert had cause to regret the part he had played in setting up the Berwick agreement.

Apart from their personal differences, the king and his erstwhile lieutenant stood for completely different things. Once he had re-established himself, David devoted his considerable energies to restoring the power and fortunes of the crown. This meant, where possible, uniform justice, centralised administration and efficient harbouring of royal resources. In all of these fields he was surprisingly successful. To Robert and his aristocratic cronies all this was an anathema, an unwarranted intrusion into their traditional rights. They particularly resented the king's foreignness. More than half of David's life had been spent in France and England, and the nobility had not forgotten his attempts to take the succession out of Scottish hands. Nor did David's financial exactions and his reliance upon 'new' men such as Sir David Erskine, Norman Leslie and Sir John Danielson endear him to his magnates.

The first sign of trouble came in 1360, when the king's English mistress Katherine Mortimer was cruelly stabbed to death. Thomas Stewart, Earl of Angus, was implicated in the crime and held in Dumbarton Castle. When in 1362 David seized Kildrummy Castle from the obstreperous Earl of Mar, aristocratic resentment simmered more fiercely. Open rebellion – 'a mighty conspiracy and sedition' of 'great and powerful men' – broke out early the next year.

It is not easy to imagine Robert Stewart as a rebel. He was generally too lackadaisical, too much a politician to risk life and position in the chancy business of armed conflict. But when the earls of Douglas and March rose against the king in January 1363, the steward offered them his somewhat half-hearted support. The issue which had finally drawn him from the fence was David's frantic love-life.

The king's childlessness was not due to impotence. Far from it. Although not producing the same results, David's sexual appetite was quite as healthy as his steward's. Indeed, the longer he was unable to produce an heir, the harder he tried to do so. His relations with Queen Joan had cooled a while ago, and when he came north in 1357 she promptly returned south, dying in England in 1362. After he had got over the tragic death of Katherine Mortimer, David fell in love again. The object of his considerable passion was Dame Margaret Logie, sometime wife of the deceased Sir John Logie, to whom she had born a son. Therein lay the root of the steward's anxiety. Margaret had proved her fertility. If she were to marry the king, as seemed very likely, there was a chance that the line of Robert Bruce might not die out after all. It was probably that alarming prospect, rather than more respectable utterances about the king's lack of appropriate counsel, which led Robert into rather shameful support for the rebels.

The uprising was a futile gesture. Lacking the stomach for a fight himself, Robert hoped to benefit from the military success of his fellow conspirators and ride a subsequent wave of popular support. When both failed to materialise, he meekly submitted to David, promising 'for the rest of my life I will be faithful to…the Lord David, illustrious King of Scots.' He had no choice but to accept the marriage of the king to Dame Margaret, which took place in Fife in April 1363. Robert then sat back, fingers crossed, to see what would come of the union.

Fortunately for the Stewarts, nothing came of it. But David was by no means done yet. He still had the English card up his sleeve, and by the end of the year, with Margaret's stomach still as flat as on the day they had married, he was playing it for all he was worth.

The purpose of the high level discussion carried out at Westminster between the English and Scottish kings and their privy councils was to settle once and for all the question of the ransom, now seriously in arrears, and arrange a lasting peace between their countries. Two memoranda were drawn up. These gave considerable concessions to the Scots, including the return of Berwick and the cancellation of all remaining ransom payments, if they would accept either the King of England or one of his sons as successor to a childless David. There was no mention of a union of governments, merely a union of crowns. Scotland would remain a separate, independent country.

These sensible if unrealistic terms were put to the three estates of the Scottish parliament at Scone in March 1364. The reaction was exactly the same as it had been the last time a similar proposition had been made. The estates came out overwhelmingly in favour of total independence and their own choice of heir to the throne – Robert Stewart:

> '…the three estates answered unequivocally …that in no way did they wish to grant or in any manner agree to the matters which the King of England and his council were seeking.'

Robert might have made a fool of himself by taking up arms against David, but he was still undoubtedly a popular man.

Thwarted a second time in his attempt to get the succession altered, David returned to domestic issues with ruthless vigour. While he was in this frame of mind, declared Wyntoun, 'no one dared resist his will'; so Robert sensibly kept his head down, afraid that a further mistake on his part might provoke the king into yet another attempt to mar his family's future prospects. Being eight years older than David, it was increasingly unlikely that he would benefit personally from this moderation. But there were now signs that David was starting to accept the inevitable and regard Robert's eldest son John, Lord of Kyle, as his heir apparent. In 1368 he made John Earl of Carrick on his marriage to Annabel Drummond of Stobhall, the queen's niece.

Even so, the Stewarts were not yet in calm waters. In 1368, having done or said something to annoy Queen Margaret, Robert and several of his sons were cast into prison. The steward was isolated for a few months with his fiery son Alexander, the future 'Wolf of Baddenoch', in the bleak castle on Loch Leven, later the prison of an even more celebrated Stewart, Mary Queen of Scots. When shortly after his release in 1369 Robert was relieved of his earldom for a while, there seemed no end to the family's tribulations.

David kept up the pressure on the Stewarts by other means too. He was tired of Queen Margaret, particularly as she had failed to do for him what she had done for her first husband. Now there was a new light in his life – Agnes Dunbar. Perhaps she would be the one to bring him the son he so desperately desired? Queen Margaret was duly divorced and given an annual pension of £100, and wealth and gifts were lavished on Agnes in preparation for her legitimately joining David's sterile stud farm. Further proceedings were delayed, however, when Margaret refused to accept her divorce and travelled to Avignon to woo Pope Gregory XI to her cause. Although David was embarrassed by her action, it had little bearing on his future. For all Agnes' obvious charms and the king's equally obvious efforts, the lady did not become pregnant.

* * *

It is surprising how the tiniest organism can exert an influence out of all proportion to its size. The exalted position of the Stewarts in 1370, for example, owed more to the invisible workings of the human reproductive system than to all the family's ambitious strivings. What would it have prof-ited them to have performed the most illustrious feats of arms and won the brightest reputations if, like the king, they had failed to provide for their succession? And now, as they stood so near yet so far from the greatest prize of all, they owed their final elevation not to any striking gesture but to the mindless life cycle of some unknown germ. On the morning of 22 February 1371 King David was suddenly taken ill in Edinburgh Castle. By nightfall he was dead.

After six generations, spanning two hundred and thirty-five years, the family of Walter Fitz Alan had finally won the crown of Scotland.

CHAPTER 9

Worst Among Equals?

I

The first fifty years of Stewart rule brought the dynasty little credit. Except when it came to family squabbles, Scotland's new leaders favoured conciliation rather than confrontation. For most of the time they were happy to amble along the paths of least resistance, leaving the ruthless to flourish and the poor and weak to fend for themselves as best they could.

The first Stewart monarch, Robert II, was no exception to the rule that good men rarely made effective kings. As we have seen, contemporaries did not speak ill of him personally; yet much of their comment implies that he was at best an undistinguished leader and at worst a useless one. When his nineteen-year rule was followed by the equally pathetic reign of his crippled, melancholic elder son, and then by the prolonged exile of his teenage successor, it appeared as if the Stewart monarchy was doomed to perpetual ignominy. Before the return of James I from England in 1424, many ordinary Scots must have wondered what they had done to deserve such a wretched and ill-fated royal house.

* * *

Robert II was the victim of his previous behaviour as well as his personality. For the first fifty-five years of his life he had worked hard – if he ever worked hard at anything – to keep in with the Scottish aristocracy. He had been rewarded with their support when David schemed for an English succession; but now that he was king, Robert found his proximity to families such as the Douglases a political shackle which he had neither the will nor the power to remove. Although attempts were made to dress the new dynasty in more glamorous genealogical robes (most notably by Archdeacon Barbour of Aberdeen in his *Stewartis Orygenale*), the family's rise from among the ranks of the baronage was not easily disguised – its very surname saw to that. Like a successful businessman permanently indebted to his original backers, Robert II was unable to distance himself from old colleagues and allies. In their eyes he was little more than the first among equals.

The Bruce kings had demonstrated that a successful monarch had to be the first above equals. But the lesson was lost on their successor. Now that he was entitled to a more elaborate hat, he saw no reason to change his pragmatic approach to affairs of state. He made this clear even before his coronation by not punishing the Earl of Douglas when he challenged the Stewarts' right to the succession. Robert chose instead to mollify the dissident Douglases with elaborate preferments: the earl was made a justiciar and warden of the East March; his son James was granted a handsome pension and given Princess Isabella, the king's fourth daughter, as a wife. As Wyntoun tactfully remarked,

> 'Thus after a rude beginning
> They made a soft and good ending.'

Such Danegeld might have bought short-term harmony, but it sent unfortunate signals to other recalcitrant nobles and did little for Robert's prestige.

To make matters worse, by contemporary standards Robert Stewart was already an old man. With advancing years his relaxed approach became more pronounced, until he virtually gave up any attempt to exercise personal control over his kingdom. This might not have mattered had his heir been capable of making up for his father's deficiencies; but since Earl John of Carrick was if anything an even more ineffectual personality, Scotland was doomed to long years of dismally lymphatic government.

* * *

The situation was not helped by the continued Stewartisation of the Scottish nobility. Like the Saudi royal family in the later twentieth century, the Stewarts spread like a creeper over and through the trellis Scottish state. Within half a dozen years of Robert's accession, the ruling dynasty held seven of the country's sixteen earldoms and was connected by marriage with almost every distinguished house in the country. Many of Robert's problems stemmed from his inability to control a family which tended to regard itself as a privileged clan above the law. Those most close to Robert were the least tractable of all, as Bower noticed:

> 'What shall I say about his sons? Some were peaceable and benign, while others were insolent and malign.'

The least attractive was undoubtedly the fourth son Alexander, who had shared his father's detention in Loch Leven Castle at the end of the previous reign. His behaviour as royal lieutenant in the north, which earned him the famous title 'Wolf of Badenoch', was so scandalous that in 1388 he had to be relieved of his post. Far from chastened by the humiliation, the Wolf spurred to new heights of barbarity.

Aware of his offspring's ambitions and potential for trouble, Robert took steps early on to remove at least one source of contention between them. He had the 1318 Act of Settlement read out at his coronation and the next day he declared John, his eldest son by Elizabeth Mure, to be his heir. To clear up any remaining 'uncertainty of the succession', two years later the estates drew up a tailzie (a document setting out the inheritance) establishing the strict order of male succession. First in line were John and his male heirs, followed by the four remaining legitimate sons (Robert, Alexander, David and Walter) and their male heirs. Having acquired the throne by statute through the female line, the king was doing his best to ensure that neither practice would be repeated. Surprisingly, his wish prevailed until 1689. It was one of his few enduring contributions to the Scottish state.

II

Robert II coped quite well for the first six or seven years of his reign. He delivered a patriotic speech at his coronation which was well received by jingoistic magnates and he courted further popularity by opening negotiations with France for a renewal of the Auld Alliance. But he did not support positive words with action, and continued to pay the English his predecessor's ransom until the death of Edward III in 1377. At home the machinery of David II's government freewheeled smoothly on for a while, driven by its own momentum rather than by any fresh impetus. Indirect (but not direct) taxes were collected relatively efficiently. Robert maintained a sensible continuity of administrative personnel, exemplified in the career of David's secretary John Lyon, who was rewarded for his services with the thanage of Glamis and the chamberlainship. Relieved at the relaxation of David Bruce's harsh and vindictive policies, and soothed by Robert's skilful pragmatism, the nobility cooperated willingly enough with the undemanding new regime.

These happy, benignant days for Scotland and her mellow-minded king did not last. By 1377 physical disability and senile dementia had produced a marked deterioration in Robert's ability to lead. Two currents converged to bring the situation to a crisis. Fighting broke out on the border with England, and from 1378 onwards there were numerous indications that, left to their own devices, the nobility were incapable of upholding an impartial or uniform system of justice.

In the spasmodic land fighting up and down the North Sea coast the king took no part. For this and his later lack of soldierly vigour he was scorned by Froissart as 'no valiant man, but someone who preferred to remain at home rather than march into the field.' Although Robert shared his grandfather's distaste for chivalric displays of machismo, there was more to his absence from the front than a simple dislike of bloodshed. He was now in his sixties (an age when even the renowned Edward III had not taken to the field) and beset by physical frailty, failing eyesight and deafness. Had Robert tried to lead his forces in person, the sight of his Don Quixote-like figure trotting aimlessly about the battlefield in heavy plate armour would have been more of an embarrassment than an inspiration.

By November 1384 things had come to such a pass that the general council of the estates was forced to act. That spring John of Gaunt, Duke of Lancaster, had marched north and held Edinburgh to ransom (he did not sack the city because Holyrood Abbey had afforded him sanctuary during the English Peasants' Revolt of 1381). The Highlands were in turmoil and the nobility acting with such impunity that in 1382 Sir James Lindsay of Crawford was permitted to go free after murdering John Lyon of Glamis, chamberlain and the king's son-in-law.

Meeting at Holyrood Abbey, the council did not criticise Robert directly, but recognised that

'our Lord the King, for certain reasons, is not able to attend personally to the execution of justice and law of this kingdom...'

Although vague, the phrase 'certain reasons' is clear indication of Robert's physical deterioration (Wyntoun called him 'feeble with age') and a tacit recognition that he was not entirely to blame for the 'offences and outrageous crimes [which] have been committed against the law for no short time.' Humble even in adversity, Robert undertook to 'reform and repair any of his actions which had been negligent'. More significantly, he agreed that

'his first-born son and heir, the Lord Earl of Carrick, is to administer the common law throughout all the kingdom.'

The king retained theoretical control over other aspects of government, including foreign affairs. Yet since for a number of years he had played a diminishing part in all matters of state (for example, in 1381 important negotiations with John of Gaunt had been conducted by his son), the agreement was to all intents and purposes an abdication.

From this point onwards King Robert fades wraith-like into the background. We are told that in 1385 his eyes were 'red bleared' and the colour of sandal wood or silk – cataracts? He spent much of his time far from the centres of government, either sheltering in Rothesay or whiling away his time at modest Dundonald Castle. The disparaging comments of Froissart, mocking a king who 'had rather lie still than ride', have coloured the judgements of future generations on an infirm old man, too gentle for the role he was asked to play. Ever the bully, Dr Johnson later added his voice to the chorus of contumely. 'Though of considerable size,' wrote Boswell of his master's visit to Dundonald,

DUNDONALD CASTLE

'we could not by any power of the imagination figure it as having been a suitable habitation for majesty. Dr Johnson, to irritate my old Scottish enthusiasm, was very jocular on the homely accommodation of 'King Bob', and roared and laughed till the ruins echoed.'

* * *

In 1385 the border conflict burst into full-scale warfare when the young Richard II and his uncle John of Gaunt advanced into Scotland. The Scots and a strong detachment of French knights chose scorched-earth tactics rather than confrontation. The cost of the policy was high: several border abbeys were sacked and Edinburgh burned, this time Gaunt sparing only Holyrood Abbey itself. Thereafter the war dragged on with a series of raids and counter-raids of which the king knew little and probably cared less. The chaos in the south was matched by mounting lawlessness elsewhere, for Carrick was no more successful at controlling independent-minded nobles than his father had been. In 1385 parliament asked him specifically to restore law and order in the Highlands, but little came of it. Three years later, instead of seeing the death of John of the Isles as an opportunity for re-establishing royal power in the north-west, the crown sent a mission to his successor, Donald, to discuss the possibility of an alliance. John of Carrick seemed to be turning out like his father: easy-going, open and generous, but without that cutting edge which successful command required.

We will never know how Prince John's career might have developed under normal circumstances. In 1388 a vicious kick from Sir James Douglas's tournament horse rendered him a chronic invalid for the rest of his life. The accident crippled his mind as well as his body. Already prone to bouts of depression, now that he was virtually housebound, John lapsed into long periods of inactivity and self-condemnation. As Robert II neared his end, the outlook for Scotland's new ruling dynasty was far from auspicious.

If the injury to John of Carrick was generally bewailed, there was one man at least to whom it seemed a heaven-sent opportunity. This was Robert Stewart, Earl of Menteith and Fife, Robert II's ambitious second son. Neither as benign as John nor as malign as Alexander, Robert was the most able of a mixed bunch. Like the rest of his family, he was 'seemly' in appearance, 'high and fair'. Eager to present a good image in public, he made sure that he was seen at religious devotions; strangely for a Stewart, it was also reported that 'in chastity he led his life'. Like his father, he was to live to a grand old age, something which probably owed as much to the fact that he 'ate and drank but soberly' as to his constitution. He was no great shakes as a military commander, but adopted a sufficiently high profile in the intermittent border frays for the uncritical Wyntoun to herald him as 'the greatest leader' of the 1385 campaign. The earl built up a substantial personal following, too, and during his father's lifetime 'the young chivalry' saw him as the man most worth following. This flair for publicity, coupled with an astute business brain and considerable administrative competence, raised Robert above his royal contemporaries and made him the outstanding Stewart of his generation.

Robert's rise to prominence had begun in 1361, when he had acquired the earldom of Menteith through a judicious marriage. Ten years later skilful bargaining had added the earldom of Fife to his honours. In 1382 he had picked up the office of chamberlain after Lyon's murder; government receipts fell away significantly thereafter. With the transference of power to John of Carrick in 1384, Robert and Archibald Douglas ('the Grim') had made a point of ensuring that the change had not affected their personal rights of lordship. Now, with the unfortunate Carrick to all intents and purposes out of the way, Robert prepared to take a further lurch up the greasy pole.

The occasion was a meeting of the three estates in general council at Edinburgh in December 1388. We cannot be sure that Robert had been planning a coup before the council gathered, but the outcome of the proceedings suggests that he may well have been up to something. The highlight of the gathering was an extraordinary document read out in the king's name. In it the seventy-two-year-old Robert II handed over virtually every branch of government to the general council and expressed the wish that his heir apparent should do likewise. Is it mere fancy to imagine the second son, on the surface all commonsense and civility, urging his senile father to take such a step? What followed certainly indicates that a document of final abdication was precisely what he had been angling for.

Having heard officially that the king was now too infirm to govern effectively and that 'his eldest son was not in his usual good health', the council appointed Earl Robert governor of the realm with a salary of 1000 marks a year. Robert's elevation was regarded with apprehension by some council members, for they gave him prime ministerial rather than royal authority. He was told, for example, not to meddle with the royal revenue, but since he was already chamberlain the instruction had a somewhat hollow ring to it. Renewable annually, the governorship was provisional upon its incumbent behaving 'well and usefully', and had to be handed back to the Earl of Carrick if and when he recovered from his illness. Even so, Robert had immense scope for furthering his limitless ambition. It is no coincidence that the very next year his son Murdoch replaced the disgraced 'Wolf of Badenoch' as justiciar in the North.

* * *

King Robert survived his surrender of authority by only seventeen months. On 13 May 1390, 'full of years' and after 'a short sickness', he passed away peacefully at his beloved Dundonald. He had brought his family to fresh heights and his amiability had undoubtedly helped to secure them in their new-found prominence. Ever the generous Stewartphile, Wyntoun chose to look on the bright side when he concluded his comments on the 'gracious, virtuous and happy' king with the words: 'A more tender heart might no man have.'

Writing a century and a half later, the perceptive John Major sought to redress the balance by drawing attention to Robert's martial and administrative failings: 'I cannot hold the aged king to have been a skilful warrior or wise in counsel'. Always of a generous and humble disposition, the first Stewart monarch would probably have concurred. A tender-hearted gentleman might have won the ladies and the praise of uncritical chroniclers, but he had not won control over a tough and troublesome state. In the end, therefore, it seems only fair to conclude that although Robert had done wonders for the Stewart dynasty, he can hardly be said to have done the same for Scotland.

III

Queen Annabella, 'a lady good and pleasant and of excellent beauty', once asked her husband Robert III (the title under which Prince John reigned – see below) why he had not made arrangements for a splendid tomb for himself. The king took umbrage, ranting on about his being but 'a stinking seed' and 'food for worms', fit only to be buried in a rubbish heap. He concluded, so the story goes, with the following remarkable exhortation:

'Bury me, therefore, I beg you, in a midden, and write for my epitaph: "Here lies the worst of kings and the most wretched of men in the whole kingdom." '

Robert's word was obeyed in death no more than it had been in life. He was buried before the high altar at Paisley.

This does not detract from the significance of Robert's memorable self-deprecatory outburst. He was not the worst monarch to wear the Scottish crown – his shortcomings were far too passive to merit such an ignominious accolade – but he was surely one of the most jejune. What nature had begun, Douglas' horse had completed. By the time the second Stewart monarch ascended the throne at the age of fifty-three he was a physical and emotional cripple. Traditionally, his ineffectiveness has been put down to the lameness which prevented him from moving easily about the kingdom: '...being bodily infirm', wrote Bower, he 'had no grip anywhere'. The king's injury undoubtedly was a problem, yet it need not have been an insuperable one. As John Major observed a century or so later,

'if that bodily infirmity which afflicted [him] were unaccompanied by any infirmity of mind, it need not have been any hindrance to his exer-

cise of the duties of a king; for he might have ridden on horseback
throughout the country.'

Robert was certainly mobile enough to put in appearances in different parts
of his kingdom from time to time, and his incapacity did not prevent him
siring children (only death, it seems, could stop the Stewarts doing that) or
making the difficult journey to Bute. His real handicap was a psychological
one. He was a profound depressive, gripped by bouts of debilitating melancholia which took the form of an almost religious obsession with his own
unworthiness.

Apart from an expedition into Galloway, during his father's lifetime John
of Carrick had made little impression as a soldier, and he probably lacked
positiveness even before his accident. The profound effect of this personal
calamity on his personality can be fully appreciated only in the context of an
age whose heroes – Earl James Douglas, Hotspur, Earl George of March and
the like – were soldiers whose deeds in battle and in the lists stirred the imagination of a chivalric society. Disability was regarded at best with pity or
suspicion, at worst with contempt. Thus, with the shadow of Robert II's
retreat at Neville's Cross already hanging over the family, the sensitive John
felt even greater shame now that he could not even take to the field. It would
have taken immense strength of character to come to terms with such a
dismal inheritance, but strength was the one quality which John's character
patently lacked.

* * *

Prince John lacked confidence even in his own name. For his coronation by
Bishop Walter Trail of St Andrews the new king announced that he wished
to be known as Robert III, not John II, believing that by avoiding the name
associated with failure in Scotland, England and France he would increase
the chances of a successful reign. It was a gesture as pitiable as it was ineffective.

Bower has a story of Robert's coronation which, if true, illustrates well the
king's personality and helps explain why, despite his obvious failings, he
remained popular in many quarters and unchallenged on the throne. Large
crowds attending the ceremony strayed into the nearby fields, trampling the
crops and doing considerable damage. When the canon granger of Scone,
Robert Logy, tried to see the king about compensation, he was turned away
before he could get an audience. Nothing daunted, the resourceful Logy
returned early the following morning with his harvesters and a variety of
crude musical instruments. Arranging themselves beneath the king's
window, they made such a din that Robert awoke and sent to discover the
cause of this cacophonic dawn chorus. When hauled before the king, Logy
explained sarcastically that since he now had no need to spend a small

fortune on harvest wages, he had decided to use the money to serenade his newly-anointed lord.

Furious at such presumption, members of the royal household demanded that the impromptu bandmaster be punished. But King Robert, 'wise man that he was', valued justice higher than a good night's sleep and ordered that the abbey be paid in full for the loss it had suffered. The tale may be apocryphal, but it contains sufficient detail to be plausible and accords well with the image of an even-tempered king loath to offend anyone, even the humblest canon. One wonders whether Robert Logy would have dared try such a trick on one of the Bruce kings.

During the reign of Robert III, lamented one chronicler, 'there was no law in Scotland. The strong oppressed the weak and the whole kingdom was a den of thieves.' The entire blame for this state of affairs cannot be laid at the feet of the monarch; apart from a brief period in 1393, Robert III was king in name only. For much of the first nine years of the new reign the guardianship of Earl Robert was renewed at periodic intervals. As when acting on his father's behalf, the earl was not keen to risk unpopularity by doing his elder brother's police work. He was more than happy to use his position as chamberlain to build up a fortune, but made no serious effort to curb the 'great deal of dissension, strife and brawling among the magnates and leading men'. Thus Scotland suffered at the hands of two leaders, one of whom could not maintain the law, and another who would not. A couple of well-known incidents illustrate well the misfortunes stemming from this sorry state of affairs.

Having lost his official position in the north in 1388, shortly after his brother's accession the Wolf Earl of Buchan became more ungovernable than ever. In May 1390 he commanded his 'wild, wicked Highland men' (believed to be 'comely in form but unsightly in dress'!) to burn Forres to demonstrate to the Earl of Moray, and anyone else who contemplated standing in the Wolf's way, just who was lord in those parts. The lesson was lost on the Bishop of Moray, who refused to continue paying Buchan's protection money. As a result, on 17 June Elgin went the same way as Forres when 'untamed people' of the Highlands left its fine cathedral a broken, smoking ruin.

Not even Robert III could overlook such behaviour. Yet rather than arrest his brother, he merely ordered him to make some sort of reparation and do penance, dressed in sackcloth, before the high altar of the Dominican kirk at Perth. This was hardly the way to tame the Wolf and his ilk.

The Highlands did not settle. Six years later the king hit upon a different way of calming the region's 'great discord', this time eschewing religious sanctions and turning instead to chivalry. Clan Chattan and Clan Kay, bitter enemies whose bloody squabbles had long disturbed the peace, were invited to meet before the king on the North Inch of Perth and settle their differences in formal armed combat.

It was an extraordinary arrangement. A field of battle was marked out, overlooked by the king sitting on a platform above the pitch. Each side was permitted thirty warriors, fully armed with swords, axes, bows and arrows, but wearing no armour. A huge crowd turned up to watch.

Just as the grim contest was about to begin, one of the participants worked out the odds against his survival and fled. Pursued by a mob of angry spectators, he made good his escape. His place was filled by a volunteer, Henry of the Wynd, a local armourer of 'savage appearance'. The diversion over, Robert ordered the battle to begin.

Some while later, after the most ghastly scenes of hacking, piercing and chopping, Clan Kay were down to one man. Since the exhausted fellow faced ten Chattans and their new recruit, the king decided that there was little point in continuing the fight and cast down his baton to bring the day's blood sport to a close. Bower believed that 'for a long time the north remained quiet.' The more objective Moray chronicler wrote otherwise: 'Homicides, robberies, fire-raisings and other misdeeds remained unpunished, and justice seemed banished beyond the kingdom's bounds'.

* * *

Robert III and Annabella Drummond had seven children. Of the four daughters, three wedded Douglases and the fourth remained unmarried. Twin boys were born on the feast of St James 1394. One, named James because of his birthday and perhaps with some thought of his great-great grandfather, survived into childhood. An elder brother, David Earl of Carrick, had been born on 24 October 1378, some eleven years after his parents' marriage. As the young man grew into adulthood there were signs that here at last was a Stewart capable of performing with some degree of competence the tasks so neglected by his father and grandfather. By 1398 the estates regarded Carrick highly enough for his name to be put forward as a possible leader of an expedition against the Lord of the Isles.

Like all his Stewart contemporaries, David of Carrick was by all accounts tall and good-looking; 'pleasant', 'mighty' and 'fair' Wyntoun called him. He was also quite well educated. The one drawback was his age. The king's illness had thrust the young earl into the political arena long before he had learned to curb his own impetuous instincts. This did not matter too much as long as his powerful mother was alive, for she exerted a strong control over her son, even using him as a front for her own causes. Chief among these was a running vendetta with governor Robert.

The queen's dislike for her brother-in-law was threefold. She resented the control he wielded at the expense of her husband, she was irritated at the way his officials prevented her from drawing the generous annual pension, and at the back of her mind lay the fear that the unscrupulous governor might try to do away with David and James and seize the throne for himself. The situation had all the makings of a classic family power struggle.

Aware of the mounting tension between Carrick and Earl Robert, in April 1398 Robert III resorted to another of his singularly ineffective schemes for smoothing over difficult situations. He hoped to submerge family animosity in a deluge of generosity by simultaneously making his son Duke of Rothesay and his brother Duke of Albany. Some significance has been read into these titles. While Prince David's dukedom recalled the Stewart's favourite offshore residence, his uncle's harked back to 'Alba', the ancient name for the whole Scottish kingdom. In historical and geographical terms the latter was by far the grander-sounding appellation. What others thought of the introduction of a new rank of nobility we cannot be sure. It is said that Archibald 'the Grim', the doughty Earl of Douglas, was also offered a dukedom; but when flatteringly addressed as 'Sir Duke', he merely muttered scornfully 'Sir Drake, Sir Drake'.

Robert's bizarre attempt to sweeten relations between uncle and nephew came to nothing, and the first round in the contest proper went to the new Duke of Rothesay and his mother. Meeting at Perth in 1399, a general council declared that

'…the misgovernance of the realm and the failure to keep the common
law is the fault of the king and of his officers'.

If this was an attempt to get at the 'officers' (ie Albany) rather than the king himself, it was deflected when Robert gladly accepted the council's blame for all that had gone wrong. Nevertheless, the upshot of the meeting was the appointment of Rothesay as the king's lieutenant for three years, with the salary and expenses once enjoyed by Albany as governor.

The move might have signalled the beginning of the end of Albany's political career. As it turned out, however, the lieutenancy proved to be Rothesay's undoing, not his uncle's. A number of events conspired to make it so.

There are indications that David had the makings of a competent lieutenant, particularly when it came to maintaining law and order; but he rarely allowed his better qualities to be seen to good effect. To begin with he found himself constrained by a special council of 'wise men', over which Albany exercised considerable influence. In going against the council's wishes or simply ignoring its presence altogether, the prince increased his reputation for high-handed irresponsibility.

Next the king and his heir managed between them to so offend the Earl of March that in 1400 he left for England and the sympathetic ear of the usurper Henry IV. Eager to divert attention away from his own arbitrary conduct, Henry demanded that the King of Scots perform the homage owing to the King of England 'since the time of Locrine, son of Brut'. This was too much even for the obliging Robert, who refused to have anything to do with such nonsense. As a consequence, Henry moved cautiously north and by

August 1400 was besieging Edinburgh Castle, bravely defended by Rothesay. When Henry's renewed demand for homage had been refused and he had scorned Rothesay's challenge to meet in an eleven-a-side set-piece battle, the English marched back to Newcastle without doing much damage. Not wishing to add to the prestige of Rothesay's lieutenancy, Albany had failed to take advantage of a favourable situation and strike at the withdrawing foe. The next year peace negotiations broke up without a settlement and cross border animosity flared yet again.

At this juncture the career of young Rothesay was suddenly disrupted by the deaths within a single year of the three figures who had kept him under some sort of control: Earl Archibald Douglas ('who in worldly prudence, courage and boldness excelled the other Scots of his day'), Queen Annabella and Bishop Trail of St Andrews. With their passing, 'dignity departed, honour withdrew and the integrity of Scotland died away'. The new Earl of Douglas, Archibald 'Tyneman' ('the Loser'), transferred his family's allegiance to the Albany camp, and the Duke of Rothesay 'gave himself up wholly to his previous frivolity'.

The nature of this 'frivolity' comes as no surprise to anyone acquainted with the Stewarts. Rothesay regarded 'other men's wives as superior to his own' and acted accordingly. His affair with the sister of the Earl of Crawford attracted much gossip, and his repudiation of the Earl of March's daughter had been the reason why the earl had taken up with Henry IV. Few expected the heir to the throne to plough a furrow of perfect chastity, but dalliance with married women and the children of the most influential aristocrats was bound to cause resentment.

In January 1402 Rothesay's term of office was not renewed. His downfall, presaged by the appearance of a 'wonderful comet', followed soon afterwards. Told that his son was preparing to seize the castle and estates of the bishopric of St Andrews and hold them until a new bishop should be appointed, as was the crown's right, the 'weak and decrepit' king was persuaded to write to Albany

> 'that the said Duke of Rothesay should be arrested by him and put into custody for a time until, after punishment by the rod of discipline, he should know himself better.'

Sadly, 'what the king proposed for the improvement of his son turned out to his harm.'

Albany and the Earl of Douglas had Rothesay arrested on the road to St Andrews. He was then taken 'mounted on a mule and dressed in a russet tunic' to Falkland Castle. Here he was held in 'a certain decent small room' until the evening of 25 March 1402, when he died in mysterious circumstances. The official line was that he had been carried off by an attack of dysentery. Rumour whispered that he had been starved to death on Albany's orders.

Several years later Albany allotted a small fortune from customs revenue to a certain John Wright. We do not know the nature of Wright's services for this reward, but it is probably no coincidence that he had been one of those responsible for holding Rothesay in Falkland. It is also said that the Albany aisle in St Giles was erected by the man whose name it bears as a penance for the death of his nephew. Whatever blame one may ascribe to an unprincipled character named Ramornie for suggesting how Rothesay might be disposed of, if the young duke was indeed murdered then his uncle must surely bear most of the guilt.

Albany and Douglas were questioned by the general council. At the end of the deliberations Rothesay was said 'to have departed this life by divine providence and not otherwise'. To his shame, the feeble King Robert accepted the decision, declaring that no one was to question it. Now only an ageing depressive and his eight-year-old son stood between Albany and the throne.

IV

After Rothesay's death Albany took over the vacant lieutenancy of the realm and diverted attention away from the circumstances of his return to power by resuming hostilities with England. He was helped by a strange but useful character who had somehow turned up in the castle of Donald of the Isles. To most contemporaries this vagabond figure was known simply as the 'Mammet', or puppet; but in public pronouncements Albany preferred the name by which the half-witted wretch knew himself: 'Richard II', the deposed King of England. As Henry IV was tied up with domestic rebellion, the pretender provided an opportune excuse to intervene over the border. Albany also hoped to deal with the Earl of March, now in harness with the bellicose Hotspur and not a threat to be taken lightly.

Albany's diversionary tactics proved painfully expensive. First the Scots suffered a sharp reverse at Nesbit Muir on 22 June 1402. Less than three months later an even greater disaster befell them at Homildon Hill when March and Hotspur overtook a prestigious Scots raiding party and captured 'the flower of chivalry of the whole Scottish kingdom'. Among their number was Albany's son and heir Murdoch and Douglas the Loser. (Having promptly changed his allegiance, a year later the ill-fated earl fought beside Hotspur against Henry IV at Shrewsbury. True to form, he had selected the wrong side and ended up Henry's prisoner, along with Murdoch.)

What the ailing Robert III thought of his new lieutenant's disastrous cross-border forays, we do not know. But other aspects of the Albany Stewarts' behaviour had begun to arouse worries even in the king's unsuspecting mind.

Rothesay's untimely death was shortly followed by that of one of the prince's confidants, Sir Malcolm Drummond, brother of the late queen and husband of Isobel, Countess of Mar in her own right. Having been kidnapped and imprisoned, Sir Malcolm had been killed 'by persons unknown'. Once again the finger of suspicion pointed towards the Albanies. If the duke himself was not responsible, then the culprit was probably Alexander Stewart, illegitimate son of the Wolf of Badenoch. After Sir Malcolm's death Alexander kept the countess under virtual house arrest in Kildrummy Castle until she finally agreed to marry him. The submission was carefully stage-managed. In the presence of the Bishop of Ross, Alexander stood humbly before the castle gates. When Isobel appeared before him he proffered her Kildrummy's keys, declaring that they were hers to dispose of as she wished. Forcibly schooled in her part, the countess promptly handed them back to Alexander. With them went the Earldom of Mar.

By 1404, when Albany's lieutenancy was renewed by the general council for a further two years, the king had finally made up his mind to try and stem the rising tide of his brother's ambition. All the royal Stewart possessions were made into an independent territorial jurisdiction, known as a regality, to prevent their falling into other hands, and the king built up a band of pensioned followers for Prince James, now Earl of Carrick. These steps might have gone some way towards securing the lad's inheritance, but they did little to safeguard his person. For a while he was entrusted to the care of Henry Wardlaw, the new Bishop of St Andrews. Finally, in 1406 Robert III decided that the only way of making absolutely sure that no harm came to his son was to send him out of the kingdom.

Bower's explanation for the king's decision to ship James to France is somewhat ambiguous:

'...when he had acquired good habits there he could, upon reaching manhood, return home in greater safety and govern his kingdom more wisely.'

There can be little doubt that 'greater safety' was far more important than picking up 'good habits' on the Continent. Had Rothesay been given the chance to grow up outside the dangerous and pressured flattery of the court circle, he might have developed into a less obstreperous young man. As it was, this opportunity now fell to Prince James, although not quite in the fashion envisaged by his anxious father.

Since the English were unlikely to guarantee the prince a safe passage over their territory, it was decided to risk the multifarious dangers of a winter crossing of the North sea. That James was to travel in February is an indication of the haste with which his journey was planned and leads one to suspect that King Robert had heard rumours of further Albany plots against the royal family. Sir David Fleming, one of the king's most loyal councillors, transported the heir to the throne safely to the Bass Rock where he was to await transport in a friendly vessel on the second leg of his passage. On the

PAISLEY ABBEY

way back from his mission Fleming was ambushed and slain by James Douglas, brother of the hostage Loser. The crime went unpunished. Whether or not Sir David's fate was related to the mission he had just accomplished is not known.

Fleming's valiant service had been in vain. The eleven-year-old prince waited on the barren rock in the company of the Earl of Orkney and a Welsh bishop for a month before he was picked up by the *Maryenknygt* of Danzig. During the delay Albany no doubt heard what was going on and possibly relayed the news to Henry IV. Forewarned or not, on 14 March English sailors from Great Yarmouth seized the *Maryenknygt* off Flamborough Head and handed over their tender prize to the authorities. King Henry undertook to relieve the French of the burden of the prince's education, allegedly asserting that the boy could learn their language as easily in his court as on the Continent. He allowed the crew which had taken the *Maryenknygt* to keep the ship's remaining cargo of wool and hides as a reward for their services.

Matters had not turned out quite as Albany had wished. James was certainly out of the way, but not conclusively so. The lieutenant would have preferred him at the bottom of the sea. Furthermore, James was as safe in the Tower of London as he would have been at the French court, for there was no way that the English would willingly harm so valuable a bargaining counter. The prince's misfortune might have brought Albany a step nearer real power, but he was still quite a leap from the throne.

* * *

While Albany was angered by the news of James's capture, the boy's unfortunate father became totally distraught. Bower recalled that it was more than the miserable man could bear:

> 'King Robert heard of his son's capture while he was sitting down to supper in his castle at Rothesay... The news broke his heart... His spirit began immediately to fade, his bodily strength ebbed away, he grew pale and such was his sorrow that he ate nothing more until he yielded up his soul to his Creator.'

He died on 4 April, Palm Sunday, 1406.

There is no avoiding the fact that Robert III had been a singularly incompetent monarch. He was condemned for having 'no grip anywhere', and 'dissension, strife and brawling' flourished throughout his reign. If we add to this the fellow's own low opinion of himself in his darkest moods, then he was undoubtedly Scotland's most ineffective king and the least worthy of all the Stewarts.

Yet an air of genuine tragedy hangs about Robert's time on the throne. There was no malice in the man. All who knew him spoke with affection of his humility, gentleness, 'sound conscience' and genuine 'love of justice', even though he lacked the will to put his principles into practice. Bower, who had probably seen Robert in old age, had fond memories of him, still handsome, with a long snowy beard and an amiable expression highlighted in bright, good humoured eyes.

It is not for us to blame this genial yet disabled man for his physical and mental shortcomings, particularly as he had acquired his position through no striving of his own. It may well have been better for Scotland if Robert had never been crowned; but that was hardly his fault. There were plenty of Stewarts who would prove better kings, but far worse human beings.

The young lad in the Tower of London was one of them.

CHAPTER 10

Fresh Horizons

I

Marooned for several weeks on a lonely rock, captured at sea by pirates and finally incarcerated in the Tower of London – James I's dramatic initiation into the adult world could have come straight from the pages of juvenile fiction. At a less superficial level, however, it was a set of brutal experiences which might well have left the youth scarred for life.

James was certainly deeply affected by what had happened to him. He later bewailed his early misfortunes in the autobiographical passages of his lengthy poem the *Kingis Quair* (see below); but unfortunately the work is too contrived and stylised an account to give us much insight into his real feelings. As far as we can tell from his subsequent behaviour, James reacted to his seizure and imprisonment with neither terror nor elation, but with a profound sense of humiliation. In time this developed into a steely determination, tinged with ruthlessness – quite alien to anything seen in his Stewart ancestors but well suited to the tasks which lay ahead of him.

James's stay in England proved personally beneficial in other ways, too. It ensured his physical safety and kept him from the dangerous exercise of power during his years of political immaturity. (His succession to the throne was confirmed in June 1406, when the General Council simultaneously appointed his uncle Albany to the post of governor.) Furthermore, the English took good care of James's bodily and intellectual welfare, knowing full well that to have held him in chains in some dripping dungeon would not only have broken the chivalric code, but also endangered the health of a prime hostage. As we saw with David II, the King of Scots was far more valuable alive than dead.

James spent only about three of his eighteen years of detention in the Tower. The rest of his time was passed in more salubrious strongholds, including the airy castle at Nottingham, the seaside stronghold at Pevensey, and Windsor, his principle residence after 1414. He was frequently permitted to attend the English court and twice went on campaign in France with Henry V, who presented him with the Order of the Garter in 1421. The previous year, wearing borrowed robes of some splendour, James had been present at the coronation of Henry's bride, Queen Catherine of France.

Unlike his father and grandfather, the exiled king was vigorous and sporty. He grew to about average height and, blessed with well co-ordinated, muscular limbs, he excelled at a number of physically demanding activities such as riding, swordsmanship, wrestling, and archery. This freedom to participate in a wide range of outdoor pursuits illustrates the generous nature of his captivity. It also raises the question of why he never tried to escape. The answer may be, of course, that he was too closely guarded, even when out riding. Yet his memories of early childhood in Scotland cannot have been very fond – might he sometimes have regarded his sojourn in prosperous and sophisticated England as more congenial than the undoubted hardships awaiting him back home? If there is any truth in this, then it would help explain his sometimes disparaging and cynical attitude when he finally returned to his kingdom.

As if to reinforce their charge's nascent anglophilia, the English arranged for James to be given a first-rate education – better than that of any Scottish royal predecessor. He was the first King of Scots whose handwriting has survived (a surprisingly pleasing script it is too), and he may even have been the first able to write more than a few consecutive words with his own pen. Tutors helped him to become fluent in English, Scots, French and Latin. Contemporaries also noted his eloquence, musical skill and attractive singing voice, remarking that he indulged in 'singing and piping, harping and other honest solaces of great pleasure and disport'. One may take with a pinch of salt, however, the sycophantic comment that he performed 'like another Orpheus'.

Begun in about 1424 but finished later, the semi-autobiographical *Kingis Quair* provides a unique insight into the creative side of James's complex personality. The poem is an extended, fairly conventional reflection on the workings of Fate, and one man's struggle to come to terms with them. In places the author flirts with sentiments worthy of his self-pitying father. One wonders, for example, whether James had in mind the depressed wailings of Robert III, as well as his own ill-fortune, when he lamented what he called his 'hard...adventure':

> ...I wold bewaille
> My dedely lyf, full of peyne and penance...
> Quhat have I gilt to faille [done to lose]
> My fredome in this world and my plesance?'

The *Quair* is as much alliterative romance as ballad, and concludes as a love poem. At the very end of his captivity James met and fell in love with Lady Joan Beaufort, the daughter of John, Earl of Somerset, son of John of Gaunt by his mistress Catherine Swynford. Since Gaunt was the fourth son of Edward III and the Beauforts had been declared legitimate in 1407, the elegant and intelligent Joan made an ideal partner for the Scots king.

James's meeting with his future bride inspired him to some of his best lines. Not surprisingly, the style and language owes more to the school of Chaucer than to any Scots versifier. Indeed, the Scotticisms might have been added after James's release to persuade courtiers that his prolonged exile had not really affected the way he thought. He recalled, somewhat fancifully, going to a window in the tower of Windsor Castle and hearing the nightingales singing below:

> 'And sing with us, away, winter, away!
> Cum, somer, cum, the suete sesoun and sonne!

> * * *

> And amorously lift up your hedis all,
> Thank lyfe that list you to his merci call.'

Then he espied Lady Joan:

> 'And therwith kest I doun myn eye ageyne,
> Quhare as I sawe, walking under the tour,
> Full secretly new cummyn hir to pleyne,
> The fairest or the freschest younge floure
> That ever I saw, me thought, before that houre...

> * * *

> Than gan I studye in myself and seyne,
> Ah suete, ar ye a wardly creature,
> Or hevinly thing in likeness of nature?'

For all its conventional imagery and stylised sentiment, the lines convey real feeling. James fell in love with the intensity of a passionate man long frustrated at his lot, and for a while all his pent up feelings were directed towards the woman who appeared heaven-sent to keep him company in his unhappiness. He was still a prisoner, but at least he now had a soul-mate with whom to share his enduring humiliation.

The couple were married in St Mary Overy, now Southwark Cathedral, on 13 February 1424. Three months later they were over the border and established King and Queen of Scotland. As concrete proof of his lasting and sincere affection for the English lady who had done so much to lift his flagging spirits, James remained faithful to Joan for the remainder of his life. In this, as well as his scholarship, the king marks a clear break in the traditions of the Stewart dynasty.

II

Robert Stewart, Duke of Albany, retained the governorship of Scotland until his death in 1420, when his office and ducal title passed to his son Murdoch. It is not clear how seriously Robert strove to secure his nephew's freedom. Aware that only the life of the young exile stood between him and the crown, he allowed himself some of the trappings of monarchy, employing his own seal and speaking of his Scottish 'subjects'. Particularly after Murdoch's release in 1415, therefore, it was undoubtedly in Robert's best interest for James to remain out of the country. However friendly a neighbour the King of Scots might have promised to be, he was also of more use to Henry IV and Henry V in England than in Scotland. Thus the policies of both the English and Scottish governments conspired with ill fortune to keep James away from his inheritance until his thirtieth year.

James retained a small Scottish household, and from the beginning of his exile he tried to keep in touch with affairs at home. It was never quite clear when a Scottish monarch came into his majority. Various ages were regarded as significant, including twelve and sixteen, and by eighteen a young man was certainly seen as old enough to play a full part in government. Around his eighteenth birthday, after some eight years of captivity, James must have been feeling particularly frustrated. In 1412 he wrote crossly to his uncle complaining that not enough was being done to secure his release. At about the same time he made a couple of gestures intended to remind the world that the true King of Scotland was still alive: he added his name to the petition to Pope Benedict XIII requesting a bull to endorse the foundation of a university at St Andrews and he wrote 'under the signet', using 'our proper hand', to confirm a pair of Douglases in possession of their lands.

Previously James had made contact with Henry IV's ally Donald, Lord of the Isles, who was in conflict with Albany over the earldom of Ross. By devious means, the governor had allowed the earldom to pass to his second son John, Earl of Buchan. Inevitably, since Donald also claimed the title, the issue had to be settled by force of arms, and Alexander Stewart (the director of the cruel Kildrummy pageant seven years before) vanquished the Islesmen at the Battle of Harlaw in 1411. The following year Donald submitted and swore allegiance to Albany. He also gave up his English alliance and, by implication, his contact with the exiled king.

James's desire to participate at long range in the government of Scotland was very understandable, even laudable. But his actions were never more than gestures and served only to increase his suspicious uncle's wariness. For all the king's fluency, his pen could never hope to match the governor's sword, and the ultimate outcome of James's correspondence was merely a bitter reminder of his obvious impotence.

Ironically, the one influential Scot with whom James enjoyed prolonged personal contact at this time was his cousin Murdoch. The king's senior by more than thirty years, Albany's eldest son had been taken prisoner by the English four years before James, and although the two men were not always held in the same place, they spent enough time in each other's company to get to know each other well. In the light of future events, it would be fascinating to know more of the relationship struck up between the scholarly and restless young king and his rather feeble elder relation.

There was a cynical, almost cruel streak to James's personality. This does not contradict the sentiments of the *Kingis Quair* – ruthlessness and sentimentality are often found on opposite sides of the same coin. He guessed correctly that Albany was going to work harder for the release of his son than for his king. Since the governor was getting on in years, therefore, James had to prepare for the possibility that one day the English might negotiate with Murdoch for the release of his master. So the king surely humoured his dull-witted cousin, perhaps even letting him win some of their many games of chess.

But even the unperceptive Murdoch was not deceived for long by such tactics. After his release, and when he had indeed succeeded his father as governor and Duke of Albany, Murdoch once confronted his ungovernable son Walter with the threat: 'Well, since I cannot control you, I will summon one who will control us both!' There was no doubt to whom he was referring. Whatever smokescreen of geniality James had put up over the chess board, Murdoch had formed a fair impression of his erstwhile companion's true nature.

* * *

The Lancastrian usurper Henry IV hoped to use his royal hostage to preserve peace with Scotland while he attended to domestic matters. But Governor Albany, who in the Mammet had a bargaining counter of his own, was not as susceptible to English bargaining as Henry would have wished. Nothing permanent came of almost annual peace discussions, and in 1409 the Scots began small-scale border hostilities. The purpose of their aggression is not clear. Albany may have been trying to force Henry to release James as the price of peace, or he was showing the English what little regard he had for their hostage. Whatever the fighting was designed to do, James remained where he was.

Others were more fortunate. The powerful Douglas was allowed home on parole in 1407. Subsequently Albany showed some political skill by making a bond with him and, at the same time, reconciling himself to the long-absent Earl of March, probably to counterbalance the Douglases. This was followed by the Albany Stewarts' success in the north and a six-year truce with England in 1412. As his uncle's position strengthened, so James's deteriorated, inspiring him to write a thinly disguised criticism of his duplicitous uncle: 'the responsibility for the delay in our homecoming rests entirely with those who should be working for us'.

Eager to be given a favourable reception by his Maker, Henry IV recommended on his deathbed that James I be released. His practical son ignored the advice. Instead it was Murdoch who benefited from the change of English monarch. Set on continental conquest, Henry V used Murdoch to secure Scotland's neutrality, and in 1416 the governor's heir was freed in exchange for Hotspur's son and £10,000. Negotiations conducted at the same time for James's release came to nothing. The king was escorted to Yorkshire in 1417 only to find that the promised Scottish hostages had failed to turn up. Small wonder that later James showed little love for an aristocracy which, judging by the experiences of his youth, he perceived to be little more than perfidious self-seekers.

It was with mixed feelings, therefore, that James heard of the sharp reverses suffered by Albany and Douglas in 1417, when they broke the new truce with raids on Roxburgh and Berwick. Even more confused emotions ran through the king's mind in 1420 when Henry V took him on campaign to France. In response to an embassy from the dauphin, the previous year the Earl of Buchan and the Loser's son Archibald had sailed to La Rochelle with a powerful expeditionary force to assist their flagging Continental ally. Their action transformed James from King Henry's 'Scottish adversary' to his 'dearest brother'. James knew that if he wished ever to be free he had little choice but to go along with this charade. He also suffered the indignity of having his campaign expenses paid for by his host.

The nadir of James's exile occurred at the fall of Melun, where he saw the vanquished Scottish garrison led out and hung as traitors for taking up arms against their king. It was a painful experience, one that even the increasingly misanthropic James can hardly have relished. He was being used as a puppet king, a pawn in England's grandiose schemes. This was brought home to him again when on 1 December 1420 he was obliged to accompany Henry on his triumphal entry into Paris.

Yet even as the captive King of Scots was being paraded through the streets of Paris, his fortunes were at last beginning to turn.

* * *

Governor Albany had died in Stirling Castle on 3 September 1420, aged eighty. Unlike his senile father and decrepit brother, he seems to have retained his mental and physical vigour to the end. Bower, invariably an uncritical fan of the royal family, waxed lyrical on the 'ornament to nature' who had ruled 'in an honourable fashion' for fifteen years. The duke, he wrote,

'...was a most patient man, both gentle and kind, talkative and friendly. He stood out among his contemporaries, attended feasts daily, spent lavishly and was generous to strangers. Furthermore, he was wise and of distinguished appearance, with pleasant looks. He could be prudent and brave; his discretion was famous and his forbearance knew no bounds.'

The eulogy is not completely ridiculous. Given his tricky constitutional position and dynastic ambitions, it was in Albany's interest to be well-liked. From his father he had inherited a superficial attractiveness, which he combined with undoubted political and social skills to ensure that potential trouble-makers were given little cause for complaint. Government finances were at best loosely controlled, allowing the Douglases in particular to enrich themselves at the expense of the customs. (More serious depredations were prevented by the governor's inability to alienate crown possessions or rights.) He was prepared to allow local magnates such as the Earl of Mar to exercise far greater regional authority than would have been acceptable to Robert I or David II. Royal justice, too, was dispensed with caution. Though not implacably wedded to a policy of appeasement – the killers of the Earl of Strathearn were swiftly brought to justice in 1413, for example – serious violence often passed unpunished, as we saw after the murder of Sir David Fleming.

Albany's wily, lenient approach did not make for strong central government. But perhaps, as during the captivity of David II, no governor could have wielded the authority of a crowned king. Albany had overcome the only serious threat to his position when he bridled the power of the Lord of the Isles, and he had held the country together during a most trying time. In terms of his somewhat limited and ignoble aims, Governor Robert's long tenure of office had been moderately successful. The future prospects of the Albany Stewarts now depended on two imponderables: the ability of the new governor to carry on where his father had left off, and the attitude of the English. Before long both were giving the Albanies serious cause for alarm.

The fall of the House of Albany began, strangely enough, with a triumph. In March 1421 Murdoch's younger brother John, Earl of Buchan and self-styled Earl of Ross, led the Scottish contingent in France to a striking victory over the English at Baugé. Henry V was prevented from moving into central France, John was made a Constable of France and the grateful dauphin commanded that the Scots were no longer to be known as 'winebags'. James was doubly heartened by the news from Baugé. It raised the prestige of the Scots in the eyes of both the French and English and led Henry V to consider releasing his hostage in return for a withdrawal of the infuriating expeditionary force.

The next year, however, muttering bitter imprecations against the Scots to the last, Henry V suddenly died. Yet again James had been proffered the cup of liberty, only to have it dashed to his feet when he tried to drink.

The Earl of Buchan's military achievements took place against a rapidly deteriorating political situation back home. Murdoch, a pleasant but incompetent man in his fifties, had few of his father's political skills. Even Bower admitted that the governor's hold on the reins of power was 'too slack'. Few respected him, no one feared him. Government finances deteriorated into chaos and lawlessness flared unchecked throughout the country. The Douglases, sensitive to the way things were moving, stood aside and began to consider how best to secure their future under a new regime.

The last straw was delivered by Murdoch's son and heir, Walter, Earl of Fife and Lennox. The irascible young earl declared that when he came to power as governor – or even as king – he would resume border hostilities with England. Wrestling with the difficulties of Henry VI's minority, the English administration responded at once: if the Scots planned to make their task still more tricky, then they would stymie them by releasing their king.

The terms for James's release were set out at York in September 1423, and finally agreed at London in December. They included a seven-year truce and the payment of 60,000 marks at the rate of 10,000 a year. Preserving the fiction that the Scottish king had never been other than a guest of the English, detained for his education and security, the huge sum was not termed a ransom but explained as what might be called tuition fees and living expenses. The litotes deceived no one, particularly as the ransom exceeded at least sixfold the actual cost of the king's upkeep.

The final agreement did not cover the Scottish forces in France, although their presence had certainly helped James's case. Indeed, he was fortunate that the negotiations for his release did not drag on into the summer of 1424. Deserted by their French allies, Buchan and his men, including the Earl of Douglas – a loser to the last – were slaughtered by the English at Verneuil on 17 August. After his wedding, at which one sixth of the ransom was waived as a dowry, in March James moved north to Durham. Here he was exchanged for twenty-seven luckless hostages and finally set at liberty.

* * *

The king who crossed into Scotland in early April was largely a stranger to his native land. Much of his education, particularly in politics and government, had been received in England, where he had studied at first hand the behaviour of Henry V, one of the most successful of all late-medieval monarchs. Furthermore, he had from time to time enjoyed the fruits of a luxury unknown in the northern kingdom and had acquired a wife and companion who shared his alien upbringing. More ominously, James had scores – real and imaginary – to settle with those whom he held responsible for his eighteen-year humiliation. However gentle had been the Stewart grasp on Scotland thus far, it did not need a clairvoyant to realise that henceforward the grip was going to tighten considerably.

Like his descendant Charles II, who endured a similarly prolonged and painful exile, once James had regained his throne there was no way he was going to be forced on his travels again. The first of an altogether tougher breed of Stewart, the new king was determined to rule – and rule hard.

III

James had no master plan for bringing his kingdom to heel. The experiences of his youth had taught him that in politics, as in life, one had to be prepared to adapt to meet changing circumstances. But this was not a repetition of the freewheeling approach of his Stewart predecessors, a mere blueprint for survival. James's studied pragmatism would be the means to effective kingship.

The twenty-nine-year old king expected a court of state and luxury, and power to govern with a considerate absolutism. After long years of embarrassing deprivation he quickly developed an obsession for money and ostentatious consumption. Given his background and opportunity for close observation of the centralised English system of government, it is also understandable why he sought to increase his personal authority over the nobility and other groups whose ambitions were potentially damaging to the fabric of a well ordered and united kingdom. This did not necessarily preclude genuine solicitude for the welfare of all his people, as long as that welfare was defined by himself.

* * *

James's first year in Scotland was probably his most tricky. As an outsider he needed time to win his subjects' trust, yet he itched for revenge on the Albany Stewarts. Personal and political instincts told him that he would not be secure in his authority until he had shown himself capable of mastering the family which had dominated Scotland in his absence. But they were a scattered and elusive target.

Albany had been well liked in noble circles. Murdoch lacked his father's subtlety and determination, but he too was not without his backers. Although Bower commented unfavourably on the second governor's leniency, he still believed him to be a 'giant among men of noble and refined character'. Murdoch's obstreperous eldest son Walter, whom Bower described as physically impressive and 'wise in speech, highly pleasing to everybody and loved by all', was even more of a threat. We are told that when denied one of Murdoch's sporting hawks, Walter snatched the bird from his father's hand and wrung its neck. This aggressive young man was a soldier, too. He commanded the key fortress at Dumbarton and had already announced that he intended to attack England if he came to power. James had every intention of denying him that pleasure. Walter was arrested on 13 May, only days after the king had crossed the Tweed. To ensure that the king did not suffer the same fate as Murdoch's hawk, James sent the young hothead to cool off behind the bars of the salt-caked fortress on Bass Rock. Exile had obviously furnished James with a nice sense of irony.

Having made his intentions clear, on 21 May James proceeded to his coronation at Scone. Here he gave a fresh twist to his tussle with Murdoch, begun over the chess board many years before. By arresting Walter so swiftly, the king had already deprived his opponent of a major piece in his game. He now followed this up by catching Murdoch in a splendid fork. It was the ex-governor's traditional right and duty as Earl of Fife to place the king on the throne. If he did so, he would deal a serious blow to his own family's ambitions; if he refused, his motives would be interpreted as treasonous.

It was with a sense of dire foreboding, therefore, that Duke Murdoch took his cousin by the hand before the assembled dignitaries of the nation and led him to the throne which he had dreamed might one day be his. One can almost hear James whispering 'Check!' as the deed was done. He was growing more secure with each day that passed.

With his power now officially sanctioned by both church and state, James met his first parliament, probably the first the country had seen for some twenty years. It was a sensible move. The king had no doubt that he alone should determine policy, but since he could not rule single-handed he understood the importance of winning at least nominal sanction for his designs from the political nation. Two matters were uppermost in his mind: taxation to pay his ransom, and the restoration of law and order, so that

'firm and secure peace might be kept and held through all the realm, and among all and sundry subjects of our… lord the king.'

A parliamentary group of 'certain persons' agreed to taxes which, had they been regularly paid, would probably have met the requirements of the ransom. Other measures dealt with lawbreaking and increased export duties, and an inquiry was instituted into the current ownership of lands once held by the crown. Within a matter of months the weight of James's rule was being felt throughout the southern part of the kingdom.

By the end of year the king was strong enough to pounce again. This time it was Sir Robert Graham (a grandson of David of Strathearn) and Murdoch's elderly father-in-law, Duncan Earl of Lennox, who were detained at the royal command. Although the charges against them were obscure and Graham was later released, the message to the Albanies was clear enough. James was manoeuvring into position for the final strike.

It was later claimed, probably falsely, that it was James's uncle, the aged Walter Earl of Atholl, who finally persuaded the king to complete his pruning of the Stewart tree. It is true that the removal of Murdoch's family made the earl heir apparent for a while – Princess Margaret, born at Christmas 1424, was debarred from the succession by the tailzie of 1373. But it is unlikely that the king needed any encouragement in his quest for revenge and security.

James was too subtle an operator to give his enemies an opportunity to dub him a tyrant, and he moved in for the kill under a legal umbrella provided by his second parliament, which met in the spring of 1425. The accusations against Murdoch and his accomplices probably stemmed from general measures enacted for 'the quiet and good governance' of the realm, or from an inquiry into how the statutes of the previous parliament were being obeyed. On 21 March James's soldiers arrested Duke Murdoch, his wife Isabella, his second son Alexander, his secretary Alexander Otterburn and his henchman Sir John Montgomery. The latter two were soon released. The fate of the others remained in abeyance. One false move, and the lion would spring.

Murdoch was taken to Caerlaverock on the Solway Firth. James may have been planning to give him an opportunity to brush up his chess during a second, presumably indefinite, spell as a hostage in England. But before the scheme could be put into effect, the king was delighted to find himself forced to take rather more drastic action.

With an impeccably crass sense of timing, James the Fat, Murdoch's only son remaining at liberty, chose this moment to launch a devastating raid on Dumbarton. He burned the town and slew thirty of its citizens, including the king's illegitimate uncle Sir John Stewart of Dundonald. This was just the sort of behaviour James was determined to stamp out. Although its over-weight perpetrator managed to scramble away to Ireland, where he spent the remainder of his life in ignominious exile, the action had played straight into the king's hands. The fugitive's family was doomed.

The detained Albany Stewarts and their henchmen were brought in irons to Stirling. Here five of the gang responsible for the outrage at Dumbarton were 'drawn by horses and hanged on gibbets' on 7 May. Seventeen days later, following a trial before twenty-one of his fellow nobles, Walter Stewart was executed on Heading Hill before the castle. It was the first state execution in Scotland for over a century. The next day the same fate was meted out to the Earl of Lennox, Duke Murdoch and his son Alexander.

Thus was concluded in James's favour the family feud which had begun twenty-three years previously with the mysterious death of his brother at Falkland.

Checkmate.

* * *

James's drastic solution to the Albany problem was conclusive, but not popular. He had acted with a savagery unprecedented in recent Scottish history. The charges brought against most of his victims were unclear; Walter, for example, had been charged with 'roborea' – presumably robbery with violence on a grand scale. Ere long people were murmuring that it had been greed, rather than justice, which had driven the king to act,

'saying that they supposed…that the king did…that vigorous execution.…because he coveted their possessions and goods.'

The rumour was not without foundation. Into the king's hands came the
earldoms of Menteith, Fife and Lennox, worth over £1000 a year, and the
£3800 owing to Murdoch from the government was quietly forgotten.

Yet avarice alone does not explain James's behaviour. His complex
motives combined cupidity and a wish to exert his own authority by making
a public example of those who flouted the law, with an unattractive, deeply
personal vindictiveness. It was as if the cancerous mortification of captivity
had grown so deep within him that only the executioner's axe could cut it
out.

IV

Unlike their English counterparts, the Scottish aristocracy were heirs to a
distinguished tradition of loyalty to the crown. The removal of a reigning
monarch was unheard of. Where else in medieval Europe could successive
kings as feeble as Robert II and Robert III have survived to pass away quietly
in their beds? But the bargain had two sides to it: in return for their fidelity
to the crown, the nobles expected to be consulted and treated with due
consideration. In a country with only a rudimentary system of formal government, the maintenance of this unwritten code of co-operation was essential
for the state to hold together. Yet neither James nor his immediate Stewart
successors liked to feel beholden to anyone, and on several occasions their
aggressive independence came close to wrecking the very machine they
drove. The fact that it managed to stay on the road was due as much to the
inbuilt conservatism of the Scottish nobility and a series of fortunately
premature royal deaths as to any skill on the part of the men at the wheel.

James was sensible enough not to confront the nobility en bloc. Instead,
as with the Albany Stewarts, he singled them out one by one, taking every
opportunity to increase his power and wealth at their expense. Drawing on
his English experience, he tried to reinforce the non-noble sector in the
unicameral Scottish parliament; he urged his magnates to reside on their
estates 'for the gracious governance of their lands by good policing'; and by
instituting the offices of treasurer and comptroller he sought to reduce the
noble hold on the great offices of state.

When James arrived in Scotland the country sported fifteen earls and a
duke, the latter title and eight of the former being in the hands of the
Stewarts. Fourteen years later there was no duke and eight of the earldoms
had been acquired by the crown, five during James's lifetime and three more
immediately after his death. James's scheming game of musical honours
began only months after his coronation, when the earldom of Buchan (and,
more questionably, the earldom of Ross) reverted to the crown with the

death of John Stewart at Verneuil. Several years later the king promised to give the Buchan estate to George Dunbar, whose restoration to the earldom of March James had refused to recognise. When Dunbar's son invaded Scotland in league with the English, however, James broke his word and kept Buchan for himself. The Ross estates remained a bone of contention between the crown and the Lords of the Isles. Although James believed they were his, he had insufficient authority in the north to enforce his claim, and after the king's death Alexander of the Isles was officially confirmed as Earl of Ross.

The earldoms of Fife, Menteith and Lennox, which James had acquired in 1425, did not remain with the crown in their entirety. The king later gave the Menteith title and some of the earldom's lands to Malise Graham, great-grandson of Robert II and Euphemia Ross, as compensation for Malise losing Strathearn to Walter of Atholl in 1427. Yet since the king kept the parts of Menteith he most coveted (including Albany's fine new castle at Doune) and he dispatched Malise south as a hostage (where he remained until 1453), James's generosity was not all that it seemed. Moreover, as Queen Joan had not yet had a son, the king also enjoyed the fruits of the old Bruce earldom of Carrick. Thus within a year of his arrival in Scotland James controlled a quarter of the country's ancient earldoms.

During the next four years James sent the Earl of Sutherland as a hostage to England, where he languished until 1444, and laid claim to the earldom of Moray. The last additions to the royal title collection came in 1435, when the crown took back March and came into the earldom of Mar on the death of Alexander Stewart, the maverick son of the Wolf of Badenoch. By the end of 1437 only the earldoms of Douglas, Angus, Ross and Crawford remained completely independent.

Even the redoubtable Archibald, 5th Earl of Douglas and nephew to the king, was not exempt from royal disfavour. In 1431 he was held for a while with Alexander of the Isles in the castle on Loch Leven. Although the reason for his detention is not clear, James had made his point – he would brook no opposition. By the end of his dynamic reign the balance of power between king and aristocracy had tipped decisively towards the crown, precisely as James had intended.

* * *

James I is supposed to have outlined his aims in this rather catchy message:

> '...let God but grant me life, and there shall not be a place in my dominion where the key shall not keep the castle and the furze-bush the cow, though I myself lead the life of a dog to accomplish it'.

Ere long it was quite clear that the king had no intention of leading a dog's life, as his lavish spending on luxuries and growing corpulence testified. But this does not make his most celebrated remark simply a clever piece of public relations.

The king's intricate, complex personality embraced the sensitive poet, the gardener skilled at 'planting and grafting fruit trees', the practical man with an interest in the 'mechanical arts', the philanthropist, the greedy big spender who kept more than half his ransom money for his own use, the despot, and the heavy-drinking hothead. As James's contemporaries found, it is an almost impossible combination to come to terms with.

Moreover, like many who incline towards despotism, there was no clear demarcation in James's mind between his own wishes and those of his subjects. Considerably better educated than the vast majority of them (he is said to have attended lectures at the newly-founded St Andrews University), he believed with some justification that only a powerful, even majestic monarchy could guarantee the well-being of the community of the realm. And for all his pompous paternalism and dubious expressions of altruism, James did on occasion show genuine concern for the welfare of even his meanest subjects.

More than once James turned his attention to the state of the Scottish church, lamenting that its 'downhill condition...fills us with apprehension'. He reprimanded Scottish monasteries for their 'somnolence and sloth', and the strict Carthusian priory he established at some cost in Perth in 1429 was the country's first new religious foundation for many years. Yet the king was more politician than saint. It was in his political interest to keep a close eye on an institution as powerful and wealthy as the church, and his demand that the clergy pray regularly for the souls of the royal family was not made solely for spiritual motives.

James, the 'lawgiver king', had a passion for regulation. Since there was a great deal to be clarified after years of gossamer-fingered government, parliament was soon issuing an unprecedented torrent of legislation, a good deal of it council-inspired. There were laws to help the economy by stipulating the size of fish nets, discouraging bark-peeling and rabbit poaching, standardising weights and measures, and regulating exports. Other measures addressed social issues, such as the siting of brothels and inns, outlawing the violent brawls which went by the name of football matches, and insisting that citizens wore dress appropriate to their social status. Further acts promoted archery and the holding of wappenschaws, literally 'weapon-showings', when able-bodied men assembled for a check on their military preparedness. Legal affairs were covered by action to limit maintenance in the courts, and to curb the independent systems of law which persisted in some parts of the country. The most laudable examples of James's paternalism were probably the steps taken to provide the poor with free legal counsel and security of tenure.

So that this redundance of regulation should not go unheeded, it was decreed in 1426 that all parliamentary acts were to be registered and circulated, and those holding heritable jurisdictions were obliged to provide themselves with competent deputies. Sessions of parliamentary committees, comprising the chancellor and 'certain discrete persons of the Three Estates', met to ease the council's legal burden. Nevertheless, the efficacy of what passed for a legal system depended very much on the king's willingness to deal with matters himself. This James was quite prepared to do. The story is told of a poor woman whose cows were stolen from her by a cateran. When, for some inexplicable reason, she then swore not to wear shoes until she had told the king of her misfortune, the robber nailed horseshoes to the soles of her feet. The king eventually got to hear of the incident. The barbarian was arrested and paraded around Perth for a couple of days with a painting round his neck illustrating his crime. He was then drawn at a horse's tail and hanged. Another tale relates how James, eager to raise the standard of behaviour at court but probably tipsy at the time, insisted that a courtier who had slapped another be held down while the injured party, upon pain of death, stab the offender in the hand. Only an hour's pleading by the queen and her ladies prevented the punishment from being carried out. Both stories may be apocryphal, but they do suggest the sort of awe in which James was held.

The dispensation of justice provided James with a useful source of income. In 1434, for example, he chastised his sheriffs for not making enough money from law enforcement. The king would no doubt have justified his action on the grounds that if court proceeds were down, not enough was being done to punish offenders. Others saw his criticism in a different light, believing James 'given to the acquisition of things'. It was not long before 'the commons...secretly called him...but a tyrannous prince.'

What was the upshot of James's efforts to control and reform his unruly realm? We may be justifiably sceptical about his attempts to alter people's social behaviour. But on larger matters, particularly law and order, he undoubtedly met with greater success. Bower believed

'He established peace within the kingdom, and he did not allow magnates or freeholders who were quarrelling amongst themselves to vent their wrath in open disturbances in their usual way.'

If James heard of an outbreak of trouble, Bower went on, he 'sent orders under his signet...for all to cease'. And cease it no doubt did. The only strictly contemporary description of James speaks of a 'fierce...far-seeing man' – not one to be trifled with.

* * *

For all his ruthless vigour, James was never able to bring the Highlands to heel. He was by inclination and upbringing a southerner, spending most of his time at Edinburgh, Stirling, Linlithgow and Perth, his favourite town.

The remote mountains and islands of the north and west were an anathema to him, and it is clear from his actions that he had nothing but contempt for those who lived there. After he had failed to bring them under control by force, he was content to leave them to their own devices, accepting that his Highland policy, if that is not too grand a title for his spasmodic interference in the region, was an unreserved failure.

In the late fourteenth century the principal Stewart in the north had been Alexander the Wolf of Badenoch, fourth son of Robert II. After the Wolf's death in 1406 his role had been filled by his natural son Alexander, who had forcibly seized the old Celtic title of Earl of Mar and won Albany's favour by thwarting the ambitions of the Lord of the Isles at Harlaw.

For the first four years of his reign James I left the situation in the Highlands as he had found it, with his cousin Mar counterbalancing the power of the Lord of the Isles, Alexander MacDonald. This untidy compromise might have satisfied the pragmatic Albanies, but it clearly did not accord with James's more ordered approach to government. Besides, there were rumours that Alexander of the Isles, whose family tradition of entering into treasonable negotiations with foreign powers James was well aware of, had approached the Norwegians. There was also the question of the disputed earldom of Ross to sort out.

James moved in the summer of 1428, employing decidedly underhand tactics. The Lord of the Isles and several of his more prominent adherents were invited to meet the king at Inverness Castle. As they arrived they were arrested. Some were imprisoned, and three of the less fortunate were 'condemned to various deaths'. Having, he believed, secured their obedience to his will, James then released his prisoners and retired south. The briefest acquaintance with the history of the region would have told him that Highlanders were not so easily tamed.

The following year Alexander MacDonald rose in furious rebellion and burned Inverness, the scene of his humiliation. Once again James gathered his forces and moved north. Some of Alexander's erstwhile supporters changed sides when they saw the royal standard, the rest were no match for the royal army. The Lord of the Isles was hunted down and taken in 'a bog in Lochaber'.

This time James was more careful. He led his prisoner back to Edinburgh, where,

'clad only in a shirt and drawers and on his knees, he offered and rendered to the king a naked sword before the high altar of Holyrood...while the queen and the more important lords of the kingdom interceded for him'.

With a theatrical display of Christian forgiveness, James accepted the sword, but to make sure that Alexander did not change his mind James locked him up in Tantallon Castle. From here MacDonald could gaze out over the sea to the Bass Rock, that bleak symbol of Stewart fortune.

Even if the Lord of the Isles was sincere in his submission, the men of the north-west had no intention of letting matters rest where they stood. In 1431 clan warfare flared into a second massive revolt, led this time by Alexander's uncle Alastair Carrach and cousin Donald Balloch. Acting on the king's behalf, the Earl of Mar met the rebels near Inverlochy and was soundly defeated.

For a while James contemplated a third northern sortie. But he had no real desire for yet another visit to the inhospitable region and he was experiencing difficulty in raising funds for another campaign. Late in 1431, therefore, he gave up all pretence of being able to master the Highlands on his own. After a second elaborate ceremony of submission, Alexander of the Isles was released and allowed to return home to resume control of his prickly lordship.

Alexander did not cross swords with the king for the rest of the reign. Before long he was openly styling himself Earl of Ross. James did not complain. He had come to realise that in some areas his predecessors' pragmatic approach had perhaps not been so foolish after all.

Finance was always a problem for James. Although normally solvent, he generally lacked ready cash and as time went on he became so engrossed with the matter that it took precedence over everything else, even justice. The seeds of his avarice, as of so many other aspects of his personality, were probably sown during his exile, and it is reasonable to assume that the Queen had a hand in the issue too. After what the couple had witnessed in England, they were both no doubt disappointed by the relatively meagre standard of comfort they found in the Scottish court. Finally, James realised that money was the foundation of power. A monarch who was constantly strapped for cash could not hope to govern effectively.

The primary sources of royal income were lands and customs' levies. James's ruthless acquisition policy meant that by the 1430s he received about £4000 a year from his estates. Customs payments gradually rose to about the same amount. When the profits of justice and other receipts were added, he had an annual income of something over £8000, rather less in real terms than that enjoyed by his grandfather Robert II. Moreover, by the time James had met the unavoidable expenses of government, such as castle maintenance, the court and diplomatic missions, he was left with a smaller disposable income than some of his wealthier subjects, particularly the Douglases.

James did not relish the situation and matters came to a head when he was faced with one-off expenses such as his ransom, military expeditions and royal marriages. Queen Joan bore her husband eight children in thirteen years. As far as the dynasty was concerned, her most important confinement took place at Holyrood in August 1430, when she was delivered of twin boys, Alexander and James. The former did not outlive babyhood, but James survived an extraordinary almond-based diet to grow up into a strong and healthy young boy, whose only blemish was a livid red birth-mark covering one side of his face.

To her husband's disappointment, all Joan's other children were girls. That meant marriage dowries. James was fortunate in having to meet only one such expense. In 1436 the twelve-year-old Margaret was shipped off to France amid much splendour to be the bride of the revolting dauphin, the future Louis XI. The cost of finding suitable husbands for the remaining girls, three of whom were employed in fostering friendly relationships with a variety of European states, fell to future governments. Isabel went to Brittany, Eleanor to Austria and Mary to Holland. Only dumb Joan and Annabella, the youngest, married Scottish husbands.

Long before the question of dowries arose, James had to pay his ransom: £66,666 (Scots) in five years. As this far exceeded his total ordinary revenue, he resorted to taxation authorised by parliament. Bower reckoned that the five percent levy on lands and goods brought in £10,000 in the first year and less in the second. When about £26,000 had been collected the scheme was dropped as too unpopular. Until 1428 the king continued to look into ways of raising the rest of the ransom, but to judge by what he did with the money already gathered he was probably more concerned with appeasing the English than actually parting with any more specie. Almost half the ransom tax was spent on foreign artillery, jewellery, luxuries for the court and an extravagant building programme at the royal residences.

Against a background of severe winters and repeated outbreaks of plague, James's conspicuous consumption and financial chicanery were not appreciated. Law and order was all very well, but not when it involved highly dubious fines on boroughs for giving false judgements in their courts. And what of the twenty-seven Scots hostages still languishing in English castles? There seemed no prospect of James ever parting with enough money to ensure their release. With such thoughts in mind, in 1431 parliament insisted that the revenue collected for the third Highland expedition be kept in a locked chest and used only for the purpose assigned to it. When the campaign was called off, the money was returned.

Worse was to follow. When asked for 2d in the £ to meet the costs of an embassy to France in 1433, 'the people began to murmur, saying that their property was manifoldly reduced by gelds of this sort'. James backed down and once again handed back what had been collected. He was losing the trust of his people.

V

Loath to meet the expenses of war and only too well aware of England's power, James tried to follow as independent a foreign policy as his relatively meagre resources allowed. The shaky truce negotiated at the time of his release lasted for most of his reign. The English realised that even if the Scots failed to pay a penny of the ransom, a campaign to punish the defaulters would cost considerably more than the sum owing, so they agreed to let the Scots exchange hostages in 1425, 1427 and 1432.

In 1428 James tested other waters by entering into discussions with France, offering 6000 men and the hand of Princess Margaret in return for the promise of land and titles. The deal was soon allowed to lapse when neither side showed much enthusiasm for it. This freed James to accept the proposals of Cardinal Beaufort, the queen's uncle, for a five-year renewal of the Anglo-Scottish truce in 1430. James had no desire to antagonise Burgundy, England's long-standing ally and master of the vital Low Country ports, and he was probably steered away from France by Queen Joan, who urged a more lasting settlement with the country of her birth.

When the Anglo-Burgundian alliance collapsed in 1435, however, James finally decided to climb off the diplomatic fence. With the English preparing for war, he approached France a second time and the following year committed himself to the Auld Alliance with a promise of 2000 troops and the hand of Princess Margaret for the dauphin. The English truce lapsed on 1 May 1436. Thereupon James called upon his wealthier subjects to provide benevolences to fund a campaign, gathered an army, and proceeded to the borders. It was the most foolish act of his entire reign.

Since coming to power James had done what he could to ensure that Scotland remained in a state of military preparedness. His martial experiences with Henry V are reflected in his announcement that 'all should practice the archer's art'. He was also the first Stewart to exhibit what became almost a family neurosis: a passion for guns. Cannon had been in use for about a century, but owing to their prohibitive expense the Scots had never been able to accumulate much of a siege train. Determined to overturn this handicap, James had purchased a number of cannon from Flanders, his most spectacular piece being a massive bronze weapon which bore the inscription:

'For the illustrious James, worthy prince of the Scots. Magnificent king, when I speak, I reduce castles. I was made on his orders – therefore I am called "Lion".'

It was soon apparent that the ordinary Scottish soldier shared neither his lord's love of cannon, nor the style of warfare which they necessitated; and the forty-two-year-old James, portly, irritable and probably hypertensive, lacked the charisma to convert them to his point of view. The consequence was a campaign of unmitigated disaster.

Following some ineffective manoeuvres around Berwick from which only the Earl of Angus emerged with any credit, by 1 August 1436 the Scots had moved on to the massive English border stronghold of Roxburgh. After his experience in France, sieges were the one part of warfare in which James felt really confident. And he was eager to demonstrate to sceptics the efficacy of his costly new artillery. The capture of Roxburgh would indeed have been a spectacular feather in his cap. But it was not to be.

When they realised that there was little immediate prospect of enriching themselves on English booty, James's soldiers began to desert by the score. His commanders were divided by a 'detestable split and most unworthy difference arising from jealousy', probably between the king and the 5th Earl of Douglas and possibly involving the queen's understandable hostility to the conflict. After two wasted weeks, the siege was called off and the Scots began packing up to go home.

At this point a well organised English relief force appeared on the scene, forcing James to abandon his artillery. Profoundly upset at the loss and irked at the dent made in his reputation, the king left the scene of his humiliation in black mood.

* * *

The disaster before Roxburgh finally persuaded a small band of James's disaffected subjects that it was time they put an end to the tyrannous Stewart before he did any more harm – there was already talk in the general council of further clipping noble wings by removing independent baronial jurisdictions. The plotters' inspiration was the hopelessly idealistic Sir Robert Graham, uncle of the miserable Malise. Robert had already twice fallen foul of the king. He had been held briefly on some unknown charge in 1424; later, in what (if we are to believe Bower) must have been a quite amazing scene, he had the affrontery to challenge James openly in parliament. Robert stood up 'with a violent... countenance', walked over to where the king sat and took hold of him with the words, 'I arrest you in the name of all the Three Estates of your realm'. He charged James with abusing and exploiting his people, thereby breaking the coronation contract between monarch and subject. The speech was followed by total silence.

Robert was arrested, deprived of all worldly wealth, imprisoned in a 'sure and hard' place, then banished. Instead of going abroad, he made his way to the Highlands where he swore to the 'wild Scottish' that he would kill the king 'with his own hands, as his mortal enemy'.

All this might have passed as the ravings of an embittered eccentric had not Graham then made common cause with Sir Robert Stewart, grandson of Walter of Atholl. The king had treated his relative well, welcoming him at court and giving him the responsible post of chamberlain, so Sir Robert's reasons for joining the conspiracy are something of a mystery. No doubt he shared Graham's dislike of James's avarice and high-handedness; he probably also resented the fact that his father had died in England after languishing there as a hostage for ten years.

There is one other possible ingredient in the cauldron of conspiracy: lingering doubts about the legitimacy of the children born to Robert II and

Elizabeth Mure. Two men in particular are likely to have harboured suspicions on this score, 'that old serpent inveterate' Walter of Atholl and his grandson, the aforementioned Sir Robert Stewart. The birth of Prince James had ended Walter's role as heir apparent. But what if the king and his young son really were of illegitimate descent? If that were the case, then the Atholl Stewarts' chance of winning the crown would not depend on the life of the infant prince. The throne would be theirs by right, immediately.

We will never know whether or not the murder of James I was a desperate bid for power by the Atholl Stewarts. Indeed, we cannot be certain that Earl Walter even knew of the plot. In the end it did not matter. It was enough that he was believed to have been party to it and he duly paid the terrible price for that belief.

Ignoring the warnings of an aged seer, whom he dismissed as 'nothing but a drunken fool', James spent Christmas 1436 at Perth. The court was housed in the town, while the royal family resided in the comfortable security of the moated Blackfriars priory nearby. They were accompanied by a close circle of friends and trusted servants, among whom was the embittered chamberlain, Sir Robert Stewart.

Sometime during the late afternoon of 21 February, Sir Robert arranged for the locks and bars of the royal apartments to be rendered inoperative and for a makeshift bridge to be placed over the moat. He then withdrew, met up with his fellow conspirators and waited for nightfall. In his band were the outlawed Sir Robert Graham and four citizens of Perth to whom the king owed money.

The king passed a pleasant evening in the company of his wife and other ladies, reading, listening to music and playing chess. Then, just as he was preparing to retire, the quiet of the night was broken by a startled cry: 'Treason!'

The warning came from the servant Walter Stratoun, who had encountered the assassins by chance as they were entering the priory. Although he was swiftly dispatched, Walter's shout gave the king time to hide.

First James looked to the window, but found the aperture too narrow. Then, snatching tongs from the fire, he levered up the floorboards of his private chamber and lowered himself into the vault below. It was not an easy task. After years of high living his athletic figure had deteriorated into 'excessive corpulence'. Later sources embellished the story by telling how Catherine Douglas bought the unfit king precious seconds by replacing the missing drawbar on the door with her arm, a brave gesture which left her disabled for life.

By the time the intruders burst into the room James was nowhere to be seen. They ill-treated the women, conducted a quick search, and then left cursing to look for their quarry elsewhere. When the coast was clear, James began to haul himself up out of his hiding place, puffing and blowing at the unaccustomed exertion. At this point the conspirators remembered the vault. They rushed back into the room to find the king, red in the face, just emerging through the floor. He promptly dropped back into the void.

This time there was no escape. Apparently the vault had been sealed to prevent the king's tennis balls from bouncing out, and if there was no hole big enough for a tennis ball to pass through, then there was certainly not one large enough to accommodate a man of James's bulk. He was trapped.

The murderers followed their unarmed victim down into the shadows. James was no coward, and backing into a corner he held off his assailants for a few moments with his bare hands. But it was a hopeless struggle. The assassins cut him down in the darkness, then fled from the building under the cover of night.

The killers were gravely mistaken in believing that news of their deed would lead to general rejoicing. However unpopular the king might have been, no one of any consequence was prepared to condone his murder. Expressing the sentiments of the whole country, the Edinburgh mob howled:

> 'Sir Robert Graham
> That slew our king –
> God give him shame.'

James I had earned more friends at his death than he had ever done during the forty-two years of his turbulent life.

CHAPTER 11

Fiery Face

I

On the whole the handsome early Stewarts were a genial lot. Whether as stewards, kings or governors, they earned the respect and often the affection of those around them. Even their faults were harmless enough – laziness, indecision and sexual profligacy are hardly the stuff of which villains are made. Surprisingly, considering the times in which they lived, before the fifteenth century few of them met with brutal deaths. Indeed, the family exhibited a remarkable capacity for longevity.

With the sinister demise of the young Duke of Rothesay in 1402, however, the long summer of Stewart tranquility had begun to draw to a close. Under the two Albanies the days had grown shorter still, until with the reign of James I the dynasty had entered an altogether darker and harsher period of its history. The family no longer stood for amiable flexibility, but for resolution and ruthlessness. In the space of two turbulent generations, the Stewarts had lost their innocence.

There were rewards, of course. Guided by a new breed of ambitious kings, the Stewarts rose to glittering heights undreamed of by less aggressive ancestors. One day the descendants of the dapifers of Dol would wear the crowns of three kingdoms and hold sway over territories stretching from Orkney to the equator and beyond. But the price of this transient worldly glory was a gnawing unease of spirit which so often haunts the mighty.

James I had been assassinated because he was believed by some to be 'so cruel a tyrant'. Only four of the next nine Stewart monarchs died in their beds – two in reasonable comfort, one in exile and one having plunged into an irreversible depression at the age of forty. Of the rest, two were beheaded, two died in battle (one blown up by his own cannon) and another was murdered. Most experienced wretched childhoods and not one reached the age of seventy.

With this in mind, some have spoken sympathetically of the ill-luck of the Stewarts. This is too generous a judgement. The truth is that the royal line begun by James I was hung for the most part with decidedly unattractive individuals, whose arrogant insensitivity repeatedly cost them the affection of their people. Only rarely did the bitter-sweet air of tragedy freshen their diverse and often bloody fates.

II

The early years of James II were, if anything, even more distressing than those of his father. Not for him the long afternoons of poetry and sport. As a boy he was abducted not once, but twice, and he was forced to witness scenes of merciless barbarity.

Having lost his father at the age of six, when James's mother remarried three years later the young king was forbidden to see her except in the presence of others. As if this was not enough, the lad also had to cope with the cruel burden of his disfiguring facial birthmark. Not surprisingly, James of the Fiery Face grew up tough and mistrustful, displaying many of his father's less attractive characteristics and few of the redeeming ones.

The young king was crowned at Holyrood. Afterwards he and his mother sheltered in the fastness of Edinburgh Castle, then under the governorship of Sir William Crichton. No popular uprising followed the murder of James I and his killers were soon brought to justice. Accused of approving his grandson's dire felony as a first step to seizing the crown for the descendants of Euphemia Ross, the venerable Earl Walter of Atholl was imprisoned alongside those who had actually participated in the murder.

We will never know whether the earl really had been privy to the plot. James's vindictive widow had been wounded at the time of the assassination and to her the question of guilt or innocence was less important than the fact of revenge. She supervised personally three days of exquisite torture for her prisoners before they were dragged off to execution. The sadistic proceedings were concluded with the lowering of a circlet of red-hot iron bearing the inscription 'King of Traitors' onto the brows of the aged Walter.

The new reign had begun as violently as the old had ended. It was not a happy omen.

Dowager Queen Joan's implacable behaviour suggests why she had got on so well with her difficult husband after the first fires of physical attraction between them had died down. Freed from her husband's overlordship, she was now proving as self-willed and resourceful as he had been. She undoubtedly helped to foster similar qualities in her son, too.

Not long after the coronation Joan tired of Crichton's over-zealous protection in Edinburgh. She forced James into a clothing trunk and under the pretext of going on pilgrimage to the White Kirk of Our Lady of Lothian she smuggled him away to Stirling Castle and the guardianship of another upwardly mobile laird, Sir Alexander Livingstone of Callendar.

For all her pluck, it was not easy for the queen mother to play a significant part in the turbulent politics of her son's minority. Her sex, her English background and her widow's status all counted against her. About the first two handicaps she could do nothing, but the third was under her control. In 1439 she remarried, taking as her second husband another Stewart, Sir James of Lorne, popularly known as the 'Black Knight of Lorne'. We are told that Sir James 'married the queen not for love but for dowry and ambition', hoping through his wife to increase his power and perhaps even get control of the king. Although the Black Knight's own career ended in failure, the couple's vigorous sons, John, James and Andrew, all played significant roles in the politics of a later generation.

Joan's matrimonial adventures did not please Livingstone. Determined to put a stop to her independent behaviour before it went any further, on 3 August 1439 he forced his way into her rooms and arrested the newly-weds and the groom's brother-in-law. The agreement then cobbled together between the two factions stuck in the young king's mind for a long time. On her release Joan publicly pardoned her captor who, in return, was granted custody over the king at his mother's expense. From the age of nine James II had to learn to make his own way in the world. His resentment at Livingstone's behaviour ran deep.

The next year James experienced his second forced removal, when Crichton's men found the boy out riding near Stirling. As he 'began to smile... they understood that the king was pleased at their arrival and was glad to go along with them'. He was promptly whisked back to Edinburgh. Shortly afterwards Livingstone and Crichton accomplished some sort of reconciliation.

Although the Keepers of Edinburgh and Stirling had control over the king's person at different times during his minority, neither they nor the boy's mother were ever the real powers in the land. That role fell to the mighty Black Douglases, descendants of the Good Sir James, Walter Stewart's mentor at Bannockburn. (The senior and junior branches of the Douglases were distinguished by the epithets 'Black' and 'Red' respectively).

Archibald 5th Earl of Douglas was the son of 'the Loser' who had fallen at Verneuil. He had survived the reign of James I with his extensive lands in Scotland and France intact and served as lieutenant-general of the realm from 1437 until his death in 1439. As well as being uncommonly wealthy, the earl was also dangerously well-connected with the royal family through judicious marriages. Archibald's wife Euphemia, for example, was Malise Graham's sister. Thus while the wretched Malise remained in England and the direct Stewart line hung on the single fragile thread of the young James II, the Douglases were only a step away from the throne. There is no concrete evidence that they plotted for the crown, but they were too ambitious for the possibility never to have crossed their minds.

* * *

For the time being the Douglases had problems of their own to sort out.

When the 5th Earl died the post of lieutenant-general, although coveted by his fourteen-year-old son William, fell into abeyance. Neither Livingstone nor Sir Alexander Crichton, chancellor from 1439 onwards, had any desire to see their new-won power undermined by a teenage aristocrat, whatever his lineage. In looking for a way out of the problem the chancellor found a useful ally in a remarkable character known to posterity as James the Gross.

'All tallow and fat', James Douglas of Balveny was the Loser's brother and great-uncle to the teenage 6th Earl William and his younger brother David. The greasy lord also stood to inherit the earldom if anything should happen to the two boys. The stage was set for a particularly nasty plot.

During the course of conversation with Chancellor Crichton James the Gross is supposed to have muttered 'this realm would be more peaceful if the Earl of Douglas and his brother had been suddenly removed'. The two men understood each other only too well. It only remained for them to find a way of effecting that removal.

With hideous cunning the two conspirators laid their trap in the form of a dinner party. The distinguished guests, including James II, were invited to meet at Edinburgh Castle on 28 November 1440. Earl William and his brother duly attended and were treated to a fine meal, the last food they tasted.

At the close of the proceedings Crichton is reported to have placed a black bull's head in the centre of the table – a symbol of the impending fall of the Black Douglases. Shortly afterwards William and David were arrested, condemned as traitors and led away to speedy execution on Castle Hill.

We do not know to what extent the events of the last three and a half years had already blunted the sensibilities of the ten-year-old king. Some said that in his distress he pleaded for the Douglas boys' lives, although he may have been simply playing a role previously assigned to him. Whatever his feelings at the time, the experience became just another lesson in the heartless art of real politics. It was an example he did not forget, either. Eleven years later the Douglases fell victim to another very similar supper plot. This time it was not the chancellor but the king himself who acted the unreliable host.

Later the shameful 'Black Dinner' became part of popular folklore, recalled in this fragment of ballad:

> 'Edinburgh Castle, tower and town,
> God grant ye sink for sin;
> And even for the black dinner
> Lord Douglas gat therein.'

But what men felt in their hearts at the time they dared not utter in public, for too many of the mighty of the land had profited by the foul deed. None more so than James the Gross himself.

The gross Lord of Balvenie was now 7th Earl Douglas. In contravention of the law the Douglas lands were not forfeited on the death of Earl William, and their new owner spent the remaining three years of his life reassembling a Douglas power bloc as formidable as anything controlled by his predecessors.

The family's lands in France had reverted to the French crown – there was nothing Earl James could do about that – and Annandale had similarly reverted to the Scottish crown. These losses were counterbalanced by the addition of the Balvenie territory in Banff, Buchan and Moray. The new earl also planned to get back Galloway, which had passed to the 6th Earl's sister Elizabeth, the 'Fair Maid of Galloway'. Shortly after the 7th Earl's death in 1443, his son and heir obtained a special dispensation to marry the Fair Maid, so bringing Galloway back under the spreading Douglas umbrella.

With the death of James the Gross, the Douglas-Crichton-Livingstone axis fell apart and the country drifted into civil war. William, now 8th Earl of Douglas, sided with the Livingstones and the influential Earls of Crawford and Ross against the Crichtons and their motley collection of allies. These included the queen mother, her husband the Black Knight, the Red Douglas Earl of Angus and Bishop Kennedy of St Andrews, James I's cousin.

The fighting began in the summer of 1444 and dragged on for about a year until Crichton and the Earl of Angus came to terms. The Queen Mother died on 15 July during the siege of Dunbar Castle. She was buried 'according to her degree' beside James I in the Carthusian monastery at Perth. The Black Knight, who had earned the hatred of the Douglases by announcing that 'the realm was poorly led' during his step-son's minority, went into exile. Joan's uncaring behaviour towards her son had no doubt put James II's filial affection under considerable strain. Nevertheless, even he cannot have enjoyed being made to tag along with the forces ranged against his mother. The responsibility for this humiliation he laid squarely at the feet of the Livingstones.

In an astute tactical ploy the general council summoned by the Douglas-Livingstone faction in October 1444 had outlawed the Crichtons and declared the fourteen-year-old James to be of age. This put royal power and authority directly into the hands of Sir Alexander Livingstone's son James, who became keeper of the royal person. Understandably, the young king deeply resented the way in which he was being exploited. But he was too canny a youth to make his dissatisfaction public just yet. For the time being, smouldering inwardly, he was prepared to wait, watch and learn.

* * *

From his vantage point on the sidelines the young king noted the chaos resulting from weak and divided government. In particular he recognised how easy it was for a powerful family like the Douglases to destabilise the realm and threaten the power of the crown. Douglas influence seemed to grow with every passing year. James the Gross's second son became bishop of Aberdeen, the third acquired the earldom of Moray through marriage, the fourth was made Earl of Ormond for his services during the civil war and the fifth controlled the Balvenie estates. The family's henchmen were rewarded with lordships of parliament, titles first mooted by James I. By 1449, when James was eighteen, it seemed that wherever he chanced to look his eye fell upon some aspect of Douglas empire. The prospect did not please him.

The war taught James another important lesson. He had seen how long it took to reduce a stoutly defended rebel castle – in fact Crichton's Edinburgh fortress never fell to its attackers. Until the king was sure of being able to overawe every stronghold in Scotland, he could never be master in his own kingdom. One of James II's first independent acts was to start rebuilding the royal artillery so depleted by his father's fiasco before Roxburgh the year before his death.

III

Whatever might have been declared in 1444, James II's true majority began on his eighteenth birthday. It was the moment he had been anticipating for years, and he lost no time in putting his ideas into practice.

Like his father on his return to Scotland twenty-five years before, in 1449 the king lacked money and, consequently, real power. Finance could be raised through taxation, trade, marriage or confiscation. Although he was in no position to employ the first, before a year had passed James had success-fully exploited all the other three. The catalyst of his early success was his marriage on 3 July to Mary of Gueldres, niece of Philip the Good, Duke of Burgundy. From a political point of view it was an excellent match, for improved relations with Burgundy would help Scottish trade with the Low Countries. Gueldres was rich, too. When at her father's expense Mary crossed the North Sea in some style, she bore promises of guns and a dowry of 60,000 gold crowns. The only snag to the arrangement was that her father, Duke Arnold, insisted that Mary be maintained in the manner to which she was accustomed. To this end James had to settle on his bride an annual income of about £5000. Moreover, being an astute businessman and perhaps also mistrusting the notoriously impecunious Scots, Arnold decided to with-hold dowry payments until Mary's settlement was in place. So for a time the king's obvious pleasure at his fortunate marriage was dampened by nagging financial worries.

Mary relished her husband's precarious position no more than he did. She wished not only to be a queen, but to live like one. That meant enjoying both luxury and security. With this in mind the royal couple worked together to increase their political and financial independence.

It is likely that James had determined to break the power of the Douglases long before his marriage. Their proximity to the throne, their three earldoms, their bonds with northern potentates and their swathe of lands from Inverness to the border made them by far the greatest single potential limit on royal authority. But James did not yet feel strong enough to strike at the trunk of the tree shading him from true majesty. With Mary's backing, he chose instead to clear away the surrounding coppice.

The king's motives for turning on the Livingstones were personal, political and financial. The family had done well out of his minority. Sir Alexander was justiciar, his cousin comptroller. James Livingstone, sometime keeper of the royal person, held the posts of chamberlain and keeper of Stirling Castle. Other members of the family controlled the royal castles at Methven, Dumbarton, Dunoon, and Doune. Despite their abundance of offices and cash (the king himself owed them almost £1000), the Livingstones' landed base was comparatively narrow and they had few supporters of unquestioned loyalty. The aristocratic Douglases, for example, showed little love for parvenu office collectors, and the 8th earl stood naively aside when James turned on his family's erstwhile allies. Only later did the Douglases realise the significance of what was going on, and by then it was too late to halt their growing isolation.

Arrested for crimes committed against the king and 'his dearest mother', the Livingstones were tried before the parliament which met on 19 January 1450. It was a tricky situation. There was not much that the accused had done that had not also been perpetrated by the Douglases, and in the end only two Livingstones (the captain of Methven and the comptroller) were executed. Several others, including Sir Alexander and his son James, were imprisoned. All offices and lands held by the guilty were forfeit.

With one blow James had settled several scores of his wretched youth. He had also restored his finances and stated what his policy as king would be. The day after the executions he announced to his father-in-law (somewhat prematurely) that he would be able to meet the cost of Mary's settlement. If anyone had harboured any doubts previously, it was now quite plain that the reign of the second James Stewart would follow closely the pattern of the first. But without the poetry.

* * *

At this point the behaviour of William Earl of Douglas is difficult to fathom. The signs were ominous, for not only had James swept away the Livingstones, but the parliament which had assisted him in his spring cleaning had issued a ferocious statute warning that henceforward rebels would be punished according to the 'quality and quantity' of their rebellion. No names were mentioned, but it is significant that both Earl William and Chancellor Crichton decided at this juncture that it would be apposite to offer the king substantial loans. Then the earl and one of his brothers went abroad, leaving family affairs in the hands of a third brother, Lord Balvenie.

Perhaps the 8th Earl believed that it would be best for him to be out of the way while the dust thrown up by the Livingstone incident had time to settle? Or did he believe that he could improve his standing by seeking papal favour during the celebrations held in Rome that autumn to mark the end of the schism? We gather that he was indeed 'commended by the supreme pontiff above all [other] pilgrims'. Whatever the reasons for William's continental jaunt, which lasted until April 1451, it was a serious tactical blunder. It gave James and the anti-Douglas faction at court just the opportunity they had been looking for.

On the pretext of recovering Wigtown and West Galloway, which the king claimed belonged to the crown rather than Earl William, in 1451 royal forces swept into Douglas territory in the south-west, flattening the castle at Craig Douglas. When the astonished earl returned to discover what had happened, he had no immediate choice but to go along with the elaborate ritual arranged for him. He made a token submission and surrendered all his lands to the king. The queen, who was obviously privy to the plot, then delivered to parliament a stirring speech in William's defence, after which almost all his lands were restored in eighteen fresh charters. The documents 'granted him all his lordships again, except the earldom of Wigtown'. That remained with the crown. It helped service James's £1300 debt and brought Mary's income nearer the expected £5000.

It had all been too simple. Within a few months James and Mary learned that though they might be able to treat a family like the Livingstones with impunity, the Douglases required far more careful handling. Over the summer there were ugly rumours of rebellion in the north, where the Earls of Ormond, Moray, Crawford and Ross were all deeply dissatisfied at the high-handed way in which the king had treated his leading magnate. John of Ross, Lord of the Isles, had another complaint. James Livingstone's daughter Elizabeth had managed to escape to Kintyre when the rest of her family were rounded up in September 1449, and shortly afterwards she had married the Earl of Ross. The next year the Livingstones lost all their lands and goods, and Earl John found to his chagrin that the king's behaviour had left him with a wife but no dowry.

In an attempt to prize apart the bond linking the Earl of Douglas to the northern troublemakers, James back-pedalled quickly by returning Wigtown and Western Galloway to his chief adversary in October 1451. If the king thought this would be sufficient price to pay for temporary Douglas loyalty, then the plan failed. With Earl William continuing to chart an independent course, early in 1452 James decided upon an altogether more drastic approach. He had not forgotten the last cruel pruning of the Douglases. The justice exercised by Chancellor Crichton at the Black Dinner of 1440 had been neither honest nor popular, but at least it had been effective. James now began to wonder whether the same desperate tactic might not work a second time.

In early January 1452 Earl William Douglas freely attended the court at Edinburgh. A month later he was invited to meet the king at Stirling. The prospect of a trip into the very centre of the Crichton web did not excite him. There had been tension between the two families since the civil war of 1444-5 and Douglas believed Sir William Crichton to have been behind the attack on his family estates in 1451. Since Stirling was in the hands of the chancellor's cousin Sir George Crichton, Douglas refused to venture there without a safe pardon issued under the privy seal and signed with the king's own hand. James duly obliged, sending the document to the wary earl by one of his own henchmen.

What exactly did James intend? The contemporary *Auchinleck Chronicle* fails to support the sanitised view of later accounts that the king's subsequent behaviour was in no way premeditated. Knowing what we do of James's cold determination to brook no opposition, it is surely likely that he had worked out his options before Earl William's visit. One of those options involved murder.

William arrived at Stirling on 21 February. The date itself was auspicious, being the fifteenth anniversary of the assassination of James I. The following day the king and the earl had talks which 'took right well', presumably because they avoided the subject of the latter's bond with Crawford and Ross. James and William dined together late in the afternoon of 23rd. They then retired at about 7pm into an inner chamber. Here, in the company of a few of his most trusted servants, the king finally brought up the question of the bond.

Details of the conversation between the two men are fictional, but it is not difficult to imagine how shallow post-prandial bonhomie rapidly gave way to acrimony when James led their talk to the matter upon which they were irreconcilably divided.

James asked William to break his bond. Douglas refused. He pointed out, quite correctly, that it was a private matter over which the king had no jurisdiction.

The king tried again. Once more the earl rebuffed him, saying that no amount of pleading would make him change his mind. Muttering something like 'Then this shall!' James drew a dagger and stabbed William in the neck and body.

Seven bystanders instantly joined in the assault. Sir Patrick Gray smashed Douglas on the skull with a pole axe, spilling his brains on the floor. The others struck wildly at the prostrate body, puncturing it a further twenty-three times.

It was later given out that the king, roused by the earl's 'stubborn obstinacy' in refusing to renounce the leagues he had made against 'the most serene royal majesty', had killed Douglas in a fit of temper. Thus William was declared 'guilty of his own death by refusing the king's gentle persuasion'.

James may indeed have been angry when he struck the earl. But a thrust to the neck suggests a predetermined desire to kill, perhaps even an attack from behind. It is not easy when standing face to face with an adversary to draw a weapon and reach up to his throat without inviting evasive action. And what about the armed henchmen who had so swiftly joined in the murder? Had they not been forewarned? In the fullness of time every one of them was handsomely rewarded.

The one picture we have of James, by Jorg von Ehingen, portrays the king as a baby-faced, well-built and fashionably dressed young man, standing confidently with his legs astride. The fiery birthmark is clearly visible covering his left cheek, while his right hand rests menacingly on the hilt of his dagger. It was sometimes possible to express in paint what could not be put into words.

* * *

Within a month of the murder James II had made a swift tour of the south-east of his kingdom, spreading his version of what had happened at Stirling and rallying his forces. He could count on the support of the Crichtons, the Earls of Huntly, Angus and Orkney, and bishops Turnbull and Kennedy. James Douglas, the 9th Earl, was an altogether less able adversary than his predecessor. He made no move until 17 March, and even then all he came up with was an empty gesture of defiance before Stirling Castle. With much marching about and blowing of horns, the earl, his brother Ormond and Lord Hamilton 'gave the king uncomely words, saying they would never again obey him or acknowledge him as king'. They then burned the infamous safe conduct and set fire to the town of Stirling for good measure. It was not the sort of behaviour to bring men flocking to their banner.

Despite the 9th Earl's uninspiring leadership and his own prompt action, the king's second attempt to crack the Douglas nut proved no more successful than the first. Nevertheless, his position when the fighting stopped in August 1452 was a good deal stronger than it had been the previous February. In May the Earl of Crawford had been defeated by the loyal Earl of Huntly. James had enjoyed some military success of his own, although his devastating raid into the south-west, when his soldiers had indulged in an orgy of indiscriminate slaughter, had alienated more than it brought round. Of greater benefit had been parliament's clearing of the king's name and its demand that Douglas appear to answer the charges against him. James had also received welcome news of a more personal nature. Following the premature delivery of her first child and the birth of a daughter, in May 1452, with supposed supernatural aid from the shirt of St Margaret (specially imported from the Isle of May), Queen Mary had been safely delivered of a son. The infant Prince James secured the Stewart succession and dampened any royal aspirations on the part of the Douglases.

James's failure to defeat Douglas outright in 1452 had been due partly to the earl's approaches to Henry VI, which threatened to bring England into the quarrel, and partly to the prowess of the Earl of Ross and his ally Donald Balloch. John of Ross had taken Urquhart and Inverness, and in July Balloch's ships had launched a series of destructive raids in the region of the Clyde. These actions had made it clear to the king that he had to isolate Douglas completely before he resorted to force again. To do this he needed time.

Hostilities were brought to a close with the signing of the oddly-named 'Appoyntement' in 28 August 1452. Earl James undertook to forgive his master for the death of the 8th Earl and to behave himself in future. For his part, the king agreed to restore all the Douglases' lands. Early the next year he even handed over Wigtown and West Galloway when Earl James obtained special dispensation to marry his dead brother's widow, the much sought-after Fair Maid of Galloway.

If the 9th Earl believed that this was the end of the matter, then he was a fool. By now wise men had learned not to be deceived by the king's innocent eyes and boyish looks. James Stewart, descendant of the great Robert Bruce, was a fighter with the instincts of a terrier who clung to his prey until it was finally brought down. His agreement with Earl James was one of a number of tactical devices employed to keep the Douglas off guard until circumstances were favourable for a third and final strike.

In 1453 Douglas was given a commission to negotiate with England. It was a surprising move. James was either attempting to lull his opponent into a false sense of security by giving him the impression that he was crucial to the administration, or, believing that the earl would enter into further treasonable discussions with Henry VI, the king was proffering him sufficient rope to hang himself. But the only upshot of Douglas's negotiations was the release of Malise Graham, nominal Earl of Menteith and great-grandson of Robert II. Perhaps the return of the royal hostage was Douglas's response to the birth of Prince James? If the earl whispered words of sweet treason into Malise's ear, however, they evoked no response: after years of captivity the wretched man was too disabled to play any active role in politics.

An unreliable but interesting tale tells that James had fallen into a depression and planned to flee abroad when he heard of Malise's release and Douglas's marriage to the Fair Maid. In one version of the story his sickness is real (he would not have been the first Stewart to suffer from profound melancholia) and was cured only when Bishop Kennedy demonstrated how a whole sheaf of arrows could be broken by snapping them one at a time. A second account had James feign his malady to deceive his enemies. Although both stories lack authenticity, perhaps the latter accords more closely with the king's duplicitous personality. As for knapping the sheaf of arrows, whether suggested by Kennedy or not, it was precisely the tactic which James adopted.

The royal party had recently been upset by the passing of Chancellor Crichton, the Crichton earls of Caithness and Moray, and Bishop Turnbull.

But Death's sword is double edged, and in 1454 it delivered a more accept-able blow when the Earl of Crawford was killed accidentally. An even more welcome addition to the 'arrows' policy was the reconciliation with John of the Isles and James Livingstone, effected by July 1454 when the latter took over the post of chamberlain.

The king's last piece of good fortune was the instability produced in England by the temporary insanity of Henry VI. Although Henry had recov-ered by February 1455, the English political nation, already riven by the York-Lancaster divide, was now in no position to interfere in events north of the border. With the English neutralised and Douglas's defensive bond in tatters, by the spring of 1455 James II was ready to bring his five-year struggle to a successful conclusion.

The king set out in March, when the ground was sufficiently dry for him to move his beloved heavy artillery. The Douglas castle at Inveravon was his first target, after which he marched south-west, back to Edinburgh, then down to the Douglas territory in Dumfries and Galloway. He was in no mood to compromise. In his fury 'he took the goods and burned the homes of all who would not join him'. Abercorn Castle made some show of resistance before it was pounded into surrender, in particular by 'a great gun' which 'a Frenchman shot right well'. Lord Hamilton soon came round to James's side, but the younger Douglas brothers – Ormond, Moray and Balvenie – fought on until defeated on 1 May by a small band of border lairds at Arkinholm by the River Esk. Lord Balvenie managed to escape. The Earl of Moray was slain in the fight. The Earl of Ormond was captured and decapitated. James was delighted to receive a present of the severed head.

But what of Earl James himself? To their great consternation his men 'knew not… where the Douglas was all this time'. When eventually he did show up, it was in England. He may have believed that only with English support could he hope to resist James's onslaught, but by the time he had persuaded the fraught Henry VI to intervene, the cause of the Black Douglases was as good as lost. The earl's lands, his castles, his title and even his reputation had gone for ever.

Parliament declared the Douglases forfeited in June, even the ungrateful (or uncomprehending) Malise voting against them. That summer the royal forces ground steadily on, taking stronghold after stronghold and even making an unsuccessful side-swipe at Berwick. Eventually only the splendid island retreat of Threave remained in Douglas hands. The castle, one of the first in Scotland to be modified specifically to resist artillery fire, was Earl James's pride and joy, and he made a desperate bid to save his headquarters by handing it over to Henry VI. The move resulted in a gift towards the cost of defending Threave and a pension for its ex-owner, but no direct assistance. The document granting the earl his allowance stated that it was to be paid 'until he is restored to his heritage, taken from him by him who calls himself King of Scots'. Did the Douglas 'heritage' include the crown? Or was the slur on King James's right to the throne merely a revival of the age-old English claim to overlordship?

King James took personal charge of the siege of Threave. At great cost the Earl of Orkney slowly wheeled the 'great bombard' (perhaps 'Mons Meg') down from Edinburgh to add its mighty voice to those already barking beside the Dee.

At the last it was probably not guns but cash which induced the garrison to surrender. Dispirited at their earl's failure to stand with them or even to attempt to raise the siege, they seem to have accepted a royal bribe to lay down their arms. James did not then destroy Threave, as he had done other Douglas castles. He chose instead to leave the puissant and strategically important stronghold intact as part of his border defences.

The preservation of Threave was a fitting gesture. The crown had not simply crushed the most notable aristocratic family in the land, it had absorbed its power and influence as well. Among the green hills of Galloway, where for so long the renowned Douglases had held sway, the writ of the Stewarts now ran undisputed. It was a triumph for the royal dynasty and for James of the Fiery Face in particular. He was still only twenty-five.

IV

Had James survived to the age of his grandfather or even his father, who knows what his combination of aggression and ambition might have achieved. As it was, in 1455 he had but five more years to live.

Coinciding with poor harvests and outbreaks of the plague, the Douglas wars had brought 'great pestilence and mortality ...through the whole kingdom of Scotland'. When the parliament which met in August 1455 had taken stock of the situation, it announced somewhat acerbically that 'the poverty of the crown is oftentimes the cause of the poverty of the Realm'. In what looks like an effort to curb the young king's arbitrary behaviour and persuade him to live off his own resources, an Act of Annexation was passed to conserve the royal demesne. Swollen by about £2000 a year from the Douglas estates, the Stewart lands were divided between those 'annexed' and 'unannexed'. The former, valued at about £6050 per annum, were not supposed to be given away without parliament's approval. The latter, worth just over half as much, could be distributed as the king thought fit. Needless to say, James was not the sort of man to feel bound by written statute and a while later he contravened the letter of the act by rewarding the Earl of Ross with annexed property.

James's conduct in other spheres was often just as high-handed. He attended to the maintenance of law and order with irregular ferocity, dismissing two chancellors when he disagreed with them. He bullied his sisters Annabella and Joan into unwelcome marriages with his henchmen. Only Isabella, widowed in 1450 on the death of Duke Francis of Brittany, refused to go along with her brother's plans. Showing common sense and a laudable independence of spirit, she remained safely out of James's reach on the Continent.

Nowhere was James's determination to ride roughshod over others more plainly visible than in the provision he made for his sons. The legitimate claims of the Erskines and the Earl of Orkney were swept aside to provide Prince John with the earldom of Mar. David was given the Douglas earldom of Moray in 1456. When the boy died the next year the king kept the property for himself, overriding the valid claims of the Crichtons and Gordons. Another son, Alexander, was made Earl of March and Duke of Albany. John Stewart of Balvenie, one of the king's half brothers, became Earl of Atholl.

It was like a re-run of the reign of James I. Small wonder that in 1458 parliament, which came up with a customary deluge of statutes concerning matters such as wolf hunting, football and archery, also slipped in a gentle complaint:

'Since God in His good grace has sent our sovereign lord such progress and prosperity that all his rebels and lawbreakers are removed from the realm..., might his Highness and his ministers now incline themselves to the quiet and common profit of the realm and to keeping justice among his three estates... so that all his subjects... might pray to God and thank Him for sending them such a prince to be their governor and defender?'

There is no record of James taking the slightest notice of the rebuke.

One reason why the king felt confident to ignore those who pleaded for more ordered government was that with skilful use of patronage he had constructed a powerful body of personal support in church and state. He appointed bishops who were in accord with his own way of thinking. Now that the Black Douglases had been wiped from the political map, other branches of the distinguished family were raised in their place. George, 4th Earl of Angus and leader of the Red Douglases, was well rewarded by the king for his loyal service, particularly at the battle at Arkinholm. In 1456 the earldom of Morton was created for James Douglas, Lord of Dalkeith. New earldoms were also found for Lord Alexander Seton of Gordon (Earl of Huntly, 1455), William Hay (Earl of Errol, 1452), Colin Campbell (Earl of Argyll, 1457 – a crucial counterweight to the pretensions of the Earl of Ross), William Keith (Earl Marischal, 1458) and George Leslie (Earl of Rothes, 1457). The earldom of Caithness was recreated for George Crichton in 1452 and then passed to William Sinclair, Earl of Orkney. When all the other changes in the aristocracy wrought by James I and II are taken into account, including the establishment of the Lords of Parliament, it is clear that between them father and son had engineered what amounted to a revolution in the upper echelons of Scottish society.

James II realised quicker than his father that the one region where the wind of Stewart change could not penetrate was the north-west. He took a strong interest in the area, visiting it in 1457 and 1458. But having crossed swords briefly with the Earl of Ross at the beginning of his majority, he now successfully reverted to his father's more conciliatory policy. When James besieged Roxburgh in 1460 Ross was fighting alongside his king.

* * *

James's final massive attack on one of England's most redoubtable fortresses followed five years of vigorous military and diplomatic activity. As mentioned, in 1455 James had diverted to Berwick some of the forces mopping up Douglas resistance, but the surprise all-out assault was called off when the plan was betrayed to the enemy. The following year James renounced the border truce and, having tested Roxburgh's defences and found them mighty indeed, plunged on into Northumberland with 6000 men on a limited but profitable raid. A more ambitious scheme to take the Isle of Man led to rebuff and a destructive counter-raid by the Stanleys in 1457. When another move against Berwick the next year proved no more successful than the first, James renewed the Anglo-Scottish truce for a further two years. The magnitude of the fortifications around Berwick and Roxburgh is indicated by the English government's willingness to allocate £2000 a year to their defence in time of war – more than James's annual income from all the forfeited Douglas estates.

James brought the same confident aggression to diplomacy as to domestic matters. He seized the governor of Iceland in 1456 and used him as a bargaining counter in negotiations with King Christian of Denmark-Norway for the cession of Orkney and Shetland to Scotland. The matter was not concluded during James's lifetime, but the eventual acquisition of the northern isles by his son owed much to the firm line established in the previous reign.

Scotland's new-found sense of purpose and importance was born out by the presence at one time or another of James's envoys in most European courts. As well as dealing with matters of trade and the marriages of numerous Scottish princesses, they also raised the rather far-fetched question of James II's claim to the French county of Saintonge, which he announced was his by the terms of the Franco-Scottish treaty of 1428. Spurred on by their dynamic young king, to whom they were loath to report the failure of any mission, Scottish diplomats enjoyed greater European prestige than at any time since the thirteenth century.

But for all his desire to cut a figure on the Continental stage, James was essentially a warrior. Unlike his aloof father, who lacked the personal touch with common people, Fiery Face was admired and respected by his soldiers as 'a fellow to every private'. He was never happier than when lining up his beloved guns, seeing that they were well positioned and checking their range. It was as if, after a childhood marred by human deceitfulness, he had made the subconscious decision to trust only inanimate objects which behaved as he bid them. It was a pitiful condition for a young man, and in the end it led to his death.

James had been planning an all-out assault on Roxburgh for some time. When in July 1460 the battle of Northampton opened England's long civil conflict known in shorthand as the Wars of the Roses, he recognised a window of opportunity too wide to be ignored. 'A great host' was swiftly raised and moved south. The mighty cannon trundled along with it.

In a matter of days the Scots had Roxburgh surrounded. As soon as the guns had been dug in, the bombardment began. James was in his element, rushing about the lines checking, encouraging and advising. Then, on the morning of Sunday 3 August, disaster struck.

James's passion for artillery made him 'more curious than became the majesty of a king'. He was probably pushing his guns beyond their limits, overloading their breeches with gunpowder in an effort to increase their range. And when the fuses were lit he preferred to stand beside the gunners rather than retire to a safe distance. As a result the impetuous king 'was unhappily slain by a gun which blew up when it was fired'.

We do not know how the exiled Douglas reacted when he heard how James had died. No doubt he permitted himself at least a smile. After all, death by accidental explosion was not an inappropriate way for such a violent life to end.

CHAPTER 12

King Cat

I

The news of James II's accidental killing was received with 'great dolour through all Scotland'. The king had been hardly an attractive personality, yet the grief at his premature death was genuine enough among his soldiers and those who had benefited from his efforts to maintain an equitable system of justice. Significantly, unlike the force his father had brought to Roxburgh a quarter of a century before, James II's army stuck to its task. As a gesture of respect to the man who had begun the enterprise, the Scots pressed on with their attack until the stronghold eventually fell, thereby fulfilling the dubious prophesy that Roxburgh would fall to a dead man.

The unhappiness of most Scots at the passing of their young Fiery Face was occasioned not so much by the loss of an individual as by the unwelcome prospect of yet another under-age king. Despite their obvious fecundity, no Stewart monarch had yet managed to leave a mature and healthy heir – a pattern, incidentally, which was not broken for another century and a half. Robert III's incompetent and chaotic reign had been followed by his son's long exile and then by the bitter factional strife of his grandson's early years. Now the cycle of minority-reprisal-rule-premature death was to revolve all over again.

* * *

Prince James was eight when his father died. A week later he was crowned James III at Kelso Abbey with some ceremony. The proceedings were attended by the nobles who had gathered for the assault on Roxburgh, and 100 knights were created at the same time. The capture shortly afterwards of Wark and Roxburgh Castles set the new reign off to a pleasantly encouraging start.

The prime influence on the new king was his mother, Mary of Gueldres. Sophisticated, cosmopolitan and a good judge of character, she was more responsible than anyone for filling the head of her good looking elder son with exalted ideas of what it meant to be a king. She lived in great splendour on the £5000 annual income provided by her marriage settlement. It was far more than any king had to spend on personal pleasures and luxuries, and she had enough left over from day to day expenses to order lavish improvements at Falkland and Stirling, where James passed most of his time. Remarkably, Mary was also responsible for beginning the construction of an entirely new castle at Ravenscraig, the first in Scotland to be built specifically to withstand artillery bombardment.

Thus until his twelfth year James dwelt in seclusion and considerable comfort. He readily soaked up flattering stories of the majesty of his European counterparts and his father's Continental ambitions. It was a dangerous upbringing for a Scottish king, and one that James never managed to reconcile with the realities of government by compromise and the careful husbanding of comparatively meagre resources. It left him permanently dissatisfied with his lot and inwardly humiliated by his lack of real power.

The king never travelled abroad, but until 1480 he repeatedly made plans to do so. This and his pacific attitude towards England added to an impression, also given by James I, that he was without real affection for his country or its people. Lacking his two predecessors' ruthlessness and his father's ability to get on with the common people, he grew ever more isolated, avaricious and inconsistent – an impossible man to work with. And the ability to work with at least some of the political nation was the key to successful Scottish kingship.

James also faced a problem which had not troubled the monarchy since the reign of Robert III. He had opportunistic and troublesome brothers of about his own age. Alexander Stewart, Earl of March and Duke of Albany, six at the time of his father's death, grew up with at least some of the qualities lacking in his elder brother. Pitscottie's comment that Albany was 'esteemed in all countries above his brother the king's grace' need not be taken too seriously, for Duke Alexander was no courtier or politician. But he built on a strong power base as warden of two marches and admiral of Scotland, and he attracted some sort of following among the hearty as a soldier and avid participator in tournaments. Five years his junior, John, Earl of Mar, was an altogether more gentle, mysterious figure, with a reputed interest in the occult. Neither Alexander nor John got on with their elder brother.

The last three pieces in the family puzzle which exercised James's mind for much of his reign were his half-uncles, the sons of Queen Joan by the Black Knight of Lorn. The senior, John Stewart, was already Earl of Atholl; the second, 'Hearty James Stewart', became Earl of Buchan in 1470; the third, Andrew Stewart, pursued an ecclesiastical career and eventually claimed the bishopric of Moray. All three were ambitious and not one of them bore much affection for their complicated nephew.

The first years of James's reign were relatively well ordered. There was some continuity of prominent government personnel, with Mary of Gueldres holding pride of place through her control of the king's person. She was assisted by a council on which sat Bishop Kennedy of St Andrews, the Bishop of Glasgow and the Earls of Angus (Red Douglas), Huntly (Seton), Argyll (Campbell) and Orkney (Sinclair). There were mutterings in James's first parliament when some nobles complained that 'there was little good done in parliament... by giving the keeping of the kingdom to a woman', and unfounded rumours later linked Mary's name with those of high-born lovers. But by and large the machinery employed by her husband continued to operate smoothly.

The overriding question of these years concerned Scotland's attitude to the civil wars in England, which re-opened in the autumn of 1460. With the exiled Black Douglas lurking over the border and English factions embroiling themselves in Scottish politics whenever they felt it advantageous to do so, the situation was fraught with difficulties. Bishop Kennedy and the Earl of Angus, both out and out Lancastrians, played the game less successfully than Mary and Argyll, who preferred a more flexible approach.

Initial Scottish assistance for Henry VI and his powerful wife Margaret of Anjou proved insufficient to prevent Edward of York claiming the English throne in March 1461 and then smashing the Lancastrians at Towton. Although the Scots were given Berwick as a reward for continuing to support Henry VI, the wisdom of the queen mother's more guarded approach was justified by a development in the spring of 1492. At the secret Treaty of Westminster-Ardtornish Edward IV allied with the Black Douglas, the Earl of Ross and the formidable Donald Balloch. Douglas and Ross became liegemen of the King of England in return for promises of vast estates in the north of Scotland after Edward had conquered the country. The agreement was followed by considerable turmoil in the north-west.

Mary's sensible attempts to negotiate with England bore little fruit because of opposition within the council, led by Bishop Kennedy. (It is possible that James III's later willingness to come to terms with the Yorkists was another example of his mother's posthumous influence.) In October 1462 the ill-fated Lancastrian entourage, headed by Queen Margaret and her ineffectual son, were back in Scotland, where Angus and Kennedy once again offered their support, the latter perhaps tempted by an offer of the arch-bishopric of Canterbury should Henry ever win back his crown. Edward IV responded by releasing Douglas on a devastating border raid.

In July the next year James was given his first taste of campaigning. He took part in a series of skirmishes which resulted in the capture and execution of Lord Balvenie, Black Douglas's brother. Despairing of ever getting any substantial support from the Scots, Queen Margaret then left for Burgundy in search of more reliable assistance, leaving her wretched husband languishing in St Andrews.

When the queen mother died in December 1462 Kennedy was left the prominent figure in the administration. He was given custody of the king the following year. Accepting the inevitable (and an English pension), in 1464 the bishop made a fifteen-year truce with Edward IV. He was not too distressed to hear the next year that Henry VI had been captured in Lancashire and incarcerated in the Tower.

Despite past differences between Kennedy and the queen mother over foreign policy, James seems to have got on well with his new mentor, the 'most able of any lord' in the council. The crown had benefited greatly from the recovery of Mary of Gueldres' dowry, and Kennedy used some of the new wealth to arrange progresses for the king so that he might be seen by his subjects. At Inverness, the furthest north he ventured, he met the unreliable Earl of Ross and confronted him with the more obvious of his misdeeds. However, since neither party was prepared for hostilities and the king was ignorant of the Westminster-Ardtornish agreement, Ross got away with confessing to only a little minor peculation and lawbreaking. The full harvest of his treason waited to be gathered later.

James was still only thirteen when Kennedy died in May 1465. Under the guiding hands of first his mother and then the bishop, the first half of his minority, although eventful, had proved relatively stable. At least the lad had not been subjected to the humiliating tugs-of-war for his person which had made his father's early life so unpleasant. But the next five years turned out to be nowhere near so easy.

* * *

Government continuity was preserved by leading figures from the era of the queen mother and Bishop Kennedy. Lord Avondale, an illegitimate son of Duke Murdoch, remained as chancellor. Archibald Whitelaw, as tactful and accomplished a servant as his twentieth-century namesake, kept his post as secretary. And Colin Campbell, 1st Earl of Argyll, justified the faith shown in him by James II by loyally serving his son in a number of positions, including justiciar, master of the royal household and, later, chancellor. Another peer whose star was in the ascendant was David Lindsay, 5th Earl of Crawford. Son of the Tiger Earl, he rose in the king's affections to become Scotland's first non-royal duke. But none of these councillors had personal control over the young king, who was in the charge of Lord Gilbert Kennedy, keeper of Stirling Castle and brother of the celebrated bishop.

It was not the Bishop of St Andrew's family who strove hardest to fill the political vacuum left by the cleric's death but the ancient Ayrshire family of Boyd, who had risen on the tide of James II's fortunes. Sir Robert Boyd had been created Lord Boyd in 1454 for loyalty during the Douglas crisis. His more able younger brother, Sir Alexander Boyd of Drumcoll, had been among the assassins present at the Douglas dinner of 1452, and by 1466 he was captain of Edinburgh Castle and chamberlain of the royal household. The post brought him close to the king, whom he is supposed to have instructed in chivalric matters.

There was nothing very chivalrous about the younger Boyd's behaviour in July 1466. While accompanying James on a sparsely attended hunting party near Linlithgow, Sir Alexander knocked down Lord Kennedy and carried off his tearful teenage master to Edinburgh Castle. (The violence of the kidnap may have been a sham, for the Kennedys and Boyds had signed a bond uniting them 'in all their causes... against all manner of persons'.) It was almost as if the story of the Stewart monarchy was being scripted by an unimaginative writer of soap operas: three under-age kings in succession had now been carried off against their will.

Raised on a diet of adulation, James III did not take kindly to the harsh manner in which his self-esteem had been so sharply punctured. However, the next scene was one of forgiveness and betrayal rather than revenge. The king offered parliament an official explanation of what had happened, stating that the Boyds had acted on royal command and that their action 'should never be called in question'. All except Sir Alexander were granted a royal remission and Lord Boyd was appointed governor of the royal person and principal executive until James reached his twenty-first birthday.

We shall never know quite what machinations had been going on behind the scenes. The parliamentary business was not only a put up job, but also the public acknowledgement that a coup had taken place within the Boyd camp. Deprived of royal forgiveness, Sir Alexander was clearly being made a scapegoat for his family's treason and before long he lost the governorship of Edinburgh Castle.

Lord Boyd was not yet in a position to dominate the government, neither was he able to control the king as closely as he might have wished. James continued to make a number of progresses around the country, acquainting himself with its geography and, more importantly, making contact with men of wealth and influence. Judging by his later conduct, he was not over impressed with what he saw.

Nothing daunted, Boyd sought to secure his future through marriage. His daughter Elizabeth was wedded to Earl Archibald Douglas, son of the 5th Earl. More significantly, Boyd's son Thomas became husband to James's elder sister Mary and was created Earl of Arran to give him the status commensurate with his position as the king's brother-in-law. Once again James wept at the Boyds' high-handed behaviour, although probably more for the waste of a precious international bargaining counter than for the fate of his seventeen-year-old sister. Perhaps also at the back of his mind was the fortunate marriage between Marjory Bruce and Walter Stewart, conducted a century and a half previously. One never knew where union with the royal line might lead.

The king's own wedding took place at Holyrood two years later, when he was eighteen. His bride was Princess Margaret of Denmark-Norway, a small, twelve-year-old girl who must have found the way she had been thrust into the adult world extremely distressing. Her considerable dower, comprising Linlithgow, Doune and widespread estates to the value of one third of the king's income, was held back until she had proved her worth by providing her husband with a son. In their last major political act, the Boyds negotiated a potentially magnificent dowry. The annual payment to Norway for the Western Isles (which had not been paid for years) was ended, and the bride's father undertook to pay 60,000 Rhenish florins, 10,000 of which were to be handed over at once and the remainder in instalments. Most significantly, the Isles of Orkney and Shetland were mortgaged to Scotland against the payments being kept up. Before long James was taking steps to ensure that the territory remained permanently with the Scottish crown.

As his father before him, with his marriage James assumed personal control of his kingdom. Egged on by the Earl of Argyll, his first important act was to take revenge on the Boyds. In the parliament of 1469 they were accused of having abducted the young king, 'traitorous vituperation and degradation of our royal authority and majesty', and 'many other treasonable actions, rebellions, crimes and transgressions'. The punishment for such a serious assortment of crimes went without saying: forfeiture of life, lands, titles and offices.

Lord Boyd was in England when the sentence was passed. Understandably, he chose to stay where he was and become a pensioner of Edward IV, along with the Black Douglas. Boyd's son, the Earl of Arran, had gone to Denmark to bring back Princess Margaret. We are told that as soon as his ship anchored in the Forth and before he had time to disembark, Princess Mary climbed aboard and told him what was afoot. Thereupon he promptly weighed anchor and sailed back to the Continent, taking Mary with him. Her brother was not amused.

That left the unfortunate Sir Alexander Boyd once again carrying the can for his family's misdemeanours. He was executed on Castle Hill and the Boyd lands were set aside to enhance the patrimony of the king's eldest son.

II

In the summer of 1482, some thirteen years after James III had broken the Boyds and taken over personal control of his realm, the king summoned the Scottish host to assemble at Edinburgh. The situation was fraught with danger. A massive English army under the command of Richard, Duke of Gloucester, had streamed over the border and was now heading towards Lauderdale.

The air was thick with treason and rumour. The enemy had already taken the town of Berwick (but not the citadel) after little more than token resistance from the Earl of Crawford and Lord Grey. James's own brother, Alexander Duke of Albany, rode beside Duke Richard at the head of the invasion force, with the exiled James, 9th Earl of Douglas, lurking ominously in the background.

Now in his thirty-first year, King James moved down to Lauder ahead of the bulk of his forces. The English were twenty-five miles away. James realised that his only chance of breaking their advance lay in taking up a carefully prepared position in the pass running between the Lammermuir and Moorfoot Hills, a desperate strategy but one which made military sense as long as the morale and discipline of the Scottish forces held. The king's plan was never put to the test.

Unbeknown to James, it was not the enemy before him he needed to fear most but the enemy within. He had alienated not only his brother Albany, but also his three half-uncles, the Earls of Atholl and Buchan, and the Bishop of Moray. For some time the sons of Queen Joan and the Black Knight of Lorne had been biding their time, waiting for an appropriate moment to pounce. At Lauder they deemed the time right. They seized the king and hustled him back to Edinburgh Castle, where he was put in the charge of the Earl of Atholl. The least popular members of the royal household received scant justice – some were hanged from Lauder bridge, the rest banished. Confused and disheartened, the Scottish army melted away.

By the time Gloucester reached Edinburgh it was quite clear that he was engaged in no ordinary invasion. The Scottish government was in total disarray. James, still commanding some support, was his uncles' prisoner within the lofty walls of Edinburgh Castle, while Albany, whom Gloucester had hoped to place on the Scottish throne as a puppet of Edward IV, had become embroiled in a family squabble of hideous complexity.

No one would have been surprised if the events of 1482 had taken place in England – in the fifteenth century king making had become almost a national pastime in that country. But such behaviour was unprecedented in Scotland's immediate past. In only a dozen years of inept and tactless personal rule the young Stewart king had succeeded in snapping the bonds of loyalty which for centuries had served to bind the people to their monarchs. It was an almost incredible achievement.

III

James was as much of an enigma to his contemporaries as he has been to succeeding generations. To some he was the idle young fop who would 'take no labour…but lie still in lust, sloth and sleep' rather than tend to the affairs of state. To others he was simply a singularly nasty piece of work inclined to slay 'both tame and wild as he was wont', whose abused kingdom fell from him as an apple falls from a rotten stalk. Both impressions are too simplistic.

James III was less ruthless than his grandfather, less vindictive than his father and certainly more vigorous than either of the first two Stewart kings, Robert II and Robert III. But he was a self-opinionated youngster, without much political acumen and 'impatient of criticism, quick to make a foolish decision and slow to revoke it'. And his dynasty's endearing geniality had evaporated long before the middle years of the fifteenth century. Finally, at the end of his reign James III had the misfortune to be replaced through armed insurrection by the only early Stewart monarch to combine competence with popularity. James IV's dashing achievements, helped by an avalanche of favourable propaganda, rapidly eclipsed his predecessor's dismal catalogue of failure. James III was not notably less agreeable than his namesakes; he was just less politically competent, and that left him struggling out of his depth.

It is not clear quite when the rift opened between the king and his brother Alexander, Duke of Albany. There were rumours as early as 1475 that the bullying borderer had tried to poison James, and in 1479 the duke was indicted for treason before parliament. His alleged crimes ranged from 'the treasonably stuffing, providing and fortifying the castle of Dunbar' to deliberately breaking the current truce with England. Some of the charges, particularly his behaviour at Dunbar, do not stand close investigation, suggesting that the king's decision to strike came after years of fraternal squabbling.

Albany was held in Edinburgh Castle, from where we are told he made a dramatic escape involving knotted bed sheets and a rope. One vivid version of the story tells how the duke lured the captain of the guard and some of his men into his room for a drinking bout, killed them when they were too inebriated to fight back, cast their bodies onto the fire and scrambled over the walls, preceded by his servant. But the fugitive had miscalculated the height of the drop and his attendant broke his leg jumping from the foot of the makeshift ladder to the ground below. With better luck, his master made a safe landing, hoisted the injured man onto his shoulder and set off into the darkness.

The duke made his way from Edinburgh to Dunbar, where he prepared his castle against the king (making a nonsense of the charge that this was one reason for his previous detention). He then sailed to France, where he was warmly welcomed by Louis XI and provided with a French wife, Anne de la Tour, to replace Catherine Sinclair whom Albany had divorced in 1478. (The son of the second marriage, John Stewart, returned to Scotland in 1515 as governor for the infant James V.) Meanwhile, back in Scotland the case against Albany was allowed to lapse and the duke waited for a propitious time to make his return.

For James's second brother, John Stewart Earl of Mar, there was no escape route of knotted sheets, real or metaphorical. He was arrested around Christmas 1479 and taken to Craigmillar Castle, perhaps because Edinburgh was now considered too insecure. What happened next? All that we know for certain is that Mar died and his lands were forfeit, meaning that somewhere, somehow, he had been found guilty of treason. Later, ghoulish stories spread about how the prince had been conspiring to do away with his brother through witchcraft and how he had been transferred to a house in Canongate where he had been bled to death in a bath tub. If this is what happened, then Mar may have been murdered or subjected to a gory but comparatively painless form of execution. Or he may simply have fallen victim to inept fifteenth-century medical practice.

The least troublesome member of James's immediate family was his wife Margaret. A contemporary portrayal of her by Hugo van der Goes – in which she appears more like a caricature of a late-Victorian Salvation Army worker than a queen – owed as much to current fashion as to any desire to capture a true likeness. It shows a thin, narrow-chested woman with an inordinately long neck and high forehead. The uninspiring effect of her weak chin is balanced by an expression of flinty single-mindedness.

It is unlikely that the king's relationship with so stony-faced an individual ever approached the passionate. On occasion he had cause to be grateful for her political acumen. They shared a sincere piety and after Margaret's death James unsuccessfully sought her canonisation. The time they spent living apart in the 1480s was probably due more to the different circumstances of their lives than to any emotional estrangement. As far as we know, despite the presence at court of 'a whore named Daisy' and reports that Bishop Elphinstone requested the king to eschew lust and stick to his queen, James had no regular mistress and sired no illegitimate children. The story that Lord Crichton had an affair with Princess Margaret in revenge for the king's seduction of his wife is titillating but almost certainly untrue, as is the rumour that the king himself shared the pleasures of his sister's bed. Equally implausible is the view that the man who 'took pleasure in women' had homosexual tendencies. In some matters, at least, James III was very much a Stewart.

The portrait of James on the same alterpiece as his wife shows an altogether better-looking individual. His face is less rounded than his father's and he wears his dark hair thick and long. A full, almost pretty mouth is set beneath a well-shaped nose and fine, oval eyebrows. The king's confident expression verges on the arrogant, although a hint of sadness flickers behind those handsome eyes.

Margaret's first child James, Duke of Rothesay and Earl of Carrick, was born in March 1473. Afterwards the queen went on pilgrimage to the tomb of St Ninian at Whithorn to thank the saint for the child's safe delivery and to avoid an immediate second pregnancy. Another James, the future Duke of Ross, was born in March 1476 and John, Earl of Mar, followed in 1479.

The other women in James's life were his sisters, Mary and Margaret, whom he appeared to regard as little more than pawns in his political games. Mary, as we have seen, fled with the Earl of Arran in 1469. When she returned to Scotland in 1471 to plead her husband's cause, she was ignored until his death then made to marry Lord Hamilton. Margaret, the younger sister, was dangled before a number of important suitors until, with a display of independence which ruined James's diplomacy overnight (literally), she accepted Lord Crichton as her lover, became pregnant and vanished from the political scene until the next reign.

* * *

Of all the criticisms made of James, the most consistent was that he was 'wondrous covetous'. Bishop William Elphinstone of Aberdeen, who heavily influenced his royal master in the 1480s and was always eager, according to the eulogistic Boece, to chip in with an appropriate moral maxim, begged James to eschew avarice. The advice was sound, not just for the well-being of the king's soul but for that of his kingdom too. In 'gathering money rather than the hearts of his barons' James undermined the pillars of his authority. The court was the political nation's spring of patronage and, therefore, of wealth. When the stream ran dry, some were ruined and many were disillusioned, and angry discontent stalked the tower houses of the great.

To give him his due, we should recognise that James faced very real financial difficulties. His revenue of about £16,000 sounds large, but steepling inflation rendered it far less than it seemed. A pound of silver worth 768 pence in 1440 had increased in value to 1,680 pence by 1483. The expanding domestic market was short of hard currency, adding to the impression that the kingdom was 'bare of money'. Parliament was as reluctant as ever to grant direct taxation, while the queen's massive endowment (including the castles at Threave and Doune, and the lordships of Galloway, Stirlingshire and Methven) reduced considerably the crown's landed income. War, particularly sporadic English naval action, compounded the difficulties. When things were at their worst 'many poor folk died of hunger'.

Then as now politics and economics ran as coupled coaches on the same train. There was no way that James could have increased his wealth without political repercussions, but he certainly had no need to be so tactless in the way he went about it. He tried to stop hoarding, and yet was widely and accurately rumoured to be the greatest hoarder of all – he was carrying £4000 in cash with him on the day he died and a further £24,000 was found stashed away in Edinburgh Castle. He failed adequately to reward his supporters for their loyalty. The acquisition of the Boyd lands in 1469 and Earldom of Ross in 1476 (see below) were no different from similar seizures by the first two Jameses; but with acts such as granting the earldom of Lennox to Sir John Stewart of Darnley in 1473 then revoking the gift three years later, the third James carried appropriation to new heights of exasperating tactlessness.

More damaging was the government's attempt to manipulate the currency. Following the Boyds' example of minting £3000 worth of copper coins in 1466, fourteen years later James sanctioned a massive issue of debased coinage. It was a desperate, foolish measure intended to help finance the imminent war with England. Its effect was to provoke the crisis which ensured that the war would never be fought. Seen as 'the cause of great dearth and hunger throughout all the country', the 'Black Money' was every-where reviled, and two years later it was worthless.

James's attention to justice was spasmodic and subjective. When his own interests were at stake he could be painstakingly attentive, even concerning himself with the fate of a single ox. In other matters the young king was woefully remiss. By the 1470s we hear of 'the great break that is now in divers parts of the realm', and by 1478 murder, treason and robbery were said to be 'common throughout the realm'. And it was not just the common cateran who was causing problems. Squabbles between high-born lawbreakers were also dangerously out of control.

As well as failing to take steps to uphold the law, James made matters worse by unashamedly exploiting the judicial process for profit. His speciality was the sale of remissions for virtually all crimes, including murder. The corrupt policy was deeply resented, as the author of the fifteenth-century poem 'The Harp' suggested:

> 'When great council...
> Has ordained straight to spare no man from justice,
> And within short time you change your intent...
> Then all the world murmurs that you are bought.'

James was certainly insensitive and even sometimes malicious. Yet care is needed before accepting all the stories about him which have accumulated over the years. This is particularly so where his close advisors are concerned.

* * *

It used to be believed that James's court was peopled by an unworthy coterie of low-born hangers-on (his 'familiars') who prevented the king from taking the advice of 'wise discrete persons'. The picture of an easily-led young king presiding over a household filled with 'unworthy vile persons' of dubious morality has undoubted salacious appeal, and provides a plausible explanation as to why 'the king... lost the hearts of many of the lords'. It is now widely accepted, however, that the 'secret servants' existed more in the imaginations of chroniclers than in historical fact.

James did have familiars at court, but there was nothing unusual in this. Royal households had always attracted young sons of the nobility, various artists and musicians, doctors, and skilled craftsmen of every description. What would have been unusual and a justifiable cause of outrage would have been for James to show such people undue favour. There is no concrete evidence that he did so. We do not even know whether Cochrane, his supposed favourite and the man later held responsible for the disastrous debasement, was called Thomas or Robert. Whoever he was, he seems to have been only an 'usher of our sovereign lord's chamber door'. William

Roger and Thomas Preston, the other familiars whom the magnates report-edly strung ignominiously over the bridge at Lauder, were of no greater consequence. The importance of the Lauder coup lay not in the execution of household menials, but in the seizure of the king.

Some did well out of James's patronage. These were generally not parvenus but men of good family, such as David Crichton (given custody of Edinburgh Castle) and the 'familiar squire' Sir David Guthrie, whose family had risen during the king's minority. Guthrie was created a baron and later became captain of the royal guard, an unusual position which suggests that quite early in his reign the king was fearful of violence against his person.

The only clear example of a low-born favourite who benefited spectacu-larly from James's patronage was the illegitimate cleric William Scheves. From a minor court official with an interest in astrology, he rose to become Dean of Dunkeld and then Archbishop of St Andrews in 1478. His sputnik-like ascendancy began with a disagreement between the government and Patrick Graham, Bishop of St Andrews and nephew of Bishop Kennedy. In search of papal support, Graham had travelled to Rome where, to the surprise of almost everyone, particularly the king, he was elevated to the exalted status of Archbishop in 1472. Understandably, James refused to recognise the appointment.

The case now became a tussle between the curia and the crown for control over the Scottish church. James held the whip hand, for the arch-bishop could do nothing without royal support, and after a while Rome decided to drop the impecunious Graham and come to an understanding with its adversary. Thereupon the first archbishop of St Andrews went mad and Scheves was appointed in his place. Excommunicated, bankrupt and insane, Graham spent his final years being shuffled around various Scottish prisons before dying in 1478. His successor, only forty when appointed, enjoyed a long and prominent career as a key figure in church and state.

Scheves turned out to be a competent churchman and a loyal servant of the crown. His elevation attracted jealous disapproval from some of his fellow ecclesiastics, particularly Andrew Stewart, Bishop of Moray; but by and large the raising of a man from obscurity to one of the highest offices in the kingdom was accepted as a legitimate exercise of the royal prerogative. His career throws an interesting light on the miserable victims of the 1482 coup. If the servants who hung over the Leader Water that July morning had been killed because they really were upstart 'untrue hearts', then surely Scheves should have been swinging beside them? No amount of excuses can disguise the fact that it was James, not his servants, whom the plotters were really after. Cochran, Preston and Roger were merely unfortunate mice caught in a trap set for a more important victim.

* * *

After his death James was criticised for being a man who 'loved solitude and desired never to hear of wars, nor of their fame'. The comment is a strange mixture of truth and fiction. In 1470, when he processed to Inverness, it looked as if the young king would prove as keen a traveller as his predecessors. But what he saw of the rugged Highlands and its independent-minded inhabitants was not to his liking. Consequently, as the years went by he passed an increasing amount of time in Stirling and Edinburgh, the latter acquiring the status of capital city during his reign.

A similar change seemed to come over James's attitude towards war. He began like a disciple of Mars himself, planning grandiose Continental campaigns the like of which had never before been even contemplated by a Scottish king. When these were thwarted, he swung to the other extreme. His desire for a secure and lasting peace with England – a sensible but in some ways shocking new policy – provoked bitter hostility among those with a vested interest in profitable cross-border raiding. Unable or unwilling to explain himself, James's foreign policy invariably alienated some powerful group or other.

In 1469 James arranged for the exposition of an extravagant pronouncement about his own authority. It claimed for him 'full jurisdiction and free Empire within this realm', or supreme power in the land. As a result, legal transactions were recorded by notaries public appointed by the king, not, as had been the case, by the emperor or pope. Three years later James had the fleurs de lys struck from the royal arms of Scotland lest it be thought to imply subordination to France. The reign's final batch of silver coins portray James wearing an impressive imperial crown.

What did all this pretension mean? At its face value it suggests a king smitten with a hopelessly inflated idea of his own importance. This is misleading. Whatever his faults, James was not stupid. He was not claiming to be able to override parliament or do without the support of his nobility. Behind his ostentatious claims lay a painful sense of his own domestic weaknesses and international inferiority. He used the word 'Empire' simply to mean that Scotland was an independent kingdom where no outside authority – imperial, papal or English – held sway. It was the same concept that Henry VIII was to employ during his struggle with the papacy in the 1530s.

Another interesting parallel with Henry VIII is the way James III almost immediately launched into a foreign policy of unrealistic aggression. Both kings came to power at eighteen, and both determined to cut a dash on the international scene. James wished to raise his profile in Continental politics. He was saved from inevitable and ignominious failure by the restraining hand of his parliament. Henry's reputation would be preserved by the fatal impetuosity of James's son, James IV.

In September 1470 James devised a way of ensuring that Orkney and Shetland would remain part of the Scottish kingdom. From Lord Sinclair,

Earl of Caithness, the crown received the Earldom of Orkney and Kirkwall
Castle. In return – and it seems to have been a fair and mutually agreed
exchange – Sinclair was given 4000 marks, the fine castle at Ravenscraig,
lands in Fife and a number of important privileges. By early 1472 the King of
Scots was Lord of Shetland and Earl of Orkney. Even if the islands' former
owners had managed to redeem their mortgage, it would now have been
extremely difficult for them to regain possession of the territory.

The first sign that James might not be content merely to consolidate his
kingdom came in 1471. First he offered to mediate in the struggle between
France and Burgundy, a scheme as costly as it was preposterous. The chances
of Louis XI and Philip the Bold accepting the good offices of an immature
and virtually unknown Scot were negligible. All that can be said in favour of
the idea is that it might have provided a suitable husband for James's younger
sister Margaret. The next year James horrified parliament by suggesting an
expedition to seize Brittany, which he claimed through his aunt, the
widowed Duchess Isabella. Two equally fantastic proposals followed. One was
aimed at the Duchy of Gueldres, the other resurrected his father's designs on
the French County of Saintonge.

No Scottish king had ever led an army outside the British Isles. James had
little military experience and inadequate resources for a large-scale attack on
England, let alone for a prohibitively expensive overseas expeditionary force.
Fearing unprecedented demands for taxation, and domestic chaos should the
king be defeated or even killed, parliament used every device it could to divert
its hot-headed king away from paths it felt sure would lead to disaster. The
nobility, terrified at the mooted 'passing' to the continent, felt unable 'in any
wise [to] give their consent'; the clergy too begged James to 'remain at home'.
James was first drawn from Brittany with the prospect of Saintonge, then
finally persuaded to abandon all his dreams on account of their economic and
political cost. The bitterness of the pill of rebuttal was slightly sweetened by
vague (and even more unrealistic) hints that he might save himself for a still
greater Continental honour – election to the imperial crown.

James now lowered his sights. However, his new target was scarcely less
controversial. While maintaining clandestine contact with Louis XI, he
determined to heal the breach with England which on several occasions had
threatened to force him into open conflict. Edward IV was eager to neutralise
Scotland in order to concentrate on a campaign in France, and James, now
aware that the cost of any war would have to be borne largely by the crown,
was eager to ease Anglo-Scottish tension. The two monarchs first met at
Alnwick in September 1473, and thereafter made rapid progress towards the
centrepiece of their new-found friendship, the formal betrothal in 1474 of
the one-year-old Prince James to Edward IV's daughter Cecily, her baby
fiancé's senior by four years. The union was sealed at a bizarre ceremony held
in Blackfriars, Edinburgh, where two proxies, the Earl of Crawford and Lord
Scrope, held hands and plighted their troth to each other. Marriage was to

follow as soon as the infant couple were old enough. A dowry of 20,000 marks (about £40,000 Scots) was agreed, to be paid in annual instalments.

Sensible though the treaty might have been, it did not receive the welcome James had anticipated. There was predictable dismay among Border lords such as his mettlesome brother Albany (who 'loved nothing so well as able men and good horses') and Angus, heirs to a strong tradition of preying off English settlements to the south. Moreover, at a time when nationalist sentiment was being fed by Blind Harry's popular poem 'The Wallace', in some circles amity with the old enemy was interpreted as a betrayal of Scotland's heritage. Still others believed Edward was not to be trusted. As if to bear out these fears, in 1475 he invaded France in alliance with Burgundy (taking Robert Boyd and the Black Douglas with him) and signed the profitable treaty of Picquigny with Louis XI.

The news came as a triple snub to James. It undermined the basis of the 1474 agreement, put into perspective the paltry sums required to buy off the impecunious Scots (the French were to pay Edward 50,000 crowns a year) and reminded James of his failure to hold a similar course earlier in the reign.

But for the time being James had other things to think about. Before leaving for France, Edward had leaked information about the 1462 Treaty of Westminster-Ardtornish in order to ensure that the Scots did not break their word and take advantage of his absence. John MacDonald, Earl of Ross and Lord of the Isles, was peremptorily summoned to parliament to answer for the 'treasonable leagues and bonds made by him with Edward King of England'. When the traitorous Hebridean failed to appear he was found guilty in his absence and declared forfeit of life, land and titles.

The next summer James followed parliamentary condemnation with military intervention. Confronted by a royal fleet and army led by Crawford, Argyll and Huntly, MacDonald surrendered. In July he 'humbled himself and obeyed the king's will, upon certain conditions'. The inveterate rebel lost Kintyre, Knapdale and the earldom of Ross, but was left with some prestige as a Lord of Parliament. His illegitimate son Angus Ogg was recognised as his heir.

Boece's claim that James had 'subdued the Highlanders' and given 'the whole country a well-established peace' is rather too generous a summary of the king's achievement. Ogg soon put himself at the head of those who rejected his father's terms and by 1481 he was in a strong enough position to be negotiating with Edward IV, thereby reviving the MacDonalds' tradition of treason. Nevertheless, James could take some comfort from the fact that in the short term he had enjoyed more success in the north than either his father or grandfather.

* * *

The crisis which led to the Lauder coup began with the collapse of James's pro-English policy. Edward paid the Scots their dowry instalments until

1479, but his agreement with Louis XI had freed him to take an increasingly aggressive attitude towards his northern neighbour. James was well aware of the precariousness of his position, showing obsequious friendship towards Edward, 'the right excellent high and mighty prince, our dearest cousin and brother, the King of England', and proposing to strengthen Anglo-Scottish understanding through the marriage of Princess Margaret to Lord Rivers, Edward's brother-in-law. The terms of the contract had been agreed upon when Margaret's swelling contours revealed the extent of her spirited and undiplomatic behaviour with Lord Crichton. Plans for her betrothal were hastily dropped.

On several occasions in the later 1470s James tried to get a safe pass to visit the shrine of St John the Baptist at Amiens. His motive was not simply religious. Alarmed by Edward's belligerence, the Scottish king desperately needed to strike up his own personal accord with Louis XI. Edward was aware of this, and for one reason or another James never managed to make his pilgrimage. Thus when sporadic fighting broke out on the Borders in April 1480 James found himself still without a secure ally abroad and with precious little reliable support at home.

The following year the pressure on James mounted when Edward dragged out the ancient English claim to Scottish overlordship, renewed his alliance with France and caused heavy damage to Scottish shipping. Serious fighting was prevented only by the Scots' lack of resources and the intervention of a papal legate.

By 1482 James's plight had become desperate. The 'Black Money' crisis was at its height. Clearly frightened at the way events were shaping, the king's uncles led a parliamentary attack on Lord Lyle, one of the crown's more loyal supporters, and demanded a restatement of the remission granted to them for misdemeanours committed during the minority. To make matters worse, the exiled Alexander now cynically shifted his attitude towards England, landing at Southampton and teaming up with Edward IV and his Douglas pensioner. At Fotheringay on 10th June Albany did homage to Edward IV and was proclaimed 'Alexander King of Scotland' by the gift of the King of England. The pretender's liege lord then promised to help his new vassal recover his kingdom. Several powerful Scottish lords, including the Earl of Angus, were also secretly prepared to swap Alexander IV for James III.

This was the situation in which James found himself as he tried to marshal his troops in Lauderdale. The measures taken to resist the invader had been impressive: wappingshaws had been held, coastal defences put in readiness and the king had even met the cost of putting 500 men in Berwick out of his own pocket.

But none of these provisions addressed the real weakness of the crown's position. The folly of James's youth had finally cost him the confidence of his people. Until his uncles struck he was unaware of the gravity of his situation, but by then it was too late to do anything about it. His crown, and even his life, were in serious danger.

IV

The crisis of 1482-3 took the form of a tripartite Stewart family scrap. At the centre was the terrified king, supported – more or less – by his level-headed wife and men such as Archbishop Scheves, Lord Avondale and the Earl of Argyll. On one flank stood the king's half-uncles Atholl, Buchan and the Bishop of Moray; on the other James's rebellious brother Alexander, Duke of Albany and self-styled King Alexander IV, backed by an English army under the Duke of Gloucester.

It was once thought that the prime mover at Lauder had been Archibald Douglas, 5th Earl of Angus. Linked to the Boyds through marriage, he was given the nickname 'Bell the Cat' (from the fable of a brave mouse which tied a bell round a cat's neck) for being the man responsible for confronting the tyrannical king. In fact the unreliable earl was closer to Albany than to the Black Knight's sons, and any idea that he was an idealist was belied by a later career of unrelenting duplicity.

James was fortunate that during the chaotic months following his arrest his best interests were served by his doing nothing, for that is precisely what he did. A kind interpretation of events might be that he was playing for time. The probable truth was that, at least to begin with, he was too shaken to do anything but look to his own preservation. Fearing 'that certain lords and people who were then with him would have slain and undone him', he charged Edinburgh's keeper John Stewart, Lord Darnley, with assembling a bodyguard to attend the king 'both night and day, to keep and defend him'. Darnley, who was in the queen's pay, did as he was bid and was later handsomely rewarded. It is a measure of James's remarkable ability to make enemies, however, that the man who had protected the king in his hour of need and acted as a mediator between him and his enemies was to be found among those taking up arms against the crown only six years later.

Gloucester and Albany reached Edinburgh in August with a small force. The city placated the invader with presents and a promise to repay Edward's dowry instalments; then, having seen Albany reach some sort of agreement with the Scheves-Avondale-Argyll triumvirate on 2 August, Gloucester moved south to resume his attack on Berwick. Isolated and depressed by news from the capital, in September Sir Patrick Hepburn surrendered the citadel to the English.

In early September Albany and his three new allies had travelled to Stirling to talk with Queen Margaret. Technically speaking Edinburgh Castle belonged to the queen, and she may have had closer contact with her husband's jailers than she would have acknowledged publicly. This made her an ideal go-between. She agreed to Albany's restoration to the earldom of

Mar and to compensation for his sister Mary for her ill treatment at the hands of the king. At the same time Margaret somehow arranged that the king should be released. Abandoned by their new master and fearing the wrath of their old one, Scheves, Avondale and Argyll took to the hills.

Albany then returned to Edinburgh and began a token siege of the castle. On 29 September, as Margaret had planned, James was released by his uncles and moved to Holyrood Abbey where he lived in what was reported to be 'great merriment' and left his family to sort out their disagreements. The queen's willingness to treat with the rebels took some explaining, and for a while relations between the suspicious king and his queen remained understandably strained. That winter Albany told parliament that he had acted against his 'dearest brother' so that his 'noble person' should not be exposed to the 'daily danger' of war. It was a pretty feeble excuse, and made no mention of the fact that Albany had returned to Scotland with an English army not to help his brother but to replace him. The nearest 'Alexander IV' came to revealing his true intentions was an unfulfilled request to be appointed lieutenant-general of the realm.

By now time was running out for the incompetent pretender. The longer the uncertainty went on, the more people reverted to their traditional loyalties. Of the rebel uncles, only the hearty Earl of Buchan seemed prepared to keep up the opposition. In late December he joined Albany and Angus at Dunbar Castle to devise a way of recapturing the king. When this failed even Buchan gave up.

A month later Albany, Angus and some of their closest followers repeated the pledges given to Edward IV at Fotheringay. In March 1483, with a display of truly Machiavellian duplicity, they made a complete submission to the restored James III. It says a lot for James's patience (or feeble grasp of political realities) that even at this stage he was prepared to accept his brother's word. Albany and his cronies were not even imprisoned: all they had to do was keep at least six miles distant from the king's person.

When the true extent of Albany's treasons leaked out in April, he admitted an English garrison into Dunbar and fled south. This is not quite the last we hear of him. The following year he returned to Scotland in partnership with the venerable Black Douglas and raided Lochmaben. The aged earl was seized and confined to Lindores Abbey. 'A man who can do no better', he observed wryly, 'must be a monk'. His partner in crime escaped to France, where the following year he was killed by a splintered lance while fighting in a tournament. His castle at Dunbar fell to the king on 6 December 1485.

* * *

One of the most extraordinary aspects of the debacle of 1482-3 was that five years later almost exactly the same thing happened again. James III was clearly not a consummate villain and his reign is unusual for its lack of severed heads. His leniency in 1483 is bewildering: ex-rebels such as the Stewart uncles, Angus, Lord Gray and many others were soon free to resume their careers. Only one Albany supporter was executed. It is most unlikely that either of the two previous Stewart kings would have been so generous.

What people seem to have found so infuriating about James, apart from his sensible but misplaced desire to get on well with England, was his unpredictability. In 1484 the Earl of Argyll was rewarded with some of Albany's lands for his steadfast loyalty. Four years later, in February 1488, he was suddenly dismissed from the chancellorship. At the same time the Earl of Crawford, another royal stalwart from the mid-reign crisis, was elevated to a dukedom. Atholl was rapidly taken back into favour, while his brother Buchan was banished for three years and deprived of most of his offices. 'Bell the cat' was given no formal pardon but appointed warden of the Middle and Eastern Marches. The old serpent had no idea, therefore, when the king might suddenly turn upon him, as he did on Margaret's lover, Lord Crichton, in 1484.

The same uncertainty pertained in the field of justice. In 1484 James said that he would sell no more remissions for three years. At the end of this period he admitted before parliament that one reason why his kingdom was 'greatly broken' by lawlessness was his own leniency towards offenders, and he declared that henceforward offenders would be 'punished extremely'. True to his word for once, he 'began to use sharp execution of justice in all parts'. This was all very well, but coupled with simultaneous moves to undermine local jurisdictions by allowing appeals direct to the Lords of Council and the reorganisation of the justice ayres, it left nobody knowing where they stood.

Two unrelated incidents sparked off the final crisis of the reign. The king was a sincerely religious man. It was reported, somewhat incredibly, that he burst into tears whenever he looked upon a representation of Christ or the Virgin Mary. By the later 1480s he had weathered a period of tension with the papacy and was once more on good terms with the curia. In 1486 he received the papal golden rose – a sign of the holy father's particular approval. The next year James and Innocent VIII came to a mutually satisfactory agreement over the method of appointment to vacant Scottish benefices and Scheves's see of St Andrews was given primatial status, equal to Canterbury. As a tangible manifestation of his faith, in 1485 James began the foundation of a new royal collegiate church at Restalrig, outside Edinburgh. To help pay for his venture he contrived, with papal blessing, to suppress the Benedictine Priory at Coldingham, then in the hands of the Humes, and allocate its revenues to Restalrig. The Humes were one of a number of powerful Border families who already found James 'hateful'. The king's latest high-handed action was all that was needed to force them into open revolt.

The second goad to rebellion was James's perceived Anglophilia.

Following the death of Edward IV in 1483, the next year James signed a truce with his successor and the Scots' erstwhile enemy Richard of Gloucester, now Richard III. Negotiations for an Anglo-Scots royal marriage collapsed with Richard's deposition by Henry VII in 1485, but a year later James followed a truce with the new king by further talk of a marriage alliance. The idea was for the 'great and tender love' between the two monarchs to be cemented by a triple union: James III, a widower since 1486, with Edward IV's widow Elizabeth Woodville, and two of James's sons with Elizabeth's daughters. To make his second son appear a more attractive proposition as a son-in-law, James created him Duke of Ross. The two kings planned to meet in July 1488 to bring their plans a step nearer fulfilment.

For the southern barons this was the last straw, and in February 1488 they bribed the keeper of Stirling Castle, who was married to a Hume, to hand over the heir to the throne. The rebels announced that the king was intending to treat his son the same way as he had treated Albany, and Prince James may already have started to mistrust his father, particularly after the favour shown recently to his younger brother.

By March James was desperately looking around for support. He sent messengers to France, England and the pope. Although the south was all but lost, his uncles, Crawford and several northern barons were still loyal. The king failed to attract Angus and is even rumoured to have approached the antique Douglas for support. 'Sir', came the supposed pessimistic reply, 'you have kept me and your black coffer in Stirling too long; neither of us can do you any good.'

Rebel propaganda gave out that the king was listening to 'deceitful and perverse council' and was 'bringing in Englishmen to the perpetual subjection of the realm'; but a quick glance at the names of their leaders shows that their motives were as much personal as altruistic. Behind the fifteen-year-old prince stood, among others, Earls Angus and Argyll, Lords Gray, Lyle, Drummond and Hailes (Patrick Hepburn), the Bishops of Glasgow and Dunkeld, and numerous angry Humes, all of whom had suffered from the king's capriciousness. Many more stood aside, afraid to enter the struggle but no doubt secretly wishing the rebels success.

In May James confirmed his opponents' worst impressions of him by agreeing terms at Aberdeen then promptly renouncing them. After skirmishes near Blackness, which resulted in Buchan's surrender as a hostage, the king returned to Edinburgh. From the capital he set out for Stirling to get hold of his wayward son. At Sauchieburn on 11 June his hopelessly outnumbered forces met those of the rebels, who had gathered presumptuously beneath a royal standard.

The battle was fought on almost exactly the same spot where Robert Bruce had crushed Edward II 174 years previously. But even the Bruce's own sword and the fastest horse in the kingdom were not enough to save James. His army was routed and the king 'happened to be slain' in the flight. A fort-

ROTHESAY CASTLE

night later his body was laid to rest beside that of his wife in Cambuskenneth Abbey.

The Scottish historian John Major, twenty-one at the time of Sauchieburn, wrote in 1521: 'You can find many kings, in this country and elsewhere, who were worse than James III'. But not many, he might have added, who were so singularly insensitive to their people's wishes.

CHAPTER 13

'Few Like Him in Scotland'

I

The rebels who had gathered at Sauchieburn beneath the banner of James 'Prince of Scotland' had sworn a solemn oath not to harm the king's person. There is no reason to doubt their sincerity. Fully aware of the hideous punishment meted out to the last Scottish regicides, they were loth to bring down similar retribution on their own heads.

But war is cruelly unpredictable. Somehow, somewhere, in the chaos of battle the king had fallen. Thus an operation to remove a cancer from the body politic had left the surgeons not with a patient restored to health, as they had intended, but with a corpse. The prince's men were almost as dismayed as their opponents. When extensive enquiries failed to discover who had killed James III, responsibility for the crime was left resting squarely on the shoulders of the rebel leaders, their fifteen-year-old figurehead included.

The unfilial behaviour of the Duke of Rothesay – now James IV – is not easily explained. Little is known of his early years, but the information we have suggests that at least until the age of nine he enjoyed a comfortable, quiet life and a good education. He spent most of his time at Stirling in the company of Queen Margaret and his two brothers. The king his father was a frequent visitor, and there is no evidence that he showed any early hostility towards his heir.

The first seeds of mutual mistrust were sown probably during the troubles of 1482. As we have seen, the queen's behaviour when negotiating with the rebels was not quite straightforward and may have led her husband to suspect, with some justification, that she had confided private anxieties about her husband's kingship to her elder son. Furthermore, it is likely that the king had resented the unusually solicitous interest shown by Albany in the way Rothesay was being brought up. Thus by the time of his mother's death in 1486, through no fault of his own the thirteen-year-old prince may well have been the subject of his father's dangerous, jealous suspicion.

Apart from offering him to foreign powers as an eligible marriage partner, James III deliberately distanced Rothesay from matters of state. This kept the impetuous youth politically naive, as well as fearful for his own safety – an easy target, in other words, for the seductive rebel propaganda of 1488. However, as his immediate reactions showed only too clearly, the manner of James IV's usurpation belied his true character, which knew more of honesty than most Stewart kings.

When he realised the awfulness of what he had done, James became 'dolorous and always taken up with his own thoughts'. He spent long hours mooching about by himself, shocked at the speed of events and unable to come to terms with the unworthy part he had played in them. Depressed and lonely, the adolescent king eventually turned in his misery to the worldly cleric George Vaus, Dean of the Chapel Royal and Bishop of Galloway, confessing that he had 'been advised to come against his father' and pressing the dean to tell him what he thought of the new government. Vaus feared that the Prince's backers would be 'utterly displeased' if what he really felt about the rebellion leaked out, so he kept his thoughts to himself. But the kindliness and under-standing he showed towards the unhappy penitent did help to salve the troubled boy's badly bruised conscience.

Never one for half measures, James decided that the penance ordained by the church was insufficient to expunge his sin. He therefore ordered the manufacture of a heavy iron chain which he wore round his waist next to the skin as a constant reminder of the shameful manner in which he had come to the throne. It was reported that as the years passed new links were added to the king's uncomfortable remembrancer, lest he grew accustomed to its weight. It is more likely, in fact, that this was done simply to accommodate James's expanding girth.

James of the Iron Belt's guilt stemmed not from regret at having taken part in the 1488 coup, which he felt had been entirely necessary, but from what he believed was a personal responsibility for his father's unfortunate death. While accepting his implied patricide with deep regret, he showed little sympathy for the personality of his victim. James endowed masses for Queen Margaret's soul in October 1488; it was another eight years before he did the same for James III. The new king was not a vengeful character. We will never know precisely what his father did to arouse such hostility in him, but it must have been dire.

The earliest portrait of the future James IV is on the same altar panel as Hugo van der Goes' depiction of James III. Behind the king kneels a child of about nine with a handsome round face full of wide-eyed innocence. If we have interpreted events correctly, six years later James was still very much the innocent abroad. He had been given a cruel introduction into the ways of the world, but several years were to pass before he finally hardened into manhood. Only then did the Scots realise what a disguised blessing the slaughter at Sauchieburn had been.

II

James IV was crowned at Scone with great pomp on 24 June. The date was the anniversary of Bannockburn and the venue where royal inaugurations had taken place since time immemorial. Both were deliberately chosen by the new regime to lend weight to the occasion. But all the ceremony in the world could not disguise the fact that the magnificent coronation had been arranged by a narrow clique for their own benefit. Scotland's magnates stayed away in droves. Only two earls attended; there was no constable and no marischal, and the crowning was not performed by Archbishop William Scheves of St Andrews, but by his bitter rival William Blackadder, Bishop of Glasgow. (The bishop's name can be spelt with a single 'd' to avoid unfortunate comic connotations.) The message was clear. The manner of the overthrow of James III and subsequent distribution of the spoils of victory had already aroused considerable disapproval.

Administrative posts and perquisites were handed out to the rebel leaders like Sauchieburn battle honours, many of the richest prizes falling to the Hepburns and Humes. Patrick Hepburn, Lord Hailes, the soldier who had tried to hold Berwick Castle in 1482, rapidly emerged as the most powerful figure in the new regime. His mastership of the household gave him control over the persons of the king and his brother James, Duke of Ross. Hepburn's military power was based on his possession of Edinburgh and (later) Threave Castles, the post of high admiral, and the wardenship of the West and Middle Marches. He took over John Ramsay's Bothwell lordship when the latter fled to England and had it elevated into an earldom in October. Numerous other powerful and lucrative positions, from keeper of the privy seal to master of the royal larder and cellar, were snapped up by Hepburn's acquisitive relations.

The dispute over Coldingham Priory was finally settled in favour of the Humes. Their leader Alexander Hume acquired Stirling Castle, the office of chamberlain and the guardianship of the king's youngest brother John, Earl of Mar. With Argyll restored as chancellor and a frantic search begun for James III's real and mythical treasures, it was patently obvious that whatever principle had first inspired them, James IV's supporters were now chiefly motivated by a pragmatic determination to seize whatever spoils of victory they could lay their hands on.

No wonder James found the whole enterprise profoundly depressing. Having joined what he thought was a revolution against corruption and false policy, and having endangered his soul by endorsing the rebels' false claim that James III had poisoned Queen Margaret, all James now saw was retribution and a sordid scramble for office. As if to confirm their lack of scruple, on 3 October the men who had chastised his father for 'bringing in Englishmen' signed a three-year truce with Henry VII. There must have been moments when James felt that not even by winding ten fathoms of chain about his waist could he atone for his lack of judgement.

Life was not all gloom for the new king. After years of relative isolation he was now the centrepiece of a European court. Stared at, feted and flattered,

he was soon learning what it was to be a monarch. Courtiers hung obse-
quiously on his every word, while hastily dispatched foreign embassies
disguised their missions of reconnaissance with kind words and presents.
Spaniards from the twin kingdoms of Castile and Aragon, masters of the wily
art of diplomacy, understood better than any the way to win the heart of a
vigorous fifteen-year-old: all his life James treasured their gifts of a splendid
Toledo sword and dagger, and wore them at his side in his last battle.

Even at this stage James was no armchair king. He knew full well that one
reason for his father's unpopularity had been the way he had cut himself off
from his people by declining to travel about the country, and within weeks of
his accession James had begun the exhausting progresses around Scotland
which became such a marked feature of his rule. By the first anniversary of
Sauchieburn he had been seen by more Scots than had set eyes on his predecessor in the previous five years.

* * *

The new Earl of Bothwell waited four months before meeting a parliament.
By October his regime had begun to settle in and he had a clearer idea of
those held by the king 'in great and high displeasure' for their unpatriotic
behaviour during the reign of James III. Bothwell was an astute politician.
Acutely aware of the hostility his success had stirred up, he dealt harshly only
with hostages (such as the Earl of Buchan) or men like Ramsay who had
already left Scotland. The Earl of Crawford and Buchan's brother John, Earl
of Atholl, escaped lightly. Crawford lost only his decorative badge of his
previous loyalty, the dukedom of Montrose. Of the four magnates brought to
justice, not one was permanently disabled.

In the long run other parliamentary business proved more contentious.
The first steps were taken to elevate Blackadder's see of Glasgow into an
archbishopric. A tax of £5000 was demanded to finance an overseas embassy
to find 'a noble princess' for the king, now deemed to be 'of perfect age' to
marry. Finally, James was exhorted to undertake justice ayres to restore law
and order in his troubled kingdom. The energetic young man was only too
pleased to continue his perambulations; but it was soon noticeable that the
so-called 'justice' being dispensed was dangerously weighted against the
regime's opponents.

Plenty of opponents there were, too. Men who had been loyal to James III,
such as the erstwhile Montrose, believed that not enough had been done to
find those responsible for the 'the treasonable and cruel slaughter' of their
late master. More worrying for the Hepburn-Hume axis were the allies of '88
who now felt excluded from power. Headed by magnates like Lord Lyle and
the Earl of Lennox, they complained that James IV was 'governed by others'
whose aim was 'to destroy our sovereign lord'. Before long the disaffected had
produced a predictable list of these 'partial persons': Bothwell, two other

Hepburns, Blackadder and the pusillanimous Vaus. On account of their family connections, it seems, the Humes were excluded, and no one ventured to criticise the young king himself.

The rebellion of 1489 gave James IV his second experience of warfare in two years. In early summer, backed by Lord Lyle and that seducer of royalty and inveterate adventurer Lord Crichton, the Earl of Lennox and his son Matthew proclaimed their intention of removing the king's false councillors. Their revolt was centred on the mighty fortress on Dumbarton rock, with the less puissant Lyle castle at Duchal and the Lennox stronghold at Crookston forming the outworks.

Bothwell did not consider James mature enough to play anything but a token part in the government's response to the threat. The king visited the Earl of Argyll's operations before Dumbarton, and he was present to see his royal artillery swiftly pound Duchal into surrender. But he spent much of the summer attending to more commonplace tasks, such as receiving ambassadors, furthering his education and enjoying himself. Plays and his new jester 'Gentle John' kept him amused at court and he burned up his phenomenal energy in pursuit of game and young ladies. When Sir John Wood defeated and captured the Tudor-backed English privateer Stephen Bull, James displayed his chivalrous nature to the world by presenting his prisoner with a gift and returning him to Henry VII. The King of Scots had no wish to give the impression that his domestic troubles were anything but a minor irritation.

While James was busy polishing his international image and broadening his practical experience, the political situation suddenly took a marked turn for the worse. Argyll was still struggling to make an impression on Dumbarton, when news came through that Lord Forbes had joined the rebellion, charging through Aberdeen and the surrounding countryside waving what he claimed was the bloody shirt of James III. He was soon joined by the Master of Huntly and the Earl Marischal, and gathered the tacit backing of others, including the three troublesome royal uncles, Atholl, Buchan and the Bishop of Moray. Earl Archibald 'Bell-the-Cat' Douglas, always reluctant to align himself with any faction, remained astutely on the sidelines.

Bothwell had already tried to pacify the rebels by broadening the council with the inclusion of Bishop Elphinstone and Constable Errol, and he now arranged for Crawford to be reinstated as Duke of Montrose. But this was not enough. His opponents came south, seized Doune and temporarily raised the siege of Dumbarton. The position remained perilous until Lord Drummond received a tip-off regarding the enemy's whereabouts and routed them in a night attack on 11-12 October near the source of the Forth. James, who had witnessed the victory, was impressed by what could be achieved by a swift attack. It was an unfortunate lesson in military daring.

Argyll's hefty guns finally brought Dumbarton to its knees in early December, so Ramsay's arrival the next year with a boatload of weapons from

Henry VII was too late to have any impact on the campaign. Besides, a new spirit of compromise was suffusing the tempers of James's feuding magnates. It was now eighteen months since the Sauchieburn affray had muddied the waters of the Scottish pond, and the murk was at last starting to settle.

The healing began in the parliament which assembled in February 1490. James personally cancelled all forfeitures made during his reign. He annulled the grants issued since his coronation and undertook to give away no further lands before his twenty-first birthday. Some of those who had enriched themselves from the coup of 1488 surrendered part of their gains, and even the traitorous arms-runner Sir John Ramsay found his way back to court.

The composition of the new privy council, including such disparate characters as Bothwell, Lennox and Montrose, illustrated well how old enemies were agreed to unite in service of the young king. Still under the close surveillance of his ministers, James resumed his judicial peregrinations, this time distributing more even-handed judgements. Despite the crucial part Lord Drummond had played in the 1489 campaign, for example, there was no remission for his son when he burned to death twenty of his family's Murray enemies in the church of Monzievaird.

For all his activity, James was not yet in close personal control of his kingdom. And he probably did not want to be, either. As a healthy, vigorous teenager the details of administration and accounts undoubtedly bored him rigid. Like England's Henry VIII, in his youth James was quite prepared to leave everyday matters to his council while he concentrated on the more glamorous and pleasurable aspects of his role. That is not to say that he was unaware of what was going on – he was too intelligent for that – but he was content not to be involved too closely. Unfortunately, this approach worked only when the king was backed by a sophisticated central administration and a civil servant as omnicompetent as Thomas Wolsey. Henry VIII was to have both. James had neither.

For a while the whines of discontent echoed on. The embassy tax was paid tardily and reluctantly, exacerbating the administration's financial difficulties. By early in 1492 only £2000 of the £24,000 left from the previous reign remained unspent. The continuing 'heavy murmour and voice of the people' about the manner of James III's death caused parliament to offer a reward of 100 marks to anyone identifying his killer. Responsible men were raising a new complaint, warning that those close to the king were trying to 'degrade and destroy' his personality by 'dissolving it in pleasure'. James was turning into a fervent, almost obsessive gambler. His card sessions lasted for days at a time and involved huge stakes. The £36 which he lost on one occasion would make a sizeable dent in most modern household budgets – in the fifteenth century it was a small fortune. And it was not just with young court familiars (who probably could not afford to play with him for long) that the king idled away his hours, but with the highest in the land. Foremost among these aristocratic card sharpers and dice rollers was that forty-three-year-old

old political fox, Archibald Bell-the-Cat, 5th Earl of Angus.

The Red Douglas had needed all his slippery skills to survive to 1492 with his power intact. The previous year, with the English alliance about to expire, Bothwell had approached France with a view to renewing the Auld Alliance. Henry VII responded by employing leading Scottish magnates, Angus among them, to urge the English cause north of the border. Although Angus was not involved in the most treasonous dealings of all – an undiscovered but unsuccessful plot by Buchan and Sir Thomas Tod to kidnap James and smuggle him into England – his behaviour was suspicious enough for the royal army to besiege his sandstone fastness of Tantallon in October. Having lost heavily at cards as he waited in vain for a breach in the castle's gigantic curtain, James gave up the siege and forgave Angus on condition that he swapped some of his Border possessions for Bothwell lands in Ayrshire. Scotland renewed her English truce in November and four months later ratified the treaty with France. By the next year Angus was not only in favour but in the council as well, as chancellor.

What did James see in Angus that he was prepared to treat him so generously? A man of the world and an intelligent master of the Scottish political scene, the earl was obviously good company. Moreover, the countless hours he spent sitting opposite the king at the gaming table had given him an excellent opportunity to study the man closely, so that by 1492 there was not a single feature of the king's character he did not understand. It was this knowledge which enabled the earl to bind himself to the king with ties far stronger than any he was able to conjure up on his own.

Angus's trump card was his niece, Marion Boyd. James first met her late in the summer of 1492 when he was passing through Angus's estates around Kilmarnock. It is not beyond the bounds of possibility that Angus knew of his niece's undoubted attraction and carefully arranged the encounter, perhaps briefing Marion in her part beforehand. But even Bell-the-Cat must have been surprised at the intensity of the bond which formed between the couple. They fell passionately in love. Over the next two years James visited his mistress whenever he could and she bore him two children, Alexander in 1493 and Catherine the following year.

* * *

It took more than the sexual energies of Marion Boyd to slake James's thirst for adventure. During the prolonged civil disruption of 1488-91 north-west Scotland had lapsed once more into the sort of independent lawlessness which had so sorely tried James's predecessors. Conversant with the Gaelic tongue, James appreciated the culture of the Highlands better than any Scottish king for generations; but his approbation did not extend to the region's politics. So in 1493, now that the south was beginning to settle, he undertook the first of several expeditions to the Western Isles.

The principle problem facing James was that power in the Highlands had become so fragmented that he found it almost impossible to know which island chief to deal with. John MacDonald, nominal Lord of the Isles, was still alive, but his authority had gone and he was seen locally as little more than a feeble crown collaborator. James arranged for his lordship to revert to the crown and in 1494 the last Lord of the Isles was reduced to the status of a court pensioner. His flamboyant illegitimate son Angus Ogg had perished at the hands of his Irish harper in 1490, and Ogg's bastard son Donald Dubh was a prisoner in the Campbell castle at Inchconnell. That left Ogg's cousins, Donald Gorme of Sleat and Alexander of Lochalsh, as seemingly the only feasible contenders for leadership in the area. Both submitted to James at Dunstaffnage in August 1493 and were knighted.

The next year a new figure came into the frame, John MacIan of Ardnamurchan. He proved his use to the government first by slaying the unreliable Alexander of Lochalsh (who had already broken the bond made the previous year), then by capturing and handing over to the crown an even more disruptive figure, Sir John MacDonald of Islay. James had made two trips to the Isles in 1494 when he reinforced his Kintyre castles at Tarbert and Dunaverty. With unbelievable effrontery Sir John had broken into the latter and hung the corpse of its royal captain from the walls before James's fleet had even disappeared over the horizon.

The king was still far from bringing the Isles to heel, but his decisive action was indicative of a new mood in the government. A sweeping Act of Revocation in June 1493 had brought back to the crown all lands alienated since the reign of his grandfather. The next March, when the king was twenty-one, he was officially released from the keeping of the Earl of Bothwell. That left only one more fetter to shake off.

Shortly after his twenty-first birthday James ended his first great romance by arranging for Marion Boyd to marry John Mure of Rowallan, thereby undermining the privileged position of Archibald of Angus. The king's days of tutelage and unalloyed pleasure seeking were over. From this time forward James IV was his own man, undisputed master of his fate.

III

Employing the well-chosen words of diplomacy, the Spanish ambassador Pedro de Ayala declared the adult James to be 'as handsome in complexion and shape as a man can be'. In other words, the King of Scots had a good physique and an unusually clear skin, but was not particularly tall or handsome. Given his mother's po-faced appearance this is not surprising. He was of medium height, with auburn hair and a longer, squarer face than either his father or grandfather. Apart from his 'noble stature', his most notable physical features were large eyes beneath fine, arching Stewart brows, a distinguished-looking nose and the full, rounded mouth of a libertine. His bachelor's beard was removed the day after his marriage – presumably at his bride's request.

What James lacked in looks, he made up for in personality. No other Stewart has received quite so much adulation. In what appeared to be a fortunate and probably unique amalgam of his family's better characteristics, he combined the charm of Governor Albany, the intelligence of James I and the bravery of Steward Walter. Erasmus lauded the 'great strength of intellect' and 'vast knowledge' of the 'much loved' king. Certainly James was a perceptive judge of character; he had been well educated, too, principally by his mother and the respected humanist scholar, Secretary Archibald Whitelaw. His excellent ear and good memory gave him a flair for languages, although it is doubtful whether he really was, as has been claimed, fluent in Scots, English, Latin, French, German, Italian, Flemish, Spanish, Danish, as well as 'the languages of the savages who live in some parts'! His appreciation of music is better documented. Not only did James attract to his court vocalists and instrumentalists from every corner of Europe, but on all but his most ascetic journeys he insisted on a travelling accompaniment of Italian musicians.

Everyone who came across the man who behaved 'as though he were lord of the world' was struck by his generosity. There were tips for ferrymen who carried him across rivers, for entertainers who made him laugh and even for the urchins who released wild ducks for his hawks. On his ceaseless perambulations he never failed to leave handsome presents with his hosts. He pressed pensions to poets and plausible cranks, annuities on loyal familiars and earldoms on the mighty. There is even a record of fourteen shillings given to a workman injured in the reconstruction of Linlithgow.

James saw to it that his court reflected this image of the liberal, cosmopolitan king. His aunt Margaret Stewart, Lord Crichton's ex-lover, was restored to favour, and when her illegitimate daughter Margaret married the wealthy Edinburgh merchant William Todrik, James met the expenses of the ceremony by selling exemptions for customs duties. The new nobility, such as James Hamilton (Earl of Arran, 1503) and David Kennedy (Earl of Cassillis, 1509) mingled with the old, and all rubbed shoulders with Dunbar's colourful assortment of

> 'kirkmen, courtmen and craftismen fyne,
> Divinouris, rethoris and philosophouris,
> Astrologis, artistis and oratouris…
> Men of armes and valyeant knychtis…
> Musicianis, minstrelis and mirrie singaris,
> Pryntouris, payntouris and potingaris…'

To court flocked chivalrous knights from every corner of Christendom. Here they met African drummers, Italian songsters, Flemish metalworkers, French scientists, German lute players, Spanish dancers, and entertainers of one sort or another from cities as far apart as London and Constantinople. Unable to remember anything like it, the Scots swelled with such national pride that a foreign visitor wryly observed that 'on land they think themselves the most powerful kingdom that exists'.

This was just the sort of impression James wished to create. But knowing what we do of his insecure antecedents, his hatred of criticism and his knack of avoiding responsibility for unpopular acts done in his name, one cannot avoid the suspicion that his skilful playing of the part of the bountiful king disguised a deep inner need for adoration.

James's obsessive restlessness was probably another manifestation of emotional fragility. A king was certainly expected to travel widely about his kingdom, but James seemed to carry the principle to ridiculous extremes, dashing hither and thither, and scarcely ever spending more than a month in one place. Ayala oversimplified when he said that 'When not at war, he hunts in the mountains'. James did hunt – tirelessly – but he also toured Scotland on justice ayres, social visits and pilgrimages. He is reported to have ridden alone from Stirling to Elgin, via Perth, in a single day. His court became famous for its tournaments, in which the king participated as a 'wild knight'. When not in the saddle, he could usually be found dancing, philandering, playing football or golf, or attending to government business with the same energy that he brought to all his activities. Only in eating and drinking did James show moderation. He did indeed appear a phenomenal figure – all vigour, dash, bonhomie and liberality. Small wonder that awe-struck subjects declared that there were 'few like him in Scotland'.

However, we have to be careful before accepting at face value the hyperbole of James's contemporaries. He was in power for longer than any monarch since Robert Bruce, and he could not but have been compared favourably with his immediate predecessors. He was fortunate, too, in presiding over Scotland during a period of intellectual and literary burgeoning which has cast a golden cultural hue over his kingship. James was no Solomon, nor even a Bruce, and Ayala's subjective claim that he had 'few faults worth mentioning' needs careful qualification.

Behind the dashing facade lay a rather different James. This was the rash and uncertain man who felt it necessary to boast that he could treat his subjects 'exactly as he likes', the compulsive gambler who could lose £70 at a sitting, and the depressive weighed down with a burden of inner guilt. He 'could not be consoled' when his wife Margaret was seriously ill after the birth of his first son on 21 February 1507, and insisted on making a pilgrimage to Whithorn on foot to plead with the Almighty for Margaret's life. And it was this James – 'courageous, even more than a king should be' – who at the age of forty would rashly chose to lead the charge at Flodden Field in person.

Furthermore, throughout his adult life James 'was greatly given to carnal pleasure', another indication that perhaps his extroversion was tinged with a need to prove himself. His first love, Marion Boyd, was replaced as royal mistress in 1496 by Margaret Drummond, daughter of Lord Drummond, James's military mentor during the 1489 autumn campaign. The king is said to have cared more for Margaret than for any other lover, and at one time he even expressed a wish to marry her. Surprisingly, her period of favour lasted scarcely more than a year. In 1497 she was packed off back to the new Drummond castle near Crieff, where she and her sisters died in mysterious circumstances five years later. James paid for masses to be said for her soul and took care of their daughter Margaret, who eventually married Lord Gordon.

In 1498 James reminded Archibald Bell-the-Cat just how little he now needed the good will of the ageing political has-been. In a sexual coup which damaged the earl's pocket as well as his pride, James stole Archibald's mistress Janet Kennedy who had recently been given Archibald's barony of Bothwell. After the birth of a son James (the future Earl of Moray) in 1499, the king rewarded Janet with the lordship of Menteith and the castle at Darnaway. The latter was a particularly well-sited gift, for it lay athwart James's pilgrimage route to the shrine of St Duthac at Tain. Henceforward the king's annual treks north offered the double delight of both physical and spiritual consolation. His other romantic attachments are less well documented. They included Isabel Stewart, whose royal daughter Jean accompanied Mary Queen of Scots to France as a governess, and sufficient other casual liaisons – real or imaginary – for most ancient Scottish families (the author's included!) to claim descent somewhere along the line from James of the Iron Belt.

In the light of James's moral failings it is tempting to dismiss as misinformation Ayala's report that the king 'fears God and observes all the precepts of the Church'. But that is just as much an oversimplification as accepting without question James's confident public persona. There was without doubt a deeply religious side to the king's personality, although it was never neatly compartmentalised. His annual pilgrimage to Tain, for example, was the result of a genuine yearning in his soul, just as his stopping off to see Janet Kennedy on the way was the manifestation of an equally strong physical desire. Indeed, in their different ways both visits may have stemmed from the same inner loneliness.

The dichotomy crops up time and again in James's dealings with the church. He once went on pilgrimage to a celebrated hermit on the Isle of May – yet spent part of the visit shooting sea birds from an open boat. He supported the strictest regular sect of all, the Observant Friars – yet was happy to use his father's indult (papal licence) of 1487 to exploit the church quite ruthlessly, placing first his brother, the Duke of Ross, then his eleven-year-old illegitimate son in the archepiscopal see of St Andrews and diverting its revenues to the royal coffers. He made a point of hearing mass before undertaking any important business; he endowed collegiate churches; he observed Lent most strictly; he spoke often of wishing to visit Jerusalem and, towards the end of his reign, of leading a crusade against the Muslims. And in 1507 he was delighted to receive from Pope Julius II a gold-hilted sword and the title 'Protector and Defender of the Christian faith'. Yet all the time he was treating the church like a government department, drawing on its wealth and filling its higher offices with loyal servants. Although such contradictory behaviour was commonplace among the crowned heads of Europe at the time, it does not make James's intricate personality any easier to understand.

* * *

Like Russia's Peter the Great, whom in some ways he resembled quite closely, James IV showed a close interest in practical and scientific matters. He was fascinated by medicine, offering 14 shillings to those prepared to let him extract their teeth, twice as much to those willing to participate in the rather more dangerous experience of being bled by him, and endorsing Edinburgh's new College of Surgeons with a royal charter in 1506. With the help of foreign metalworkers he took up his grandfather's passion for artillery and turned Edinburgh Castle into one of the foremost gun foundries in Britain. When in 1507 the Edinburgh burgesses Walter Chapman and Andrew Millar established Scotland's first printing press, James welcomed their enterprise for the help it would give in disseminating 'books of our laws, acts of parliament, chronicles [and] mass books'. Understandably, lighter works proved far more popular with the reading public.

More amusing (to the onlookers at least) was the king's financial support for Doctor Damian, a Renaissance Heath Robinson character whose attempt to fly from the ramparts of Stirling Castle with a pair of home-made wings ended unceremoniously in a dungheap. Damian blamed his failure on the presence in his apparatus of hen feathers which, he explained, like the birds from which they came, naturally gravitated towards the earth. A less plausible story tells how James marooned two infants on Inchkeith with a dumb woman to see what language they would adopt. Always keen to embellish a good tale, Pitscottie believed they came to the mainland speaking Hebrew.

James would be known as the 'father of the Scottish navy' if the child had survived infancy. He loved ships, acquiring thirty-eight of them for his fleet and bequeathing two new dockyards to posterity. Realising better than any other Scottish monarch how important a strong navy was in defending his country's shipping and shores, and how useful it was as a means of overawing the Western Isles, he allowed naval expenditure to rise year by year to an astounding £8,000 per annum. His finest creations, the *Margaret* and the *Michael* were inspired by Scotland's failure in 1502 to mount an effective expedition to help his grandfather, King Hans of Denmark. The *Michael*, a

£30,000 vessel of perhaps 1,000 tons, 200 feet in length and carrying a crew of 300 and 1,000 soldiers, was the pride and joy of Scotland's royal admiral. Adorned with the whistle and chain of his office, he oversaw every detail of her construction. When the 'great ship' was ready in 1512 he even fired a gun at her to see if she was stout enough. Fortunately, 'the cannon injured her not'. For a few brief years Scotland ranked as a naval power in northern Europe and her leading sailors – Sir Andrew Wood and the three Barton brothers (Andrew Barton once presented James with a barrel-full of heads removed from Flemish pirates) – acquired a formidable reputation in the North Sea. But everything depended on the drive and ambition of the king. After James's death the *Michael* was sold to the French and allowed to rot, and the rest of his fleet soon perished through lack of attention.

Education was another of James's practical concerns. His support for parliament's 1496 'Education Act', which made it theoretically compulsory for the elder sons of barons and freeholders to be schooled from the age of nine, was granted not because of any idealistic belief in the virtues of learning but because he hoped that 'knowledge and understanding of the laws' would lead to an increase in 'justice... through all the realm'. Having been well educated himself, James saw that his own children received a similar advantage. He did not live long enough to supervise the education of his legitimate offspring; but he paid for the royal bastards Alexander and James to spend several years in Padua, Siena and Rome, where they encountered some of the finest minds of their day and absorbed the liberating spirit of the Italian Renaissance.

James was a prodigious builder on land as well as at sea. During his reign a number of royal castles were strengthened or reconstructed, and he furthered his household's domestic comfort by raising a secular tower beside the abbey at Holyrood and adding to Linlithgow palace. His finest work was at Stirling, where he was primarily responsible for the castle's impressive Forework and for setting out the formal courtyard known as the Upper Square. On the eastern side stands his Great Hall, a gigantic cavern of a building, heated by five huge fireplaces and covered with a hammer-beam roof of magnificent proportions. There endures no finer symbol of James's kingship. Awe-inspiring, impractical, out-of-date even before it was completed, the Hall's Italianate ornament and medieval form tell more than any portrait about the reckless showman who ordered its elevation.

IV

'Since the present king succeeded to the throne', wrote Ayala in 1497, the Scots 'do not dare quarrel with one another as much as they used to, especially since he came of age'. If the Spanish ambassador had known more about the sorry state of affairs preceding James's accession, he might have been rather more positive about the king's law-keeping abilities. It was his labours in this sphere above all others which led ordinary citizens to speak of James as their 'noble and gentle prince' who maintained the 'great favour of his people'.

Much of James's success in bringing lawbreakers to heel was due to his unstinting personal efforts on interminable ayres. The subjective judgements of his youth were soon forgotten as year after year he dispensed swift and fair, if somewhat ruthless sentences 'without respect to rich or poor'. As one might expect with James, he usually managed to mix business with pleasure. One of his best-known escapades occurred in 1504, shortly after an accord with England, when he cantered about Eskdale with Lord Dacre, hanging one day, hunting the next, and all the while surveying disputed border territory. When James could not be present in person – not even he had the ability to pursue every criminal in the land singlehanded – matters were left to the equally amateur efforts of local barons, sheriffs and justices. James oversaw one significant legal development: councillors and judges assembling to hear cases on a regular basis, marking the emergence of the Court of Session and Scotland's permanent judicature.

It was to the king's advantage to keep judicial matters under close personal control, for this allowed him to see what was happening (and not happening) and gave him a chance to raise extra cash. Profits of justice had always provided the Stewart kings with useful income and at one time or another they had all played the system for profit, particularly by selling remissions. James III's exploitation of the law in this manner had been a principal source of discontent. It is perhaps surprising, therefore, to find his son employing similar tactics, although rather less blatantly. He sold remissions for lesser crimes, avidly collected composition fines and arranged for trials to be delayed, sometimes for years, on payment of respites. It was a clear example of the governmental system in which, as Ayala observed, the king 'lends a willing ear to his councillors and decides nothing without asking them – but in great matters [and financial ones] he acts according to his own judgement'.

Once he had Scotland under control, James had little time for parliament which he rightly regarded as a potential obstacle to his authority. He preferred to govern unfettered, keeping in touch with the political nation through the less formal channels of court, council and personal contact. The estates met only thrice after 1496, each time to attend to specific issues, which in 1504 and 1506 meant Highland forfeitures.

After three further visits to the Western Isles in 1495, James seemed to be bringing the region to heel. Three years later, however, greed and impatience led him to undermine most of his earlier achievement so that when he died the Isles were still very much wayward outer planets in his otherwise ordered solar system.

The great Highland and Island revolt was sparked off by the Revocation, signed at Duchal Castle in March 1498 during James's final spate of visits to the north-west. The act required all the king's charters to be renewed and a fee paid for the privilege. Grumbles of resentment swelled into rumbles of revolt in 1501, when the eleven-year-old Donald Dubh (whom the government bluntly described as that 'bastard son to Angus of the Isles bastard') was somehow released from Argyll's custody and handed over to the MacLeods. The Islanders 'are almost gone wild' remarked one observer when he saw the 'great abuse of justice' which followed. Royal castles were attacked, the king's officers slain and rebel raiders swept down as far as the Clyde. An attempt to quieten the storm by parading the ancient John of the Isles round his former haunts was thwarted when the last of the great MacDonalds died in 1502.

James, who had always been reluctant to venture far into the hostile Hebridean maze in person, declined to visit the turbulent region. The job of restoring law and order fell first to the Earl of Argyll. When he proved unequal to the task the command passed to a man with first-hand experience of rebellion, Alexander Gordon, 3rd Earl of Huntly, who as Master of Huntly had been a prominent rebel himself in 1489. This time he stood at the right end of the royal cannon, and with the assistance of the new Earl of Arran and the ships of Sir Andrew Wood he patrolled about the Western Isles, battering Dubh's fortresses into submission one by one. The principal rebel, Torquil MacLeod, was never taken, but Dubh was seized and incarcerated at Stirling after the fall of Stornoway Castle in 1506.

The king took steps to see that the trouble did not recur. He established royal justices and sheriffs at Inverness-Dingwall and Tarbert-Campbeltown, on the fringes of the danger zone. Celtic law was banned and James made grants to the lowlander bishops of the Isles and Argyll to assist them in taming the 'wild people' of their diocese. Nevertheless, although the Islanders had been made to 'tremble with terror' by James's seaborne artillery, their watery province remained as distant as ever from the full force of James's authority. The Stewarts had finally broken the MacDonalds without filling the power vacuum their collapse had created. 'None of the former kings have succeeded in bringing the people into such subjection as the present king', crowed Ayala in 1497. One wonders whether he would have said the same ten years later.

Court, castles, palaces, ships, diplomacy, war – James IV's expenditure was colossal, perhaps rising to over £44,000 a year by the end of his reign. He never had enough to do all that he wanted – what king ever did? – and in the end his quest for quick profit was to prove his undoing. But before that his ability to raise vast sums of money without incurring his subjects' hostility was one of his greatest achievements.

By squeezing all he could from customs, justice (he went as far as demanding remissions for crimes committed in the previous reign), rents and other traditional sources, James received a substantial revenue which he augmented by exchanging traditional leaseholds for a system of feuing – not unlike the modern practice of selling off council houses. However, what really brought in money was a series of one-off devices and payments. Having taxed the country almost annually for the first ten years of his reign, after 1497 the king eased up in his general demands, finding it easier to raise 'spiritual taxes' (like the £9000 levied in 1512) from the second estate alone, or special levies such as the 1513 'tax on spears'. The revenues from the see of St Andrews were a welcome addition to his coffers, as were his moderate dowry from Henry VII (see below) and proceeds from the 1498 Revocation – he charged up to £1000 for charter renewal.

The perceptive Ayala noticed this hand-to-mouth existence. He commented that the King of Scots 'is not able to put money into strong boxes' and that on occasion he was even compelled to meet immediate needs by pawning or selling off some of his most valuable possessions. This was why James, always the gambler, was driven to risk tapping those most dangerous of all sources of finance: diplomacy and war.

V

The invasion of Italy by Charles VIII of France in 1492 began a new chapter in the story of European international relations. Henceforward the continent would be dominated for over a century by a struggle for hegemony between France and the Spanish-Imperial axis. Whether she liked it or not, given her traditional friendship with France and her long-standing animosity towards England, one of France's bitterest foes, Scotland was bound to be drawn into the conflict. James understood the rules of the new game very well and did his best to play it to his country's advantage. But he seriously overestimated the strength of his hand, and in the end he lost almost everything he had laid on the table.

James's ace was his bachelorhood. As early as 1492 Spain had offered the Scots a marriage treaty to wean them away from France, but when the prospective bride turned out to be merely an illegitimate daughter of King Ferdinand the proposal was scornfully rejected. The Spanish need not have worried, for the last thing the Sauchieburn regime wanted was to add to their difficulties by provoking external aggression, and the truce with England was extended first to April 1494, then to April 1501. Henry VII's unwillingness at this stage to offer James a more prestigious wife than the daughter of the Countess of Wiltshire ensured that the peace did not lead to a more substantial alliance.

James was in no hurry to marry. The presence of his healthy brothers ensured the security of the succession and he was finding native girls quite able to meet his physical and emotional needs. He knew that if he bided his time, and found a means to put pressure on Henry, he would one day secure a far more important bride than any offered so far.

As luck would have it, in 1495 there turned up on James's doorstep just the figure the king needed to persuade Henry to take the Scots more seriously. The man was Perkin Warbeck, a Flemish pretender to the English throne who, after one or two false starts, had eventually decided that he was

Richard of York, the younger of the two Princes in the Tower. James did not believe him for a moment, but since Warbeck and his motley crew of hangers-on were backed by the dowager Duchess of Burgundy and had other useful Continental connections, he decided after some debate to go along with the charade and see what he could get out of it.

The plan worked well. In return for moderate expenditure and providing the impostor with the hand of Lady Catherine Gordon (hardly a suitable bride, whatever her charms, for a king of England), James drew the spotlight of European attention and even managed to make a financial gain. Spain dispatched Ayala to find out more about this ambitious young Scot who was daring to thwart their schemes. Henry VII tried to woo the Duke of Ross from supporting his brother's designs with the gift of a crossbow, and then urged Ramsay and Buchan – still England's pensioners – to kidnap the Flemish charlatan and bring him to England. When the plot came to nothing, Henry talked for the first time of a possible marriage between the King of Scots and the English princess, Margaret. James had no reason to trust Henry at this stage; so, in return for an offer of Berwick and 50,000 marks, he prepared to help Warbeck invade England.

With Ayala tagging along beside him, in 1496 James made a wary yet profitable raid into the valley of the Til. He then returned to his hawking. The only members of the assault party who found the venture distressing were Warbeck, who attracted not one English subject, and the king's Spanish shadow, who had seven of his entourage killed or wounded. Ayala was amazed at the way James had led his forces: 'I saw him throw himself into the most dangerous situations..., so that sometimes I had to hang on to his clothes to pull him back... . He doesn't take the slightest care of himself'. History has furnished these remarks with an ominous authenticity.

The next year was more frustrating for all parties in the conflict. Henry's massive retaliatory invasion was diverted by a rebellion in the West Country, James's 'great raid' (Mons Meg and all) had to be aborted when his funds ran out, and a counter-raid by Thomas Howard, Earl of Surrey, was broken up by bad weather. Realising at last that he was being used by James merely as a ploy in his military and diplomatic manoeuvres with England, Warbeck boarded the aptly-named *Cuckoo* and sailed for Cork, Cornwall and eventual execution.

The Warbeck campaigns were popular in Scotland and did James's ego a power of good. Ignoring the crucial part that luck had played in his survival, he now believed himself a great soldier, boasting correctly that very few of his predecessors had twice challenged the English on the Border and returned unscathed. It has been remarked that a salutary defeat at this stage of the king's career might have saved him from disaster later on. But as far as his dynasty was concerned, the successes of 1496-7 were just what was needed, for they set up the most momentous marriage in Stewart history.

With Ayala's belated mediation, a seven-year Anglo-Scottish truce was agreed on 30 September 1497, followed the next year by negotiations to turn it into a long-lasting understanding sealed by a royal wedding. The details were settled by the end of 1501, and on 24 January 1502 the Treaty of London was signed, proclaiming perpetual peace between Scotland and England. Henry VII's fears of the possible consequences of a Scot ascending the English throne had been overcome, and a marriage between James IV and the twelve-year-old Margaret Tudor was arranged for the next year, when the girl would be of connubial age and the necessary papal dispensation obtained (the couple shared the same great-great-grandfather). Margaret was to receive a dower worth £12,000 a year and her husband a dowry of £30,000, payable in annual instalments by 1505. Nine months later James came to Glasgow Cathedral to swear to observe the treaties made in his name the previous January. It is said that with his usual desire to do everything at breakneck speed he signed the document before reading it. When he came to do so, he found that he had implicitly accepted Henry VII's far-fetched title of King of France. He immediately made a written declaration that he had not seen the word 'France' and demanded an amended copy of the original agreement. It was clear from the beginning that 'perpetual peace' meant different things to different people.

Margaret left England in June 1503 and arrived at Dalkeith in early August. Here she was visited daily by her husband-to-be, who showed off before her like a love-struck schoolboy, performing cowboy leaps into his horse's saddle from long range and forcing the wretched animal into a variety of spectacular tricks normally associated with a circus ring. Whatever else the princess might have thought of James, his peacock-like display left her in little doubt about his potential as a lover. The wedding was as lavish a ceremony as Scotland had ever seen. Crowds flocked into Edinburgh from far and wide, eagerly thronging the streets to catch a glimpse of the exquisitely dressed young English bride. The king, at the peak of his manhood, looked more noble than anyone could remember. Later there was dancing, singing, music and even a poem by William Dunbar, the 'Thistle and the Rose', to celebrate the occasion. The wine bill alone came to a formidable £2,000.

But the sour English embassy, heirs to centuries of contempt for the Scots, refused to be impressed by this strained extravagance of a second-rate court. Margaret was not happy either, and was soon writing to her father about how lonely she was in a cold land of uncouth unsophisticates. James, too, was clearly disappointed with his glum, unattractive wife. Before long he was speeding north to assuage his frustration in the shrine of St Duthac – and the bed of Janet Kennedy.

* * *

The peace of 1502 lasted better than many might have expected. Henry met his daughter's dowry payments on time and did what he could to control the sporadic friction which inevitably cropped up between the two mainland British kingdoms. James was similarly willing to see the accord last; besides, for much of the time he was too preoccupied with other matters, particularly the Highland rebellion, to cause his father-in-law trouble. Yet the success of the new policy was entirely dependent upon the good will of both parties, and when Henry was succeeded by his aggressive son Henry VIII in 1509 it was not long before Anglo-Scottish relations began to slip back into their old channels of mistrust and hostility.

Faced with excommunication if he refused, Henry VIII renewed the Perpetual Peace but was not inclined to smooth over minor difficulties the way his father had done. He would not hand over the Englishman responsible for the death of the Scottish warden of the Middle March, and he rejected the request for compensation when Sir Andrew Barton, whom he termed a mere pirate, was killed at sea in a fight with the Howards. He even alienated his sister, the Queen of Scotland, by holding on to the legacy of jewels left her by Henry VII.

There were other family tensions, too. Between 1509 and 1516, when Henry's wife Catherine gave birth to the Princess Mary, Queen Margaret of Scotland was heir presumptive to the English throne. In 1509 she and James had tactlessly reminded Henry of this by christening their second son Arthur, an obviously British (rather than Scots) name. The fact that Henry's elder brother had also been an Arthur made the gesture doubly insensitive. Margaret's political importance was highlighted by the death of her husband's brothers in 1503 and 1504, and by the death in infancy of all her six children, except Prince James, born in 1512.

From the moment he came to the throne, Henry VIII had talked of invading France. Virtually all his predecessors had done so and to the young king it was a mark of virility that he should maintain the tradition. Ferdinand of Spain was delighted to egg him on. Realising what a dilemma he would be in if Henry had his way, James floated the idea of an international crusade against the Turk, led by himself. He knew it did not have a chance of getting off the ground. Nevertheless, it was a useful way of drawing attention to himself as a statesman guided by principles higher than mere aggressive dynasticism.

By 1512 James had to make a decision – Perpetual Peace, the Auld Alliance or, perhaps, judicious neutrality? Henry showed no sign of offering the Scots anything in return for their neutrality, and even allowed his parliament to raise England's age-old claim to Scottish suzerainty. Louis XII, on the other hand, was promising everything if James would support him: weapons, cash, backing for James's crusade and, if needed, endorsement of his family's claim to the English succession. Furthermore, with the bulk of the English forces on the Continent, James reckoned he would have a good chance of making a substantial profit out of a quick, well-planned Border raid. After all, he had done it before and the embarrassment of excommunication which would follow his breaking the 1502 treaty could be sorted out by subsequent diplomacy.

James was no callow, impetuous youth. He was a monarch with years of experience under his iron belt, and he eyed the stakes long and hard before coming to a decision. In the end, compared with Henry's contemptuous reliance upon a piece of paper, the French offer proved too good to resist. In July 1512 James signed up with Louis. It was a risk, to be sure, but one that appeared eminently worth taking. James had only to wait for Henry to leave for France and then crash over the undefended border to make 1513 the most glorious year of his reign.

English ambassadors arriving at the Scottish court in 1513 with instructions to reach some sort of last minute accord found the minds of the Scots already made up. Henry sailed for France on 30 June, and Louis gave concrete form to his promises by agreeing to hire the Scottish fleet for £22,500 and, later, by sending James money, munitions and men. When Bishop Elphinstone called for Scottish restraint, he was shouted down for speaking 'stupidly', 'like an old man'. The air was thick with diplomatic insults, too: the King of England declared himself to be 'the very owner of Scotland' and the King of Scots said he was Henry's heir. The time for compromise had passed.

The largest Scottish army ever assembled was summoned to meet on 14 July . The cannon, drawn by 400 oxen, were trundled down the hill from Edinburgh Castle to meet them. Having dispatched his best gunners with the fleet to France by the northerly route, James paid a flying visit to Tain and left his capital for the south on 19 August. Undaunted by the failure of Lord Hume's premature 'Ill Raid', he forded the Tweed on 22 August and swiftly took the substantial English strongholds at Norham, Wark, Etal and Ford.

By this stage of the campaign James had achieved virtually all he had set out to do. He had fulfilled his bargain with Louis XII and seized considerable booty – some of his soldiers had already deserted with their loot. He had no plans to press on to Berwick or to face the approaching English army under the Earl of Surrey in open battle. Besides, he had paid his artillerymen only until 9 September.

The seventy-year-old Surrey might have been ridiculed by the Scots as 'an old crooked earl lying in a chariot', but what he lacked in physical strength he made up for in guile. He knew his proud adversary well and goaded him to remain in the field with taunts about the death of Barton a few years previously. James took up the challenge. Installing his army in a strong defensive position on three hills at a site near the River Til traditionally known as Flodden Field, he waited for Surrey to make the first move.

* * *

For all his skirmishing success and prowess in the tournament, James had never before fought a large-scale battle, and his lack of experience showed in three terrible errors of judgement. First, he failed to attack his enemy when they divided in order to cross the Til. The manoeuvre severed the Scots' route home and compelled them to turn to face the foe. While ideal for blasting down castle walls, James's 'marvellous large pieces of ordnance' were not easily repositioned on the uneven, slippery countryside.

Then James made his second, most serious mistake. After a brief artillery duel, in which the smaller English field pieces proved more accurate than their less wieldy Scottish counterparts, 'keeping no order among his men' he urged them to leave the security of their hillsides and charge the enemy. The calamitous order was given at about 4pm on the wet, blustery afternoon of 9 September.

Numerically the two sides were well matched, each having about 20,000 men. But the weather hampered the Scottish archers, leaving the outcome of the conflict in the hands of their companions armed with towering pikes and swords. Manipulated by well-trained soldiers fighting in close formation, the pike was unbeatable – no army in the world could penetrate such a porcupine of deadly bristles. Wielded by the undisciplined Scottish volunteers, however, the weapon was a liability. The rough ground compelled James's five scilltrons to break up before they reached the enemy and at close quarters the pikemen had no answer to the deadly chopping and thrusting of the English halberdiers.

The king led the Scottish charge in person, his third and fatal error. He battled to within a spear's length of Surrey. There, pierced by an arrow and with a gaping halberd wound in his side, James of the Iron Belt fell lifeless onto the damp English grass.

'O what a noble and triumphant courage was this', remarked the English chronicler Edward Hall, 'for a king to fight in a battle as a mean soldier'. James had played the hero to the last.

King James IV by an unknown artist.
Intelligent, energetic and creative,
'James of the Iron Belt' was undoubtedly the most heroic
of the motley band of Stewart kings.

No contemporary painting does justice to the magnetic attraction of Mary Queen of Scots. In this 1578 picture by an unknown artist she was certainly past her best.

Mary II – a portrait in the style of Wissing.
Earnest, dull and devout to the point of obsession,
in a cynical age Mary's transparent sincerity won her
a considerable following.

Thomas Hawker's candid portrait of Charles II,
one of the few later Stewarts who did not suffer from acute melancholia.

Edward Bower's portrait of Charles I.
The King's total lack of political instinct may have earned him the
posthumous title of martyr, but it brought a legion of misfortunes
upon his unhappy kingdoms.

James VI as a young man, attributed to Adrian Vanson.
The King's instinctive astuteness more than compensated
for his lack of charisma.

The Young Pretender in old age (1785), by Hamilton.
Crushed by drink and depression,
at the time of this portrait he had only another three years to live.

The last of the Stewarts:
Cardinal Henry Benedict Stewart,
'Henry IX' in the eyes of God but not of men.

CHAPTER 14

'La Douceur et la Force'

I

By 1513 the Stewart monarchy seemed trapped in a frustrating game of political Snakes and Ladders. Time and again it had progressed painstakingly over the squares of Scottish politics until it landed on the long snake of premature death, slid swiftly back to minority and had to begin its climb all over again. Of all these regressions, Flodden was undoubtedly the most depressing.

On that blustery September day the Scots had lost not only their 'mightily lamented' king, but the Archbishop of St Andrews, nine earls, fourteen lords of parliament, a bishop, two abbots, numerous chiefs and lairds, and thousands of ordinary countrymen. The significance of the disaster did not sink in immediately, and at first the depleted administration called for a fresh effort to avenge the defeat. But when it came to exchanging aggressive posturing for action, remarkably few were prepared to come forward. James IV had worked wonders in building up his subjects' confidence, only to smash his own handiwork beyond repair in a final act of folly.

* * *

James V inherited his crown at the age of nineteen months. He was presented by his pregnant mother at a small-scale 'Mourning Coronation' in the Chapel Royal at Stirling on 21 September, then hurried back to his cradle while the faction-riven aristocracy sought to conduct his minority in their best interests. Over the next fifteen years James was treated more like a totem than a human being, by turns forgotten and flattered, begged and threatened, educated and abandoned, closeted and captured. It is hardly surprising that he turned out the most insecure and unpleasant Stewart of all.

The king might have enjoyed a more settled childhood had his mother been prepared to eschew politics in favour of her domestic responsibilities. But Margaret was a Tudor, with all that family's passion and selfish ambition. Four months after the birth of a posthumous son by James IV she married 'for pleasure' the dashing and attractive Archibald Douglas, 6th Earl of Angus, grandson of the 5th Earl (Bell-the-Cat) who had recently died. Having joined James IV's final campaign with some reluctance, the elderly Bell-the-Cat had withdrawn in tears before Flodden on account of his age, leaving his son and heir to fall beside the king. Margaret's remarriage officially deprived her of the role of tutoress to the infant James V, assigned to her in James IV's will; but as she had locked herself away in Stirling Castle with her son, for the time being there was not much that anyone could do about her truculence.

Two other relatives featured prominently in the early part of James's minority. One was James IV's knightly favourite James Hamilton, 1st Earl of Arran, the son of James III's sister Mary (who was still alive) by her marriage to Lord Hamilton. The second was John Duke of Albany, the dark-bearded and handsome French son of James III's troublesome brother Alexander. The new Albany had kept in touch with James IV, but spoke only French and had no great love for the country to whose throne he was now heir apparent. Nevertheless, he was able, honest and conscientious, and 'to the exceeding joy of all good men' he arrived in Scotland on 16 May 1515 to assume the governorship.

During the passage from France Albany had mugged up on Scottish affairs by reading chronicles. Knowing that he could hardly govern for James V if he never saw the lad, he sent messengers to Stirling asking Margaret, now carrying Angus's child, to hand the king over. Furious, the queen mother replied by lowering the portcullis in the emissaries' faces. When Albany turned up shortly afterwards with an army she sought to divide the besiegers by dressing her three-year-old in his crown and robes of state and parading him round the battlements. The device failed, and after personally handing over the keys of Stirling to Albany, James was escorted to his father's unfinished palace at Holyrood. Margaret did not see him for another two years. After various adventures, she fled to England where the week following her arrival she gave birth to Margaret Douglas, the mother of Lord Darnley. Angus was not with her. Already tired of his overbearing and increasingly portly wife, he had taken up with the daughter of the Laird of Traquair.

Meanwhile, all was not going smoothly for Governor Albany. In 1516 his Francophile policy provoked a rebellion by Arran and others, after which he tactfully reconciled himself to his opponents and adopted their more aggressive attitude towards France. In 1517 he returned to the country of his birth to see what he could wring from the new king, Francis I. The governor came up with an unratified renewal of the Auld Alliance at Rouen, and a rather unsatisfactory French suggestion that James V could one day marry whichever Valois princess was left after the Spanish had taken first pick. Although the proposal eventually bore fruit, at the time French princesses were the last thing on the mind of the five-year-old King of Scots, who was being shuffled around the countryside to deter kidnap attempts by agents of the self-styled 'protector' of Scotland, his uncle Henry VIII.

At England's request, Albany was detained in France for four years. In his absence James welcomed back his mother, but was distressed to find her still preoccupied with her love life rather than with her lonely son. She now wished to divorce Angus, or 'Anguisshe' as she called him, basing her demand on the extraordinary claim that James IV had still been alive when she had remarried. (It was widely rumoured that James had slipped off to Jerusalem after the Flodden disaster, to return one day to save his people. In fact, the English had found his naked body on the battlefield and taken it by way of Berwick to lie unburied – James had died excommunicate – in the Carthusian house at Sheen outside London.) When it came to divorce the Tudors never showed much affection for the truth, and Margaret pursued her case at the Curia with resourcefulness, even befriending Albany at one stage in the belief that he could incline the pope to take her seriously.

James's distress increased further when his mother's 'ungodly living' with a new lover, Henry Stewart, attracted widespread criticism; and his emotional insecurity was matched by renewed fears for his physical safety when Henry VIII and the Emperor Charles V allied in 1521. At this point Francis I allowed Albany to return to Scotland to rekindle Franco-Scottish friendship. The Treaty of Rouen was ratified and Princess Madeleine suggested as a suitable partner for James V. But the mood in Scotland had changed. When Albany marched south the Scots were either unwilling to cross into England (1522) or merely tagged along as spectators behind the governor's French reinforcements (1523). As far as James was concerned, however, the situation brought most welcome attention. His mother had given up her pragmatic friendship with Albany and was unusually solicitous in trying to wean her son away from the governor's influence, and uncle Henry sent his nephew a fine dagger and a gorgeous coat of cloth of gold to remind him how pleasant the English were and how unnecessary it was to fall out with them.

There was more to come. Following Albany's passage to France in May 1524, Margaret and Arran hit on a way of obviating his return by prematurely 'erecting' the fourteen-year-old James into the kingship. This was duly done in July. Henry VIII showed his approval by paying for the boy to have a personal bodyguard of 200 men-at-arms.

Albany's withdrawal allowed the return of Angus, whom the governor had banished. It was not long before the separated couple were at each other's throats again. Early in 1525 they met across Edinburgh – Margaret (and Arran) in the castle, Angus (and Lennox) in the town – and several spectators of the compelling Burton-Taylor-style row were killed when Margaret's cannon took ill-aimed pot-shots at her husband.

That summer an attempt was made to end the incessant feuding among the leading magnates by allowing each in turn to act as host to the king. The ludicrous scheme collapsed in November when at the end of his period of duty Angus refused to surrender his royal guest. James was, in effect, a prisoner of the Red Douglases.

Angus had James 'erected' again, took him on wide-ranging justices ayres and allowed his mother occasional visits, as long as there were no soldiers in her retinue. But for two and a half years the boy had no personal freedom. Angus sanctioned his every move and kept him under close observation day and night. To make the detention more palatable, and hoping to turn the king into a malleable adolescent fop, Angus spoiled him terribly. He was loaded with every conceivable present: horses, guns, bows, robes, jewels – whatever James asked for was provided. And when he showed signs of tiring of these trinkets, Angus introduced him to the more intoxicating pleasures of the flesh. Thus James whiled away his teenage years with whores and hawkers, trapped in a net of cloying candyfloss.

Like the Livingstones during the minority of James II, Angus overplayed his hand. By 1528 he was chancellor and the only earl regularly attending the council. His avaricious followers had swarmed into almost every lucrative post available, from castle keeperships to master of the royal wine cellar. And while James obviously enjoyed some details of his captivity, he grew to hate his captor. The alienated nobility stood aside, waiting for chance to strike. In 1526 two attempts to free James by force both failed. During the second any doubts the king might have had about the true nature of his position were dispelled when, at a crucial point in the fray, Angus's brother George laid a hand on James's shoulder with the grim words

'Bide where you are sir; for if they get hold of you, we will seize hold of you, be it by one of your arms… and pull you in pieces rather than part with you.'

But part James eventually did, fleeing in disguise from Edinburgh in May 1528. At Stirling he met up with his mother, now divorced from Angus and married to Henry Stewart. After creating his new father-in-law Lord Methven (or 'Muffin' as Margaret was soon calling him), in July James re-entered Edinburgh at the head of a huge host. Summoned for treason, Angus barricaded himself in Tantallon until it was agreed that if he gave up all his castles he could pass unmolested into England, which he wisely did. James V was free at last.

II

The precocious seventeen-year-old king, whose personal rule began as soon as he had driven his hated step-father from the capital, was a difficult, contradictory youth whose looks mirrored his complex personality. Of middle height and dignified bearing, he was not quite handsome. Traditional Stewart features – fine brows, thick auburn hair and an aquiline nose – were set against the pale complexion and tight mouth inherited from his unlovely Tudor mother, and his straggly beard was carefully clipped to disguise an irresolute chin. But it was the eyes which gave him away. Cold blue-grey and slightly hooded, they flickered and darted like a snake's, watchful, mistrusting. Pierre de Rousard saw James in 1537 when the king was twenty-four and politely summed up his paradoxical appearance in the following couplet:

> 'La douceur at la force illustroient son visage
> Si que Venus et Mars en avoient fait partage.'

As a baby James's ill-health had caused his mother and father great anxiety, obliging them to employ a string of wet nurses to provide milks to match his fluctuating needs. Although he toughened later, he lacked his parents' extraordinary physical robustness, and there are signs that he began to weaken shortly after his twenty-fifth birthday. Moralising contemporaries believed this debilitation stemmed from the sexual excesses into which Angus had initiated him. Gifted with the Stewarts' undoubted physical magnetism, James fathered seven known illegitimate children, three before the age of twenty. Later, by confessing his 'lapse' and playing up his 'paternal feelings', James successfully petitioned Clement VIII

> 'to dispense with the defect of birth, so that the boys may be promoted
> to holy orders with some relaxation as to age'.

Four royal bastards were found benefices in the church, while James Stewart, a son by his favourite mistress Margaret Erskine, was created Earl of Moray and played a major part in the politics of the next two reigns.

Since Angus's syllabus for his stepson's education had concentrated almost exclusively on the sensual ('the exercise of baser passions'), James's academic development had been cut short in 1525. Before then he had been given a sound grounding by a number of tutors. These included David Lindsay, the kindly master usher at Stirling who had playfully carried the young king around on his shoulders and imbued him with a life-long appreciation of music, and Gavin Dunbar, whom James made his chancellor in 1528. The king was undoubtedly quick-witted, but his lack of formal education put him at a disadvantage on the international stage, where most of his royal contemporaries – Francis I and Henry VIII in particular – displayed an ostentatious grasp of Renaissance arts and learning. James spoke halting French, and his need for an interpreter to converse with an Italian bishop suggests that his spoken Latin and Italian were not up to much either.

With the exception of his father, few of James V's ancestors on either side were notably pleasant, and what breeding had begun an unsatisfactory upbringing had completed. The result was a deceptively inaccessible man. Shrewd, secretive and highly strung – at times almost hysterical – he manifested his deep-seated insecurity not in exhibitionism or drinking, but in an intense vindictiveness and in a tawdry need to prove himself with endless, obsessive fornication.

* * *

James set about tidying up the mess of his minority with a devastatingly successful combination of ruthlessness and skill. First, he had to find some money, for his revenue was down to about half that enjoyed by his father fifteen years previously. Inflation and the falling exchange rate of the Scottish pound (now worth $\frac{1}{4}$ of £1 English) compounded the problem. It was not just the royal household which was feeling the pinch; in 1527 a baker was still awaiting payment for bread he had supplied the court in 1517!

The fundraising devices James employed were as varied as they were effective. By tightening control over the royal estates he increased their income to some £15,000 a year. The profits of justice, customs and feudal rights were exploited to the full, and in giving his natural children such lucrative benefices as Melrose Abbey and Coldingham Priory he was able to divert substantial church wealth into his coffers. By 1540 his ordinary annual revenue alone had risen to about £46,000. Incidental receipts brought in even more. When he ran short of cash he bullied wealthy nobles into making one-off payments, euphemistically termed 'benevolences'. In 1530 the Earl of Huntly lost 2,000 marks in this manner. The customary Act of Revocation, issued with supreme confidence from distant Rouen in 1537, brought in the usual fat crop of compositions. Lord Gray's cost him 10,000 marks. Taxation of the secular estates was rare, although James was granted £20,000 in 1535 to woo his French bride. As far as the king was concerned it was a good investment, for his two marriages brought substantial dowries as well as plentiful rich gifts. James even managed to get Francis I to meet the expenses of his 1536-7 French expedition, thereby releasing the parliamentary grant for other purposes.

The parsimonious king's greatest financial coup came in 1531. Anxious to keep James within the Roman Catholic fold, Clement VII demanded that the Scottish church make a massive payment to fund a college of justice and strengthen the state generally. Faced with howls of ecclesiastical protest, James commuted the levy to £72,000, to be paid over four years, and a further £1,400 a year for the judges' salaries. Intended matching funds for the salaries from his own pocket never materialised. When the college finally received parliamentary sanction five years after the funds for its foundation had been collected, it turned out to be merely a poorly endowed version of the court of session, staffed by almost exactly the same personnel.

James spent like a northern Croesus, his household alone soaking up about £10,000 a year. There were extravagant card games and lavish apparel, rich new crowns for the king and queen, and pensions for scholars such as Hector Boece, whose imaginative *History of Scotland* the king had translated into Scots by John Bellenden. The finest hunting hounds were imported from England and tended by eight keepers and a 'master dogger'. When David Beaton went on his frequent diplomatic missions to France he invariably carried a royal shopping list of expensive luxury items such as French harness. The ageing queen mother demanded huge sums to be kept in the manner to which she was accustomed. James's grand tours to various parts of the kingdom, particularly his great expedition of 1540 round the north and west, were also very costly.

The only item of expenditure which left a lasting impression was James's building programme, amounting to almost £5,000 a year. He added a Continental-style gatehouse at Falkland and employed French masons on the new palace block at Stirling Castle, whose facades were one of the earliest attempts at classical architecture in Britain. Linlithgow, where the arms of Scotland, France and the Emperor were emblazoned together on the gate, was by all accounts even more impressive – Mary of Guise said that she had not seen its like outside the chateaux of the Loire.

The king did not part with all his income. He accumulated a treasure of some 300,000 livres in

'gold and silver, all kind of rich substance, whereof he left great store and quantity in all his palaces at his departing'.

By 1539 such avarice led an English agent to report ominously: 'This king inclineth daily more and more to covetousness'.

* * *

Like his father, James V combined a scandalous private life with a sincere public faith. He shared James IV's appreciation of the strict Observant Friars, went on pilgrimage to Our Lady of Loretto near Mussleburgh, was assiduous in his personal devotions (with good cause), and shared many of his contemporaries' liking for religious relics and special holy men, even when he knew them to be charlatans. But by the third decade of the sixteenth century mere surface compliance with the customs and rituals of the Roman Catholic Church was not enough. The rapid spread of Protestantism over northern Europe during the 1520s required every ruler to make up his mind on the question of reform. The English government first used the appearance of Lutheranism to put pressure on the pope to accede to Henry VIII's request for a divorce; when this failed, Henry was persuaded to adopt those aspects of the new movement which benefited his monarchy and treasury, taking over control of the church and seizing much of its wealth. James was tempted to follow suit, even if only for financial reasons: the church's revenue is estimated to have been at least £250,000 per annum. But his internal authority never matched that of his uncle and, as we saw in the case of the court of justice, he decided to turn the church's weakness to his pecuniary advantage rather than abandon the institution altogether.

What James described as 'the foul Lutheran sect' was established in eastern Scotland before he began to rule in person, although he did not take positive steps against it until 1533-4. Even then persecution was spasmodic rather than concerted, with political and religious motives often overlapping. In 1541, for example, a stage-managed heresy trial was used to find the Anglophilic Sir John Borthwick guilty in his absence. The king was reputed to have kept a blacklist of over 300 nobles against whom he could bring heresy charges if and when policy demanded.

James knew of the clergy's manifold faults and weaknesses. In 1530 he admitted to the pope that 'the ecclesiastics are out of hand', and later he wrote of their 'dishonesty and misrule… in wit, knowledge and manners'. Parliament's belated attempt to strengthen the ecclesiastical hierarchy in 1541 received his approval. But generally he chose to exploit the church by emphasising its dependence upon royal protection rather than pressing for reforms which might have reduced his income. The pope agreed to extend James III's indult, giving the King of Scots almost total control over church patronage. James delivered the clergy one of his most blatant and public reminders of their dependence on him after a Twelfth Night performance of Sir David Lindsay's anticlerical 'Satire of the Three Estates' in Linlithgow Palace. The familiar's piece so impressed the audience that when it was over the king turned to the bishops present and warned them that he would feed them to Henry VIII if they did not mend their ways. They did not reform, of course, and James had no real wish for them to do so; but the threat had made it quite plain who stood between them and possible penury. When asked why he did not follow his uncle's example and dissolve the Scottish monasteries, James confidently replied, 'What need I to take them to increase my livelihood, when I may have anything that I… require of them?' It was the ultimate short-term vindication of his Machiavellian approach to ecclesiastical affairs.

Secular magnates fared little better than the clergy. After 1532 no earl sat in the royal council, and during his entire reign the king did not create a single hereditary lord of parliament. He turned instead to well educated men of more lowly birth, such as lawyers and clerics. Since the king had little to fear from creations who owed their advancement to him alone, he loaded them with responsibilities and favours. By 1536 a contemporary was describing the clerical diplomat David Beaton as 'the abbot whom one might call the king himself', although Beaton would have been the first to deny any such pretension.

The families traditionally accustomed to serving the king, who had been so skilfully wooed by James IV, now found themselves out in the cold, particularly if they showed friendship towards the Red Douglases or questioned the government's anti-English, pro-papal policies. Border lords were humiliated by the handful: Buccleuch, Maxwell, Hume, Johnstone, Scott and Bothwell were all warded or imprisoned at one time or another. Argyll was also locked up, Crawford lost much of his inheritance and his son, 'the wicked master', was compelled to renounce his right to succeed. Harsher, almost sadistic treatment was reserved for Angus's family and their close sympathisers. James persecuted Comptroller Colville and Lord Advocate Otterburn simply because they communicated with his ex-father-in-law. In 1537 he caused public outrage by burning alive the beautiful Lady Glamis, Angus's sister, for supposedly conspiring to poison him. Five days later the unfortunate Master of Forbes who happened to have married another of Angus's sisters was hung, drawn and beheaded on the accusation of plotting to shoot the king. The barbaric method of his execution was hitherto unknown in Scotland.

Cupidity as well as vindictiveness inspired James's enmity towards the nobility. When the Earl of Morton failed to produce a male heir, James ordered him on pain of death to hand over all his lands to Douglas of Lochleven, who then passed them on to the king. Sir James Hamilton of Finnart, a natural son of the 1st Earl of Arran, was dealt with even more peremptorily. A highly favoured master of works, Sir James had accumulated a considerable fortune through royal service when, in August 1540, he was suddenly arrested and executed on the twin charges of corresponding with Angus and scheming to murder the king. Neither charge was substantiated and men whispered that he had been removed so that James could get his hands on his servant's gold. Many Stewart kings had been hard masters, but none had approached the sheer punitive malevolence of James V. As one Englishman observed: 'So sore a dread king and so ill-beloved of his subjects was never in that land'.

There was, however, another side to the king's unpredictable strictness. It did at least serve to quell the debilitating lawlessness which had re-emerged during his minority. George Buchan remembered that James was not above remaining in the saddle 'night and day, in the coldest winter, [to] catch... robbers... unawares', and 'with a small party he would march against the fiercest thieves... and... force them to surrender'. As a result of such efforts the defenceless were said to dwell 'quietly and in rest, out of all oppression and molestation of the nobility and rich persons'. There is also evidence that James worked hard to protect his subjects' interests overseas. His correspondence is full of letters such as that written in 1530 to the Dutch government demanding justice and compensation following

'... a grievous complaint from wives of certain fishermen, who, for no other reason than that they were Scots, were run down and drowned while fishing in the Orkney seas by certain Hollanders in a slightly larger vessel.'

In due course James acquired a reputation as a poor man's king, 'easy of access, even to the poorest'. He encouraged this by wandering about disguised as the 'Goodman of Ballinbreich' to catch the latest gossip and get to know better his more lowly subjects. Suggestive of a deep insecurity, the rather demeaning pastime also appealed to the deceptive side of his nature and allowed him the thrill of seducing country girls incognito. Apart from the usual parliamentary legislation to uphold the peace and some efforts to improve the courts, his government's only specific measure to help the disadvantaged was a revival of the advocate for the poor. Otherwise ordinary citizens relied, with some confidence, on James's vicious reputation to protect them from lawbreakers.

The campaign to 'staunch all theft and rieving within this realm' began in 1528 when James turned his attention to the Borders. Here there was 'no justice' and raiders had recently wrecked fifty-two parish churches. Matching force with force, James sent in Highlanders to hunt down all the vandals and freebooters they could lay their hands on. With grim humour, the king wrote to Francis I of France that 'some find it a little difficult to accustom their necks to the yoke'. As well as many smaller fry, the first sweep brought in Scott of Tushielaw and Cockburn of Henderland, two well-known plunderers. They were followed by the notorious Armstrongs of Liddisdale, a family whose criminal exploits were every bit as spectacular as those of R. D. Blackmore's Doones.

Like their fictional Exmoor counterparts, the Armstrongs too have been immortalised in literature. Although we cannot be sure whether the subject of the famous ballad 'Johnnie Armstrong' was the John peremptorily executed in 1529 or the 'Black Jock' rounded up by the government in 1530, it mattered little as far as James's reputation was concerned. He rejected an offer of help from one of the family with a terse 'What wants this knave that a king should have?' and had Simon Armstrong condemned to death by quartering. Later, the ballad maker had James dismiss Johnnie's pleas for clemency with the words:

> 'Away, away thou traitor straing,
> Out of my sight soon mayest thou be.
> I granted never a traitor's life,
> And now I'll not begin with thee.'

The riever's reported rejoinder bitingly summed up local reaction to the harsh and insensitive drive for obedience: 'It is folly to seek grace at a graceless face.' The king might have brought peace to the Borders, but his uncompromising methods alienated local society. As early as 1531 Bothwell had told the Earl of Northumberland that he could put Henry VIII on the Scottish throne with little trouble, and when in 1542 James demanded military support from the men of his southern frontier he found them understandably loth to obey.

James used similar tactics to overawe the Highlands. Mistrusting the Argylls, the traditional royal lieutenants in the area, he relied instead on Alexander MacDonald of Islay, his half-brother the Earl of Moray, and the 4th Earl of Huntly, James's companion during Angus's supremacy. In 1528 the king granted 'letters of fire and sword' to Moray, calling on him to exterminate all Chattans except women, children and priests, who were to be deported. Fortunately, as far as we can tell the ghastly execution was not carried out. An unsuccessful rebellion by Donald Gorm of Sleat in 1539 led the next year to James's circumnavigation of the north and west in twelve heavily-gunned ships. The chiefs were completely overawed by this show of force and allowed their sons to be taken away for their education. The Highlanders knew that if there was any future trouble in the region there would not be much chance of the lads ever returning.

The strongest vindication of James's policy came in 1536, when he crossed to France secure in the knowledge that he was leaving a submissive kingdom in which 'every man that hath any substance fear[s] to have a quarrel.' But such passive loyalty was never enough. Eight years later James discovered that he had his people's obedience, but not their love.

III

James's skills were ideally suited to the duplicitous world of international diplomacy and for most of his reign he exploited Scotland's fortunate position to great advantage. He became so adept at riding the surf of European politics, however, that in the end he believed he controlled the waves themselves, and so came tumbling down.

All James's instincts told him that he would be better off sticking with the Auld Alliance than trying to revive his grandfather's pro-English stance. Henry VIII's troubles with Rome left him decidedly exposed, especially as the man he might normally have looked to for support against France, the Habsburg Charles V (King of Spain and Holy Roman Emperor), was pledged to root out all forms of European heresy. Henry had also earned James's undying hatred by harbouring Angus and his friends.

But there were significant factors complicating the situation. Margaret, the queen mother, remained more or less true to the country of her birth and constantly used her influence to advance her brother's cause. There was also the religious issue. A growing number of Scots, particularly in the south and east, approved of Henry VIII's attacks on the church, leading them discretely to question James's alignment with the forces of Catholic reaction. Finally, the idea of accord with England had lost its novelty, and the impact of Flodden had fostered a feeling in some circles that perhaps it would be better for Scotland to draw a curtain over centuries of animosity and learn to live at peace with the English. Aware of all this, James still decided that his best course was to take as much advantage as he could of England's weakness. For several years the policy served him well.

James began by signing an extended truce with Henry VIII, then seeing which European ruler was prepared to make him the best offer of a wife. He inclined towards France, still bound to Scotland by the Treaty of Rouen and where Albany remained a useful Scottish agent. But he was happy to try elsewhere to get a better deal. The initial running was made by Charles V, eager to employ James's weight against England. Although nothing came of negotiations for a Habsburg marriage, James persuaded Charles to renew a favourable commercial treaty with the Low Countries, send him much needed munitions and award him the coveted Order of the Golden Fleece (May 1532). James also believed that Charles offered to recognise him as heir presumptive to the English throne.

Albany had opened the French bidding in 1529 by suggesting that Catherine de Medici, the grandniece of Pope Clement VII, would make a good partner for James. The match never materialised, but Clement compensated James with the generous cash deal over the court of justice. In the meantime, brandishing his proposed imperial link and making tactful remarks about 'the age-old friendship' between Scotland and France, James went back to Francis I and asked for the hand of the young Princess Madeleine. Francis was genuinely solicitous of the welfare of his frail thirteen-year-old daughter, believing quite correctly that her constitution was totally unsuited to Scotland's damp and chilly climate. He was also unwilling to offend Henry VIII by giving away his best prize to a Scot. Consequently, he proposed that James make do with Mary of Vendôme and 100,000 crowns.

This brought the king of England into the bargaining. Henry's vulnerability now that his ecclesiastical revolution was nearing its climax enabled James to exploit the situation to the full. In 1534 he gratefully accepted Henry's offers of the Order of the Garter, lifelong peace and funding for a proposed three-way summit between England, France and Scotland. Henry even went as far as hinting that he might acknowledge James's claim to the English succession, as long as James recognised Henry's marriage to Anne Boleyn. This James was prepared to do, although since he refused to commit himself to a wedding with Princess Mary the succession question remained in abeyance. In fact James had no real interest in an English wife and at one stage he thought seriously of marrying his current mistress, Margaret Erskine. The scheme fell through only when Margaret failed to get papal dispensation for a divorce from her husband.

* * *

By 1536 the situation had altered again. Henry VIII's first two wives, Catherine of Aragon (Charles V's aunt) and Anne Boleyn were now dead, allowing Henry to come to terms with the emperor. This persuaded Francis I to turn to the Auld Alliance. Attracted by a flattering portrait of Mary of

Vendôme, in July James suddenly set sail for France to take a look at the lady's 'reputed personal qualities' for himself. Strong gales caused his first trip to be cancelled. Nothing daunted, James set out again on 1 September with half a dozen ships and an entourage of about 500. The voyage showed a furious Henry VIII, who had planned to meet James at York that autumn, just how cynically the King of Scots had been dealing with him over the last couple of years – less than twelve months previously James had made his uncle a present of a master falconer and six fine falcons as a token of his friendship. Henry's sister Margaret was even more upset. Having spent £20,000 in preparation for the York conference, which was to have been the culmination of years of underhand diplomacy, she was 'at the most displeasant point she could be'.

James, too, met with disappointment. He landed at Dieppe on 10 September and went disguised as John Tennant to the court of the Duke of Vendôme to sneak a glimpse of his prospective bride. What he saw made him demand 20,000 more livres of dowry, the Order of St Michael and trading privileges for Scotland. The unfortunate Mary was plain and hunchbacked. So, his first target 'happening not to please his fancy', James turned again to 'his dearest Madeleine', now sixteen. In explaining why James chose to marry the lean and tubercular princess, who had already been turned down by a number of suitors because there was 'little hope that… [she] would have children', some have claimed that he fell in love with her. But spontaneous affection was as alien to James's personality as open-handed generosity. It is more likely that he agreed to marry Madeleine, and accept her dowry, not in spite of her illness but because of it. In selecting a doomed wife he knew that before long he would be free to bargain for a second bride – and a second dowry.

To begin with Madeleine was equally hard-headed about the proposed deal. 'At least I shall be queen for so long as I live', she remarked, adding 'that is what I have always wished for'. And that is just about all she got. The couple were married in Notre Dame on New Year's Day 1537 and five months later, after a long delay at Reims occasioned by Madeleine's failing strength, they landed at Leith. Falling on her knees and kissing Scottish soil as she stepped ashore, the new queen strove hard to like her new home. But try as she may, the place and its people depressed her unutterably. She wrote home pitiably of her 'sweet France' and the 'ashes of patience' she was obliged to endure. As predicted, the unaccustomed weather wrecked havoc on her fragile constitution and seven weeks after her arrival, broken in spirit as well as health, she passed sadly away.

James went through extravagant formal expressions of grief; yet when David Beaton left for France to bear the news of Madeleine's death to Francis I he also carried his master's instructions to treat for another French bride. James had done well out of his first French connection. Shortly after his marriage the Pope had sent him a sword and cap, and Francis had met all the

Scots' expenses as well as providing James with the first instalment of a dowry of 100,000 gold crowns and sufficient gifts to warrant two extra boats for his return journey. The cynical king of Scots now determined to repeat the operation.

During his Continental excursion James had been impressed with Mary, the intelligent and extrovert daughter of Duke Claude of Guise-Morraine, and the news that she had been widowed in June 1537 had tied in nicely with reports of Madeleine's ebbing strength. Now that the queen was dead, there was no time to be lost. Mary of Guise was a fine figure of a woman, in every way the antithesis of poor Madeleine. She was tall, shapely and handsome, with blue eyes and shining red-gold hair. She was tough, too, and Beaton reported that, like a strong wine, she 'may endure travel well'. Above all, Mary had proved her fertility by bearing her first husband two sons. Henry VIII already had his beady eyes on her, giving Mary the opportunity to quip that her neck was a good deal more slender than her body.

Nevertheless, probably contrary to Mary's own preference, Francis I plumped for another Scottish match. After a proxy marriage in France on 18 May 1538, Mary left her surviving infant son Francis and crossed to Scotland to marry James at St Andrews on 19 June. She was a formidable acquisition for the Scottish court, not just in terms of her personality and accomplishments but because she brought another six-figure dowry. In personal terms the union was not a success, although the queen's brave public face disguised how much she missed France and her little Francis. James's disregard did not help. Never satisfied for long with a single lover, however voluptuous, he was soon slipping off to an alternative bed at Tantallon.

But when in 1540 and 1541 Mary gave birth to two sons, James and Arthur, her husband's triumph seemed complete. Over the course of a dozen years he had secured the succession, brought his kingdom to heel and 'wonderfully enriched' himself. By any standards it was a considerable achievement.

* * *

Nemesis first struck in April 1541, carrying away both the royal princes. She also destroyed James's position on the Continent by reopening the animosity between Francis I and Charles V, obliging them both to turn to Henry VIII for support. This reduced Scotland once more to the status of a third-rate offshore power whose fate was of little concern to the major European monarchs.

Understandably, Anglo-Scottish relations had deteriorated following James's snub to Henry in 1536, and when James got back from France in 1537 he had been incensed to find his mother trying to divorce her Muffin and reunite with the exiled Angus. James cancelled the divorce proceedings and managed to seize Margaret five miles short of the border as she was attempting to flee into England. As long as Henry VIII feared Scotland's use as a springboard for a Catholic invasion, he had to tread warily in support of his sister's idiosyncratic Anglophilia, and he worked hard to persuade James to follow his example and assume governorship of the Scottish church. But by the summer of 1541 Henry was no longer the religious pariah of Western Europe, and he was free to give vent to his true feelings towards his wily northern neighbour.

During the remaining six months of 1541 events slipped further from James's control. He was increasingly unwell, possibly as the result of falling from his horse some three years before. In October he was distressed not to reach his mother's bedside before she died of a stroke. When an English herald was killed on the border and James failed to keep a second appointment with Henry VIII, Anglo-Scottish relations deteriorated sharply. Having waited for James at York for twelve days before returning south, Henry's foul mood was not improved when, on arriving home, he was told of his fourth wife's infidelity. He muttered darkly that he had the same 'rod in store for him [James] as that with which he beat his father'.

By 1542 'there was not a certain peace, nor yet an open war'. In August an English raiding party which included Angus and his brother was successfully ambushed at Haddon Rig by the Earl of Huntly, although the two exiles managed to get away. In November Henry VIII resurrected England's overlordship claim and sent the Duke of Norfolk on another raid. When the English troops grew mutinous and retired, James was keen to seize the initiative and pursue them over the border. But his call to arms was widely ignored. Local people 'exclaimed marvellously' when they were forced to contribute to the army's upkeep. The disaffected nobility, particularly those with Protestant sympathies, were loth to march against the English. And around every hearth the memories of Flodden came swelling back with awful warning. Norfolk returned to England unharmed.

James was livid. He cursed the 'feint hearted' magnates, disbanded the army and raised another privately with the help of a handful of loyal supporters. His health was now giving serious cause for alarm: 'I have been very ill', he wrote, '... such as I never knew in my life'. At night he was haunted by terrifying dreams. In one the ghost of Sir James Hamilton assaulted him and cut off his arms.

Mistrusting more traditional councillors, James was now leaning heavily on the advice of personal favourites, men such as David Beaton (created a cardinal in 1538 and archbishop of St Andrews in 1539) and the familiar Oliver Sinclair, 'the most secret man living with the King of Scots'. It was hardly a trio to inspire the nation to fresh heights of military prowess. The new army of about 18,000 men left Edinburgh on 21 November and divided in two. Beaton and the Earl of Moray based themselves at Haddington, as if preparing to march down the east coast, while James, Sinclair and Lord Maxwell proceeded further west. At Lochmaben James was taken ill again, leaving Sinclair and Maxwell, quarrelling bitterly, to advance on a small English force near the River Esk.

Although outnumbering their foe by three to one, the ill-led and divided Scots who gathered on Solway Moss had no stomach for a fight. Many surrendered before they had struck a blow in anger, and Maxwell is reported to have done his best deliberately to disrupt the Scottish ranks. The result was a chaotic rout in which the favourite Sinclair was captured.

The effect on James was devastating. 'Sudden fear and astonishment came over him' and he despaired that 'he could never recover his honour again'. Illness and a series of personal and political disasters had reawoken the depression which always slumbered in the Stewart soul, making the king 'so abashed that he cannot perfectly determine what he should do'. He rode first to Peebles, then to Edinburgh, then on to Linlithgow, where he spent a week with his heavily pregnant queen. He finally came to rest at Falkland, took to his bed and refused to make arrangements for the forthcoming Christmas celebrations, saying that he would not live to enjoy them.

Some reports speak of a sudden change of heart, of tearful confessions of guilt and invitations to Angus to return home. But it was all too late. The last blow was the news that Sinclair was in English hands. 'Is Oliver tane?' James asked. On seeing the nodded reply, he sighed 'All is lost.'

The end came on 14 December. Muttering enigmatically (and incorrectly) 'It came with a lass; it will pass with a lass', the seventh Stewart king turned his face to the wall and died, aged 30. He was buried beside Queen Madeleine in the Abbey Church at Holyrood.

IV

The second lass of James V's parting prophesy was his daughter and heir Mary, born only a week before his death. As it turned out, the Stewart dynasty did not pass with Queen Mary, although she came closer than any of her predecessors to bringing the family down; and, paradoxically, it was Mary's volatile personality and turbulent reign which first brought the Stewarts worldwide celebrity. Fame, it seems, is a fickle judge. In singling out Mary for stardom it passed over the claims of many more worthy – not least Mary's splendid grandfather, James IV – and settled on the Stewart who cared least for Scotland. And history, with similar inappropriate partiality, remembers her as Mary Queen of Scots.

In 1542 Mary's disastrous career lay unrevealed. The chief concern at the time was whether the weakly baby queen would survive at all, much current opinion believing that she would not. Nevertheless, careful nursing brought her through those dangerous early months so that when the precious infant was unswaddled from her voluminous covers before Sir Ralph Sadler in March 1543, the English emissary was able to report back to his king that 'it is as goodly a child as I have seen of her age, and is likely to live'. Four months later the baby was moved to Stirling Castle, in whose royal chapel she was crowned Queen of Scotland in September. News of the unusual ceremony, at which the royal insignia were carried on the tiny queen's behalf by select members of the aristocracy, was reported all over Western Europe. Barely nine months old, Mary was already the focus of international attention.

* * *

As soon as the Scots learned that they were to be governed by a queen they began wondering whom she would marry. It was, of course, a question of paramount importance; and as the months slipped by and Mary survived the perils of sixteenth-century babyhood to grow into a bonny, high spirited girl of undoubted attraction, the task of finding her a suitable partner grew ever more pressing.

Mary's minority was quite as chaotic as those of her Stewart predecessors. Indeed, if anything it was more so because of her sex and the divisive issue of religion. In simplest terms, the political nation was split between those who favoured a Protestant, pro-English position, and those who wished to stick to the Auld Alliance and Roman Catholicism. Initially the former faction was led by a number of powerful 'English lords': a combination of sometime exiles, such as the Earls of Angus and Bothwell, and men like Lord Maxwell who had been captured at Solway Moss but released by Henry VIII to promote his cause in Scotland. Opposite them stood James V's shuttle diplomat Cardinal David Beaton, the queen mother, and others of a conservative, Catholic or anti-English persuasion. Somewhere between the two groups hovered the uninspiring 'Mr Toad' of Scottish politics, James Hamilton, 2nd Earl of Arran. Because he was heir presumptive (being the great-grandson of James II), Arran was created governor general of Scotland and tutor to the queen. He brought no distinction to either position. Mary of Guise, whose considerable political acumen was sadly under-employed during the 1540s, scorned him as simple and 'the most inconsistent man in the world; for whatever he determineth today, he changeth tomorrow.' Despairing of the bribery, backbiting and treachery which lay so sordid around him, in 1543 Sir George Douglas moaned that 'the world... [was] so full of falsehood, that he knew not whom he might trust.'

The man most Scots first learned to distrust was Henry VIII. Guided by the 'English lords', in 1543 Arran allowed the Bible to appear in the vernacular and accepted Henry's Treaty of Greenwich, which proclaimed a lifelong peace between England and Scotland cemented by the future marriage of Queen Mary with Prince Edward. But when Henry was slow to ratify the agreement and started suggesting that Mary should move to England at once, not at the age of ten as had been agreed originally, he confirmed Scottish nationalists' suspicions that he was really trying to take over Scotland entirely. Denouncing Greenwich, Beaton and his faction came back to power, leading a converted Arran with them. In December they renegotiated the Auld Alliance. Fears of Henry VIII's true intentions had led to Mary being moved to Stirling's breezy fastness from the relative insecurity of Linlithgow.

Henry's response was as terrible as it was typical. Throughout southern and eastern Scotland towns, villages, abbeys and churches were all indiscriminately 'put to fire and sword'. 'Burn Edinburgh town!' roared the king to his lieutenant, the Earl of Hertford, continuing

> 'Sack Leith… putting man, woman and child to the sword, without exception…. Spoil and turn upside down the Cardinal's town of St Andrews… sparing no creature alive within the same'.

Over two years Hertford conducted what became known euphemistically as the 'Rough Wooing' of Queen Mary – a series of devastatingly destructive raids designed to force Beaton's government to come to terms. In all the centuries of cross-border fighting Scotland had never experienced anything like it.

Surprisingly, Hertford's wooing did not unite the Scottish nation, either for or against the English, for by now religious divisions had cut too deep to be easily plastered over. In 1546, shortly after Beaton had burned the godly Protestant preacher George Wishart, the cardinal himself was killed by reformers. His mutilated body was hung over the castle wall at St Andrews then pickled in salt and preserved in a dungeon. Calling in vain for English assistance, the rebels held the castle against the government until compelled to surrender by French troops in July 1547.

The death of Henry VIII the previous January had brought Hertford, now Duke of Somerset, to power in England as lord protector for the young Edward VI. The news of the reformers' defeat at St Andrews provoked Somerset into launching the last ever full-scale raid into Scotland by an English army. The military outcome was sadly predictable: Arran's forces were smashed at Pinkie in September. While Mary was hurried to safety at the island priory of Inchmahone, Somerset established a base at Haddington and set about occupying as much of southern and eastern Scotland as he could. Among those inclined towards Protestantism the English troops were not unwelcome, leaving Arran no alternative but to turn to France once more for help.

The formal approach which Arran made to Henry II in January 1548 irretrievably altered the course of Mary's life. Already at war with England, France was only too pleased to help the Scots, as long as their queen was pledged to marry Dauphin Francis and shipped to France without delay. As his potential allies were holding his son as an unofficial hostage, Arran accepted the terms. Mary's future was sealed at the treaty signed in the

Franco-Scottish camp outside Haddington on 7 July 1548.

In February Mary had been transferred to Dumbarton, from where it would be easy to pick up a ship travelling down the west coast to France. Henry II sent his own galley to collect her. Accompanied by a miniature household of her own, young and old, legitimate and illegitimate, the six-year-old Mary Stewart went aboard on 29 July to await a favourable wind. Her mother bade her a tearful farewell. Still only thirty-three, Mary of Guise was heartbroken to lose her second child and desperately wished to travel with her to France, where she had spent her happiest days.

The breeze swung round on the night of 6-7 August. The next morning, its great oars dipping rhythmically into the rippling Clyde, the vessel bearing the infant Queen of Scots pulled for the open sea. Thirteen years Mary was away; when eventually she returned to Scotland it was as a complete stranger.

CHAPTER 15

Mother and Son

I

The royal galley carrying Mary Queen of Scots to France held a safe but stormy Atlantic course to the west of Ireland, then eased round to the east and put in at Roscoff on 13 August 1548. No cheering crowds greeted the child-queen, as they would do the Bonnie Prince five generations later, for the precise whereabouts of Mary's disembarkation had not been arranged in advance. But warm reception or not, the lively six-year-old seemed to take at once to the land she had heard her mother speak of so often and so fondly; and France took the little Scots queen to her heart with equal speed and fervour.

The years which followed became something of a dream sequence in Mary's life. King Henry II's 'most perfect child', she was first the pert, pretty waif whom the French believed had been rescued from barbaric Scotland for them to civilise – an exotic plant displayed for the wonderment of high society. Then she was the tall, elegant and vivacious teenager, whose sensual, hooded eyes and unmistakable Stewart sexual magnetism wrought havoc among all the men she met. Finally, in a ceremony of staggering magnificence she married Dauphin Francis on 24 April 1558. Fifteen months later, on the death of her greatest admirer, Henry II, she became queen consort of France. For ten years Mary had been the darling of the court. Flattered and spoiled to a degree that would have turned far wiser heads than hers, at sixteen she was still alarmingly immature and unrealistic.

By the courtly standards of the day, Mary's formal education was satisfactory. She was carefully instructed in such ladylike arts as music and dancing; she became fluent in several European languages; and her immensely astute and powerful uncle, Charles Cardinal of Lorraine, introduced her to the subtle skills of statecraft. The end product was a woman who would have made a charming and helpful partner to a king ruling in his own right – as it was intended she should be to Francis II. But it was a hopeless grounding for one destined to govern Scotland. The distressing minorities of successive Stewart kings, teeming with violence and intrigue, might not have taught five Jameses the finer points of diplomatic etiquette, but they were left with no illusions about the realities of power. For her part, Mary was given no insight into the complexities of Scotland's very personal political system, where the crown, for all its grand pronouncements, stood at the heart of a web of interdependent allegiances. Besides, she was raised to think of France as her homeland, and Scotland as a remote and unimportant province on the inclement north-western frontier of Europe. In 1551 a French visitor had described her homeland as mere 'desert'.

For eleven years the extent of Mary's involvement in Scottish politics was limited largely to agreeing an unconstitutionally premature Act of Revocation in 1555, sending her mother blank sheets with a large 'MARIE' inscribed at the bottom, and three weeks before her marriage irresponsibly signing an agreement which, in French eyes, virtually handed over Scottish sovereignty to the King of France. There is little purpose or justice in blaming Mary for what she did or did not do. But her French upbringing goes a long way to explaining what went wrong when she was finally called upon to be queen in more than just name.

* * *

As far as the French and the majority of Mary's subjects were concerned, the situation in Scotland improved steadily after the queen's departure. The English were driven out by 1550, when peace was made with Somerset's less aggressive replacement, the Duke of Northumberland. In 1549 Arran was tied firmly to the French cause with the flattering and enriching title of Duke of Chatelherault, and when Mary of Guise crossed to France the next year to see her daughter she was accompanied by a gaggle of Scots noblemen who were only too pleased to be 'bought... completely' by the French crown. After the Paris parliament had declared Mary to be at 'her perfect age' in 1554, Chatelherault was eased out of the governorship with golden handshakes and his position passed to the queen mother. By 1555, with the fervently Roman Catholic Mary Tudor on the English throne and her co-religionist Mary of Guise skilfully governing her daughter's kingdom with French aid, it seemed as if Guise guile was succeeding where centuries of English bludgeoning had failed.

In the later 1550s the Scots appeared to get themselves even deeper into French toils when their commissioners followed agreement to Mary's marriage to Dauphin Francis with an offer to him of the Scottish crown matrimonial in November 1558. But beneath the surface strong currents of resentment were gathering. The regent's high taxation demands – £60,000 for Mary's wedding, for example – were not popular. In 1557 Scottish soldiers refused to cross the Tweed to support a French campaign in northern England. A short while later the first Protestant bonds (or 'bands') were drawn up. When four of the eight commissioners negotiating Mary's marriage died in mysterious circumstances, it was plausibly rumoured that they had been done away with by the French because they had learned too much. Finally, in November 1558 the upsurge of Protestant and nationalist sentiment was given new heart by the accession of the anti-Catholic Elizabeth I to the throne of England.

In the new year events moved more swiftly. Before April 1559 Mary of Guise had worked hard to hold the Scottish nation together behind the French alliance. But the Franco-Spanish peace of that month freed Mary, like Henry II in France, to turn her attention to the problem of domestic heresy. The inspirational John Knox returned to Scotland on 2 May. Mary brought in more French troops, and by the autumn her administration was engaged in a spasmodic, low-key civil war with the English-backed Protestant Lords of the Congregation. The rebels occupied Edinburgh in October, accepted Elizabeth I's formal backing at the Treaty of Berwick in February 1560, and with the help of their allies bottled up the French in Leith.

At this point Mary of Guise, whose 'singular wit' and 'mind very propense to equity' had earned her broad respect from all parties, might yet have salvaged something for France from the Scottish maelstrom. But on 11 June 1560, 'worn out with sickness and grief', she died. She could shield her daughter no more. Mary Queen of Scots was now responsible for her own kingdom.

* * *

Most Stewart monarchs had shown a precocious desire to get their hands on the reins of government as soon as they possibly could. Not so the seventeen-year-old Mary. By remaining in France for fourteen months after her mother's death and failing to provide Scotland with a legal government during that period, she laid up considerable troubles for herself. The Protestants negotiated the Treaty of Edinburgh in July 1560, by which French and English troops were obliged to withdraw. They then proceeded to the Reformation Parliament, which abolished the authority of the papacy, outlawed the mass and annulled all ecclesiastical acts issued since the reign of James I. Although Mary refused to accept either the treaty or the revolutionary acts, her recalcitrance made no difference. Scottish government was going ahead without her.

As long as Mary was Queen of France she might have been excused for letting Scottish affairs take a subordinate place in her priorities. Three days before her eighteenth birthday, however, she suffered the second serious bereavement of the year when her anonymous little husband Francis II died at the age of sixteen. The king and queen had been close childhood playmates and their married relationship was probably more akin to that of brother and sister than husband and wife. Sullen and highly-strung, the immature Francis had doted like a lap dog on his lovely wife, while Mary soaked up his adulation and responded with similarly innocent affection. Although genuinely distressed at his death, she had lost a friend, not a true lover. Some sort of genital malformation (perhaps undescended testicles) had prevented Francis' 'parties generatives' from performing 'aucune action' than passing water. To all intents and purposes, therefore, Mary was still a sexual and political virgin. It was a dangerous condition for a passionate young woman with heavy responsibilities.

Francis' death left Mary at a loss to know what to do. She was no longer queen of France, and it was soon clear that she was not going to be allowed to get her old title back by marrying Francis' successor, Charles IX. She said she ought to be Queen of England, because the Roman church's refusal to recognise the marriage of Henry VIII to Anne Boleyn rendered Elizabeth illegitimate in Catholic eyes; but at this moment no conservative power was prepared to back her claim with force. Finally and indisputably, she was Queen of Scotland. But Scotland was just about the last place on earth she wished to visit.

The French grew restless. In vain Mary looked around for a Continental husband to rescue her from having to perform her duty. At last, having been refused a safe conduct from her cousin Elizabeth I, Mary set sail for Scotland on 14 August 1561. When the French Duke of Albany had reluctantly left home in 1515 to undertake a similar mission, during the voyage he had prepared for the task ahead by immersing himself in Scottish history. In stark contrast, as the French coastline disappeared into the mist, Mary stood morosely on deck muttering to herself over and over again: 'Adieu France, adieu France, adieu donc ma chere France... '. It was hardly an auspicious beginning to the greatest challenge of her life.

II

Leith was shrouded in thick fog when Mary came ashore on 19 August, a week earlier than expected. She was greeted warmly by a hastily assembled reception committee and a mob of gawping bystanders. Without doubt all but the most misogynous and Protestant Scots were delighted to see their queen again, for she had been away for thirteen years and not since 1542 had the country experienced the rule of an adult monarch. Besides, Mary made a most favourable early impression, as George Buchanan admitted

> 'the excellency of her mien, the delicacy of her beauty, the vigour of her blooming years, and the elegance of her wit, all joined in her recommendation'.

Today we would describe Mary as highly attractive rather than beautiful. Her most prominent feature was her height – about five feet ten inches, very tall for the time. Although embarrassing for an ordinary girl, the queen's ability physically to dominate virtually all women and most men was a useful asset in her armoury of regality. Moreover, far from being gangly or cumbersome, she carried herself with the easy fluency of a natural athlete schooled in courtly graces. As well as her height, she inherited her mother's much admired fair complexion, fine figure and red-gold hair. From the Stewarts she acquired a rather large nose, a fashionably small mouth and those heavy-lidded, sexy eyes which drove at least one frustrated young man into raving insanity.

Mary's physical attributes were such that, had she a personality to match, there was almost nothing she could not have achieved. But alas! her capti-vating shell concealed a character lacking in almost all the qualities required of a successful monarch.

The saving characteristics of the queen's immediate Stewart predecessors – their political intelligence and doughty single-mindedness – both passed her by. Instead she inherited the family's least valuable traits: a painful need for adulation, a tendency to bewail her lot and, above all, a pitiable predis-position towards melancholy. Highly strung and passionate, Mary alternated between bouts of vigorous exercise, which more than once drew her to exclaim that she wished she were a man, and long periods of nervous exhaus-tion, during which she was incapable of performing any duties. The condi-tion, which we would now diagnose as manic depression, had killed her father, and ran back at least to Robert III. It came upon her when she most needed to be on top of affairs, 'after any great unkindness or grief of mind', and was accompanied by tears, protestations that she wished she were dead and psychosomatic pains in her right side.

A tactful and iron-willed woman might have managed to extend her authority over Scotland, as Elizabeth I did over England. But not a spoilt, inexperienced depressive like Mary, raised in a culture which regarded her paltry kingdom as 'the arse of the world'. It was a situation almost bound to lead to disaster.

* * *

From a political point of view Mary's inheritance could have been worse. The nation rallied to her. Even if she was not up to the task of giving positive personal direction (which she was not), the council had plenty of experience of managing the day-to-day affairs on its own. And the naive queen had the sense to lean heavily on two moderate councillors of undoubted ability: Lord James Stewart, her half brother by Margaret Erskine, whom she created Earl of Moray in 1562, and William Maitland of Lethington, 'a young man of penetrating judgement'.

The religious position was more tricky. Benefiting from historical hind-sight, numerous commentators have suggested how Mary might have coped with her 'very ticklish' inheritance. Like her Catholic namesake, Queen

Mary of England, Mary Queen of Scots might have worked firmly and tactfully to reverse the creeping Protestantism of the previous thirty or so years;
or, more pragmatically, she might have accepted the inevitability of some
form of Protestant kirk and used her power and influence to ensure that it
remained as moderate and accessible to royal control as the Anglican church
taking root further south.

Unfortunately for Mary, she did neither. The result was a period of drift,
when the queen maintained her private Catholicism while her subjects
moved further and further from the faith of their ancestors. It was a curious,
unsatisfactory situation, in which uninterestedness masqueraded as tolerance. Mary confusingly assisted the new kirk by allowing it to collect one
third of the revenues enjoyed by the old. She attended mass when others
were being prosecuted for doing likewise. In 1562 her reliance upon
Protestant councillors provoked a revolt of the Catholic Gordons, which
resulted in the death by heart attack of the overweight George Gordon, Earl
of Huntly, and the execution of one of his sons. The following year she did
nothing but burst into hysterical weeping when verbally assaulted by the
mysogynous rantings of John Knox. Not surprisingly the great European
Catholic families – particularly the Habsburgs and Valois – looked askance at
what was going on and had serious reservations about whether Mary would
make a suitable bride for a prince of their own religion.

Mary's problem was not simply that she was out of her depth in the world
of administration and politics, though that was serious enough; it was also
that she just did not enjoy being in Scotland. And, unlike her mother, her
sense of duty was insufficiently developed for her to try to make the most of
her lot. She recovered her Scots tongue, but as yet she spoke no English and
thought only in French. She went on progresses round the country as much
for the exercise and adulation as out of any sense of obligation. Parliament
met from time to time, yet accomplished little of moment. The council, too,
gathered regularly; but while it sat in one part of Holyrood Palace, the pretty
young queen, indifferent to its deliberations, remained in another, amusing
herself with her Continental favourites.

The situation was ripe for scandal. When a lovestruck French poet was
found concealed in the queen's bedchamber not once, but twice, tongues
began to wag. Tales of a court 'immersed in vice' spread like the plague
around the palaces, inns and street corners of Europe. As far as we know, they
were all largely without foundation. But ultimately that was not important.
What did matter was that Mary had neither the dignity nor wisdom to scotch
them at source, and so her reputation suffered.

Mary's court was her refuge from the harsh Scottish climate and even
harsher strictures of puritanical Protestant sermons. When she could, the
lonely queen sheltered here with a select coterie of musicians and poets,
dressmakers and artists, lamentably trying to recreate the world she had left
behind. Among her friends and flatterers she was supreme, their mistress and

inspiration, the witty conversationalist, the singer and the lute player of grace and sensitivity. Sometimes languishing in secluded despair, sometimes the life and soul of the company, she dreamed of the day when someone would rescue her from her chilly northern exile.

Mary identified two possible escape routes: the throne of England and marriage. Both she pursued assiduously.

The first was perhaps the most attractive, although the least likely. Mary's cousin Elizabeth refused either to die, or to name Mary as her successor. That left only the remote possibility of an armed invasion of England on Mary's behalf by one or more Catholic powers. With France in religious turmoil and Philip II of Spain hoping that Elizabeth might return her kingdom to the Catholic fold of her own accord, Mary was given little encouragement from either quarter.

For several years a marriage outside Scotland seemed a more realistic possibility. Since the death of her impotent Francis, Mary's name had been linked to a galaxy of European bachelors, including the kings of France, Denmark and Sweden, and various members of the Habsburg dynasty. Sadly, the most promising of the latter, Prince Don Carlos, went insane in 1562. At about the same time a similar fate befell another suitor, the infatuated James Hamilton, Earl of Arran, son of the Duke of Chatelherault. To Mary's obvious distress, there was now no long line of ardent suitors hammering at her door in quest for her hand. Moreover, her ambiguous religious policies and the malicious stories circulating about her private life were making it increasingly unlikely that she would ever marry a crowned head and so find her way out of Scotland, at least by the wedding route.

In 1564 Elizabeth put forward one of her own admirers, Robert Dudley, Earl of Leicester. Negotiations for the unlikely match went cautiously ahead until the following spring, when suddenly and spectacularly they collapsed.

Mary had fallen in love.

The queen could not have chosen a less suitable target for her passion, either personally or politically. Henry Stewart, officially Master of Lennox but more generally known by his courtesy title Lord Darnley, was the son of the 4th Earl of Lennox and Margaret Douglas, the daughter of Margaret Tudor and her incompatible Angus. As Darnley was second only to Mary in succession to the English throne, Elizabeth's disquiet at his liaison with the Queen of Scots jeopardised the Anglo-Scottish accord built up by Moray and Lethington. At home Darnley's elevation was bound to cause disquiet among his fellow magnates.

This would have mattered little had Darnley been a man of some calibre. Instead, he proved if anything an even worse candidate for high office than the queen herself. What Mary saw in him was a tall, handsome and well-built young man who, when he deigned, could be charming and even amusing in a superficial way. He had benefited from a good education and had literary pretensions. But what more objective observers saw was either 'a pleasant twit' (Mary's uncle) or, more accurately, an arrogant and spoilt young fop with an unpleasantly vicious streak in him. Although it did not take Mary long to realise her terrible mistake, by then the damage had been done.

Darnley had been raised in England during his father's lengthy exile and first travelled to Scotland early in 1565. His initial meeting with the queen took place at Wemyss Castle, Fife, in February. Mary was much taken with 'the lustiest and best proportioned long man that she had seen', and like all men Darnley was irresistibly drawn by the queen's sexual magnetism. From the outset the relationship between the two was unmistakably physical.

At Stirling two months later Darnley fell ill with measles. Mary visited him, attending to his needs and remaining at his bedside until late at night. By the time her lover had recovered, Mary was hopelessly lost. She created him Earl of Ross in May and Duke of Albany on 20 July. Ignoring constitutional niceties, a week later she declared him to be King of Scotland. The couple were married the next day, 29 July, at about 5.30 am in the chapel royal. Such was their eagerness to live together, they had not even waited for the necessary papal dispensation.

* * *

Two months before Mary's disastrous marriage Thomas Randolph commented on 'the pitiful and lamentable estate of [the]… poor queen'. She was, he perceived

'so altered with affection towards the Lord Darnley, that she hath brought her honour in question, her estate in hazard, her country to be torn in pieces… '.

It was a piercingly acute observation.

Although he had acted as a Protestant in England, 'King Henry' (as he was now styled) was nominally a Catholic, and after her marriage the queen attempted to bring about a belated revival of the royal couple's faith. Coming after years of vacillation, the new policy provoked more suspicion and hostility than fervour, and helped to persuade those who had stood by Mary thus far that her marriage dangerously threatened the political and religious status quo. The result was a rebellion – the Chaseabout Raid – in the late summer of 1565 which ended with Moray and Chatelherault fleeing into exile. Dashing about southern Scotland on horseback with all the vigour of a true Stewart, the Raid brought out the very best in Mary.

From this time forwards events acquired a tragic momentum of their own. Increasingly disillusioned with her king, now revealing himself to be little but an irresponsible, immature and drunken lout, the pregnant queen turned for solace to her coterie of household familiars, prominent among whom was an ugly but talented Italian musician, David Riccio, recently appointed her

French secretary. Never able to resist testing her coquettish charms, Mary took to sitting up late with her bewitched servant. A new wave of malicious gossip began to circulate. More sinister, and ultimately less innocent, was the queen's growing political dependence upon the unpopular Protestant magnate James Hepburn, Earl of Bothwell.

The upshot of Mary's injudicious flirtations with her 'stranger Italian' was the wretched man's murder. The Protestant lords implicated in the Chaseabout Raid had not found it difficult to persuade Darnley of the sexual nature of his wife's relationship with Riccio, and on 9th March 1566 the secretary was dragged from his mistress' supper table in her private apartments at Holyrood and bloodily stabbed to death amid pitiful screams of 'Sauvez ma vie, madame!' The body lying in an adjacent corridor, mutilated with over fifty wounds and with Darnley's own dagger still protruding from it, was a grim symbol of Mary's four years of vapid government.

The queen learned nothing from the Riccio incident, except that her husband was probably even more vile than she had previously imagined. The murder did, however, inspire her to an uncustomary burst of political energy. By the summer she had dropped her Catholic crusading and reconciled herself with the Chaseabout Raiders. The birth of Prince James on 19 June brought considerable personal and national relief. But the replacement of Riccio by his brother Joseph and Mary's continued dependence upon Bothwell did not suggest that the new tranquillity would endure for long.

Indeed, it did not. Darnley was now a major personal and political embarrassment. Drunk by night, morose by day, he ostentatiously refused to attend James's christening on 17 December, thereby suggesting that he was not the boy's father. He attempted to undermine his wife's position further by complaining to the pope and Catholic crowned heads of her failure to restore the old religion. As early as November 1566 Mary was discussing how she might be rid of her infuriating husband.

The queen was increasingly brought low with physical and, presumably, psychosomatic illnesses closely resembling those which had afflicted her father and other Stewart ancestors. In her depression she wept frequently and on occasion wished she were dead, or back in France. Never acute, her judgement deteriorated still further. The situation was complicated by the fact that she was again pregnant, presumably by Darnley as the result of some fleeting reconciliation, but possibly by the aggressively masculine Bothwell.

Smitten with a debilitating attack of syphilis, early in 1566 the 'king' was moved to Kirk O' Fields House, Edinburgh, to recuperate. Here Bothwell arranged for his removal from the political scene with an assassination as spectacular as it was mysterious. At about 2 am on 10 February Kirk O' Fields House was blown sky high. Darnley's unmarked body was found strangled in the garden. Whether Mary was privy to the plot we will never know for sure. What was important at the time was that Bothwell 'was then more, as was reported, familiar with the queen's majesty than honesty required.' And, even after a stage-managed trial in which the overpowering earl was found innocent of the murder, 'it was heavily rumoured that he was guilty thereof.' Once again, Mary's half-innocent flirtations (to give her the benefit of the doubt) had landed her in serious trouble. Moreover, instead of lying low and waiting for the tumult to pass, as Elizabeth I wisely advised, Mary protested her innocence and resumed her favours to Bothwell and his supporters. When on 24 April Bothwell appeared to waylay the queen on her journey from Stirling to Edinburgh, carried her off to Dunbar and married her at Holyrood three weeks later, events seemed only to confirm people's most malicious suspicions.

Whether Mary had been forcibly abducted by Bothwell and raped, or whether she had submitted to the advances of her swarthy adventurer and enjoyed a few gaudy nights with him, within days she was running with tears of remorse and threatening to kill herself. It was of no avail. Mary Queen of Scots had become a national liability. Headed by a group known as the Confederate Lords, the nation rose in revolt and defeated the royal army at Carberry on 15 June. Bothwell galloped off, literally, into the sunset. He ended up in Denmark, where he died eleven years later, insane and chained to a pillar in the darkest of dungeons. Mary was imprisoned in the island castle of Lochleven. 'Burn her! Burn the whore!' the Edinburgh mob had yelled when she had been brought back to the capital. Never had a Stewart fallen so low.

Mary was now twenty-five. Although she had another twenty years to live, her days of liberty and majesty were all but over. In July, a few days after she had miscarried with twins, she was compelled to abdicate, and five days later, on the 29th, her infant son James was crowned King of Scotland. Her half-brother James, Earl of Moray, became regent on 22 August.

Employing her celebrated charm – always her most potent weapon – for almost the last time, on 2 May Mary escaped from Lochleven dressed as a countrywoman. Supporters flocked to her. But deserted at the last moment by the puissant Earl of Argyll and out-generalled by Morton's commanders, her forces collapsed without a fight at Langside on 13 May. Mary now despaired of Scotland. Ignoring those who advised her to make a further stand, she shaved her head and fled south in disguise towards the border, '92 miles across country without stopping or alighting'.

Aboard a fishing boat crossing the Solway Firth, Mary suddenly had misgivings about the wisdom of her choice of refuge and she asked the crew to alter course for France. But the vessel was too small and ill-equipped for such a voyage. At about 7pm on 16 May 1568, therefore, born by winds and currents as impersonal as Fate itself, Mary Queen of Scots landed at Workington. When she heard of her cousin's arrival, Queen Elizabeth was not amused.

III

Mary's decision to flee to England, whose legitimate monarch she persistently claimed to be, was as stupid as any she ever made. It was taken on the spur of the moment and against good advice, and once made could not be revoked. Within two weeks of her arrival, despite her tearful protests, Mary was placed under a house arrest from which only death released her nineteen years later.

It is difficult to see what other course Elizabeth's government could have taken. They had no wish to give the impression of approving rebellion, but welcoming Mary at court would have opened a Pandora's box of political and personal rivalry. Allowing her to return to the Continent would have dealt a trump card to England's Catholic enemies. And sending her back to Scotland (if the Scots had wanted her) would have jeopardised burgeoning Anglo-Scottish friendship. So Mary was doomed to fret away her remaining years in a variety of Midland stately homes and castles.

Elizabeth's first move was to hold a three-way conference (between herself, Mary and Moray) in 1568-9 to examine the charges against the fugitive queen. In fact the device was merely a cover-up, giving Elizabeth an excuse to do nothing. The 'bosom serpent' Mary was not permitted to attend in person, and despite the evidence of the notorious Casket Letters, which seemed to implicate her in Darnley's murder, in the end the deliberations were inconclusive. Moray returned home with a £5,000 English loan in his pocket. His half-sister remained a prisoner.

Mary was never permitted to spend more than two years in a single place. Some of her residences were a good deal more congenial than others. Chatsworth and Sheffield Castle she found pleasant; the cold chambers and corridors of Tutbury Castle, the bleak and rambling medieval pile near Burton upon Trent where she ended up in January 1585, depressed her unutterably. Her health always gave cause for concern, and within a few years the woman of 'an alluring grace, a pretty Scottish accent, and a searching wit, clouded by mildness' had given way to a portly and stooping middle-aged arthritic, whose false hair, mean mouth and tight, lined face bore little resemblance to the girl whose beauty had broken so many hearts. From 1573 onwards she paid trips to Buxton spa, where the waters seemed to alleviate her physical suffering.

For most of her captivity Mary used her own money to maintain a rudimentary court, and her household of some forty souls always addressed and treated her as queen. Initially she took exercise and corresponded freely, although her letters were scrutinised by the English secret service. Much of her time was spent writing, working on delightful embroidery, gossiping – and plotting. And this, at the last, proved her undoing.

It was dangerous enough for Elizabeth's government to have so emotive a symbol of Catholic monarchy as Mary living on English soil, but when she made her hosts' predicament even more trying by involving herself in a succession of treasonous plots, in the end she left them with little option but to remove her.

Mary was implicated first in the 1569 Revolt of the Northern Earls, then, two years later, in the Ridolfi Plot. With the international situation fast deteriorating, the Catholic Throckmorton Plot of 1583, which aimed to destroy Elizabeth and replace her on the English throne by Mary, was far more serious. When it was followed in 1586 by a similar hot-headed Catholic venture known as the Babington Plot, Elizabeth's council had had enough. The conspiracies themselves were probably not too dangerous, and Mary's commitment to their rasher actions is questionable. But it was not a time for legal niceties or quibbles. No matter how naive her approach, the Queen of Scots was a conspirator. Secretary Francis Walsingham monitored (and possibly doctored) Mary's supposedly secret correspondence, presented his evidence, arranged a commission to try her, and then waited for Elizabeth to put her signature on her cousin's death warrant.

Loth to take responsibility for the life of a fellow sovereign, Elizabeth prevaricated. Finally, on 1 February 1587 she signed. The warrant was hastened to Fotheringay, where Mary had been transferred the previous September. There, before an audience of some 300 packed into the great hall, at about 10am on Wednesday 8 February 1587, Mary Queen of Scots was beheaded.

Her life in ruins, Mary had decided that only in the manner of her passing could she hope to win the approbation of posterity. It was an isolated yet brilliant decision, and for once she played her part faultlessly. Dressed in deep red, the liturgical colour of martyrdom, she met her execution with great serenity. Her final major political act had been the first she had not bungled, and so she died true to her motto: 'In my end is my beginning'. The Stewarts had found their first martyr.

* * *

Mary had soon revoked the abdication forced upon her in the summer of 1567, and to her dying day she insisted that she was Queen of Scotland; but her son James VI maintained with equal resolution that he was King of Scotland. So for twenty years two Stewarts claimed the same throne, an awkward family predicament and one which was repeated a little over a century later.

James, who could never remember not being king, spent much of the first twelve years of his life at Stirling. He made his earliest official appearance in public at the age of five, when his supporters employed him to sanction a gathering of the estates called in his name. After he had made a short speech and noted with childish innocence that the parliament building had a hole in its roof (an observation shortly afterwards interpreted as oracular profundity), the boy was returned to his studies. Supervised by the elderly Protestant scholar George Buchanan and the milder Peter Young, these appear to have been rigorous in the extreme, with the result that James grew up the most scholarly of all the Stewarts. In adulthood he recalled with a mischievous twinkle in his eye that he had learned 'Latin before Scotis'. Certainly he acquired an outstanding fluency in the classics and other languages, so that he could simultaneously translate from Latin, French, Scots and English. Before his teens he could recite 'a great part of the Bible by heart' and was equally conversant with 'the history of almost every nation'. Visitors could not but be impressed by this royal prodigy. To one he was 'the sweetest sight in Europe... for strange and extraordinary gifts of wit, judgement, memory and language'. To another, who met James in 1584, he was 'for his years the most remarkable Prince that ever lived... : he understands clearly, judges wisely, and has a retentive memory.' In short, he was better educated in political and academic matters 'than anyone else in his kingdom'.

The king's impressive academic achievements were not matched by a corresponding emotional development. Raised in a dour, largely male-dominated household, James was deprived of the affection necessary to develop a sense of personal security. He grew up with homosexual proclivities that offended his intolerant contemporaries, and his craving for affection could lead him to 'indiscreet and wilful' dependence upon male favourites. From the age of seventeen he drank heavily. He also took readily to the deceit required of a successful politician. Before his mother's death he was such a 'great dissembler' that Queen Elizabeth, the most astute double-dealer of all, was driven in frustrated fury to denounce him as 'that false Scotch urchin!'

For all his quirky learning (which included a strong interest in witchcraft), pedagogy and political duplicity, James remained transparently human. Genuinely aware of his own faults and frailties, he once observed, 'I, James, am neither a god nor an angel, but a man like any other'. Although not physically robust, he loved hunting and hawking. His manners did not meet the refined standards of Continental courts, and he was untidy, short-tempered and sometimes shockingly bawdy. His most endearing feature, apparent from an early age, was a sharp sense of humour.

One day, having spent hours studying the fifteenth-century machinations of Archibald Bell-the-Cat, James and his pupil companion the young Earl of Mar grew irritatingly noisy in their play. The tyrannical Buchanan, busy at his writing, ordered the boys to be quiet. Quick as a flash, James wondered out loud who would bell the schoolroom cat. Buchanan beat the boy soundly for his effrontery. The Countess of Mar, the royal governess and the nearest thing in James's life to a mother figure, objected. 'I have whipped his arse,' retorted Buchanan, 'you can kiss it if you like!' Scholarship was not the only thing the king picked up from his misogynous old tutor!

Buchanan, whose writings played a major part in the popular vilification of the 'Bawd' Mary Queen of Scots, must bear some responsibility for James' unfilial attitude towards his mother. Throughout his early years the only picture James knew of Mary was of a murdering Catholic adulteress. As a result of this and her desertion of him when he was barely a year old, James's lack of sympathy for Mary's predicament was hardly surprising: 'She should drink the ale she had brewed' is his supposed reaction on hearing of her arraignment in 1587. Long before, the youth's instinct for survival had taught him that it would profit him nothing to expend emotional energy on a political liability who recognised him merely as 'Prince of Scotland'. The only time mother and son came close to seeing eye to eye was during the early 1580s, when James flirted with his mother's proposal for an 'Association' in which they would rule Scotland as joint monarchs.

James's personal rule began shortly after Mary's execution. Prior to this his minority had been as troubled as those of any of his Stewart predecessors. The turmoil remaining after Mary's flight into England took a while to die down. The anglocentric Earl of Moray survived as regent until shot through the stomach by an assassin in January 1570. There followed a period of civil war, in which English soldiers assisted the supporters of the infant king, and two further regents, including Darnley's elderly father, came and went. By November 1572 the Protestant James Douglas, 4th Earl of Morton, had won the regency. With the surrender of Edinburgh Castle and its garrison of the queen's supporters the following May, Mary's cause in Scotland was lost for ever.

When he was twelve, the age at which his grandfather had first been 'erected', James began to exercise some personal influence on government. Having been persuaded to dismiss Morton, he became besotted with Darnley's Catholic cousin, the charming and sophisticated Esme Stuart, Lord d'Aubigny, who arrived in Scotland from France in 1579. Another star in the ascendant was that of the 'wise and learned' Captain James Stewart, an arrogant soldier of fortune who 'thought no man his equal'. Aubigny obtained the earldom of Lennox in 1580 and James Stewart that of Arran the following year.

The Lennox-Arran axis was broken in August 1582, when a faction of prominent Protestants seized James in the Ruthven Raid and held him under house arrest. To the boy's intense distress, Lennox returned to France where he died the next year. Arran survived the coup and re-emerged as a prominent figure in the administration after the king had succeeded in escaping from the Raiders in 1583.

By now 'an old young man', James was maturing rapidly as a politician. He skilfully pursued a middle way in religion and politics, supporting the Black Acts of 1584 which curbed domestic Presbyterianism and made his government more attractive to Elizabeth. Consequently, after he had formally rejected Mary's proposed 'Association', the way was clear for an agreement with England, finalised in 1586. The league, which brought James a much-needed £4,000, was born of practicality, not sentiment, and as such proved remarkably durable. On news of his mother's execution James made formal gestures of complaint, ordering his court into mourning and severing diplomatic links with England. With a little persuasion, however, he soon accepted that Elizabeth had not been personally responsible for what had befallen at Fotheringay and within a few months Anglo-Scottish relations were back on a relatively even keel.

James's true reaction to Mary's demise was probably not so much sorrow as relief, even delight. One source has him making a great public show of grief, but in private coming out with the gleeful exclamation: 'Now I am sole king!' Indeed he was. And if his luck held he would one day be King of England too. It was a glorious prospect, without parallel in Stewart history.

Part III

Rulers of
Three Kingdoms
and of None

CHAPTER 16

Rex Pacificus

I

Whitehall, London. It is about two o' clock on the cold, overcast afternoon of Tuesday, 29 January 1649.

A high black-draped scaffold has been erected against the outside wall of Inigo Jones's magnificent banqueting hall. Near its centre stands a low block. A number of people are gathered on the platform: soldiers, clerks, a cleric, a heavily built fellow in disguise holding a large axe, and a small, elegant man with a beard and long hair, simply dressed in a doublet and cloak. It is the king, Charles I.

Around the scaffold troops of cavalry stand guard. Beyond them stretches a huge multitude of people, warmly wrapped against the weather and straining forward for a glimpse of what is happening. The king appears to be talking, but he is too far away for those in the street to catch his words.

After a while Charles removes his upper garments; then, feeling the chill, he resumes his cloak. Having looked at the block and exchanged some words with the executioner, he raises his hands in prayer.

An awesome quiet descends on the scene, broken only by the occasional snorting and stamping of the horses.

His short prayer over, Charles pauses, gazes short-sightedly around him, carefully takes off his cloak, and kneels – almost lies – at the block. The executioner stoops to make sure that the small neck is clear of hair, then takes a pace back and grasps the axe firmly in both hands.

Charles signals that he is ready. The axe rises high above him and falls, straight and true. There is a sharp thud as it severs the king's neck and embeds itself into the wood below. A second, duller sound follows as the head rolls heavily onto the wooden boards. The body gives a few involuntary twitches, then is still.

After a few seconds' silence the crowd breaks into an awful, long-drawn-out groan. Before it has died away mounted soldiers are clattering into the street, shouting at people to go home. On the scaffold Charles's stiffening body is picked up and carried carefully inside, leaving souvenir hunters to gather what grizzly remnants they can and tearful mourners to dip their handkerchiefs into the king's rapidly congealing blood.

* * *

FOUNTAIN COURT, HAMPTON COURT

The fatal blow delivered on that cold January afternoon did not bring the Stewart dynasty to an end. The Scots and the majority of the king's English subjects were appalled at what had happened, and eleven years later a Stewart was back on the throne.

* * *

No matter what men wished, however, the clock could not be turned back. A lesson had been learned, albeit in a violent and unpopular manner: the Stewarts, indeed all kings, were personally expendable. Charles II took it to heart, but not his brother, James VII and II. And so, twenty-eight years after the monarchy's restoration, a reigning Stewart was again deprived of his throne. This time it was done carefully and without bloodshed, yet even more conclusively. Neither James nor his descendants ever wore the crown again.

II

The young James VI, who had gradually gathered the reins of Scottish govern-ment into his hands during the mid-1580s, possessed few of the characteristics we have come to associate with his family. He was a scholarly, perceptive man of words rather than deeds. Arthur Wilson observed that 'few escaped his knowledge, being, as it were, a magazine to retain them'. James loved to show off this learning in debate, particularly in defence of a *via media* in religious and political matters. On one famous occasion in 1596 his broad-mindedness so annoyed the Presbyterian leader Andrew Melville that the divine was driven to seizing the king by the sleeve and reminding him that he was but 'God's silly vassal!' With a remarkable show of tolerance, God's vassal allowed the comment to pass unpunished.

Unlike his eye-catching parents, James was

'of the middle size; more tall than low, well set and somewhat plump, of a ruddy complexion, his hair of a light brown.'

A wispy beard and moustache concealed a small mouth, similar to his mother's, from whom he also acquired hooded eyes which in later life protruded from his rounded visage. His nose was long, like his grandfather's, and although not handsome he was still sufficiently good looking in 1617 to have been flatter-ingly described as of a 'sweet face'. Unusually for a Stewart, he was physically lazy (except when it came to hunting, for which he had an unquenchable passion) and he liked nothing better than to withdraw with a few friends 'to places of... solitude and repost'. When pressed by obsequious English courtiers, he once exclaimed in angry frustration: 'God's wounds! I will pull down my breeches and they shall also see my arse'. To the astonishment of his new subjects, accustomed to his predecessor's frosty formality, James's bawdiness had survived the journey from Edinburgh to London intact.

James lacked his ancestors' inordinate sexuality. We do not know whether his much-discussed relations with attractive young men went further than fond words and petting. Stemming from an inner desire for affection on the part of a man who once self-indulgently described himself as 'alone, without father or mother, brother or sister', they usually took the form of a rather pathetic paternalism. In 1586 he was believed to be 'very chaste and yet desirous of marriage', and he had no trouble fathering children.

Although James retained the academic interests which Buchanan had worked so assiduously to instil in him, he rejected his teacher's avant-garde belief that a monarch's powers were limited to his subjects' material welfare in favour of the more orthodox view that the king was 'God's lieutenant[s] upon earth'. This was not a blueprint for self-seeking absolutism, for no sensitive king raised in the Scottish political system could possibly have contemplated such a goal. *Basilikon Doron* (1599), the published statement of James's political philosophy written to instruct his son Henry, is marked by the wit, realism and responsibility of a man who was 'ever for the medium in every thing'. An all-powerful monarch, James believed, was essential to hold the state together, guiding and serving his people like a father. In a paternalistic age the simile was readily understood; the royalist Thomas Wentworth took it up three years after James's death when he explained to the Council of the North, 'Princes are… indulgent, nursing fathers to their people'. As James reminded the English parliament in 1610, 'were he a foolish father that would disinherit or destroy his children without cause, or leave off the careful education of them'. This was perhaps an arrogant way of putting it; but the underlying sentiment was concern, not tyranny.

* * *

In theory the neurotic and precociously intellectual young king was well positioned to govern in the manner he advocated. Despite the antics of his mother and the questioning of Presbyterians, the institution of monarchy was still widely popular, and the Black Acts of 1584 had confirmed the royal power 'over all estates as well spiritual as temporal'. To deny this authority was treason. But after forty-odd years of what James disparagingly referred to as rule by 'women, little children and traitorous and avaricious regents', a yawning chasm had opened between concept and public practice. James's task was to close the gap before it swallowed him up.

The first step had been achieved before James's majority: a provisional compromise with the kirk by which it accepted limitation of its authority to the religious sphere in return for recognition of its Presbyterian structure and the authority of the General Assembly. The king's next move was to tackle the nobility, wallowing in the 'feckless arrogant conceit of their greatness and power'. In this, as in so much that he undertook in the early part of his reign, James drew heavily on the support of his non-noble chancellor Sir John

Maitland of Thirlestane. A survivor of the Arran administration, Maitland had already been instrumental in forging the links with the kirk and arranging the league with Elizabeth. From now until his death in 1595 he employed his blunt but powerful tactics against the 'unbridled liberty' of the aristocracy. James did well to rely on such a servant. Not only was Maitland highly competent, but his direct tactlessness made him extremely unpopular (to the Earl of Bothwell he was a mere 'puddock-stool of a knight'), which shielded the king from criticism which might otherwise have come in his direction.

The plan to 'bridle the earls' came in two parts. Firstly, the king and chancellor deliberately set about creating a *noblesse de robe*, favouring men of the class of lawyers and lairds. 'Simple soldiers and gentlemen', James called them, 'whom he could always… ruin… as easily as he had made them'. Secondly, the king determined to 'reduce' the nobility 'to their duty' and 'good order'. But it had to be done 'little by little', and he could begin only when they gave him the opportunity. He did not have long to wait.

Guided by his academic instincts, James veered away from extremes of religion, once saying that he would be 'sorry to punish… [men's] bodies for the error of their minds'. This, coupled with a fear of assassination and a desire to avoid papal excommunication, led him to treat Catholics with a leniency which shocked less open-minded contemporaries. The exiled Catholic Archbishop of Glasgow was restored to favour and made ambassador in Paris, while nearer to home the handsome young Catholic Earl of Huntly, recently married to Esme Stuart's daughter, enjoyed the sort of high favour once lavished on his father-in-law. James was deeply upset, therefore, when Elizabeth's ambassador gave him written proof that Huntly, Crawford and Errol (the 'Northern Earls') had written to Philip II expressing their sympathy at the failure of the 1588 armada. The last thing James wished to do was upset Elizabeth and so jeopardise his chances of winning the English succession. Huntly was deprived of his post of captain of the guard and imprisoned for a while.

Instead of learning their lesson, the Catholic magnates rose in a half-hearted revolt aimed primarily at the detested Maitland, and had to be broken up by force. In 1592 Huntly again overstepped the mark by leading an attack which resulted in the murder of the 'bonnie' Earl of Moray, the darling of the ultra-Protestants. For the third time James inclined towards leniency, and the recalcitrant earl was detained only temporarily. But when at the end of the year the Catholic George Kerr was found leaving for Spain in possession of blank sheets of paper signed with the names of the Northern Earls, even James's patience ran out. Under torture Kerr revealed details of a supposed Catholic plot. The king moved north in force and after further prevarication presented the Catholic troublemakers with the choice of exile or conversion. By 1597 they had accepted the latter. James's extraordinary leniency, which must have caused his more forceful royal ancestors to turn in their graves, had finally achieved its end.

It was not just the Catholic nobility which gave James problems during his first ten years of personal rule. Even more humiliating was the disruptive behaviour of Francis Stewart, 5th Earl of Bothwell. Descended from an illegitimate son of James V, and nephew of Queen Mary's overbearing third husband, from whom he inherited much of his brilliant, enigmatic personality, for six years this most contradictory of Stewarts terrorised his young master most mercilessly. Part scholar (a facet of his personality which James found attractive), part rake, part bully, he first rebelled in 1589. Two years later, imprisoned on charges of seeking to harm the king through witchcraft, he escaped and made a night raid on Holyrood house. A few months afterwards he narrowly failed to seize the king. By July 1593 he was back at Holyrood, browbeating the cowering king into promising a fair trial on the witchcraft charge. Dissatisfied with the outcome of this confrontation, Bothwell made a final raid in April 1594 before going into exile on the Continent. The king's handling of the turbulent earl had been motivated as much by timidity as policy; in the end, however, he had ridden out the tempest and emerged with his authority enhanced.

The last noble threat – the Gowrie Conspiracy – came during the final summer of the century. John Ruthven, the twenty-two-year-old 3rd Earl of Gowrie, was heir to a long-standing squabble with the ruling Stewarts. His grandfather Lord Ruthven had been among Riccio's murderers, and his father, 1st Earl of Gowrie, had led the humiliating Ruthven raid and suffered execution in 1584. The dashing 3rd earl had not endeared himself to the king by having some sort of contact with the impossible Bothwell and by dabbling in the black arts while completing his education abroad. Like many of his contemporaries, James had a fearful fascination for the occult and had even written a treatise on the subject under the title of *Daemonologie*. The young earl had cut quite a dash when he returned from his sojurn on the Continent, and further angered James by opposing royal policy in parliament. The crown also owed him a considerable sum of money.

Matters came to a head on 5 August 1600 when the king was out hunting near Perth. Among his fellow sportsmen was Alexander Ruthven, the earl's attractive younger brother who for a while had been in high favour with the king. Somehow, perhaps lured by the scent of gold, James was persuaded to drop in on the Ruthvens at Gowrie House. After dinner, when Alexander and the king were alone, something occurred which caused James to scream for help. Armed royal retainers rushed to his assistance and the Ruthven brothers were slain.

Some have claimed that the king had deliberately engineered the incident to remove awkward opponents. James himself pointed out the unlikelihood of such a suggestion

'It is known very well that I was never blood-thirsty. If I would have taken their lives, I had causes enough; I needed not to hazard myself so.'

If we take the king at his word (not always a wise thing to do), then the fracas was either a bungled assassination plot, or, more likely, merely a sudden quarrel which had flared out of control.

Whatever the true origins of the bloodshed, James was quick to turn it to his advantage. He ordered all Edinburgh clergy, hitherto somewhat lukewarm in their support, to offer up prayers for his deliverance. All except one did as they were bid and for many years 5 August, as 5 November later, was celebrated as an important royal anniversary.

James's approach to his kingdom's endemic lawlessness was quite unlike that of his blunt forbears, but it was just as successful; indeed, since he favoured cooperation above coercion, ultimately his achievements proved more hard wearing. He understood the need for effective, broad-based conciliar administration and regularly attended council meetings, enjoying their atmosphere and participating in the discussions. In 1601 the Englishman Sir Henry Wotton reported favourably that James 'is patient in the work of government, [and] makes no decision without obtaining good counsel'.

The Scots were deluged with an avalanche of declarations, proclamations and explanations, exalting the monarchy and exhorting them to uphold the law. Some were little more than empty words. James did not reform his country's creaky and still rather subjective legal system. His declamatory paternalism met with little success in the Highlands and Islands, and nowhere did he participate personally in the type of posse activity favoured by his less timid grandfather. Nevertheless, on the Borders, where the new accord with England was a real boon, his rule was keenly felt. In 1588, for example, he borrowed artillery from Carlisle to overawe Lord Maxwell. By the end of the century the Border culture of raid, tower house and vendetta was at last beginning to die out. Elsewhere, as well as making examples of recalcitrant magnates, he supported the law enforcement agencies whenever possible and bound troublemakers to keep the peace on pain of huge financial penalties. After ten years of personal rule James's skilled and sensitive midwifery had brought forth the child everyone had been longing for: a 'delectable time of peace', without precedent in living memory.

The king's achievement was all the more impressive because he had gelded religious as well as political opponents. His approach to the kirk, initiated by Maitland and similar to that used with the Northern Earls, involved giving the Presbyterians sufficient rope to hang themselves. Parliament confirmed the Presbyterian kirk in 1592, although the institution was still debarred from politics and received no further endowment. Understanding that the fiery aggression of Andrew Melville and his band of zealous young Presbyterians had to be handled carefully, over the next five years James marked time. He had to deal with the Catholic threat first and did not want to take steps that might lose him Elizabeth's subsidy or draw unfavourable notices from the pulpit.

By 1596, however, the year of Melville's celebrated sleeve-plucking incident, the presumptive demands of the extremists had gone too far. They had tried to influence foreign policy, attacked James's queen for her 'vanity', dubbed Elizabeth an atheist, questioned the authority of the council and challenged the king's view that his 'free' monarchy was answerable to God alone. In December a popish scare in Edinburgh led to riots and gave James the chance he needed. The capital was fined. Slowly, almost imperceptibly, the king shifted administrative responsibilities onto the shoulders of his bishops. At the same time he tightened his management of the General Assembly, summoning it to meet at short notice and away from centres of ultra-Protestantism. He also made a habit of appearing in person and gave financial assistance to moderates to help them attend. By 1603 the Assembly was yet another scalp hanging at the belt of Scotland's remarkable 'urchin'.

The most ominous trophy missing from James's collection was solvency. Despite regular grants of parliamentary taxation, his 'excruciating' poverty remained a constant source of embarrassment and weakness. Unlike Mary of Guise and Queen Mary, he had no French cash to fall back on. Faced with a paltry annual revenue of about £15,000 sterling, in real terms appreciably less than that enjoyed by James V, a ruthless king might have found alternative sources of income. A careful one might have harboured his resources more wisely. But James was neither, and his cavalier extravagance only made the situation worse. He tried borrowing and asking members of his household to meet their own expenses; he debased the coinage; he even resorted to personal deprivation, at one time going without his customary afternoon quart of wine. None of it did any good.

Even Elizabeth, by European standards a royal pauper, seemed fabulously wealthy by comparison. The £4,000 pension she paid James made it hard for her to balance her books; but to the recipient, who comprehended only books of words, not figures, and to whom the concept of financial balance was an irritating irrelevance, the sum was absolutely essential. When it was due the king's normal manner of addressing his cousin – 'Madame and dearest sister' – was replaced by an effusive:

> 'Right excellent, right high and mighty princess, our dearest sister and cousin, in our heartiest manner we recommend us unto you'.

Once, when after three begging letters the money had still not arrived, James bleated:

> 'If ye think my friendship worthy that annuity, remember *qui cito dat bis dat.* [He who gives quickly, gives twice.] Let not the circumstances of the giver disgrace the gift... '.

Elizabeth kept her purse tightly shut. James resorted to threats. This was quite the wrong approach, and in response to the queen's furious riposte James whined hopefully, 'I perceive sparks of love to shine through the midst of the

thickest clouds of passion that are there set down.' This was the sort of grovelling Elizabeth had been looking for, and in the end she paid up.

His English pension apart, James's only sizeable windfall was the £150,000
dowry which came his way on marrying Princess Anne of Denmark. The event
was the most conventionally romantic of his reign. After the usual wrangling
over the terms of the marriage contract, the couple were wed by proxy in
Copenhagen on 20 August 1589. When the pretty, blonde-haired Anne's
attempt to reach Scotland was foiled by storms in the North Sea, on 22
October James set out from Leith to bring his bride home himself. He arrived
safely and married his 'little wiffe-waffe' at Oslo on 23 November. The pair
remained in Scandinavia until the following April, enjoying what was by all
accounts a riotous yet happy honeymoon. Upon their return Anne was
crowned in as lavish a manner as James could afford, which involved pouring
'a bonny quantity of oil' over her right arm and breast. She then settled down
in her role as queen, wife and mother, brightening the court with her charm
and extensive artistic patronage.

Anne was her husband's junior by eight years, virtually a child when she
married. At first the relationship worked well and, finding female charms not
as unappetising as he had feared, the king played the ardent lover with some
enthusiasm. His months abroad, removed from the sinister atmosphere of plot
and assassination which had so distorted his childhood, were some of the most
carefree of his life. But the passion did not last. Back in Scotland he soon tired
of his lively but scatterbrained and unacademic queen, and by the time of her
death in 1619 the couple had drifted far apart. James found solace in the
company of handsome young men; Anne turned to the arts, the Roman
Catholic church (which she joined in the 1590s) and her children. In 1594 the
birth of a male heir, the attractive Prince Henry, was received 'as if the people
had been daft for mirth'. Two further children, Elizabeth and Charles, survived
into adulthood. Unhappily for the Stewarts, Henry died of typhoid in 1612 and
the succession passed to his younger brother. Few deaths have had such
profound consequences.

As the sixteenth century drew to a close the 'northern Solomon' was
proving the most successful governor of his dynasty. The kirk was quiescent,
the nobility calmed, his kingdom at peace, and the succession assured. Having
thus far triumphed in practically every sphere in which his mother had blun-
dered, James was now concentrating on the area of her most singular failure –
acquisition of the English crown.

II

The relationship between Elizabeth I and James VI was one of mutual personal
hostility tempered by expediency, like an unhappy marriage held together for
the sake of the offspring. Towards the close of her life Elizabeth accepted that
the King of Scots would have to succeed her – he was both a Protestant and her

nearest male blood relation, being descended from Margaret Tudor by her marriages to both James IV and the Earl of Angus. Nevertheless, Elizabeth was loth to acknowledge her own mortality and never publicly recognised James as her heir. The furthest she went was to declare that she would do nothing to prejudice his eventual succession. Her security and vanity were better served by keeping James in the dark, or at least in the shade, and on occasion she was prepared to thicken the obscurity by delaying or reducing his blessed pension. As we have seen, James desperately needed Elizabeth's money and backed away from offending her lest she break her silence and renounce him. To that end he had accepted his mother's execution and acted against those subjects, such as the Northern Earls and the Presbyterians, who had deliberately offended the English queen.

By the turn of the century James's principal ally at the English court was Elizabeth's secretary Sir Robert Cecil. When early in 1601 – probably with James's knowledge – the wayward young Earl of Essex rose in futile revolt against his difficult old queen, Cecil carefully kept James's name out of the subsequent trial. After this James and he conducted an extensive correspondence. For security reasons important figures were referred to by coded numbers: the king was 30, the secretary 10 and his ailing mistress 24. The two men also worked to prepare a climate of opinion at home and abroad in which James's accession to Elizabeth's throne would be taken for granted.

Queen Elizabeth died early in the morning of Thursday, 24 March 1603. It is rumoured that on her deathbed, with an enigmatic movement of the hand, even she finally acknowledged her successor. A few hours later Sir Robert Carey was in the saddle, riding hard to the north. Reaching Holyrood house late on Saturday, he was taken into the king's presence. Exhausted and dishevelled, he knelt before a smiling James and greeted him as king of three kingdoms: Scotland, England and Ireland.

467 years had elapsed since Walter FitzAlan had left England to take up residence in Scotland. Now, fourteen generations later his direct ancestor was to return south as king. The Stewarts were on the threshold of the most prestigious phase of their extraordinary history.

* * *

Government is government, whatever the country, and after sixteen years as an adult monarch James had proved himself a notably successful practitioner of its wily arts. He knew he had done well, too. And now, in his mid-thirties, he was supremely confident of his ability to manage the affairs of three kingdoms as capably as he had those of one.

His confidence was not ill-founded. The basic machinery of government in Scotland and England was not dissimilar, and Irish administration was subordinate to the English privy council. The religious difficulties James had confronted in Scotland had parallels in England and the language barrier was more of an irritation than an obstacle. Moreover, for over a century policy makers in both countries had been coming round slowly to accept that co-operation rather than conflict best suited their mutual interests.

But English politics was considerably more sophisticated than Scotland's. The wealthier country was more tightly governed, more centralised. It operated according to different traditions and was blessed, or cursed, with a parliament accustomed to having a greater say in matters than its Scottish counterpart. The difficulty of handling a racially and religiously divided Ireland only added to the complexity of James's task. Nowhere in Europe did multiple monarchies have an easy ride. Despite the ecstatic welcome afforded the new king during his journey south, which he mistakenly believed was levelled more at himself than at his office, it remained to be seen whether James would be able to adapt his tactics and style to suit all his subjects, new and old. It was also open to question whether, once the honeymoon was over, the English would take personally to their extravagant, quirky and pedantic new sovereign.

* * *

'Many Scots', wrote John Major in 1521, 'are accustomed, though not openly, to compare the Stewarts to the horses in the district of Mar, which in youth are good, but in their old age bad.'

This derogatory aphorism was based on the lives of Robert II, Robert III and James I, since by Major's time no other Stewart monarch had survived beyond the age of forty. Not so James VI, however, who for a long time was held up as the perfect example of his family's propensity to equine deterioration. The view used to be that with advancing years he declined from a distinguished governor into a timorous and bawdy old fool with the political acumen of a self-important village schoolmaster. The change, significantly enough, was thought to have begun when he succeeded to the English throne.

James's reputation was mutilated between the Scylla of popular Anglo-Scottish animosity and the Charybdis of his son's incompetence. The mangled and unwholesome body was then put on public view in one of the most brilliant character assassinations in the English language. Only in the last quarter of a century or so have forensic historians working on the battered remains been able to recreate something akin to a true likeness of the eccentric yet gifted king.

The average seventeenth-century Englishman held the Scots (and most other foreign nationals) in deep contempt. Their xenophobic dislike of 'Caledonian bores' or 'northern adjectives' was the product of ignorance, centuries of warfare in which the English had singularly failed to bring Scotland to heel, and arrogant hatred for a smaller, poorer nation. No one expressed English prejudice better than Sir Anthony Weldon, who accompanied James on a trip to Scotland in 1617-18 and then wrote a secret treatise on what he had seen.

> 'First, for the country, I must confess it is good for those that possess it, and too bad for others, to be at the charge to conquer it. The air might be wholesome but for the stinking people that inhabit it; the ground might be fruitful had they but the wit to manure it.'

Scottish men he satirised as blasphemous, lascivious, violent and stupid barbarians. The women were no better, mere 'monsters':

> 'to be chained in marriage with one of them, were to be tied to a dead carcass, and cast into a stinking ditch'.

So when James and his Scottish followers arrived in England they walked into a mire of prejudice. However they conducted themselves – and even on his best behaviour the king was hardly a model of decorum – they were bound to attract criticism, particularly as in uniting the British crowns James, a Scot, had triumphed where so many heroic English kings had failed.

The second problem facing anyone trying to make a clear evaluation of James's kingship is the inescapable fact that a Great Rebellion rocked his kingdoms a mere seventeen years after his death. Surely, scholars presumed, such a momentous event must have had deep-rooted causes? So they combed James's reign in search of them and came up with rows with parliament, prodigality and personal indiscretions which seemed to fit the bill. Elizabeth, on the other hand, the romantic heroine of the cloistered academic, was let off lightly. The political causes of the mid-century turmoil, so the received truth ran, began with the rule of an unsophisticated, bigoted outsider – the 'wisest fool in Christendom'.

This is where Weldon, dismissed from the household after the discovery of his scurrilous anti-Scottish manuscript, put in the heaviest boot of all. His witty satire *The Court and Character of King James* was published in 1649, when the author was dead and the Stewart monarchy had been replaced by a republic. It was vitriolic, unkind and inaccurate; above all, however, it was memorable. The pantomime king leaps from the page: 'fat enough', 'tongue too large for his mouth', with skin 'as soft as Taffeta Sarsnet' and 'legs... very weak' so that he was 'ever leaning on other men's shoulders'. The character shredding is even more effective than the physical mockery. We have a king 'naturally of a timorous disposition' who 'loved not the sight of a soldier'; the drunkard inclined to 'repent with tears' after a night's debauchery; the slut who 'never washed his hands' and 'would never change his clothes until worn out to very rags'; and the mean-spirited misogynist, 'crafty and cunning in petty things', 'very liberal... of what he had not in his own grip' and 'ever best... when furthest from the queen'. So compelling is this portrait that it hung unchallenged in people's minds for generations. It is one of the curious injustices of history that the reputation of James's incompetent mother Mary Queen of Scots has generally been kindly treated, while that of her genial and infinitely more capable son has been vilified unmercifully.

IV

England was James's Promised Land. To get there he had spent the best years of his life scraping, grovelling and scheming, and now that he had achieved his goal he was determined to enjoy himself. In the words of a foreign observer, he wanted 'to have nothing to do with other people's business and very little to do with his own', but was content 'to devote himself to his books and to hunting, and to encourage the view that he... [was] the real arbiter of peace'. His few positive political aims – to enhance further his authority in Scotland, end England's long-standing war with Spain and amalgamate his inheritances into the single kingdom of Great Britain – were intended to make his life easier and more pleasant. He had no wish to reform or stir up unnecessary trouble.

It was a dream manifesto. The first three years of James's English kingship revealed just how tricky a situation he had inherited, his initial successes and failures setting the tone for the rest of the reign. Some things went well, very well. He recalled that on his slow journey south (he wished to avoid arriving in London before Elizabeth's funeral) 'all the ways betwixt Berwick and London were paved with people', 'their eyes flaming nothing but sparkles of affection'. The popularity did not evaporate, and sixteen years later there was genuine rejoicing when he recovered from a bout of serious illness. To the relief of all but a handful of merchants whose fortunes depended upon the profits of war, peace was formally agreed with Spain in 1604. And having met a deputation of disaffected puritan ministers, James presided over a successful religious conference at Hampton Court which settled a number of issues troubling those who found the Anglican compromise difficult to stomach. An even happier outcome of the meeting was James's commissioning of a new translation of the Bible. Completed in 1611, the Authorised Version endures as one of the outstanding works of literature in the English language – an unexpected gift from a 'Scottis man'.

But not all was sweetness and light. There were three plots against the king. The two in 1603 were trifling; the third, the celebrated papist 'Gunpowder Plot' of 1605, was more worrying and forced James to support harsh measures against all Catholics. Equally disruptive of the king's pleasure was the attitude of his first parliament. Far from translating their expressions of pleasure at James's succession into practical help, MPs swiftly reverted to the sort of prickly nit-picking which had marred proceedings under his predecessor. They proved fearfully possessive of their ill-defined privileges and baulked at voting the government the finance it required. Most wounding of all was the irrational scorn they poured on James's sensible proposal for union with Scotland.

Matters were not helped by what was going on at court, that superficial yet vital centre of the country's social and political life. Scots plagued the place, arousing deep English suspicion and jealousy. Patronage and gifts, so long distributed in careful cupfuls by Elizabeth, poured forth in streams. Even James admitted later that his early years 'were… as a Christmas'. Inspired by postwar delight and relief at the passing of the old queen's strict regime, banquets, masques, plays and concerts abounded. The costs of every department soared. Standards of behaviour slipped. And over the whole backbitten, sordid show presided – when he was not away hunting – the complacent, alien king.

* * *

Like many experienced politicians, James was increasingly drawn towards foreign rather than domestic matters. He also realised, unlike his son, that nothing destabilises a regime so much as war, particularly an unsuccessful one. This was especially relevant to England, where the king was unrealistically expected to 'live of his own' and so had to fall back on the generosity of the political nation to fund military campaigns.

Throughout his double reign the 'Rex Pacificus' adopted the role of arbiter of Europe. In doing so he overestimated England's power and underestimated residual antipathy towards the Catholic powers, notably the old enemy Spain. The marriage in 1613 of his daughter Elizabeth to Frederick, the inept Protestant Elector Palatine, was the first span of a proposed family bridge across a divided Europe. James hoped to follow it with a similar union between one of his sons and a Catholic royal house. But a French match came to nothing and the Spaniards thought less of James's scheme than they made public. He maintained his moderate position after the outbreak of European war in 1618, and when he was still talking rather than acting after Spain had seized his daughter and son-in-law's principality, his pacifism began to take on the unwelcome hue of pusillanimity. Right at the end of the reign, after Prince Charles had returned humiliated from a supposedly incognito peep at the Spanish infanta, it was clear that James's designs had failed. Nevertheless, even Weldon, his most ferocious critic, had to admit that the king had 'lived in peace, died in peace, and left all his kingdoms in a peaceable condition'. It was not a glamorous achievement, but it was one for which most of James's subjects were quietly most grateful.

English men and women also had cause to be grateful for the skilful manner in which James, the Supreme Governor of the Church of England, piloted his fragile vessel between the rocks of religious dissent. Raised as a predestinarian Calvinist, he was also a confirmed erastian and Episcopalian, a position he summed up in his famous maxim: 'No bishop, no king'. His experiences with Melville and his followers had brought home to him the political danger posed by an independent church operating alongside the crown rather than under it. At the same time James was not foolish enough to believe he could demand absolute uniformity of belief. What men thought in their hearts was their affair; what they did or said in public was his.

Thus guided, James did what he could to enhance the status of the clergy, promoting men of learning and wisdom but keeping at arm's length intelligent enthusiasts such as William Laud, Bishop of St David's, who James warned 'loves... to bring things to a pitch of reformation floating in his own brain'. In practical matters James was against bringing anything to a pitch. In due course, when it was clear that the scare of 1605 had been hatched in the hearts of a handful of unrepresentative recusant hotheads, anti-Catholic legislation was enforced less vigorously. When the 1618 *Book of Sports*, a manual of activities suitable for the Sabbath, was found to cause widespread offence to puritan sensibilities the king revoked his order that the book be read aloud from the pulpit. From its inception the Anglican church had been a moderate, compromise institution. A king wedded to the *via media* was just the sort of guardian it required, and under James's careful stewardship it thrived.

* * *

In discussing the possibility of an eventual union between England and Scotland, Henry VII, that most astute of politicians, had predicted that 'the greater will draw the latter'. And thus it turned out. When James bid a tearful farewell to his people in 1603 he had promised to return to them every three years. He did so only once, in 1617-8. He boastfully explained to the English parliament that he had broken his word because he had no need to travel north more frequently

> 'here I sit and govern it [Scotland] with my pen; I write and it is done, and by a Clerk of the Council I govern Scotland now, which others could not do by the sword.'

Like many other of James's sweeping pronouncements, the remark held a germ of truth wrapped in a shell of exaggeration.

Through his Edinburgh council James continued the work begun before 1603. The service nobility, 'lords of erection', were increased by a further twenty-nine creations. The battle for law and order went on with greater assurance now that the king was secure from physical intimidation of the kind practised by Bothwell and the Ruthvens. In 1613 Lord Maxwell paid the ultimate penalty for committing 'murder under trust', while in the Highlands a variety of violent and disreputable measures to curb lawlessness met with some success. The Scottish parliament, dominated by the Lords of the Articles and never more than a poor relation of its aggressive English counterpart, remained quiescent. The kirk, too, was cajoled and pushed towards erastian uniformity, a process which culminated in the General Assembly of 1618 accepting the Five Articles of Perth. These involved, among other measures, lay confirmation by bishops and the obligation of communicants to kneel.

Yet a selection of individual incidents and measures does not convey the whole truth about Scotland during the king's absence. He might have believed that he had only to write for things to happen, but in fact they often did not. The Articles of Perth, for example, were widely resented and not strictly enforced. As the post took a week to travel from London to Edinburgh, many day-to-day decisions devolved to the council. The system worked because 'Blessed King James', a Scot who knew his country intimately, was personally popular in Scotland and did not strive too assiduously to promote uniformity between his diverse realms. His son, a naturalised Englishman with little first-hand knowledge of Scottish affairs, had an almost pathological obsession with conformity, particularly in religion. Therein lay the seeds of his downfall.

* * *

One of James's greatest disappointments with the English, whose land he perceived to flow with milk and honey, was that they were so reluctant readily to grant him an appropriate share of their wealth. The problem of getting the most lightly-taxed nation in Europe to accept the cost of government was rooted in history and would have taken a political genius to sort out amicably. Elizabeth's parsimonious housekeeping had kept matters under control until war forced her into a deficit of some £400,000 by the end of her reign. By 1625 the debt had risen to over £1 million. The predicament had political (and constitutional) implications not simply because James was unable to live of his own, but because he gave the impression that, apart from the brief period of Lionel Cranfield's treasurership (1621-24), he had no real desire to do so. He considered it more important to cut a dash than costs. The doubling of the court's musical establishment, the quadrupling of wardrobe expenses and the throwing of a £3,300 Twelfth Night banquet of 1,600 separate dishes hardly seemed the gestures of man concerned with his overdraft.

The most celebrated effort to put the royal finances on a surer footing was Cecil's proposed parliamentary Great Contract of 1610, a scheme to swap certain of the king's feudal revenues for an assured annual income. When it foundered on popular ignorance and intransigence the lord treasurer's career received a blow from which it never recovered. Other revenue-raising devices, such as the sale of honours and monopolies, loans and royal backing for the hare-brained scheme of Alderman Cockayne to reorganise the cloth trade, all produced as much acrimony as cash. Perhaps, within James's limited terms of reference the government's hand-to-mouth existence did not matter too much. Drastic financial reform, ultimately the only realistic long-term solution, would have been even more painful, so James was happy to muddle through. As long as the country was at peace and there was no religious ingredient in the tension, then his political instincts were sufficiently sharp to prevent things getting too out of hand.

The same applied to James's relations with the English parliament, the Commons in particular. He did not like a body which questioned his view of monarchy, ruined his scheme for union with Scotland and kept him always short of money. On one occasion he actually wondered out loud why his ancestors had ever allowed such a cantankerous institution to come into being. But needing it as a point of contact with the localities and as an occasional source of funds, he understood that he could not dispense with it altogether, and by and large he handled it quite well. Parliament met infrequently, sitting for a little under three years during his twenty-two-year reign. Ministers kept an eye on what was going on, and generally proceedings turned ugly only when hostile court factions carried their squabbles into the chambers, as happened in the parliaments of 1614 and 1624-5.

If James is remembered for anything, it is for his favourites. His fondness for handsome young men amused contemporaries, horrified the Victorians and interests modern historians. The details of what James got up to with his menfriends does not concern us. What is important is whether or not they mattered. From one point of view, they did not. Of James's English favourites, only George Villiers exercised extensive political influence. The rest were primarily sideshows to whom the king turned, like a hobby, for relaxation and solace. But they were significant because their presence tarnished the image of the king. One incident scratched that image particularly deeply.

On Cecil's death in 1612 two factions vied for power, one based around the powerful Howard family, the other cobbled together by an unpleasant schemer named Sir Francis Overbury. Overbury's best hope for advancement lay in the presence in his group of the flaxen-haired Scot Robert Ker (or Carr), the king's current favourite and royal secretary. Things started to go wrong for Overbury when Ker entered into a passionate affair with Frances Howard, the dissatisfied wife of the oafish Earl of Essex. In 1613 malicious gossip blossomed into glorious scandal when Frances commenced proceedings for divorce on the grounds of her husband's impotence. Details of the case, real and imaginary, were the talk of the decade. To the cost of his reputation, James assisted his favourite's lover in her quest and imprisoned Overbury, who was arguing vehemently against the divorce, in the Tower of London. He died there in September. Lady Essex won her case and married Ker on Boxing Day. That, for a while, was where the story rested.

However, in 1615 James was given clear evidence that Ker and his wife had instigated Overbury's murder by poisoning. The following year they were duly tried before the House of Lords, found guilty and sentenced to death. Ever loyal to old friends, James pardoned them. He insisted only that they be held in the Tower, from where they were released in 1622. It was not really the sort of behaviour expected of 'God's lieutent upon earth'.

* * *

Ker emerged from the Tower to find James besotted with George Villiers, Marquess of Buckingham and the last, possibly the most able and certainly the most significant of all his protégés. By now the perceptive king of 1603 was deteriorating into a rather sad old man. He was overweight and drinking too much. His teeth had started to fall out, he had painful piles, and a combination of gout and arthritis made movement difficult. Physically and emotionally he leaned on Buckingham, his 'Steenie' or 'sweet child and wife', as he had leaned on no one else. It was not an edifying sight. Nor was Buckingham's rise to political pre-eminence healthy for the body politic.

James's shrewdness never left him entirely, and as long as he was around he upheld some sort of political balance. But the end was now near. In the spring of 1625 he suffered a series of convulsions. Towards the end of March he had a stroke, and on the 27th, half suffocating in his own phlegm and lying in a bed besmirched with the results of uncontrollable dysentery, he died. So horrible a death was common in the days before modern medicine. But James, an uncommon king if ever there was one, surely deserved better.

Sir Simon d'Ewes was surprised at the general 'slight and disregard [at] the loss of so mild and gentle a prince'

> 'For though it cannot be denied but that he had his vices and deviations... ; yet, if we consider his virtues and learning on the other hand, his care to maintain the doctrine of the Church of England pure and sound... , and his augmenting the liberties of the English... , we cannot but acknowledge that his death deserved more sorrow and condolement from his subjects than it found.'

And the same writer showed greater perspicacity than most of his contemporaries by prophesying that 'the ensuing times might yet render... [James's] loss more sensible, and his memory more dear'.

CHAPTER 17

'That Man of Blood'

I

Legend tells that King James was once wakened in the night by screaming in the bedchamber of his second son, Prince Charles. When the king went to see what was happening he found the child's nurse Marioun Hepburn in hysterics.

'What's the matter with ye, nursie?' enquired James kindly. Marioun sobbed that while she dozed a mysterious dark stranger had entered the room and cast a dark cloak over the prince's cradle. It was a sinister omen, she wailed, 'na canny'.

Fascinated by evil and its manifestations, James was inclined to agree with her and predicted of his son: 'If he ever be king, there'll be no good of his reign. The devil has cast his cloak over him already.'

* * *

Although the incident is apocryphal, Charles Duke of Albany was indeed raised in shadow. As a sickly two-year-old he was considered too frail to accompany James VI's triumphant journey into England in the spring of 1603, and this pall of physical disability was never entirely lifted. Charles suffered from rickets in his childhood and although he strengthened later he grew up short, probably not much over five feet one inch, and thin-legged like his father. More awkward was a nervous speech impediment which caused him to stammer his way through public pronouncements. He was well educated, but lacked James's incisive intelligence. The contrast between the reserved, narrow-minded son and his garrulous, witty father could hardly have been more pronounced, or more embarrassing for the sensitive young prince. Other family comparisons exacerbated his early feelings of inadequacy. His popular elder brother and sister were bright adornments of the court. Henry Prince of Wales, the Protestant paragon seven years his senior, was an approachable extrovert; his elder sister Princess Elizabeth inherited her mother's appealing vivacity and good looks. Henry's death in November 1612 and Elizabeth's marriage three months afterwards both came too late to alleviate the impression in Charles's mind that he was the runt of the Stewart litter.

The prince reacted by retreating into himself. As a consequence, despite the abundance of first-hand information about him, he remains the most remote of all the Stewarts and an almost impossible man to fathom. Because he appeared aloof in public, he has sometimes been thought cold. But to certain individuals he showed profound affection. His relationship with his father, for example, was always warm. James had a long private talk with his 'sweet son' shortly before his death and the 'Baby Charles' gave his father one of the most lavish funerals London had ever seen, accompanying the coffin (carried on a hearse designed by Inigo Jones) on foot from Denmark House to Westminster Abbey. Never a vindictive man, Charles was not upset by the unseemly attention which James had poured upon Villiers, whom the old king once professed to love 'more than anyone else'. Indeed, from the prince's later teens until Villiers' assassination in 1628 the royal favourite remained Charles's own 'true constant and loving friend'. He may have filled the role once played by Charles's brother Henry, to whom the prince had been deeply attached. Finally, after a shaky start Charles grew to love his French wife Henrietta Maria with a single-minded devotion unseen in a Stewart marriage since James I. His wedding to the diminutive fifteen-year-old daughter of Henry IV took place in 1625, following the collapse of the Spanish match and shortly after the death of James I. For several years Charles was irritated by the apparent superficiality of his doll-like bride, and on occasion they refused to speak to each other for days. But the removal of Villiers and a succession of pregnancies broke down Charles's barriers. As the circumstances of his kingship became ever more troubled, he discovered in Henrietta Maria a toughness he had hitherto overlooked and found in family life a comfort generally lacking elsewhere. It was part of his tragedy that he was never able convincingly to translate his sincere paternalism from the domestic circle to the world of his subjects at large.

In the darker corners of the court it was whispered that Charles's father was not the King of Scots but one Bedy the Dane, a former friend and admirer of Queen Anne. James, who had endured similar stories about his own paternity, ignored the calumny, and there is enough of the Stewart in Charles's appearance to support his confidence. The long nose and face of his great-grandfather James V are faithfully reproduced in Van Dyck's superb portraits. The mouth is small but fleshy and unconvincing; the hooded eyes, so alluring in Mary Queen of Scots, in Charles appear disdainful, while the perfect brows of his ancestors have given way to straighter, thicker lines. Despite its frame of magnificent dark auburn hair and the most elegant of beards and moustaches, it is not a particularly handsome face. Neither is its appeal increased by the aloof expression with which it was generally painted.

Charles was probably the most astute patron of the arts ever to occupy a British throne. In England the tradition of royal patronage of literature, painting, architecture and music had lapsed somewhat under the parsimonious Elizabeth. It was revived by James and reached a remarkable apogee under his son. Some have claimed that the king's support of geniuses such as Inigo Jones and Van Dyck alienated him from the majority of his subjects, who mistrusted the court's new classicism and heavily intellectual allegory. While it is true that during the Civil War philistine Parliamentarians scorned the king's costly 'old rotten pictures and broken-nosed marbles', this was wartime propaganda, the grasping of any stick to beat the enemy. The truth is that however divisive his other behaviour, Charles's artistic example set standards which were widely adopted and went some way towards creating a national culture which transcended political frontiers. The three largest collections of Van Dyck paintings outside the court were all in the hands of men who later fought for Parliament.

Charles's ability to carry his subjects with him did not extend to church matters. His devout (but not bigoted) Anglicanism was inextricably tied to his belief in the Divine Right of Kings: as God had placed him over his kingdoms, so too He had entrusted him with the welfare of the churches in England, Ireland and, most controversially, Scotland. To question the authority of the king in either sphere was to question God's judgement; or as Charles himself put it, 'princes are not bound to give account of their actions, but to God alone'. In theory this was similar to his father's position. The difference was that James, the pragmatist, realised the folly of trying to marry theory and practice, whereas the idealistic Charles was obsessed with the creation of order and uniformity. In December 1642 he told James Hamilton that he would rather die a martyr than abandon his principles. James was the survivor; Charles was not, and he got his martyrdom.

Indecisiveness was not one of Charles's faults. But willingness to act with resolution is of little use unless accompanied by sound understanding and judgement, neither of which Charles possessed. Together with his reserve and the sort of obstinacy often found in the narrow-minded, this made the king almost as vexing to his supporters as to his opponents. To the last, for example, Charles insisted that 'sovereign and subject are clean different things' – a far cry from his father's patently frail humanity and an impossible position from which to negotiate with those who rejected the monarchy's divine origins. Equally trying was Charles's attitude to the day-to-day business of government. Although James spent more hours in the saddle than at his desk, he was an intelligent and swift enough worker to ensure that he kept abreast of what was going on. Not so Charles, who alternated between wasting hours pouring over the minutiae of his in-tray, and days on end when he showed no interest at all in matters of state. Charles was the first Stewart king to come into his inheritance in the prime of life. As in the case of his grandmother Mary Queen of Scots, one wonders whether the tough schooling of a troubled minority might not have better prepared him for the task which lay ahead.

II

The problem with presenting a balanced account of Charles's kingship is that everyone knows how the story will end before it has begun. Consequently there is a tendency to view his reign either as a long slide through constitutional breakdown, civil war and defeat to execution, or as an uneven roller coaster path, punctuated with significant 'turning points', to the same end. There was nothing inevitable about Charles's bloody fate. Chance and coincidence probably played as great a part in bringing it about as politics and economics. Furthermore, the tale's settings and characters were continually changing, involving court and courtiers, parliament and MPs, battlefields and commanders. The only constant actor was Charles himself, by turns victim, hero, king and pawn in the greatest of all Stewart dramas.

The reign got off to a bad start. Against a darkening economic background, Charles's government allowed itself to be drawn first into an unsuccessful war with Spain, then in 1627 into a contemporaneous and equally disastrous conflict with France. Both campaigns required a good deal more money than parliament was prepared to grant unconditionally. In the spring of 1625 a paltry expedition to liberate the Palatinate disintegrated around Breda. That autumn another costly but ill-disciplined force was humiliated before Cadiz. In 1627 a venture led by Villiers himself, now Duke of Buckingham and Lord High Admiral, failed dismally in its attempt to relieve the Hugenots besieged in La Rochelle. The three disasters provided a focus point for rising discontent.

The Tudor and Stuart courts were riven with factions, each striving to corner the market in the limited number of valuable crown perquisites, privileges and pensions. Elizabeth and James more or less maintained a balance between the competing groups. But in elevating Buckingham, that 'gilded bottleneck of patronage', to a position of unprecedented power, Charles drove frustrated parliamentarians to voice their disappointment in constitutional terms, most famously in the 1628 Petition of Right. The dissent was not all empty rhetoric either. Beneath the personal squabbles and posturing lay barely perceived issues of great magnitude. If MPs accepted the Divine Right of Kings, then how could they in all honesty criticise Buckingham, whom God's lieutenant had appointed? Did Charles have the right to override *habeas corpus*, as he did in 1626 when he imprisoned several gentlemen for refusing to part with the loan demanded in place of unforthcoming parliamentary subsidies? And, even more fundamentally, were parliaments really an integral part of the English system of government, or merely devices summoned by the king to help him in his office – 'altogether in [his]... power for their calling, sitting and dissolution'? With one eye on European developments, the administration's opponents (whom Charles said were but a 'few members') claimed that the very existence of a representative institution was at stake. The king, on the other hand, thought that it was parliament which was overstepping traditional boundaries. The squabbling ended in 1629 when Charles dissolved his third troublesome parliament in four years, arrested the most recalcitrant members and determined, for a while at least, to rule without the dubious assistance of his assembled Lords and Commons. Peace with France and Spain swiftly followed.

* * *

The government of England and Scotland depended ultimately upon co-operation between the crown and the political nation. As in Elizabeth's final years, so during the later 1620s war had placed that relationship under severe strain. But with the return of peace, tension subsided and Charles's southern kingdom entered upon an eight-year period of comparative prosperity and stability.

These were undoubtedly the best years of Charles's life. Apart from a light attack of smallpox, he enjoyed excellent health. With each year that passed his relationship with Henrietta Maria deepened in affection, nurtured by mutual delight and pride in their growing family. Six of their nine children survived into adulthood: Charles, Mary, James, Elizabeth, Henry and Henriette Anne, whose births spanned the fourteen years from 1630 to 1644. Although the young princes and princesses spent long periods apart from their parents, Charles and Henrietta Maria found more time to spend with their offspring than was usual for a royal couple; they took them for walks and on occasion enjoyed the sort of pleasant family evenings normally associated with Victorian households. The many portraits of Charles painted at this time are suffused with a serenity which borders dangerously on self-satisfaction.

It was not just Charles's domestic affairs which gave him cause for optimism. Since Buckingham's death he had no favourites, and chose instead to head his own administration. Assisted by a small group of efficient ministers, notably Archbishop William Laud, Lord Treasurer Richard Weston and Thomas Wentworth, President of the Council of the North and Lord Deputy in Ireland, he set about imposing the sort of order in church and state which so appealed to him. There was little new in the undertakings of Charles and his council; their aim was rather to breathe fresh life into old devices. 'Thorough' was their catchphrase, not 'Reform'. The royal finances were straightened out, so that by 1637 revenue had risen to over £1 million, an increase of fifty percent over that of 1625. This was the result partly of better management and partly of careful exploitation of the crown's traditional sources of income. The latter policy was not always popular, but only Ship Money caused serious opposition, and then not until Charles's 'Personal Rule' was already foundering on other shoals. Further measures sought to reinvigorate local government and improve the militia, while after a few years of tireless if tactless labouring in Ireland, Wentworth felt confident enough to tell Charles that he was 'as absolute here as any prince in the world can be'. For neither the first nor last time an English politician had gravely misunderstood that most complex of islands.

Charles was convinced that the 'best profession' of the Christian religion lay with the Church of England, yet he showed none of his father's passion for theology and claimed to have no quarrel with anyone acknowledging Christianity's fundamental beliefs. He accepted alike his wife's Catholicism (even gently chiding her when she missed mass) and the Presbyterianism of his tutor, Thomas Murray. And he was annoyed by the intolerance and presumption of MPs who attacked the cleric Richard Montagu for denying predestination and the fundamental nature of the doctrinal distinctions between Roman Catholicism and Anglicanism. In 1628, in a gesture that was bound to be misinterpreted, Charles appointed Montagu to the see of Chichester.

Still more open to misinterpretation were the efforts of Charles and Laud in the 1630s to tidy up the Church of England. What the king and his arch-bishop sought, they said, was manifest uniformity according to the Elizabethan settlement of 1559; all they succeeded in doing was opening up old wounds. Their efforts to control preaching, clean up churchyards ('in many places... extremely annoyed and profaned'), convert communion tables into railed-off altars at the eastern end of the church, increase the emphasis on ceremonial generally and support church courts might not strike us as particularly contentious. Punishments for offenders were few and usually quite mild. But taken altogether the measures gave some worshippers the impression of creeping Popery, a surreptitious scheme 'to alter and subvert God's true religion by law established in this realm'. By itself the dissent of a minority in one kingdom, albeit the most influential one, need not have caused Charles undue anxiety. But taken in conjunction with other sources of friction and, above all, with a major revolt in Scotland, it was very serious indeed.

III

The causes of the Great Rebellion against the Stewart monarchy are as complex and controversial as any event in British history. Whether the rebellion grew out of diverse and deep-rooted socio-economic changes or not, it first manifested itself in Scotland, where for all their vagaries the Stewarts had been held in the highest esteem for centuries. How on earth did Charles manage to dispel centuries of goodwill so quickly?

The king's Scottishness was limited to the trace of an accent in his voice and a romantic fondness for the country of his birth. By the time of his accession the Scotsmen with whom he came into regular contact, such as Sir William Alexander, Earl of Stirling, and the Marquis James Hamilton, were primarily English courtiers. When true Scots met the king they were astounded at his ignorance of his native land. That ignorance bred mistakes, which in turn bred resentment and, eventually, resistance.

Charles did not visit Scotland for eight years after his accession, governing in the meantime by remote control from London. It was not a tactful decision, for in the eyes of many Scots the Stewarts were primarily kings of Scotland for whom the English throne was an added perquisite. Mismanagement made the situation worse. The Scottish privy council was staffed by unsuitable ministers, and it was not long before the Scots were feeling that they were governed by a king who knew little about them and cared less. The upper echelons of society resented Charles's sweeping Act of Revocation and continued domination of parliament by the Lords of the Articles. Persistent direct taxation and the high cost of the king's belated Scottish coronation drew more widespread criticism. But as with the English, the Scots were most deeply upset by Charles's religious policies.

The appearance of a growing number of bishops on the privy council, culminating in the appointment of Archbishop Spottiswode as chancellor in 1635, was a clear indication of the direction Charles wished to take the kirk. His use of the alien English liturgy at all services in Scotland, particularly at his coronation, and the high-handed manner in which Lord Balmerino was dealt with for objecting to contentious Church Acts fanned the smouldering resentment. Flames first appeared in 1635 when the king issued a Code of Canons designed to bring the kirk more into line with Anglican practice. With the publication of a new prayer book the following year the king found himself with a full-scale conflagration on his hands. The canons assumed a 'Royal Supremacy in Causes Ecclesiastical' which had never been established in Scotland, and ignored presbyteries and the General Assembly.

The Prayer Book drawn up by Charles and his Scottish bishops was essentially non-controversial, although details of the communion service and references to 'ornaments' raised some hackles. What really infuriated the Scots was its introduction on the authority of the crown alone, without consent of either parliament or an Assembly. The new liturgy was first used on 23 July 1637 in St Giles's, Edinburgh. Amid cries of 'the mass is come amongst us!' a rather muscular woman (perhaps a man in disguise) hurled a stool at the unfortunate minister. A riot ensued. In a matter of days the protest had spread throughout the country. Charles responded with instinctive obduracy: 'I mean to be obeyed'.

One reason why Charles was such a difficult man to deal with was that time and again he adopted what seemed to be a resolute stand only to back down later. This resulted in his opponents having no clear idea what he really believed, and so drew them into pressing for further concessions. This is precisely what happened in Scotland in 1637-8. Having said that he would not give way to the rebels' demands, when the Scots organised themselves beneath a revolutionary National Covenant in the spring of 1638 Charles empowered his cousin Hamilton to negotiate with the Covenanters 'until I be ready to suppress them'. Controversial seventeenth-century ecclesiastical innovations were withdrawn and a Covenanter-dominated General Assembly met in Glasgow Cathedral in November. When the Assembly proved far more radical than Hamilton had anticipated, he tried in vain to dissolve it. His command was ignored and the members proceeded – illegally – to dismantle the whole kirk hierarchy, including bishops, which Charles and his father had put in place. The king determined to fight. It was not a sensible decision.

Charles had no standing army and could not lay his hands on enough money to raise one. The Scots were well led, reinforced by professional soldiers returning from the Continent and fired by a heady mixture of nationalism and religious fervour. To make matters worse, Charles's nine years of personal rule had raised so many doubts in the minds of the English that for one of the few times in their history they were unwilling to assist their king in a proposed conquest of Scotland. Consequently, the so-called 'Bishops' Wars' of 1639 and 1640, the king's first experiences of warfare, ended in his total humiliation. Far from blowing away the 'small cloud in the north' they served only to increase its size and spread it south. By the Treaty of Ripon signed in June 1640 Charles made further concessions to the Scots, whose forces now occupied the north of England, and agreed to pay them £300,000. That meant summoning an English parliament.

When the Long Parliament met in December 1640 no Englishman of any consequence thought that the disputes between the king and the political nation would lead to war. Furthermore, war would have been a physical impossibility because at the time Charles commanded virtually no support. The Cavalier party emerged in response to the growing radicalism of the king's parliamentary opponents. But that radicalism was at least partially forced upon them by the fact that at no stage did they feel able to trust the king. There is no point in holding any individual responsible for forging the complex chain of events which led to civil war, but through his refusal to accept that kingship was as much about politics as principles, Charles certainly added more links than anyone else.

A few examples must suffice. Many MPs could not bring themselves to trust a king who had expressed the fullest confidence in Lord Deputy Wentworth, even bringing him over from Ireland in 1639 to deal with the Scottish crisis, only to sign the death warrant of 'one of the fairest flowers of his garland' in May 1640. Equally conflicting signals were received later the same year when Charles seemed to agree to a humiliating constitutional settlement with the Scots, then intrigued to do away with Argyll, Hamilton (now with the king's enemies) and other Covenanting leaders. The same vexatious king made a convicted felon Lieutenant of the Tower of London in December 1641 and, stung by his wife's taunt of 'Go, you coward! and pull these rogues out by the ears, or never see my face more', brought soldiers into the Commons in January 1642 to arrest opposition leaders. The

Parliamentarians still said that it was the king's false advisors they mistrusted, not Charles himself. But in their hearts they knew this to be a fiction. By the summer of 1642 the gap between the two sides had become unbridgeable and Charles, who had left London immediately after his failure to arrest the Five Members, raised the royal standard at Nottingham on 22 August. A day or so later it blew down in a gale.

* * *

Charles made a good soldier. His leadership was strong and brave – sometimes almost inspiring – and he showed a competent grasp of tactics. He might have been more responsible than anyone else for the outbreak of war, but he cannot be blamed for losing it. In the end he was defeated by an enemy with a stronger strategic and logistical position, backed by superior financial resources, control of the sea and, latterly, by a large and well organised force of Scots. The king's best chance of success lay with a series of swift victories culminating in the capture of London. This he failed to accomplish.

Following the inconclusive engagement at Edgehill, near Warwick (23 October 1642), the royal army moved via Oxford towards the capital. Charles's nephew Prince Rupert, the most experienced Cavalier general, seized a Parliamentary outpost at Brentwood; but Charles then found himself outnumbered 2:1 by the trained bands of London and retired to his Oxford headquarters to consider peace proposals and plan the next year's campaign.

The negotiations with parliament came to nothing and Charles confirmed his enemies' impression that he was not to be trusted by reaching an agreement (of no military moment) with the Irish Catholics who had risen in bloody revolt against their Protestant overlords in 1641. The royalists had some military success in 1643, notably in the north and west, but their campaigns were not sufficiently well co-ordinated to threaten the parliamentary strongholds in the south-east. The most significant events of the year were parliament's reorganisation of its resources and its ambiguous agreement with the Scottish Covenanters, known as the Solemn League and Covenant. The League bore its signatories two fruit: one sweet, one bitter. The first was a considerable strengthening of parliament's forces in the north of England, enabling them to overwhelm Prince Rupert's army at Marston Moor on 2 July 1644. The second was the defection to the king of the outstanding commander James Graham, Marquis of Montrose. For a year Montrose waged a remarkable Highland campaign against the Covenanters until finally defeated by David Leslie's veterans at Philiphaugh in September 1645. By this time Charles too was in dire straits. Unwisely risking his main army in battle, in June he had been overwhelmed by Parliament's New Model Army at Naseby. It was a devastating blow to the royalists. The king recognised as much himself when he wrote a month later: 'I must say there is no probability but of my ruin'. At such times the age-old Stewart melancholia returned with a vengeance.

Over the next nine months the Cavalier war effort fell apart. Commanders surrendered or fled abroad. Common soldiers fended for themselves as best they could and one by one the royalist strongholds passed into parliament's hands, until even Charles's Oxford headquarters was threatened. To avoid capture the king fled the city in heavy disguise on 27 April 1646. Eight days later, placing his trust in the innate loyalty of the Stewarts' oldest subjects, he suddenly appeared at the Scottish army camp near Newark. His days of freedom were over.

IV

The royal family was now widely dispersed. The queen, who would never see her beleaguered husband again, had been set up by her family in the palace of St Germain-en-Laye near Paris, where she continued to work vigorously on Charles's behalf. Never one to cast principal aside lightly, at this juncture even she had the political common sense to see that the king's stubbornness had become a liability. In letter after letter she urged him to make concessions, whether he meant to keep them or not, until Charles finally begged her: 'For God's sake leave off threatening me... '. In this mood the king gave the impression that he was prepared to die rather than abandon his principles.

Henrietta Maria's eldest daughter Mary, married to William, Prince of Orange, was living in the Netherlands. Henriette Anne, the baby of the family affectionately known as 'Minette', was safely with her mother. In the spring of 1646 the teenage Charles, Prince of Wales (his more formal title of 'Prince of Great Britain' was rarely used), managed to slip away from the West Country to the Scilly Isles. After further adventures and a generous slice of luck he too eventually found his way to St Germain. At the end of the Civil War that left three royal children – James, Duke of York (aged fourteen), Princess Elizabeth (aged twelve) and Henry, Duke of Gloucester (aged six) – prisoners of state in England. They were well treated and permitted to see the king quite frequently, although their visits caused Charles as much pain as happiness. Early in 1648 James gave his guardians the slip during a game of hide-and-seek and was smuggled away to the Continent disguised as a girl. Elizabeth and Henry were allowed access to their father right up until the time of his death, bidding him a tearful farewell the day before his execution. Elizabeth died in detention in 1650 and Henry was granted compassionate exile three years later. To the great distress of his surviving brothers and sisters, he died of smallpox shortly after the restoration of Charles II.

* * *

Charles's behaviour during the last three years of his life is not easily understood, although the outline of what happened to him is swiftly told. He
remained with the Scots in the north of England until early in 1647, when
he was handed over to parliament and transferred to Holdenby House in
Northamptonshire. In June he was seized by a troop of soldiers under the
command of Cornet Joyce and taken to the army's headquarters at
Newmarket. That autumn he moved with the army to London and was
detained in Hampton Court, from where in November he escaped to
Carisbrooke Castle on the Isle of Wight. However the castle's governor
Colonel Robert Hammond was less sympathetic to the king's cause than
Charles had anticipated and he was once more detained. When the army had
suppressed a series of regional revolts and defeated a Scottish invasion, the
radical rank and file began openly condemning the king as 'Charles Stuart,
that man of blood'. He was transferred via Newport and Hurst Castle to
Windsor, where he remained until 19 January 1649. His last moves were to
the capital itself, trial in Westminster Hall and finally the scaffold in
Whitehall.

Sometimes Charles gave the impression that he was willing to come to
terms. He entered into compromise agreements with the Scots when on the
Isle of Wight, and with parliament several months later. But on other occasions he dug in his heels, telling his captors 'You cannot do without me. You
will fall to ruin if I do not sustain you.' As so often before, such equivocation
drove to distraction all who sought to negotiate with him. The Scots gave up
in despair in 1647. The army commanders, most notably Oliver Cromwell,
followed suit at the end of 1648. Both had concluded, albeit reluctantly, that
there was simply no point in talking to the king any more. Even at his trial,
just before the sentence of death was pronounced, Charles changed tack for
the umpteenth time, crying 'I have a plan... for a lasting peace... '. But the
court had had enough and refused to listen. It is a measure of Charles's almost
unbelievable political ineptitude that when his kingdoms were in turmoil,
split from top to bottom by social, political and religious divisions, he failed
to take advantage of the situation and secure his release.

Even the view that Charles courted martyrdom does not hold much water.
It might explain why on 20 March 1648, when careful plans had been made
for his escape, he refused to leave the Isle of Wight. But it does not explain
the several genuine efforts to get away which ended in failure, or the pathetic
outburst at his trial, or the confession made in October 1648 after he had
struck a bargain with parliamentary Presbyterians

> 'the great concession I made this day – the Church, Militia and Ireland
> – was made merely in order to my escape [sic], of which if I had not
> hope, I would not have done'.

At his trial Charles refused to recognise the authority of the tribunal or to answer the charges levelled against him. Technically speaking his stance was correct, for the only legally constituted courts were the king's. Yet he was wrong to believe that 'the freedom and liberty of the people of England' were on trial with him. Those determined to get rid of him were no more tyrants than he had been, and the government of the interregnum was probably more competent and humane than its precursor. In the rhetoric of the court which had tried him Charles was executed for being a 'traitor and murderer' who had attempted 'to introduce an arbitrary and tyrannical government'. In fact he was condemned to suffer death 'by the severing of his head from his body' on 27 January 1649 because, like his equally infuriating grandmother Mary Queen of Scots, he had left his captors with little alternative.

CHAPTER 18

The Politician and The Papist

I

At the time of his execution Charles I had three sons: Charles, James and Henry. The latter, as we have seen, died suddenly at the age of twenty, having outlived the restoration of the Stewarts by only a few months. But Charles and James survived the dangers of war and sickness to determine their dynasty's fortunes for a further forty turbulent years, at the end of which the family split irrevocably and the senior branch was once more languishing on the Continent.

* * *

After a few enjoyable sporting months on Jersey, in June 1646 Charles moved to St Germain at his mother's request. Here, to his intense frustration, he marked time for two years in the cloying, formal atmosphere of the queen's court. He played the part of the dutiful son with instinctive charm but was irritated at the way Henrietta Maria failed to consult him over matters of policy, and he reacted coldly to her efforts to marry him off to 'La Grande Mademoiselle', the formidable daughter of her brother Gaston, Duke of Orleans. This painful exile within an exile ended in July 1648 with Charles's departure for The Hague and the company of his sister Mary and her husband William, now stadtholder of the Calvinist United Provinces. For the first time in his life the prince was free to exercise real authority. He soon discovered, however, that it was one thing to plan action and quite another to put it into operation.

The events of the previous eight years had splintered the ranks of the royalists and their sympathisers into numerous, generally hostile factions. Somehow Charles had to reconcile these if he was to stand any chance of restoring his family's fortunes. Among his closest supporters were his Roman Catholic mother and her French backers, the flamboyant but politically inept Prince Rupert and the hot-headed young Duke of York. Other nominal backers were the Calvinist Dutch, optimistic Irish royalists, dispirited Cavaliers and disaffected English parliamentarians. The king could also expect help from a variety of Scots, whose adherence to the Stewart cause ranged from the unquestioning loyalty of Montrose, through the pragmatic support of Hamilton, John Maitland of Lethington and those who had reacted against the English army's seizure of power by entering into the Engagement in the winter of 1648, to the stricter and more wary Covenanters led by Archibald Campbell, the squint-eyed and fanatical 8th Earl of Argyll. Not surprisingly, it was quite beyond the capacity of the eighteen-year-old prince to produce a coalition from such a motley, squabbling crew. Indeed, when his restoration did come about it was less the result of his own efforts than of developments within England over which he had virtually no control.

Nevertheless, Charles did what he could. In the summer of 1648 he relieved James, Lord High Admiral since the age of four, of his command over the English naval vessels which had recently mutinied and come over to the royalists. The move was only the first of several embarrassing confrontations between the two brothers. Charles then led the fleet on an unprofitable patrol along the coast of south-east England. The rest of the year was largely taken up with an attack of smallpox and infatuation for Lucy Walter, the 'brown, beautiful, bold but insipid creature' who was the first of Charles's many mistresses. The former affliction left him less scarred than the latter: he was never able to shake off rumours that he had secretly married his lover, and James, the son Lucy bore him in April 1649, hung like a deeply-loved albatross round Charles's neck for the remainder of his life. Shortly before receiving his son, Charles lost his father. The news of Charles I's execution reached the Continent in a newspaper report and was tactlessly relayed to his successor by Dr Goffe, one of the royal chaplains. Going up to Charles in the middle of a crowded room, Goffe simply addressed him as 'Your Majesty' for the first time. The young man burst into tears. Rarely thereafter did he allow his emotions to get the better of him in public.

Understandably furious that the regime in England should have beheaded their king without even consulting them, Charles's Scottish subjects swiftly recognised Charles II and entered into protracted negotiations to install him in his northern kingdom. Charles was as suspicious of the Covenant and its dour adherents as his father had been. But he had outstayed his welcome in the United Provinces, and having heard that Cromwell had smashed the royalists in Ireland and that the dashing but unpopular Montrose had been defeated and executed by his Covenanting opponents in Scotland, on board a vessel lying off the Moray coast Charles reluctantly agreed to his hosts' stringent terms and proceeded ashore. Within days he was wishing with all his heart that he had never come. A poisonous cloud of mutual mistrust hung over his relations with the Covenanters. They froze him from their councils and subjected him to endless petty insults and humiliations. 'Nothing', Charles retorted later, 'could have confirmed me more to the Church of England than their hypocrisy'.

The Scots were unable even to provide Charles with the military security he needed. Fresh from his Irish campaign, Cromwell swept north, destroying the Covenanting army at Dunbar on 3 September 1650 and occupying Edinburgh and a large part of lowland Scotland. The engagement at Dunbar enabled the king to increase his personal authority and he was crowned at Scone on 1 January 1651; but the area under his control was dwindling almost daily. By the summer, finding virtually all of his kingdom apart from the Highlands in English hands, he led his army past a contemptuous Cromwell, over the border and down into England. Like the similar journey made almost a century later by Bonnie Prince Charlie and his Jacobites, it was a brave but ultimately hopeless gesture. Holed up in Worcester, Charles's outnumbered and depleted force was annihilated by Cromwell's professionals, again on 3 September. The king fought with remarkable bravery then fled from the battlefield. Assisted by immense good fortune and the innate loyalty of dozens of his subjects – including many Catholics – he remained at large for six weeks until in October he finally found a captain prepared to ferry him from Shoreham to the relative security of France.

By the age of twenty-two Charles had already experienced more adventures than befall most people in a lifetime. The effect on him was marked. He had learned to dissemble, to act and to conceal. He was convinced of the untrustworthiness, even unpleasantness of the great majority of the human race, particularly Scots and Presbyterians. Those who were not cheats were foolish idealists, like his father and Montrose, who invariably came to sticky ends. Above all, he was now certain that there was only one person who truly deserved his unstinting care and attention: himself.

* * *

There must have been times during the next eight years when Charles wondered whether he would ever return to the kingdoms which were his by right. By the end of 1653 there was no territory left, not even the American colonies, which still regarded him as its king. Despite its problems, Cromwell's regime had become a relatively stable part of the European scene, powerful enough to attract an alliance with Cardinal Mazarin's France in 1655. As more and more countries closed their doors to him, Charles and his paltry, impecunious court toured like a shabby circus in search of a sponsor. In 1654-5 it travelled from France to Germany and then, following its ringmaster's decision to become a pensioner of Spain, on to a more permanent site in the Spanish Netherlands. As well as doing what he could to keep his cause alive, Charles filled his days with vigorous exercise, playing games, chasing women (including La Grande Mademoiselle – this time it was she who went on the defensive) and dancing, at which he excelled. He did not, as some reported, resort to 'low debauchery'; nor was he a spendthrift. Always aware of his role as a king, albeit without a kingdom, as far as his circumstances allowed he carried himself with dignity and notable courtesy.

James Duke of York, younger and less immediately concerned than his brother with the prospect of the dynasty's restoration, went his own way for a while. After failing to augment his income through marriage, he signed up for the army of the brilliant French general Turenne and enjoyed himself hugely as a brave if somewhat naive cavalry officer. His antics were terminated by Charles's Spanish alliance, which forced James to surrender his French commission and join his erstwhile enemies in their dismal campaign in the Low Countries. The switch engendered another painful fraternal row.

Just how crucial the genius of Oliver Cromwell had been to the stability of the English republic became apparent immediately after his death, which occurred with remarkable coincidence on 3 September 1658. In Brussels Charles waited with mounting frustration as the strange pattern of shifting administration and royalist revolt unfolded. Then in January 1660 General George Monck crossed into England from Scotland with a large and disciplined body of troops and set in motion the train of events which culminated in the king's return. Now that he was once more the man of the moment, Charles was permitted to return to the United Provinces. From here on 4 April he issued his conciliatory Declaration of Breda, setting out the terms under which he would accept restoration: a general amnesty, liberty of conscience, a fair land settlement and arrears of pay for the army, with the tricky details to be worked out by parliament. Promising everything but guaranteeing nothing, the Declaration met the needs of most interested parties, and on 25 May 1660 Charles II stepped ashore at Dover to a tumultuous, almost hysterical welcome.

* * *

On catching a glimpse of himself in a mirror Charles is supposed to have remarked, with a rare burst of truthfulness, 'Odd's fish! I am an ugly fellow.' He was certainly the most unhandsome of all the Stewarts whose features have been recorded. His long, fleshy face was like a caricature latex puppet fashioned out of his ancestors' least prepossessing features: heavy brows over cold, dark eyes, a large putty nose, thick lips which curved at the edges into a smirk, and a bulbous chin. His hair was black, his complexion unfashionably swarthy. Elsewhere nature had been kinder to him. According to a poster issued during his escape from Worcester he was 'above two yards high', very tall for the seventeenth century and a characteristic perhaps inherited from his great-grandparents. For much of his life he kept his lean, muscular figure in good trim. A keen, almost obsessive sportsman, like many of his dynasty, he was in the habit of taking long fast walks twice a day, and rode and sailed as well as any man in the country.

The torch of Stewart sexuality, which had burned uncustomarily low during the previous two generations, was fanned into new flame by Charles's ardour. Not since James IV had such a passionate lover sat on a British throne. Like James, Charles treated women as a yuppie might treat his motor cars; easily dissatisfied when they started to show signs of wear and tear or when a new model appeared, he changed them often and rarely regarded them as anything other than convenient amusements. They and their offspring cost him a good deal of money and sometimes not a little personal and political embarrassment, but only one or two, most notably Louise de Keroualle, the long-standing favourite of his later years, influenced affairs of state. The rest of the beautiful collection, whose unmistakable charms were sometimes recorded for posterity with titillating frankness by court painters, were little more than playthings.

The king's obsession with sexual conquest – perhaps the most obvious manifestation of his selfish narcissism – caused most suffering to his wife, the prim Roman Catholic Portuguese princess Catherine of Braganza. Their marriage took place in 1662, cementing the move away from Spain which had been signalled the previous year by the wedding of Charles's young sister Henriette Anne to the Duke of Orleans. Unsophisticated, convent-educated and accompanied by a dreary entourage of ladies 'for the most part old and ugly and proud', Catherine was hardly the sort of bride to divert Charles for long from his philandering ways. The best he could say of her looks was that there was 'not anything in her face that can in the least shock one'. Nevertheless, he was kind enough to her for a few weeks and professed to finding his first night with her most agreeable.

The felicity did not last. Before long the queen's home-grown harridans were packed off back to Portugal and replaced by English ladies-in-waiting, among whom was the ravishing Barbara Palmer, Countess of Castlemaine, very much the mistress in current favour. The queen's misery multiplied when, despite the king's efforts which proved only too successful in other beds, she failed to conceive a child. Court gossip was not slow to read more into the situation. It was rumoured that Edward Hyde, Charles's principal minister and now Earl of Clarendon, had arranged his master's marriage in the knowledge that Catherine suffered from a continual 'bloody flux', and so was unlikely ever to bear children. The queen's predicament did indeed suit Hyde well. In September 1660 his daughter Anne had married Charles's heir, his brother James, Duke of York, and given birth to his child the following month. Seven other children followed. Two of them, Mary and Anne, eventually succeeded to the throne.

By the 1670s Catherine knew that she would never win the heart of a husband from whose bed she was almost totally estranged. Charles continued to treat her with charming civility – as he did all who did not cross him openly. He resisted the temptation of divorce and resolutely stood by his queen when she became the subject of popular anti-Catholic suspicion. But he did not change his behaviour. For her part, Catherine, whose affection for Charles was painfully genuine, learned to live with his waywardness, although it always upset her. She knew him well enough to realise that she had a better chance of keeping in his favour through dignified detachment than confrontation. Her brave attitude is well exemplified in a story from the 1670s.

Wishing to spend time enjoying the saucy delights of that 'bold merry slut' Nell Gwynne, the king sent a message to his wife that he was ill and so could not be with her. Catherine, impossibly naive or simply jealous, took him at his word and hastened to visit him on his sick bed. When the revellers were warned of the queen's approach, the naked Nell gathered up her clothes and hastily secreted herself behind a wall hanging. In her haste she left a slipper behind on the floor.

Entering the royal bedchamber and seeing Charles beneath the sheets and the offending slipper in the middle of the room, the queen realised at once what had been going on. Sighing, she turned and left, explaining that she had no wish for the pretty fool who owned the slipper to catch cold and so be taken with a genuine illness.

We are told that as Charles lay dying he sent Catherine a message begging her forgiveness for all the wrong he had done her. He may have meant it, or it may have been just another example of his unfailingly good manners. With Charles one never knew.

II

In some parts of the country the magnificent nation-wide party sparked off by Charles's return lasted for over a week. There was a stupendous amount of drinking and no end of singing, dancing, parading and other jollifications. But when the jubilation had died down and the country sat nursing its collective hangover, it was soon apparent that the Restoration brought as many problems as it solved. It was not possible simply to put the clock back to, say, January 1637 and pretend that everything which had happened thereafter was an easily forgotten aberration. Men (including a king) had died for dearly held causes. The institution of monarchy had been questioned and the authority of parliament enhanced. Much land had changed hands, all kinds of Protestant churches had sprouted, some with deep roots, and in various parts of Charles's kingdoms a new class had tasted power. The world had been turned upside down, and now that it was the right way up again it was clear that not all the bits had fallen back into their former positions. It was a new era, requiring a new approach. Where that approach would lead, whether to a Continental-style absolutism or to a different form of government altogether, depended very much upon the people involved, particularly King Charles.

The thirty-year-old king understood all this. Somewhere at the back of his shifty mind there lurked a shadowy image of his ideal form of government, in which he exercised easy, total control over church and state. He referred to it when he was unsure which course to take, but it was never a sustained practical goal. His first objectives were to survive with as little aggravation as possible, and enjoy himself. To these ends his policies were cautious and pragmatic. Whatever else happened he was determined 'never to go on his travels again'.

Charles did survive – to that extent he was successful – and during the last years of his reign he enjoyed as much authority as his father and grandfather had ever done. Yet his journey to the haven of the 1680s was a rough and sometimes perilous one, and certainly not helped by his shortcomings as a political helmsman.

It did not take long for the cracks papered over during the summer of 1660 to open up again. Coming so swiftly after a period of godly moral austerity, the king's lifestyle did not help. Nor did the fact that however much Charles tried to reward ex-royalists there remained many, particularly those who had voluntarily sold land and possessions, who felt let down by the restoration settlement. More ominous was parliament's unwillingness to give the king all the powers he sought. The prerogative institutions abolished under his father were not reinstated. In 1664 a new Triennial Act, by which parliament was supposed to meet at least once every three years, replaced that of 1641. And Charles found that supposedly adequate financial provisions did not bring in anything like as much as had been anticipated.

The administration's most serious setback arose over the religious settlement. Misjudging the mood of their Anglican supporters, Charles and Clarendon sought a broad-based church. Parliament and the bishops looked for a more exclusive institution, and by 1665 they had got their way. With a series of restrictive acts, misnamed the 'Clarendon Code', they excluded all but Anglicans from local office and set up a church firmly tied to the prevailing social and political establishment, thereby instituting the Tory parson-squire partnership which dominated the English countryside until well into the nineteenth century. In 1662 Charles had tried to counter parliament's initiative by resurrecting the royal power to dispense with unwanted laws, but the legislature did not support his ill-considered Declaration of Indulgence and it was dropped.

1660 saw the restoration of royal authority in Ireland and Scotland as well as England. The Cromwellian union of the three nations was dissolved. To the chagrin of Irish royalists, who in 1649 had recognised Charles II before any other of his British subjects, much land in Ireland remained in the hands of those who had held it under Cromwell. A minority Anglican church was re-established and the country governed in the king's name by his viceroy. Charles never visited Ireland and knew little of its people or their ways. His comparative disregard for a nation which had suffered more than any other at the hands of his enemies added yet another bitter chapter to the tragic history of Ango-Irish relations.

In theory the Scottish restoration returned the country roughly to the situation prevailing in 1633. The 1661 Act Rescissory annulled all legislation made since that date and a number of religious statutes reinstated an

Episcopal Presbyterian church, minus its General Assembly. Yet a third of the clergy refused to accept the new arrangement and Charles's reign was punctuated with nonconformist rebellions. Nevertheless, thanks largely to the corrupt yet effective practices of ministers such as Commissioner John Maitland, Duke of Lauderdale, the authority of Charles – the 'only Supreme Governor of this Kingdom, over all persons and in all causes' – had increased markedly by the time of his death in 1685.

Given the unpopularity of Charles's government by 1665, it now seems almost unbelievable that he should have risked making the situation worse by launching into war. But that is precisely what he did, formally instituting hostilities against the Dutch in March. The naval conflict was costly and ended two years later in humiliation when a Dutch fleet sailed up the Medway, set fire to three capital ships and withdrew, taking the king's flagship with them. By the time the Treaty of Breda was signed in July 1667 the joyous summer of 1660 had become a distant, almost cruel memory. It was certainly so for Clarendon. Out of favour with his master, dismissed from office and assailed on all sides in parliament, he fled abroad in November 1667 to avoid impeachment.

The next few years are traditionally associated with a ministry known as the Cabal, an acronym formed from the initial letters of the ministers Clifford, Arlington, Buckingham, Ashley Cooper and Lauderdale. Recent research suggests not only that Arlington played a far more prominent part than the others but that the king himself was responsible for most important decisions. Eager to govern with as few limitations as possible, his policies assumed Byzantine complexity. 1668 saw a Triple Protestant Alliance with Sweden and the United Provinces. Two years later, needing French money and fearing that if he did not abandon his fellow Protestants then the Dutch would, Charles had reverted to the camp of the mighty Louis XIV. The covert and open agreements between the two monarchs were devious, uncertain and open-ended. Charles made promises about restoring his realms to Roman Catholicism and a firmer commitment to helping Louis fight the Dutch. Submitting to ministerial pressure, two days before the outbreak of war in 1672 Charles issued a second Declaration of Indulgence, designed to help both Protestant and Catholic dissenters.

After the fall of Clarendon Charles had worked hard to curry favour with the 'Cavalier' parliament, still intact from 1661. In 1670 he had even resorted to the crude but effective bribe of allowing members to drink away their animosity at his expense in the royal wine cellars. Such extravagance was good public relations but bad financial management – in 1672 the impecunious exchequer was obliged to announce a temporary halt to all interest payments on money it had borrowed.

In Parliament Charles's second Dutch War was initially well received. But not so the second Declaration of Indulgence. He withdrew it in March 1673 and parliament pushed through a Test Act banning all Roman Catholics from holding public office. This was particularly embarrassing for the king as it obliged his brother James, the dull-witted heir to the throne, to make public his previous conversion to the Roman faith and resign his post of Lord High Admiral. Yet more alarming in Protestant eyes was James's marriage in the same year to a fifteen-year-old Roman Catholic protégé of France, Mary of Modena. Anne Hyde, who had died in 1671, had left James with daughters. Now he had a new and healthy young partner there was a very real chance of his establishing a whole line of Catholic kings. It was a prospect to strike dread into every Protestant heart.

England's expensive but largely unsuccessful participation in Louis's Dutch war ended in 1674 with the Treaty of Westminster. There followed four years of relative tranquillity. Thomas Osborne, Earl of Danby, a pompous, pallid Yorkshireman of administrative and political acumen, worked diligently to restore some semblance of order to government accounts and skilfully managed the troubled Cavalier parliament. With Louis XIV, whose lavish bribes lined the pockets of just about every Englishman with political influence, Charles played his usual vicissitudinous game. The marriage of James's elder daughter Mary to William of Orange in 1677 and the arrival of English troops in the United Provinces to assist the Dutch against the French invader were Charles's way of reminding Louis not to take him for granted. They also helped calm Protestant anxieties, which had recently been further stirred by the king's passionate involvement with two formidable French beauties: Louise de Keroualle, Duchess of Portsmouth, and Hortense de Mancini, Duchesse de Mazarin and niece of the celebrated cardinal.

* * *

The comparative calm of the years following the Treaty of Westminster was deceptive. Charles's all too public private life continued to offend on financial as well as moral grounds. Years of political deception and double-dealing had created an atmosphere of credulous uncertainty in which rumour and truth merged, like colours on a palette, into a dark sameness. The king was in possession of an army in the Netherlands. His wife, his brother and others about him shared the same faith as Louis XIV, that daunting personification of Catholic absolutism and might whose ambitions had shaped European international relations for the past seventeen years. Into this fertile soil fell seeds of a fantastic story – the Popish Plot.

It was of little consequence that no actual plot existed in the summer of 1678. What mattered was that a credulous, frightened populace was prepared to believe that there was one. The hoax peddled by the extraordinary liar Titus Oates and his side-kick Israel Tongue was just plausible: there was a Popish design to kill the king and establish a Catholic despotism. Chance happenings and fortunate discoveries gave the story full credibility. On 22

October the body of Sir Edmund Berry Godfrey, a magistrate to whom Tongue and Oates had made sworn statements of their discoveries, was found in a ditch on Primrose Hill. In all likelihood he had been murdered. Further investigations revealed an ex-secretary of the Duke of York in possession of treasonable letters, and a dismissed ambassador to the French court showed that Danby had been negotiating with Louis XIV while simultaneously asking parliament for funds to go to war with him. Perhaps because Charles never believed for one moment that there was any truth in the plot rumour, he was slow to realise its destructive potential and he failed to destroy the monster at birth. As a result, by the end of 1678 he had a full-scale political crisis on his hands.

Truth, of course, was the plot's first victim. Others soon followed. The first of many innocent Catholics was executed on 21 November. A Second Test Act prevented all Roman Catholics except the Duke of York from sitting in parliament. Intent on impeaching Danby and muttering against the heir to the throne, the Cavalier parliament was finally dissolved on 3 February 1679. Its replacement, the first Exclusion parliament, proved even less amenable to the king's wishes. By the middle of May Danby was in the Tower and the Duke of York sheltering on the Continent. Attempts were made to draw the queen into the Popish 'conspiracy' and parliament discussed an Exclusion Bill to bar James from the succession on account of his religion. The diminutive Anthony Ashley Cooper, Earl of Shaftesbury, the brilliant but embittered ex-minister whom Charles dubbed 'Little Sincerity', had built up a powerful party of Exclusionists (the Whigs) around the Duke of Monmouth, Charles's son by Lucy Walter. Although Charles continually denied it, Monmouth maintained that his parents had secretly married, making him the true (and Protestant) heir to the throne.

The crisis lasted until the summer of 1681. In the interval there were two more parliaments and two more unsuccessful Exclusion Bills. The heads of unfortunate Catholics continued to roll, the last being that of the Catholic Archbishop of Armagh in July 1681. Shaftesbury plotted. Charles prevaricated. Monmouth, vain and wholly unsuited to his role, progressed around the country as the Protestant saviour. In the end, however, the political nation held firm and the Exclusion movement, like the Plot scare, dissolved. The prospect of a Roman Catholic monarch was frightening, even to the king's Tory supporters; but it was not worth fighting over. For his part, Charles emerged from the whole sordid episode with little credit. For three years he had largely lost control of his kingdom. Torn between love for his son and dutiful concern for the rights of his brother, he had failed to give a consistent lead to his supporters. But in the end he had survived; and that, ultimately, was always his prime concern.

The third Exclusion parliament, which had gathered at Oxford in the first week of April 1681, was Charles's last. Thereafter, not through any grand design but because he never needed to summon them, he ruled without the services of his Lords and Commons. The economy was expanding, providing him with an unprecedentedly large income, and he was still receiving subsidies from Louis XIV. After a protracted stay in Scotland, James returned to the English court. In November 1682 Shaftesbury was driven into exile in Holland. Monmouth, whom Charles was reduced to labelling a 'beast and blockhead', followed in his mentor's footsteps fourteen months later. Oates was fined £100,000 and cast into prison. Where possible other Whigs were removed from office, a process facilitated by granting new royal charters to fifty-one English boroughs. Maintaining his personal control of government, Charles avoided war and its accompanying political and economic dislocation. By the beginning of 1685, therefore, only four years after the collapse of the Exclusion movement, it seemed as if the authority of the Stewart monarchy had never stood higher.

Then, suddenly and painfully, Charles II died. On 2 February he took to his bed with a kidney complaint. Three days later, during his last evening on earth, he was quietly received into the Roman Catholic church by Father Huddlestone, whom he had first met over thirty years before during his escape from Worcester. The death-bed conversion remains a mystery. It might have been pressed on a befuddled and ailing Charles by his eager brother. Or Charles might have refrained from adopting his mother's faith until he was sure that he would not have to face the political consequences of his action. Whatever the explanation, it was an appropriately enigmatic gesture from a man who had spent most of his life behind a mask of charming inscrutability.

After Huddlestone had withdrawn, Charles bade farewell to his family, legitimate and otherwise. He begged James to care for the Duchess of Portsmouth and indeed said 'Let not poor Nelly starve', although these were not his final words. Growing feebler by the hour, at dawn on the morning of Friday 6th he asked for the curtains round his bed to be drawn back and the casement to be opened. Two hours later he became unconscious and at 11.45am, his body already beginning to fester, he breathed his last.

III

The death of Charles II on that grey February morning dealt his dynasty a blow from which it never recovered. For the first time in the Stewarts' long history the head of the family had not left a legitimate heir of his own body. There was a fine double irony in the situation. Firstly, it was extraordinary that the most lascivious Stewart of all, father of countless bastards, should have let down the dynasty in this manner. Secondly, how strange that a man so unprincipled as Charles should have baulked at casting aside Queen Catherine in favour of a more fruitful marriage partner. Since he knew his blinkered brother only too well and understood what dangerous passions his Catholicism could ignite, one can only conclude that Charles had been content to die as he had lived, caring largely for himself and little for the welfare of his subjects.

* * *

Every now and again the Stewarts inevitably came up with a monarch whose political antennae either lacked sensitivity or were seriously deficient in some other way. James III, Mary Queen of Scots, Charles I and his son James were all thus deformed. The shortcoming cost them their thrones and, except for James VII and II, their lives as well. Yet it was the latter's failings which ultimately had the most enduring consequences, for neither he nor his direct descendants ever won back the crown he lost.

James was simply the wrong man in the wrong place at the wrong time, although it took a while for the political nation to realise this. At first many had understandable misgivings about the intentions of a devout Roman Catholic, whose religion was automatically associated in the popular imagination with arbitrary rule. If we are to believe Bishop Gilbert Burnet, the new king's accession aroused 'few acclamations of joy'. But after a lifetime in politics even James's underpowered imagination was able to comprehend his subjects' worries, albeit dimly, and in an effort to allay them he announced promptly that he was not 'a man for arbitrary power'. He further promised:

'I shall make it my endeavour to preserve this government both in church and state as it is by law established.'

Events would show whether he meant what he said.

Physically James resembled the late king quite closely, although the features which had looked so unprepossessing on Charles combined rather more harmoniously in his brother. As a young man he had been considered good-looking; even now, at the age of fifty-one, he still made an impressive figure. He was tall and well-built, with glorious shoulder-length hair that retained some of its deep chestnut lustre. Brown eyes and a large nose, less prominent than Charles's, sat easily on his long Stewart face above a firm chin and a fleshy, sardonic-looking mouth. James was painted often and well. The majority of the portraits, particularly the later ones, offer little hint of the personality beyond the canvas, apart from a haughty expression which verges on the vacant. Perhaps in only one picture, Sir Peter Lely's magnificent depiction of James as Duke of York which now hangs in the Scottish National Portrait Gallery, has the artist managed to suggest his subject's true nature. The duke is glancing to his right, unsurely, with a tight-lipped and obstinate look on his face. It is not the countenance of a man at ease with the world around him.

James liked order. He 'kept a constant journal of all that pass'd' and managed his household well. He had made an efficient Lord High Admiral and when king held his court on a far tighter rein than Charles had ever done. Military life suited him ideally – he was never happier than when striding about in uniform inspecting troops. Disliking 'private ease', he thrived on physical exercise and hard work. As sovereign he believed his task quite straightforward: God had created the world and charged kings with the task of governing it. They ought to have their subjects' best interests at heart, but only God could punish them if they acted wrongly. Rebellion, therefore, was akin to sacrilege. Moreover, since James held Roman Catholicism to be the only true faith, he saw it as his sacred duty to repeal England's penal laws and Test Acts, thereby freeing people to worship as they wished. In such circumstances, he believed, there would be no need to re-introduce Catholicism by force – once its obvious correctness was plainly visible his subjects would flock back to the papal fold of their own accord. That, anyhow, was the theory, simple and clear cut.

It was people that James found difficult to fathom. He could just about cope with men and women in clearly defined roles, like soldiers, sailors and servants. But lacking both insight and basic intelligence (even Charles scorned his brother's 'sotise' – stupidity), courtiers and politicians were an anathema to him. With his predecessor's quick-witted companions he had felt particularly awkward and embarrassed. On occasion he even found it hard to come to terms with himself. Although by nature puritanical, in his youth he had almost as many sexual adventures as his brother. But in complete contrast to Charles, James's lapses left him stricken with guilt – since his brother's mistresses were notoriously plain, Charles observed unkindly that they must have been given to him by his priests as penance. It was the uniquely talented but amoral George Villiers, 2nd Duke of Buckingham, who best summed up the difference between the royal pair. 'The King', he quipped when Charles was still on the throne, 'could see things if he would, and the Duke would see things if he could.' There was a great deal that James did not see.

* * *

It took the new king about ten months to lose the confidence of his English subjects and slightly longer for his ham-fisted policies to have the same effect in Scotland. His first Scottish parliament confirmed his 'solid, absolute authority', voted him a substantial revenue and agreed to severe anti-Covenanter laws. Rebellions against the popish king were swiftly and easily suppressed. But in 1686 the second parliament baulked at repeal of anti-Catholic legislation, forcing James to fall back on his royal prerogative to grant toleration to his fellow religionists and, by way of sweetening the pill, Presbyterians as well. Such blatant stretching of royal authority bred as much suspicion as relief, so that when James needed the support of his northern subjects in 1688-9 he found a goodly proportion of them unwilling to respond to his call.

James's English parliament had assembled on 19 May 1685. Heavily Tory but by no means subservient, its members were heartened to hear their sovereign declare: 'I will keep my word and undertake nothing against the religion which is established by law'. But the proviso 'unless you first break your word to me' had an ominous ring about it. So did James's remark that if parliament would not back his policies, 'You may be sure that I shall find means to do my business without you.' In the king's principal 'business', the advancement of Roman Catholicism, neither the Lords nor Commons were prepared to support him. Parliament was prorogued in November 1685 and never met again while James was master of his realm.

Despite his parliamentary trouble, James's position had by now strengthened markedly. He had been voted satisfactory supply and on 5 July his army had crushed the rebellion of the Duke of Monmouth at Sedgemoor. The

EDINBURGH CASTLE

inadequate duke, at this point more of a traitor in most people's eyes than a Protestant martyr, was executed on 15 July. About 300 of his supporters were condemned to death in the 'Bloody Assize' of Judge Jeffreys, whom James tactlessly made lord chancellor when he returned from the west. The royal army was enlarged and its efficiency improved, and the first wave of Catholic officers appeared in its ranks. The English might not have liked what James was doing, but there did not seem any easy way of stopping him.

James believed that his victory at Sedgemoor had been a sign of divine approval for his regime, and over the next two years he pressed ahead vigorously with his pro-Catholic policies. To do this he was obliged to exploit his powers in a manner which gave the impression that he was seeking to alter England's system of government, which – consciously at least – he was not. Part of the problem lay in the nature of the Restoration settlement. It had left the English constitution awkwardly plastic, not a finished article, fired and glazed. In Charles's hands it had begun to take on a definite form. Eager to improve on his brother's design, however, James seized the still malleable material with such haste and lack of dexterity that the vessel fell apart in his hands.

The principal instruments employed by James to further the lot of Roman Catholics were two medieval prerogative rights: the dispensing and suspending powers. The former allowed the crown to exempt individuals from the operation of specified laws, the latter enabled him to suspend the operation of a law entirely. In practice there was considerable overlap between them. Both had been the source of vociferous complaints during the Personal Rule of Charles I and the reign of Charles II, whose Declarations of Indulgence had sought unsuccessfully to exploit them in the interests of religious freedom. Unhamperered by parliament and backed by a 13,000-strong army based on Hounslow Heath, James resurrected the dispensing power to appoint Catholics to offices in the armed forces, the universities, the church and the government. His right to do so was upheld at appeal by the court of King's Bench in 1686. Formal relations were re-established with the papacy and policy was increasingly determined by the notoriously opportunist and mistrusted Robert Spencer, 2nd Earl of Sunderland, and a royal Catholic Council. JPs who would not support James's aim of repealing the Test Acts and penal laws were dismissed, many replaced by Catholics. All over the country murmurs of discontent arose. If the king persevered on his papist course, sooner or later there was bound to be a showdown. And James did persevere. Relentlessly.

In April 1687 he issued a Declaration of Indulgence, suspending the operation of all laws against Catholics and Protestant dissenters. It was not a popular move. Anglicans were furious that the head of their church should have betrayed them in this way; dissenters were suspicious – did a convinced Roman Catholic really want to see a multitude of Protestant congregations worshipping openly, or was the move merely a step on the road to universal

Catholicism? For the first time Sunderland expressed doubts about the wisdom of James's impetuous career towards toleration. On the other side of the North Sea James's Protestant nephew William of Orange was growing anxious too. Son of Charles I's daughter Mary and married to another Mary, James II's daughter, William regarded England's possible conversion to Catholicism with horror. If James's wishes were fulfilled then the right of William's Protestant wife to succeed her father would be jeopardised and England would be unlikely to support the Dutch in their struggle against Louis XIV. The stadtholder also feared lest James provoke a successful republican rebellion, which also might deprive Mary of her inheritance and himself of an ally. By April 1688 William was letting it be known that

> 'if he was invited by some men of the best interest... to come and rescue the [English] nation and religion, he believed he could be ready by the end of September to come over.'

On 27 April James re-issued his Declaration of Indulgence with the demand that it be distributed by Anglican bishops and read in every church in the land on two consecutive Sundays. Many denied the validity of the order in council under which the command came, and seven bishops, including Sancroft of Canterbury, were detained on charges of seditious libel. Before their trial James's opponents received another blow. On 10 June Queen Mary, who hitherto had been plagued by a series of unsuccessful pregnancies, gave birth to a healthy baby boy. When he heard the news James fell to his knees and wept tears of joy and thanksgiving for most of the night. His subjects were less jubilant, and a rumour soon spread that the baby was not the queen's but had been smuggled into her bed in a warming pan. Whatever the child's origin, the spectre of a dynasty of Catholic kings now loomed before the fearful nation.

The king's unalloyed happiness at the birth of his son and heir, James Francis Edward, did not last. Encouraged by judicial condemnation of the dispensing power, the jury at the trial of the seven bishops returned a verdict of not guilty. Shouts of delight echoed round the courtroom for half an hour. Bonfires were lit throughout the land and even the soldiers on Hounslow Heath could scarce forbear to cheer. Seven dignitaries, both Whig and Tory and including Charles II's lord treasurer Danby, wrote to William of Orange formally inviting him to invade England. 'Nineteen parts of twenty of the people', they suggested by way of encouragement, '... are desirous of a change'. It was just the tune William had been waiting to hear.

Several weeks passed before it dawned on James that his nephew and son-in-law was serious in his intention to invade. First he panicked, then he cracked under the strain. Sunderland was dismissed, the writs issued for what the king hoped would be a packed, favourable parliament were withdrawn, Catholics were relieved of their posts and old town charters restored. But all to no avail. James's subjects would not trust a man who had broken the promise made at his accession to defend the Church of England and the constitution. Instead they looked cautiously towards William, who tactfully announced that he was coming only to permit the calling of 'a free and lawful Parliament'. Sped by an easterly 'Protestant wind', the Dutch fleet sailed on 1 November and landed at Torbay four days later. The anniversary of the 1605 Gunpowder Plot was an auspicious date for the arrival of a Protestant saviour.

At this point James's leadership failed utterly. He was the anointed king, he had a powerful army to command and most of the political nation were waiting on events before deciding which way to jump. The king made up their minds for them by withdrawing into a dithering, morbid timidity. Control over the country's administration slipped from his hands. Hundreds deserted to William's camp, including Princess Anne and the up-and-coming John Churchill, the future Duke of Marlborough. Worn out by fruitless overwork and racked by indecision, James slithered into a bleak and uncomprehending introversion: Why was God allowing this to happen? What terrible sin had he committed to deserve such humiliation? When he took to musing at length on the fates of his father and other dispossessed monarchs it was clear that the old Stewart depression had surfaced yet again.

On 9th December the queen and her baby son left for France. James hung on in London for two more days, then set out by night in disguise to make the crossing himself. But his luck had now deserted him completely, and he was recognised and detained by Kentish fishermen on the lookout for fleeing Catholic priests. For three days, fearing for his life and weeping copiously, James was detained at Faversham. On the 15th he was taken back to London. Fortunately, at this point the wishes of the king and his successor coincided for the first and only time. No one was in the mood for martyrdom. James wanted to escape; William needed him out of the way. So the monarch whom no one wanted was taken by barge to Rochester, from where he was permitted to slip away by sea during the night of December 22-23. He landed at Ambleteuse in northern France on Christmas morning and joined the queen at St Germain shortly afterwards.

Thus was concluded the reign of the last Stewart king, the shortest (only 1418 days) and least glorious of the family's entire history. That James II should have overturned his 'great advantages' in so brief a period was to Bishop Burnet 'one of the strangest catastrophes that is in any history'. Perhaps if the bishop, himself a Scot, had recollected the comparison his countrymen were wont to make between the Stewarts and the horses of Mar he would not have been so surprised. Not since James IV had a Stewart monarch been held in appreciably greater esteem at the end of his reign than at the beginning. After five hundred years of political prominence and remarkable personal dynamism, the Stewart dynasty was slipping into a palpable, self-inflicted decline.

CHAPTER 19

Romans Without Countrymen

I

The Stewarts had always had their fair share of family disputes, most notably between the Albanies and crown in the early fifteenth century. But only twice before 1688 had a reigning monarch been successfully ousted by their offspring. Exactly two centuries previously James IV had overthrown his father at Sauchieburn, and seventy-nine years later Mary Queen of Scots had been forced to abdicate in favour of her son James VI. On both occasions the new monarch had been more a figurehead than a prime mover in the coup. At the time of his accession James IV had been a fifteen-year-old youth, while James VI had been only months old when he was proclaimed king in 1567.

Although a mature woman of twenty-six at the time of the revolution of 1688-9, Mary II was scarcely less of a symbol than the two previous Stewart usurpers. But not so her husband William of Orange, soon to be crowned alongside his wife as William III (or, technically speaking, William III of England and William II of Scotland). The arrangement had profound consequences for the Stewart dynasty. William and Mary ruled jointly – a partnership never officially accepted with Mary Queen of Scots and Lord Darnley – so if they had had any children they would have founded a new royal line, perhaps the House of Orange. After William and Mary the succession passed to Queen Anne, James VII and II's younger daughter by Anne Hyde. If Anne's children had survived, they too would have founded a new royal house. As it was, following Anne's death in 1714 the new royal dynasty was neither Orange nor Denmark, but Hanover, descended from James VI and I's daughter Elizabeth.

This did not mean the end of the Stewarts. The family lived on in exile, still claiming the crowns of Britain and Ireland *de jure*, and the last two chapters of this book are largely taken up with their attempts to win back the position which James VII and II had so feebly relinquished. But thrones are sooner lost than won. It would have taken a man of exceptional qualities to regain what was his by right, and the 'kings over the water' were not of that ilk. At the last, however, it was neither folly nor foe which brought the family to a close, but biology. After centuries of promiscuous fecundity, their most celebrated talent finally gave out. When neither of James VII and II's grandsons left an heir the story of one of Europe's most illustrious dynasties was finally over.

* * *

While the exiled King James mooched about St Germain-en-Laye, musing on the apparent unfairness of life and striving to come to terms with the startling sequence of events which had cost him his throne, the subjects he had deserted were trying to fill the vacuum created by his flight. Not surprisingly, it was the English, instigators of the 1688 coup, who managed most successfully. There were three questions to answer: how to explain James's disappearance, who was to replace him and what alterations needed to be made to the constitution to ensure that monarchical power would never again threaten the wishes of the ruling oligarchy. The first problem was solved by declaring, falsely, that James VII and II had abdicated and thereby left the throne vacant. William and Mary settled the second by letting it be known that one would not serve without the other. William said that he desired to govern 'in his person' and 'for the term of his life', not merely as 'his wife's gentleman usher'. Mary dutifully supported his demand and the two were crowned king and queen. The arrangement was a fudged political compromise, for even if James had abdicated and his son had indeed been smuggled into his wife's childbed in a warming pan, then Mary was his sole rightful successor. Although William had Stewart blood in his veins (his mother had been the eldest daughter of Charles I), only by accepting the radical idea that parliament had the power to rearrange the succession could he be considered the rightful king.

The settlement of 1689 altered the constitution less than one might have anticipated, although the Bill of Rights (October 1689) did away with some of the more contentious aspects of the royal prerogative as exercised by Charles II and his brother. What really changed the balance of power between crown and parliament was the way in which an unpopular monarch had been summarily replaced at the wish of the political nation, thereby rejecting the notion of divine right once and for all. The revolution was cemented in place by subsequent financial restrictions placed on William and further legislation, such as the 1694 Triennial Act and the 1701 Act of Settlement. By the end of the century England had an embryonic party system, annual parliaments, a national debt and cabinet government. When the last Stewart monarch died in 1701 the system of government had changed permanently and significantly from the one he had failed to manage only twelve years before.

On the face of it the situation in Scotland was more favourable to the exiled James. It was the English rather than the Scots who had driven him out, so in theory he was still King of Scotland, although he had never been crowned as such. William was asked to act as temporary executive and a convention parliament met to resolve the matter. Both kings sent letters setting out their positions. William's was tactful and conciliatory, James's brief and threatening. Clearly the King of St Germain had learned nothing from the experience of 1688. His supporters (Jacobites) then made the mistake of withdrawing from the convention and, having declared James's throne forfeit, parliament invited William and Mary to succeed him. They accepted with pleasure on 11 May 1689. Parliament proceeded with a settlement not unlike that in England, except that it incorporated religious changes which restored Presbyterianism and put the ecclesiastical clock back to where it had stood in about 1592.

For a number of reasons the Jacobite cause found more ready support in Scotland than in England. The Stewarts were, after all, originally a Scottish family and their demise had been forced upon them primarily by the English aristocracy. Although the first Jacobite revolt collapsed after the death of its leader Viscount Dundee at the Battle of Killiecrankie in 1689, the Stewart cause was not forgotten. William's distant, alien government became deeply unpopular. The new king's complicity in the massacre of Glencoe (1692) and in the failure of the Darien Scheme, a disastrous attempt to found a Scottish trading colony in Central America at the end of the century, confirmed many Scots in their hatred of the Dutch usurper. By the turn of the century many of the Stewarts' oldest subjects, particularly the Highlanders, were inextricably and tragically tied into the death throes of the dynasty which their ancestors had fostered so long ago.

But it was to Ireland that James first looked in the hope of regaining his crown. Shattered and depressed, initially he showed no inclination to go anywhere, let alone to a remote and notoriously lawless island on the Atlantic seaboard, now divided by civil war. But his paymaster Louis XIV, at war with England, thought the Irish card worth playing and in March 1689 James landed at Kinsale to a hearty welcome. The plan was to bring Ireland to heel and then cross over to the mainland with a loyal Catholic army. The south of the country was soon under James's control, but the Protestant north was determined to resist to the last man. The situation demanded decisive leadership and administrative efficiency. James provided neither. Lethargic and defeatist, he listened to advice from virtually anyone prepared to give it, then invariably chose the wrong option. His forces, though numerous, were ill-disciplined, poorly armed and worse led.

Feeling secure enough on the English throne, in June 1690 William gathered 15,000 soldiers and crossed to Ireland to deal with the situation in person. He brought with him a considerable artillery train and plenty of cash. Unlike the last time he had confronted William, in November 1688, James did not turn and flee. But he might as well have done so for all the resistance he put up. When the two armies met on the banks of the River Boyne on 30 June, James was outmanoeuvred and swiftly defeated. His gesture of defiance over, he reverted to type by losing his nerve and hastening back to Dublin, beset by nosebleeds and desirous of nothing but the secure comfort of St Germain. Refusing to contemplate further resistance, he sailed for France on 3 July. From this point onwards it was difficult for anyone, friend or foe, to take him seriously.

II

Queen Mary II did not excite anyone very much during her lifetime; she has not had much success with subsequent generations either. The most powerful emotion she stirs in most hearts is pity. A brief look at her life confirms this as probably the most appropriate response.

Anne, Duchess of York, gave birth to Mary Stuart on 30 April 1662, 'at which', observed Pepys in his diary, 'I find nobody pleased'. It was not an auspicious start. James was fond of his little daughter and showed her an affection unusual in royal households. But after the duke's conversion to Catholicism and remarriage to Mary of Modena, Charles II demanded that Mary and her sister Anne be moved to a separate establishment at Richmond House to prevent their coming into contact with their father's religious contagion. The rest of Mary's childhood was spent in comparatively trivial pursuits. Her formal education consisted largely of rigid indoctrination in the Anglican faith, suggesting that if she did succeed to the throne her husband was likely to exercise her sovereign powers.

The man chosen to fill that role was her cousin William, stadtholder of the United Provinces, whom she married on 4 November 1677. They made an odd-looking couple. Mary was fifteen, large (almost six feet tall and heavily built) and possessed of a certain buxom handsomeness. The twenty-six-year-old William was of medium height, thin, pale, eagle-nosed and asthmatic. Mary wept uncontrollably for almost thirty-six hours when she was told who her future partner in life would be.

The first few years of Mary's married life fulfilled her worst expectations. She was shipped off to Holland, where she was not popular. William was cold and reserved, preferring the hard life of the army camp to the more conventional pleasures of his wife's bed. Notwithstanding her husband's latent homosexuality, Mary had two apparent pregnancies. The first ended in miscarriage, the second in nothing at all. Thereafter she never conceived again. For solace she turned to religion, her piety developing into a somewhat disapproving priggery as she grew older.

Mary's devotion to the Church of England, coupled with a sense of her own unworthiness and a compelling desire to do what was right in the eyes of God and her husband, saw her through the traumatic experience of turning against her father in 1688. She was also helped by the fact that the steely William, whom she had soon come to regard with a pathetic, almost dog-like adoration, had by this time warmed towards her. Indeed, at her death he was to announce that he had 'never known one single fault in her'.

But in the hectic days of 1688-90 William was too busy with affairs of state to pay much attention to his lonely wife, who sadly observed that she was 'very much neglected, little respected, censured of all, commended by none'. She missed Holland, writing dismally that 'I shall always remember the tranquillity I enjoyed there and that I shall never find here'. She too had inherited the Stewarts' unfortunate disposition towards melancholy. To make matters worse, Mary and William fell out with Princess Anne and her dim-witted husband George of Denmark, for whom William had no time at all. He was even more censorious of Anne's confidante Sarah Churchill and her brilliant but dangerously slippery husband John. After 1692, with an unattractive display of Jacobean obstinacy, Mary refused ever to speak to her sister again.

In time the attitude of the English towards their new queen became less hostile. Although she had little influence on politics, she acted as a sensible regent during William's frequent absences on the Continent and with his approval exercised a concerned patronage over her beloved Church of England. Otherwise her days were spent in gossip, religious observation and puritanical attempts to improve the moral tone of the court and high society. Her eventual demise was never far from her thoughts: 'I do not know what will happen to me but, life being so uncertain, I prepare myself for death.' Bishop Burnet believed 'she seemed to desire death rather than life', and a violent attack of smallpox fulfilled her wish on 28 December 1694. She was thirty-two. The nation mourned the passing of one of its more worthy, if uninspiring servants.

For a while William was stricken with grief and remorse. His English wife had always been more popular in her native land than himself – not a difficult achievement – and her death had deprived him of just about his only true friend in a country he regarded as 'devilish… dirty and wicked'. But he was nothing if not single-minded. His obsession was the preservation of the Dutch republic against the might of Louis XIV's France. To that end, since Louis was the prime supporter of the exiled James, the English needed William as much as he needed them, and so the pragmatic partnership survived.

The mistrust on either side was mutual and not without foundation. The Tories, who had always found the revolution of 1688 difficult to square with their consciences, were on the whole unsympathetic to William, particularly after Mary's death, and they disliked his costly foreign wars. The Whigs were less hostile to the king's military exploits but keener on tipping the new balance of power between crown and parliament in favour of the latter. Wise men of both parties kept a finger in the Jacobite pie through clandestine contacts with St Germain. For his part William never came to terms with the political system then emerging in England. Parliament he found a tiresome nuisance, party politics an anathema and legislative control of royal finance unbelievably irritating. No one was ever left in any doubt that wherever his sickly body might be, his heart was always amid the poulders and windmills of Holland. Neither did his personality make co-operation any easier. In an age when most politicians displayed a suave and sophisticated cynicism, William's dogged honesty, aloofness and icy self control won few admirers.

The dull siege war with France dragged on until 1697. The king was personally brave but no great commander. His only success of note was the capture of Namur in 1695, a fortress town which he had lost to the French three years previously. The last years of his life were spent trying to arrange for a peaceful partition of the Spanish empire to follow the imminent death of the childless Spanish king, Carlos II. William's diplomacy came to nothing. When Carlos died in 1700 France laid claim to his inheritance, and by the beginning of 1702 the intrepid stadtholder king was again making preparations for war with his old enemy. This time, however, he never took to the field. On 21 February 1702 his favourite horse tripped on a molehill in the grounds of Hampton Court and threw William to the ground, breaking his collar bone. Complications arose from the fracture and a fortnight later he was dead. In several parts of the realm there was public rejoicing. 'No king', commented a contemporary, 'can be less lamented than this has been'. The Jacobites were especially delighted. For many years they drank toasts to 'the little gentleman in a velvet waistcoat' [the mole] who had so neatly removed the hated harbinger of all their woes.

* * *

King James had not survived to hear of William's death. After his Irish fiasco he had returned to France a man broken in spirit if not in health – he still managed to father a daughter, Louise Marie, born in June 1692. He dreamed of returning to his lost kingdoms and kept in touch with most leading English politicians, but he was able to offer them little more than token leadership. Naval expeditions in 1692 and 1696 went the sorry way of most seaborne attacks on the British Isles and an unsuccessful assassination attempt on William, intended as a precursor to the second assault, only provoked the king to declare publicly that he was the 'rightful and lawful king'. James had already convinced himself that he would be restored only if God willed it, so when the British destroyed his fleet in 1692 he sighed that the 'hand of God had appeared very visibly' in the action. The 1696 failure was dismissed with similar fatalism: 'the good Lord did not wish to restore me'. It was not what his supporters wished to hear.

The cause of the 'king over the water' was far from hopeless during these years. William was unloved and his wars unpopular. Had James been able to recapture some of his youthful vigour or, best of all, accept the church for which his father had died, then he would have stood a good chance of being the subject of a second Stewart restoration. But he was too old, too set in his ways to catch the cross-Channel current running in his favour, and by 1697 it had turned against him once more.

At the peace of Ryswick (20 September 1697) Louis accepted William as *de facto* king and undertook not to support those wishing to undermine his authority. Bitterly disappointed, James could only shrug his shoulders and mutter resignedly, 'God's will be done'. The faith for which he had sacrificed everything was now just about all he had left, and he drifted deeper and deeper into a senile saintliness. His spiritual devotions became obsessional. As well as attending mass twice daily and making frequent visits to the monastery at La Trappe, he scourged himself, took to wearing iron spikes round his thighs and would have indulged in yet more painful mortification of the flesh had those about him not urged restraint. The court at St Germain, well provided for by an annual pension of about £45,000 from King Louis, took on a depressed, lacklustre air. The diverse assortment of Jacobite hopefuls, heads stuffed full of 'chimeras and noise and nonsense', squabbled and plotted to no effect. In 1698 it was reported that 'King James looks mighty old and worn and stoops in his shoulders, the queen looks ill and melancholy'. The end was not far away.

In March 1701 James had a stroke which left him partly paralysed. Blood from painful stomach ulcers filled his mouth and splattered onto his clothing. On 1 September his condition grew worse. He was seized with convulsions and fits of violent shaking. On the afternoon of 5 September he died. His body was embalmed and cut up and the various parts distributed around France as holy relics. God's will, James presumably would have said, had been done.

III

The deaths of King William and King James left three characters on the Stewart stage, all children of the melancholy exile. At St Germain were James the 'Pretender' (the erstwhile 'warming pan baby') and Louise Marie, his son and daughter by Queen Mary of Modena; on the British throne sat Queen Anne, Anne Hyde's second daughter. The queen's last surviving child, William Duke of Gloucester, had died in 1700 at the age of ten. Louise Marie followed him to the grave twelve years later. So when Anne breathed her last on 1 August 1714, of the original cast only the Pretender remained.

One of the royal Stewarts' great strengths, or strokes of good fortune, was that they had generally managed to come up with a competent monarch just when their dynasty most needed such a figure. Thus the dynamic James I succeeded the ineffectual Robert III, James VI was able to untangle the mess left by his wayward mother, and Charles II had sufficient political skill to right the ship of state overturned by his obstinate father. And now, with the politically myopic James VII and II out of the way, Jacobite eyes turned hopefully towards his son. Sadly, their gaze met with no hero. The family's dynastic good fortune had given out at last.

Physically 'James VIII', as his supporters dubbed him, was unmistakably a Stewart. Tall, thick-lipped and long-faced, he closely resembled both his father and his uncle, although he was more slender and rather less athletic than either of them. His personality was not such a propitious mix. In his dogged dullness and inclination towards depression he took after James VII and II and Charles I rather than the more flexible and worldly Charles II. He was not the Roman Catholic crusader his father had been, but his faith was quite as unshakeable and remained a major obstacle against his ever regaining his ancestors' thrones. Above all, though, he was boring. He inspired no one and some, his wife included, were driven to distraction by his lack of spark. In sum, although James would probably have made an ideal constitutional monarch, he lacked the wit, imagination and drive ever to get himself into such a position.

James's upbringing was strict and narrow. He encountered few children and grew up with little understanding of Britain or how the majority of her people lived. Ever mindful of the sins of his youth, his father raised the boy by the rule book, filling his head with inflated notions of his own importance and of the need to live a blameless life. 'Consider that you are come into the world to glorify God, not to seek your pleasure' the dying king had told the thirteen-year-old boy. The message stuck. So did other passages from the old man's last testament, such as the warning: 'Kings not being responsible for their actions, but to God only, they ought to behave themselves in every-thing'. And then there was the most dire pronouncement of all, bred of the father's obsessive inner guilt: 'Nothing is more fatal to man, and to the greatest men (to speak with a deep-bought experience) than to be given over to the unlawful love of woman'. Being of an impressionable age as well as unimaginative and dutiful by nature, James took it all to heart.

In 1701 Louis XIV had recognised the thirteen-year-old James as the rightful heir to his father's three kingdoms. When William III had heard the news he had 'gone red in the face and pulled his hat down over his eyes'. The king of France also undertook to supervise and subsidise the boy's education until he came of age. The emphasis was now on practical pursuits, such as the mastery of languages and mathematics, and the physical skills considered necessary in a king of that period: riding, shooting, dancing and fencing. James proved a willing enough pupil and became an impressive adornment at the court of the ageing Sun King. But nothing the young man saw or experi-enced ever undermined the stern precepts with which he had first been imbued.

Fenelon, who observed James at close quarters in 1709, has left us with an interesting pen-portrait of his subject:

'In a word, the King of England is generous and unselfish, unwaver-ingly reasonable and virtuous. His firmness, his equability, his self-possession and tact, his sweet and gentle seriousness, his gaiety devoid of boisterousness, must win him the favour of all the world.'

This was James at twenty-one. It seems a fair, even flattering picture. But the words are chosen carefully. Fenelon does not say that James did win everyone's favour, only that he ought to have done. That he did not is explained by the qualities Fenelon omits: wit, intelligence, human understanding and, most glaring of all, charisma. Fenelon had drawn a worthy bank manager, not a history maker.

James had several opportunities to make a significant impact on European affairs. The first came in 1708. Britain and France had been at war over the Spanish succession for six years, and although the royal navy and the brilliant generalship of John Churchill, now Duke of Marlborough, had brought the anti-French coalition unprecedented military success, the costly war was not universally popular. It was resented most deeply in Scotland. The previous year economic circumstances had forced the Scots to accept a mistrusted political union with England, fanning nationalist sentiment and reviving Jacobite aspirations. It was, therefore, to Scotland that James the Pretender (a nickname coined by his half-sister Queen Anne) looked for a bridgehead into Britain.

The plan, known to English spies from the outset, was for James to sail with 5,000 men and 28 ships to the Firth of Forth, land in Edinburgh, seize the castle and assemble an army for an invasion of England. Louis XIV gave the venture his backhanded blessing by telling James that 'the best I can wish you is that I may never see your face again'. James's sister, the sprightly Louise Marie, bade him gather in himself 'all the virtues of our ancestors' and 'conquer or die'. As it turned out, he did neither.

French administration of the expedition was incompetent and Admiral Forbin, the naval commander, unequal to the task he had been allocated. James suffered from sea-sickness and an unfortunately timed attack of measles. Having reached the Forth too late to rendezvous with Scottish Jacobites, his fleet was driven back by an English squadron under Admiral Byng then dispersed by bad weather. Displaying typical Stewart bravery, James had pleaded to be put ashore in a small boat to try to win his throne singlehanded. His request was turned down. When the battered and dispirited flotilla returned to Dunkirk in April the surviving crew and soldiers 'crept on shore... more like rats than men'.

James spent most of the remaining years of the war fighting in the French army as the 'Chevalier de Saint George'. Just as his father had thoroughly enjoyed serving under Turenne some sixty years before, so these were some of the Pretender's happiest times. He liked soldiering and was quite good at it, as long as he was carrying out orders rather than giving them. Gunfire held no terrors for him and in the rough and tumble of camp life he forgot for a while the onerous responsibilities which weighed him down during the more reflective periods of his life.

But the war could not go on for ever. Exhausted and bankrupt, Louis XIV finally made peace with the allies at Utrecht in April 1713. The treaty obliged him to accept the Hanovarian succession and compel James to leave French soil. The unemployed Chevalier became more depressed than ever. The previous year his sister had died of smallpox. The loss of his 'special ornament and joy', he wrote, was the worst of 'the many misfortunes which... we have endured'. At twenty-three he was already coming round to his father's view that life was one long series of disasters. From France 'Jamie the Rover' (no other Stewart collected such a fine catalogue of nicknames) made his miserable way to the small provincial town of Bar, in Lorraine, where the castle which had once sheltered Mary Queen of Scots was put at his disposal by the friendly duke.

James's gloomy prospects were brightened by one powerful ray of hope. After the peace of Utrecht a number of British politicians, including the great Marlborough, had gone out of their way to keep in touch with the court at Bar. Gradually their communications became more frequent, more flattering. This upsurge in interest in the king over the water had nothing whatever to do with what James said or did. Its explanation was less flattering: Queen Anne, overweight, rheumatic, gouty and erysipelatous, was dying.

* * *

Like her sister Mary, Anne did not belong to the senior line of her dynasty. But the last Stewart monarch played too important a role in shaping her family's future for her to be dismissed in a sentence or two.

Physically Anne's life was a natural disaster. At eighteen, when she married George of Denmark, she was a large, handsome woman with a shapely figure and a face which, although unmistakably Stewart, was not without a certain winsomeness. Her hands were celebrated for their beauty. Her complexion, scarred by a childhood visitation of smallpox, was less attractive. She was also desperately short-sighted, which made her screw up her face into a frown whenever anyone unfamiliar came into her presence. The effect on those who did not know her was offputting. What looks and good health the queen had enjoyed in her youth were destroyed by eighteen pregnancies, seventeen of them in the first seventeen years of married life. Her weight increased alarmingly, her skin deteriorated into an unsightly red blotchiness and she became so crippled that she could hardly walk. Most of her babies were stillborn and the survivors died young. It was a situation which would have broken many a lesser woman.

But Anne was tough. She was comforted by intense personal friendships with women and, until his death in 1708, by her pliable and adoring fat husband. Of greater consolation was her sincere Anglican faith. Yet what really seems to have kept her going, especially in her later years, was a devotion to her country. She was the first British monarch to understand and accept the position of constitutional monarch, a new role which she did much to create. It ranks as one of the Stewart monarchy's greatest gifts to the modern world. She made mistakes, of course, and on occasion she could be downright awkward: she insisted, for example, that her ministers were her own choice and she regarded them as personal servants. Nevertheless, she never forgot that parliament was the supreme body in the land and that it was her task – by no means an easy one – to help translate its often disparate wishes into effective action. To that end she refused to become unyieldingly attached to any one party; indeed, like most of her contemporaries she abhorred the very idea of party. Balance and moderation were her watchwords. She would not allow Sophia of Hanover or her son George to set foot on British soil during her lifetime, and she was even prepared to promise the Jacobites her support 'at the proper time'.

Despite the Pretender's fawning plea 'to meet me in the friendly way of composing our difference', the proper time never came. Shortly before she died Anne appointed ministers whom she knew would invite George, now elector of Hanover following Sophia's death, to wear the British crown after she was gone. As Anne had rejected her father in 1688, so she turned aside from her Catholic half-brother in 1714, on both occasions making the painful decision to put her country's welfare above that of her family. It was what being a constitutional monarch was all about. James never understood it at all.

IV

The Pretender had to move fast if he was to take the best advantage of the uncertain situation prevailing after Anne's death. The stage was bare, and if James could get onto it quickly there was just a chance that he would succeed in capturing the audience before the debut of the Elector of Hanover. The queen died on Sunday 1 August 1714. The elector, now George I, landed at Greenwich seven weeks later. 'James VII and III' disembarked at Peterhead, Scotland, on 23 December 1715. It was as classic a piece of historical unpunctuality as once could ever hope to find.

It is not fair to blame James for everything that had gone wrong. The most serious criticism that can be levelled at him is that he had not planned carefully for Anne's demise. When it came all he was able to do was issue a manifesto saying that as 'the only born Englishman now left in the royal family' he should be invited to ascend the throne, and send vague messages to the Scottish Jacobites that he would soon be among them. The reward for his capture was raised from £5,000 to £100,000. Hanovarian spies reported his every move. In vain James looked around the European powers for a backer. The winter of 1714 slipped into the spring of 1715, and still the Pretender had not moved.

James's problem was not unlike that of his uncle Charles II during his exile in the 1650s. He had supporters, but Jacobitism, as Royalism, meant different things to different people. It was a catchall phrase adopted by anyone with a social or political grievance against the Whig/Hanovarian regime. As such it embraced not only conservative academics, displaced Tories, Catholics, Nonjurors (those whose consciences had not permitted them to swear the oaths of allegiance to William and Mary) and Scottish nationalists, but social outcasts such as highwaymen and debtors as well as xenophobes who disliked being ruled by a German-speaking king. If he was to get his throne back, the Pretender somehow had to weld this rag-bag of disaffected negatives into a coherent movement, something he was never able to do.

Probably only one man had the political and military skills necessary to lead the Jacobites to success. This was James Stuart, Duke of Berwick, the illegitimate son of James II and Marlborough's sister Arabella. It is one of the sadnesses of Stewart history that most of the family talent went to James the bastard, not James the Pretender. Born in 1670 and graced with his title (harking back to the scene of Walter III's fourteenth-century triumph) in 1687, Berwick had distinguished himself on the side of the French during the War of Spanish Succession, and towards the end of Anne's reign he had worked hard for the Jacobite succession. But now, bound by his French citizenship to adhere to the terms of Utrecht and uncertain of the Pretender's abilities to plan and lead an invasion of Britain, he refused to commit himself to his half brother's cause. Indeed, when he learned of James's scheme to land in Scotland he was scornfully dismissive: 'to believe that with the Scots alone he will succeed in his enterprise has always been regarded by me as madness.' Shortly before his departure the Pretender foolishly condemned his most able supporter as 'a disobedient servant and a bastard too'.

James eventually sailed in December 1715. By this time George I's government had successfully quashed Jacobite riots in England and rounded up their ringleaders. Louis XIV was dead and the regency of the Duke of Orleans was even less keen than the old king had been to break the terms of Utrecht. But James had recently acquired the services of the talented Tory exile Henry St John, Viscount Bolingbroke, architect of the Utrecht settlement. Acting as the Jacobite Secretary of State, it was Bolingbroke who had found a 200 ton ship for his new master and sent him off into the stormy North Sea with three attendants.

Completely out of touch with 'James VIII', who was still marooned at Bar, the Earl of Mar had raised the Jacobite standard in the Scottish Highlands the previous August. Initially the rebellion had attracted considerable support, but after an indecisive battle with Hanovarian troops at Sheriffmuir on 13 November the movement had lost impetus. 'Bobbing John' Mar turned out to be an indecisive commander and ineffective leader. Unsure which way to move, he had kept his disorganised forces hanging about waiting for the arrival of their figurehead from the Continent. That autumn James had given his watchers the slip and crossed France in disguise to St Malo. Here, tired, depressed and complaining that he had 'no idea what is happening', he had wasted more precious weeks before moving north to Dunkirk dressed as a sailor and eventually embarking for Scotland.

The arrival of Jamie the Rover proved the kiss of death for the 1715 Jacobite revolt. The long awaited saviour proved as uninspiring as the weather, which was cold and grey. The situation was difficult enough already, but James made it worse by producing no clear plan of action and showing so little regard for the men about him that many started to pack up and go home. 'We saw nothing in him that looked like spirit', noted one of them bitterly. 'Our men began to despise him; some [even] asked if he could speak'.

Uncommunicative and sullen, James put the worst possible interpretation on everything that happened, observing morosely 'It is no new thing for me to be unfortunate'. He was ill, too. Never able to cope with pressure, he was laid up with attacks of a psychosomatic ague. For a few weeks he held gloomy court in the royal palace at Scone. Then, as enemy troops under the Earl of Argyll tightened the net about him, he fled north to Dundee and Aberdeen. In February he boarded the *Marie Therese* and sailed back to Flanders with a few supporters. 'Old Mr Melancholy' never set foot in Britain again.

* * *

From this time forward James's lot went from bad to worse. He fell out with Bolingbroke and never re-established his once close relationship with Berwick. His mother died of cancer in May 1718. Ejected from Lorraine, he hauled his paltry court around southern Europe from Avignon to Turin, Parma and Modena, before it finally ended up in Rome. His choice of advisors remained wretched and he became ever more depressed and withdrawn with each passing year. He came to life briefly in 1719, when Spain, then engaged in a hopeless war with Britain, France, Austria and the Dutch, decided to join the Jacobite game. The venture was even less successful than the fiasco of 1715. A small Spanish force landed on the Hebridean island of Lewis and crossed to the mainland before being compelled to surrender in the castle of Eilean Donan. The main Jacobite fleet was destroyed by a storm before it left Spanish waters.

Three weeks after hearing the fate of his Spanish armada and on the same day as British warships were pounding Eilean Donan into submission, James got married. He had wanted to take this step for some time but had never managed to find a suitable bride willing to throw in her lot with him. The longer he waited, the less good a prospect he seemed. So by 1718 he had Charles Wogan, a dashing survivor of the 1715 rebellion, combing Europe on his behalf. The bride whom Wogan eventually came up with was Clementina, the seventeen-year-old daughter of the Polish prince James Sobieski. The Pretender was pleased with the choice. By all reports Clementina was not only pretty and lively, but a devout Catholic and likely to boost the flimsy Jacobite finances with a substantial dowry. To lure the impressionable Clementina south, Wogan indulged in a little fanciful embellishment of the truth, making out his master to be a hero, an exciting soldier-king in exile who would one day come into his own and wear the crown of one of the most powerful countries in Europe. The romantic image of the Jacobites as swashbuckling adventurers was leant further credence on Clementina's journey. Keen to prevent the match, George I had his ally the Emperor of Austria detain the Polish princess at Innsbruck, before she could cross the Alps into Italy. Wogan came to the rescue, whisking her over the Brenner Pass and down to Rome, where she waited for James to arrive from Spain. A proxy wedding took place on 9 May 1719 and the real ceremony at Montefiascone four months later.

The marriage was not a success. At first James was delighted in his bright-eyed petite bride. She, on the other hand, was disappointed in her lanky, lugubrious husband almost from the moment she first set eyes on him. Neither in nor out of bed was he anything but a bore, and within a year or so the couple were squabbling openly, to the scandalous delight of all Europe and the ruin of the Jacobite cause. 'Their tempers are so very different', commented one observer, '... that tho' in the greatest trifles they are never of the same opinion, the one won't yield one inch to the other.' James withdrew deeper into himself, Clementina developed a dangerous religious mania, and they spent several years living apart. Eventually, in 1735, her health ruined by continuous fasting and nervous exhaustion, Clementina died. It seemed as if everything James touched crumbled to dust in his hands.

The Stewart dynasty was not finished yet, however, for Clementina had been a mother as well as a wife. In their less hostile moments she and James had contrived to conceive two sons. The first, born on 31 December 1720 and christened Charles Edward Louis John Casmir Sylvester Severino Maria Stuart, showed signs of possessing many of the heroic qualities his father:

> 'The Prince of Wales is one of the finest children I ever saw and daily gives remarkable instances of wit and vivacity uncommon to his age. The beauty of his person and his genteel behaviour make him the idol of the people'.

From his earliest days there was something rather special about the boy known to history as Bonnie Prince Charlie.

CHAPTER 20

'The Last of the Royal House of Stewart'

I

Deeply suspicious of the glittering ranks of the triumphant, the British have a curious tendency to find their heroes and heroines among life's failures. This is certainly the case with the Stewarts. Only two members of the family are international celebrities. The first is Mary Queen of Scots, a woman of undeniable star quality but a political disaster if ever there was one. The second is the Bonnie Prince who illuminated the European sky with comet-like brilliance for barely fourteen months, then receded into dark and ignominious ruin. He too had the ability to captivate. The world took his story to their hearts and turned him into one of the great romantic figures of history.

* * *

Charles Edward Stuart was born on the last day of January 1720. The birth was widely celebrated by Jacobites and Anglophobes throughout Europe and the prince enjoyed a few years of warm devotion from both his parents. He was strong and healthy, too; 'one can't see a finer child' noted a contemporary of the three-year-old boy. His problems began shortly afterwards. The rows between his pedantic father and highly-strung mother were soon the talk of Roman society. Eight months after the birth of Prince Henry in 1725, Clementina, perhaps suffering from post-natal depression, left her husband for the shelter of the convent of Santa Cecilia in the Trastevere.

At this distance it is perhaps unwise to speculate too positively on the effect this separation had on the development of the two boys Clementina left behind. After all, the childhoods of most Stewarts had hardly been models of domestic tranquillity and affection. Some were toughened by their early experiences, others were permanently damaged by them. All we can safely say is that in Charles's case, given his family's increasing propensity towards depression over recent generations, the childhood trauma cannot have helped his chances of developing into a balanced, secure individual. He grew to hate his father and dislike his brother, a pretty little boy favoured by Clementina and James alike. To Charles women were an enigma; although he enjoyed numerous sexual affairs (he was, after all, a Stewart), he never established an enduring loving relationship with a member of the opposite sex. For his part, Henry was terrified of ladies and became homosexual, the celibate Roman Catholic priesthood eventually providing him with a welcome refuge from the world of obligatory marriage. For whatever reason, Fate did not equip either of the last two Stewarts with qualities commensurate with the taxing historical roles demanded of them.

It was several years before Charles's shortcomings became apparent, at least to almost everyone except his pessimistic father. The prince was quick-witted, active and, above all, charming. The Italian tour he made in 1737, aged sixteen, was an outstanding success. Women doted on him, men were awed by his considerable skills as a horse rider and marksman. The only thing he could not do was swim. Almost six foot tall, he danced with the grace of a swallow and hunted like a lion. Always believing that some great task lay before him, he kept himself in tip-top physical condition, honing his robust and muscular body to the peak of fitness. The effects of heavy drinking, a habit he had developed by the early 1740s, were offset by strenuous exercise and, as far as we know, before 1746 he refrained from taking advantage of his obvious power over women.

Charles was good-looking, but a pointed chin and high forehead prevented him being heart-stoppingly so. He had the typical nose, lips and long face of his ancestors. His eyes were large and brown, his complexion ruddy, his hair reddish. The man's special attraction, however, stemmed from that indefinable animal magnetism which over the centuries had been such a marked family characteristic. As the Jacobite Murray of Broughton wrote of the prince in 1742

'[that] which shines most in him and renders him, without exception, the most surprisingly handsome person of his age, is the dignity that accompanies every gesture. There is indeed such an unspeakable majesty diffused through his whole mien.'

The Pretender, certainly jealous of his elder son's charisma, found faults where others did not. Charles was intelligent, but not in any way intellectual. His mind, like that of his great-uncle Charles II, was fast and broad-ranging without being reflective – 'a good deal thoughtless' James called him. As a youth the prince resented disciplined study and once threatened to kill a demanding tutor. Letter-writing was always distasteful to him. He had little time for religion of any persuasion. All this was a grave disappointment to his careful, pious father, who never ceased trying to inculcate Charles with some of his own more sober (literally) virtues. In his strange way James probably always loved his 'Carluccio'; but it was the love of a manufacturer for his own product rather than for an independent creation, and the manner in which he expressed his affection – endless well-intended rebukes and homilies – served only to alienate his sensitive and vulnerable son. By 1745 the breach between the two was unbridgeable.

Henry 'Duke of York' turned out to be much more a man after James's own heart. In 1729 he had written 'I am really in love with the little duke, for he is the finest child [that] can be seen'. Contemporaries agreed, and for a year or so the second son was 'the more popular of the two [brothers] in Rome'. But Henry grew from a merry, hazel-eyed child into a short, somewhat dumpy and plain adult. His mind, less sharp than Charles's, was more cunning and academic. Its classic manifestation is the incredibly tedious diary he kept in later life. As a teenager he doted on his elder brother, unsuccessfully trying to emulate him in all he did. Later he went his own way, drawing closer to his father in a partnership of self-righteous indignation against the prodigal elder son. Henry was not a particularly pleasant man but he had foresight, cunning and self control, and as a prelate in the Roman hierarchy his careful manner earned him the respect of several more worthy ecclesiastical contemporaries.

* * *

It is ironic that Charles is remembered for his association with Scotland. Since the reign of James VI and I, with the possible exception of Queen Anne, no Stewart had shown much regard for the country from which they had sprung. Although born there, Charles I had no time for the subjects who had first plunged him into civil war. Mary II had never visited her northern realm and had showed little interest in the place. James VII and II had been a stern governor of Scotland during his brother's reign but had not returned there as king. The Scottish experiences of Charles II and the Old Pretender had left them with unhappy memories of a dismal land of foul weather and uncouth citizens. And before his experiences in 1746 the 'Young Pretender' (as Charles came to be known) shared the general European view that Scotland was a remote and relatively uncivilised appendage of England, peopled for the most part, particularly in the north, by unreliable and lawless tribes. The romanticisation of Scotland, and of the Highlands in particular, began as an unlooked for result of Charles's adventures there.

Reports of smouldering Jacobitism in the Highlands reached the exiled Stewarts in the later 1730s. The War of Austrian Succession broke out in 1740 and four years later England and France were again at each other's throats. It was to England rather than Scotland that Louis XV first looked in the hope of finding a chink in the Hanovarian armour, and towards the end of 1743 he began to plan a large-scale invasion of the south-east. He was wary of involving the notoriously unsuccessful and troublesome Stewarts too closely in the preparations and demanded that they keep off French soil while France was still technically not at war with her island neighbour. The suspicion was mutual. James was afraid that the French saw the Stewarts as mere 'scarecrows', useful for frightening the Hanovarians but not real contenders for the British crown, and so he refused to let Charles leave

Rome. Itching to get involved, however, the prince escaped on his own initiative and after a perilous journey across Europe turned up at Versailles in February 1744. He never saw his father again.

The sudden arrival of the Pretender's son in France immediately put George II's government on its guard. Most leading English Jacobites were incarcerated or closely watched. It proved an unnecessary move, for spring storms so battered the French invasion fleet assembled at Dunkirk that the expedition was abandoned. Charles was furious. He felt betrayed by the very country that should, he believed, have been his keenest supporter, raging that 'a blind man could see that France was only making sport of him'. There was some truth in the accusation, since the French were indeed more concerned to defeat the English than restore the Stewarts. Understanding, quite correctly, that an invasion of England would be a terribly risky under-taking, they now wanted the Jacobites to conquer Scotland, break the Act of Union and hold the country as a sharp thorn in England's northern flank. That done, the French might have seriously reconsidered a direct assault in the south. But neither James nor Charles would be content with Scotland alone. With them it was 'tout ou rien'.

On 16 January 1707 the Scottish parliament had accepted the terms of union with England by a large majority. On hearing the result of the vote Chancellor Seafield had remarked sadly, 'Now there's ane end of ane old song'. Technically speaking, he was correct. But although its last words had been sung, the tune of Scottish nationalism was still whistled hopefully into the Highland breeze. It now carried over the sea to Charles. The prince picked it up, hummed it to himself and carefully harmonised it with his own Jacobite air. Not until December 1745, when it was too late to do anything about it, did the Scots fully realise how their melody had been exploited. Four months later both scores were torn to shreds on Culloden Field.

By the end of 1744 Charles had become obsessed with the idea of a Scottish expedition. If necessary, he said, he would make the journey with a single footman, even by canoe! His reasoning was straightforward. To take the whole of Britain he needed French support. But the French, with whom the prince squabbled endlessly, would not move until they had definite news of a substantial uprising. Since the English Jacobites waited on the French, Charles had no alternative but to start in the Highlands, where he would be able to draw on conservative-nationalist sentiment to build up a loyal following. So for purely pragmatic reasons, not through any sentimental desire to return to the country of his illustrious ancestors, Charles set his heart on Scotland. His ultimate success still depended on the French. When they failed to take advantage of his incredible early triumphs, he was doomed.

The expedition came close to collapse almost before it had started. Deprived of French backing, Charles scraped together enough funds for an invasion fleet of just two vessels, the 64-gun *Elizabeth*, carrying 700 men and plentiful arms and ammunition, and the 16-gun frigate *Doutelle*. Both ships left Belle-Isle on 22 June 1745. Before they reached Scotland the tiny armada ran into HMS *Lion*. The *Elizabeth* was so badly mauled in the ensuing fight that she had to turn back, leaving the prince to continue in the *Doutelle* with a handful of followers. On 23 July 1745 he arrived on the Hebridean island of Barra with just eleven companions.

The news of Charles's clandestine departure broke like a thunderclap in Rome and Paris. Neither James nor Louis XV gave him a chance. Nor did some of the first Highlanders with whom he made contact, and one of them had the effrontery to tell him to go home. 'I am come home' was Charles's prompt reply. It was, of course, a palpable lie. But it was a charming one, and within a few weeks of setting foot on Scottish soil the young exile's powerful magnetism had drawn around him a substantial following of devoted clansmen. Slow to react at first, the London government eventually realised just how serious the prince's threat might be. George II returned from Hanover to find the English much taken up with a new, appropriately patriotic song – 'God save great George our King' – later adapted into the National Anthem. Soldiers were ordered back from the Continent and a price of £30,000 was put on Charles's head. The prince responded by offering £30 for George II. (His scornful gesture was mistaken for meanness and the reward was later raised to match that of the Hanovarians.)

Charles's soldiers were successful in their initial skirmishes, forcing the Hanovarian regulars under General Cope to withdraw. On his rapid progress south the prince continued to make a favourable impression on almost everyone he met. His men adored him. Their only complaint was something of a compliment: Charles was so fit and strong that even sturdy Highlanders grumbled that he marched too quickly for them. So far, so good.

On 4 September Charles entered Perth, where he proclaimed his father King James VIII and III. Recruits continued to pour in. The most notable acquisition was Lord George Murray, a fifty-one-year-old veteran of both the '15 and '19 Jacobite revolts and a first-class commander. Whatever his talents as a soldier, however, Murray had too much of the Old Pretender in him for Charles's liking. The general said what he thought; the prince hated to be gainsaid. It was not long before the clashes between them had started to undermine the effectiveness of their cause.

From Perth Charles moved on south. Skirting round the stronghold at Stirling, which he could not hope to take swiftly without heavy artillery, on 17 September he entered the capital in triumph. His popularity knew no bounds. Men and women flocked to greet the man who was now becoming universally known as 'Bonnie Prince Charlie'. Nevertheless, the 2,400 strong Jacobite army was not allowed to enjoy its success for long. News came in that Cope's force was advancing towards them from Dunbar, and both Murray and Charles (seeing eye-to-eye for once) realised that if they were to retain credibility as a fighting force they had to meet and destroy the enemy in battle.

The two small armies met at Prestonpans on 20 September 1745. Murray's generalship and the ferocious fighting of the Highlanders brought Charles a great victory: against seventy-five Jacobites killed or wounded, Cope lost over 2,000 men killed, wounded or captured. The prince, who until his arrival in Scotland had no more than six hours military experience, played little part in the fighting and was horrified by the slaughter which followed his men's breakthrough. 'Make prisoners!' he yelled in an effort to stop the killing. 'Spare them, they are my father's subjects!' The outburst was not provoked by cowardice or squeamishness, but out of a genuine concern to end the suffering. Clemency and kindliness (when sober) were two further characteristics of Charles which added to his swelling popularity.

The victory at Prestonpans left the Jacobites divided. Murray argued that the army should remain in Scotland. The great fortresses at Stirling and Edinburgh still held out; several powerful clans, notably the Campbells, Rosses and Munros, were resolutely Hanovarian; and the French had not yet sent the reinforcements which Charles had promised from the day he arrived. The prince, on the other hand, was all for pressing on into England. He was sure foreign help would come any day, particularly as an envoy from Louis XV had been with the Jacobites since 14 October. It would be fatal for the rebellion to lose momentum, he argued, for its strength lay in speed and surprise. London, he concluded, was the only target worth aiming at. On 30 October the council accepted Charles's plan by a narrow vote and the following day his force of 5,000 infantry and 500 cavalry set forth in two columns. To appease Murray they took the western route into England (roughly along the modern A74/M6), not the more direct, eastern one (A1) which Charles had advocated.

Professing himself willing to 'fly through fire and water' to help his brother, Duke Henry had left for France two and a half weeks before Prestonpans. His appearance on French soil, however well-intentioned, did his family's cause more harm than good, for the twenty-year-old Henry had developed into a pious prig with few diplomatic skills. After a hopeless inter- view with the ultra-cautious Louis XV, the duke was given nominal command of the invasion force slowly assembling in the Channel ports and packed off to Dunkirk, where he remained in scandalised impotence until he heard of Charles's eventual defeat.

The progress of the Scottish army in northern England was at the same time heartening and disappointing. In bad weather they made remarkable progress, reaching Kendal by 23 November, Lancaster two days later and Derby by 4 December. No Scottish raiding force had ever been so far south before, and there was little sign of opposition. But there was no sign either of the expected reinforcements: no news of a French move and only a trickle of recruits from the countryside they passed through. From one point of view the future prospects seemed almost too good to be true. From another they were darkly ominous. At Derby, 120 miles from London, the commanders paused to take stock.

* * *

The Derby conference, held on 'Black Friday', 6 December 1745, was the turning point not only in the story of the '45 Rebellion but also in Charles's whole career. After a long and acrimonious debate the Jacobite leaders determined to overrule their prince and return home. Charles had warned them: 'You ruin, abandon and betray me if you do not march on!' and when the vote went against him he announced that henceforth he would take all decisions himself and hold no more councils.

On balance it now seems probable that the decision to withdraw was the wrong one. The Hanovarian forces were not as numerous nor as well-prepared as their enemies believed. London was in chaos. The French were at last preparing to send over substantial assistance. The Highlanders, by no means the ill-disciplined mob they are sometimes made out to be, were 'never... in higher spirits notwithstanding their long and fatiguing march'; they would have been more than a match for any troops sent against them. One more battle might have decided the issue, and there was no reason why it should not have been won by the prince. But it was not to be. The Scots were understandably more concerned with maintaining their own liberty than with restoring the king of England. Conventional military thinking, as voiced by the experienced Murray, held that it was folly to advance deep into hostile territory unaided by adequate intelligence and with several enemy strongholds intact in the rear.

The Bonnie Prince was never the same man again. He could still be magically charming and on occasion his old enthusiasm illuminated the increasingly gloomy Jacobite landscape. But his single-mindedness was gone. All too often he appeared sullen and depressed. He drank too much, slept late and, after his return to Scotland, he finally broke his self-imposed celibacy. His decline was not unlike that of a modern young media star who, after astonishing initial success, fails to cope with the pressures and inevitable subsequent reverses of his meteoric career and slides into tragic decline.

After skilfully beating off Cumberland's pursuing force, the Scots crossed the border into Scotland on 31 December, Charles's birthday. During the next three months the prince was laid low with consecutive bouts of 'flu, pneumonia and scarlet fever. It is perhaps indicative of the fragility of his personality that failure-induced stress now left him open to illness; hitherto, when things had being going well, he had enjoyed the most robust of health. It was with a young lady who nursed him through his sickness, Clementina Walkinshaw, that he had his first known affair.

With Charles temporarily sidelined, the Jacobites met with mixed success. Inverness, Stirling and Edinburgh (which had swiftly reverted to the

Hanovarians on the departure of the prince's army for England in 1745) held out against them. But the organisation of a second Scottish army of some 4,000 men and the arrival of 1,100 Irish regulars from France gave them sufficient strength to overwhelm the Hanovarians at Falkirk Muir on 17 January. Unfortunately for the Jacobites the victory was not as complete as it might have been and shortly afterwards, again to Charles's disgust, Murray decided to lead his men into the Highlands. 'Good God!' thundered the prince, 'Have I lived to see this?' The withdrawal above the Highland line, like the retreat from Derby, made some tactical sense; but from the point of view of Jacobite strategy and morale it was a disaster. The 'Butcher' Duke of Cumberland now commanded the Hanovarian forces in Scotland. Observing his enemy's retreat, he moved carefully and cautiously in pursuit. Like an experienced trapper, he was in no hurry. He would wait until the time was right, then pounce.

In the early spring of 1746 Jacobite hopes revived when they seized a number of key strategic outposts and occupied Inverness. This was not the turning of the tide, however, but a last rogue wave before the waters of Charles's fortune withdrew to the horizon and beyond. At the end of the month a ship bearing French soldiers, weapons and money ran aground and its vital cargo fell into enemy hands. On 8 April Cumberland left Aberdeen and began a slow advance to the north-west. Charles had no option but to fight. The chances of victory, never great in the first place, were reduced by a number of crucial errors. First the Jacobites missed the opportunity of gaining time by holding the line of the River Spey; when they gave battle many of their better troops were still scattered about the Highlands and took no part in the fighting. Then Charles rejected Murray's advice and chose to face the enemy on Culloden Moor, a battlefield ideally suited to Cumberland's artillery. The night before the fray the Jacobites launched an abortive night raid on the Hanovarian camp, leaving them exhausted, or even asleep when the battle began. Finally, the clans squabbled over which should have pride of place in the front line of battle. When the fighting began the MacDonalds, sulking on the left, refused to obey the order to attack.

Weary, dispirited, outnumbered and outgunned, Charles's army was cut to pieces. When it was clear that no hope remained, Charles was 'forced off the field by the people about him'. The butchery continued for hours as Cumberland's men hunted down real and suspected Jacobites and slaughtered them by the score. Over the ensuing months the whole of the Highlands was subjected to a cruel orgy of murder, rape and devastation. Within a few years the clan culture which had enabled Charles to raise an army almost overnight had been destroyed. Ever afterwards the prince gave out that he had been betrayed by his commanders – it was his way of coming to terms with the terrible guilt he felt at having led so many brave men to their deaths and triggered the annihilation of their way of life. When on the run after Culloden he was frequently tormented by nightmares, more than once crying out in his sleep: 'Oh God! Poor Scotland! Poor Scotland!'

The story of Charles's escape belongs as much to the realm of romance as history. Culloden was fought on 15 April. A fortnight later, travelling by night and resting by day, the prince had made his way to the west coast where he sailed for the Outer Hebrides. For the next six weeks, assisted by loyal islanders who showed nothing but scorn for the £30,000 reward (at least £1 million in modern terms) on their prince's head, he flitted round the Western Isles enduring the most unspeakable hardships with outstanding fortitude. The seas were thick with British ships, the islands crawling with Redcoats, militiamen and spies. For the most part he slept in the open or in smelly cattle byres. He was seasick. He was starved. He was continually beset with dysentery. He was eaten alive by midges and lice, the scars of whose feasting he carried for the remainder of his days. Yet 'meagre, ill-coloured and overrun with the scab' he was never once heard to complain.

Neither did the prince lose his celebrated charm. When crossing to Skye disguised as Flora MacDonald's Irish servant 'Betty Burke', his small boat ran into stormy weather. To keep the company in good heart Charles sang several songs to them, including the well-known royalist lyric

> '... Then look for no peace,
> For the wars will never cease
> Till the king shall enjoy his own again.'

After a while, lulled by the singing and soothed by the rocking of the boat, Flora fell asleep with her head in Charles's lap. He sat up all night watching over her like a father, covering her face with his hands lest one of the sailors should inadvertently stumble over her in the darkness. On another occasion he confessed to one of his companions:

> 'When I was in Italy, and dining at the king's table, very often the sweat would have been coming through my coat with the heat of the climate; and now that I am in a cold country, of a more piercing and trying climate, and exposed to different kinds of fatigues, I really find I agree equally with both.'

Such is the stuff of which legends are made.

But legends are at best only half truths. There was another side to Charles's behaviour at this time which boded ill for the future. He was subject to manic mood swings, from profound depression to wild euphoria. And he drank too. Whatever he could lay his hands on – brandy, wine, whisky – he consumed with the relish of a man who wanted to forget not just the dire conditions of his present existence, but the whole sorry chain of events which had brought him there.

Having made his way back to the mainland in early July, Charles skulked around the western Highlands for a further two months. Several times he came within an inch of capture. While making his way out of a Redcoat cordon on the night of 18 July he passed so close to his hunters that he was able to listen to their conversation. But his luck held. In September he heard that two French warships were looking for him along the western coast and he made his way to Loch nan Uamh. From here, the very point where he had set foot on the mainland in 1745, Bonnie Prince Charlie went aboard *Le Prince de Conti* before transferring to *L'Heureux*. At 2am on 20 September the vessels quietly raised their anchors and eased their way westwards towards the open Atlantic. The six hundred-year-old link between the Stewarts and Scotland had been finally and irrevocably severed.

III

Charles 'left France an adventurer and came back a hero.' For a few glorious, heady months he could do nothing wrong. The world was his oyster. As the story of his adventures had spread far and wide he became the most famous man in all Europe. Crowds, especially of women, swarmed to see him. Invitations poured in and every night he was the guest of honour at some special banquet or ball.

The prince's admirers waited to see what he would do next. Would he return to Scotland or would he invade England directly? Nothing seemed beyond his already legendary abilities. The political reality, however, was very different. Louis XV cooled rapidly, his government proving no keener than it had been in 1745 to invest time and money in the Jacobites. Charles grew tetchy, even downright rude. Surrounding himself with 'low people', he threw himself into an orgy of debauchery which only embarrassed his French hosts even more. He fell out with his brother Henry, blaming him for not bringing reinforcements to Scotland when they were needed. The 'sad and silly' Old Pretender, in 'great pain and anxiety' after Culloden, had been overjoyed at his son's escape; but he could not resist bombarding him with long and tedious letters of instruction. By 1747 these had become overbearingly moralistic: '... my dear child, I must tell you plainly that if you don't alter your ways, I see you lost in all respects.' This was the truth Charles did not want to hear, least of all from his father. Never an avid letter writer at the best of times, the prince contacted James even less than before; and he made no plans to visit Rome.

Henry and his father concocted a cruel revenge. After a few weeks service in the French army at the siege of Antwerp, in April 1747 Henry secretly left Paris and travelled to Rome. Here, following a pre-arranged plan, Pope Benedict XIV made him a cardinal. To show that he had received no empty title, the 'Cardinal of York' announced his intention of being ordained a priest as soon as possible.

The news smote Charles like a pile-driver. In his fury he announced that henceforth he had no brother and never wished to hear his name mentioned. Henry's move was tantamount to admitting that the Jacobite cause was lost. Never under any circumstances would the English accept as their king a Roman Catholic cardinal, and an ordained Papist priest to boot.

To Hanovarian propagandists Henry's folly was as welcome as it was unexpected; 'by putting on the Cowle', gloated Horace Walpole, Henry 'has done more to extinguish his party than would have been effected by putting to death many thousands of deluded followers.' To Charles it was 'a dagger through my heart'. The beating of that heart was now all that stood between the Stewarts and inevitable extinction.

A further blow fell the following year when, on 18 October, Louis XV made peace with Great Britain and commanded Charles to leave French territory. He refused. His father joined the struggle, writing 'I... order you, both as your father and your king, to obey without delay Louis XV's order... to leave his dominions.' Still Charles refused. Eventually he was seized in a small-scale military operation and taken via the Chateau of Vincennes to Avignon. Only two years after his triumphal return, the hero of the '45 had become a drunken liability.

* * *

From this point onwards the careers of the three remaining Stewarts – James, Charles and Henry – followed very different paths. James maintained his court of shadows at the Palazzo Muti in Rome for another eighteen years. He was a sad figure, clinging to empty ritual and hollow honours. To the Romans he was 'the king here', to distinguish him from the real 'king there'. Even in 1740 the Whig Thomas Gray had found James unattractive, having

'extremely the looks and air of an idiot, particularly when he laughs or prays... .the first [of which] he does not often, the latter continually'.

Now, gape-mouthed, vacant and stooping, he was hardly an awe-inspiring figure.

Nevertheless, though he was becoming increasingly frail, at least until 1762 the Old Pretender's mind remained reasonably acute. His thoughts often turned to his 'dearest Carluccio' whom he never saw. For long periods, along with the rest of Europe, he had no idea where his wayward son was. He wrote letters, of course, filling them with the same unconvincing mix of affection and didacticism, and occasionally Charles replied. Their cordial correspondence was generally taken up with disputes of one sort or another. In 1762, for example, James had tactlessly asked his son, 'Is it possible you would rather be a vagabond on the face of the earth than return to a Father who is all love and tenderness for you?' This was one of the letters which evoked no reply. The gap between father and son was as wide as it had ever been.

By 1765 it was obvious that James had not long to live and Cardinal Henry tried to effect a reconciliation between the dying man and his heir. Eventually Charles relented and set out for Rome on his birthday. It was too late. The Old Pretender died at 9.15 pm the following day, aged seventy-seven. The phantom reign of the uncrowned 'James III and James VIII' had lasted longer than any other British monarch.

'I am not an apostle,' James had once declared to calm the fears of English Protestants. An apostle of Rome he might not have been, but he had never ceased to be an apostle of the Divine Right of Kings. That had been more than enough to condemn his Jacobitism to the archive of history's lost causes.

* * *

By this time Cardinal Henry of York, his family money boosted by lavish funds from benefices in Spain, France and Italy, was enjoying the highly agreeable life of a distinguished Roman Catholic prelate. In 1758 he had been made titular archbishop of Corinth. Three years later, aged thirty-six, he had been enthroned as Bishop of Tusculum, a post which entitled him to reside in the splendid old palace-fortress of La Rocca in Frascati. His appointment as vice-chancellor of the Vatican in 1763 had brought with it a luxurious dwelling in the capital, the Cancellesia Palace, and he had become a familiar sight plying back and forth in one of his sixty coaches between Rome and Frascati, enveloped in a white cloud of espicopal Tuscan dust. Relations with his father had not always been cordial, particularly when the two still lived together; but once Henry had a place of his own the two had got on rather better.

Henry mellowed with age and easy living. Now that he was safe from the need to marry, his obsessive piety gave way to more formal expressions of faith. He discovered a taste for luxury, too, collecting works of art and a fine library of books. He became known as one of the region's great entertainers, holding feasts at Frascati which were the talking point of Roman society. On one occasion Henry's lavishness almost killed him. The incident occurred when he crammed so many guests into the dining hall at La Rocca that the ancient timbers supporting the floor gave way, depositing everyone into the stables below. One man was killed and the cardinal was saved from a similar fate by landing on the roof of his own coach. Nothing daunted, Henry had the entire palace rebuilt at his own expense. It survived much as he left it until destroyed by bombs during the Second World War.

To be fair to Henry, it should also be recorded that he used his wealth for charitable purposes, earning a beneficent reputation for his spending on religious foundations and the poor of his diocese. When, after many tribulations, he returned to Rome in 1800 he was warmly received by the populace not as a cardinal or a king but as the 'Protector of the Poor'. But perhaps he needed to buy favour in this way, for he had little of his ancestors' natural charm. Pope Benedict XIV once remarked that if all the Stewarts were as boring as Henry, he was not surprised the English had driven them out.

As a young man Henry had been told by the Duke of Richelieu: 'You may perhaps gain the Kingdom of Heaven by your prayers, but never the Kingdom of Great Britain'. Henry knew this to be true. While never renouncing his family's theoretical claim to the British crown, he was too attached to the Roman church and his comfortable lifestyle to do anything practical about it. All he wanted was a quiet and peaceful life and, by and large, that is what he got. For many years the only cloud on his otherwise uncluttered horizon was the increasingly embarrassing behaviour of his infuriating brother and what Henry termed his 'nasty bottle'.

* * *

After his expulsion from France Charles fell into new depths of depression and debauchery. To his father's intense disappointment he refused to contemplate marriage until the restoration of the Stewarts. But that did not stop him from indulging in a number of tempestuous affairs, all of which ended unhappily. First he fell in love with one of his cousins, Louise de Bouillon, a sexy young rebel whose husband was away in the army. Then came Madame de Talmont, an experienced woman in her forties who hoped for more emotional commitment from the prince than he was able or willing to give. The couple finally broke off their relationship when Charles's drunken behaviour degenerated into violence. Interspersed between these more serious relationships were several casual couplings whose details have not been recorded.

By this time Charles was an international gypsy, travelling about the Continent in various disguises and under a number of assumed names. In 1750, believing George II to be on the point of death, he even smuggled himself over to London and secretly abjured Roman Catholicism in favour of the Anglican church. But the king did not die and Charles found English Jacobites unwilling to stir themselves on behalf of a volatile and overweight alien, whatever his reputation. After a stay of only two weeks the prince was back in France. His religious conversion had been about as convincing as his periodic promises to give up drinking. Over the next three years he worked intermittently on a hare-brained scheme to assassinate the 'King of Hanover' and take over London. Hardly surprisingly, the plot was uncovered by English spies and came to nothing.

Meanwhile in 1752 Charles had for some reason asked his old amour Clementina Walkinshaw to come and be his official mistress. It was a strange request, for he had not seen the woman for six years and no longer cared much for her. Nevertheless, Clementina answered the call and stayed with her prince, despite his moodiness and drink-inspired cruelty, for the next eight years. In 1753 they had a daughter, Charlotte, of whom Charles became obsessively fond. When Clementina could stand her partner's impossible behaviour no longer and moved out, taking her daughter with her, Charles broke down completely. His pain was made even harder to bear when he learned that Charlotte and Clementina had been sheltered by his father.

The flight of his mistress and daughter coincided with a humiliating time for Charles politically. Two years after the outbreak of the Seven Years War in 1756, the French had suggested that he might consider another Scottish adventure. Charles would not hear of the idea. Not only did he mistrust Louis XV, but nothing on earth would persuade him to return to the country where he had been so humiliated. There was another, deeper motive for his refusal: unacknowledged guilt at the terrible suffering he had brought upon 'poor Scotland' the last time he had been there. He simply could not face a reunion with those wretched clansmen. As a consequence, when the French planned to invade Britain in 1759 the Stewarts were given no part in the operation. It was just as well, for Louis's fleet was destroyed by Admiral Hawke at Quiberon Bay before it set out.

* * *

Over the next decade Charles deteriorated rapidly. Until 1765 he remained in drunken isolation at Bouillon. His mood swings became more pronounced, his drinking more frenetic. Following the death of his father he lived in Rome under the name of Baron Renfrew (a title which harked back to the Stewarts' first Scottish estates), trying in vain to persuade the pope to recognise him as Charles III. By the age of fifty the Bonnie Prince had been replaced by a swollen-legged, stooping man with a 'heavy and sleepy' expression on a face 'bloated and red' with alcohol. His whole demeanour was 'melancholic [and] mortified'. In this condition he at last decided that it was time he married, and after much searching a suitable bride was eventually found for him. In many ways Louise of Stolberg was more than Charles had dared hope for, and certainly more than he deserved. She was an eighteen-year-old, blue-eyed princess of good looks, charm and considerable intelligence. The marriage was celebrated at Macerata on 17 April 1772.

For a while life with Louise brought out the best in Charles. He laid off the bottle and rediscovered some of his old vivacity. There were even moments when he asked himself why he had waited so long before marrying. Louise, unfortunately, did not share her husband's euphoria. Even though she had married for money and status, she still harboured hopes of more romantic pleasures from the relationship. Alas! The girl found Charles pathetically disappointing as a lover and as a companion. While she grew bored and flirtatious, the prince reverted to his old ways, downing six bottles of Cyprus wine a day. His legs swelled alarmingly and grew pusy. By 1777 he had become physically abusive towards his wife, barricading her in her bedroom and demanding that she participate in sordid sexual deviations. Three years later, in love with a dashing young poet of the Byronic variety and revolted by the beatings and grotesque gropings of a suppurating husband whom she regarded as merely 'an old walking relic', she ran away to a nunnery. Unaware of the existence of the poet, partly out of Christian charity and partly to spite his brother, Cardinal Henry granted her a pension. Charles, hypertensive at the best of times, almost burst with rage: 'It is not possible that such a man was a brother!'

Quite why Charles survived for so long remains something of a mystery. His constitution must have been remarkable. In 1783 he lay insensible for three days. His memory went, his lungs clogged, one of his legs blew up to half the size of his body, excruciatingly painful haemorrhoids made movement a misery, but still he clung to life. The one bright light in his sodden, semi-conscious existence was his daughter Charlotte, who returned to nurse him in 1784. A few months after her reappearance she used her charm, inherited from her father along with her rather plain appearance, to effect a reconciliation between the last two Stewarts. Once again Henry – never the brightest of men – had been deceived by feminine wiles. Believing Charlotte to be as pure as the driven snow (the only sort of woman with whom he felt comfortable), he had allowed himself to be persuaded that it was his duty to make peace with Charles before he died. The cardinal might not have been so keen on the idea had he known that for many years Charlotte had been the mistress of the Archbishop of Cambrai and had born him three children.

By the end of his life Bonnie Prince Charlie, the Young Pretender, was neither bonnie nor young nor, really, a pretender. Even he had come to realise that the Jacobite cause was finished and he spent his final two years in Rome, where he had been transferred in 1785, as the Count of Albany. When he eventually passed away in his daughter's arms at 9am on 30 January 1788, 'Charles III' had long since predeceased him. The end of the dynasty was nigh.

IV

As we have seen, Cardinal Henry had never been much of a Jacobite. He had done his bit in 1745 by going to France and trying to persuade Louis XV to aid his beleaguered brother, but thereafter his heart had not really been with the cause. In 1784 he had issued a memorial stating that 'We have no intention of ever renouncing... [Our] right of succession and fealty', and after Charles's death he changed his title from 'Cardinal Duke of York' to 'Cardinal called Duke of York', implying that 'Duke of York' was now an incognito. He also insisted on his servants calling him 'Your Majesty' and occasionally he touched for the King's Evil. Yet really these were little more than token gestures. His position was best expressed in the medal he had struck in 1788. One side bore the inscription 'Henricius Nonus Magnae Britanniae Rex' (Henry the Ninth King of Great Britain); but the caveat on the obverse was equally important: 'Non Desideriis Hominum, Sed Voluntate Dei' (Not in the Eyes of Man, but of God). It was a nice compromise which satisfied most parties. In English eyes the last of the Stewarts had become more of a tourist attraction than a threat.

Had he been born at any other time the cardinal would no doubt have spent the remainder of his days in Tuscan tranquillity, as he said he would do in 1792 when the pope formally recognised George III. But the demise of his brother Charles had marked the end of an era in more ways than one. The following year saw the outbreak of the French Revolution and Europe thrown into unprecedented turmoil. Henry was unavoidably caught up in the storm, parting with considerable wealth to help Pope Pius VI pay his tribute to Napoleon I in 1796, and then narrowly escaping with his life when French troops sacked his diocese. Accompanied by two servants, the 'infirm and destitute' cardinal fled south to Naples. From here he crossed in a small ship to Messina. There is no evidence for the story that about this time he was entertained to dinner aboard HMS *Viscount* by Admiral Nelson.

In 1799 Henry made his way via Calabria and Corfu to Venice. His life was in ruins. Many believed he was dead. Then, just when it seemed as if he would perish in impecunious exile, he received help from a most unexpected source. His case was taken up by Sir John Hippisley, MP, a friend whom he had got to know in Rome some years before. Through Cardinal Borgia, Sir John learned of Henry's plight and brought it to the attention of the English public. 'It is greatly afflicting', he pointed out, 'to see so great a personage, the last descendant of his Royal House, reduced to such distressed circumstances...'. *The Times* joined in, noting that 'the Cardinal of York' was 'exposed to the shafts of adversity at a period of life when least able to struggle with misfortune'. Unaware that the British government owed the Stewarts £1.5 million from an unpaid jointure of Mary of Modena's, George III kindly allowed Henry an annual pension of £4,000. 'I am', wrote Henry when he heard of the gesture, 'in reality at a loss to express in writing all the sentiments of my heart'. So the last of the Stewarts ended his days in comparative comfort, supported by the regime his family had striven so hard to overthrow. No wonder Henry found it difficult to put his thoughts into writing.

White-haired and saintly-looking (rather like the first Stewart king, Robert II), the cardinal survived to the age of eighty-three. He breathed his last on 13 July 1807. In theory the Stewart claim lived on in the person of his heir Charles Emmanuel, King of Sardinia, senior descendant of Charles II's beloved sister 'Minette'. In reality, however, the last sad note of a very old song had finally died away.

* * *

The Stewarts might have been dead, but they were by no means forgotten. Even during Henry's lifetime the romantic imagination was rehabilitating the Scottish Highlands and endowing those who had peopled it with virtues they would never have recognised in themselves. Shortly afterwards, fired by the pen of Sir Walter Scott, all Scottish history was receiving similar treatment. The Prince Regent was keen to leap aboard the fashionable bandwagon and in 1819 he commissioned Canova to design a Stewart monument for the Chapel of the Virgin in St Peter's, Rome.

Two thirds of the way up a broad tapering pillar of Italian marble the busts of the Old Pretender and his two sons are finely carved in half-relief. The inscription reads: 'Regiae Stirpis Stvardiae Postremis' – 'The Last of the Royal House of Stewart'. Below, guarded by two sorrowing angels, stands a broad portal. Its doors are shut tight, representing the end of a story. Even as he worked, however, Canova knew that his imagery was only partially correct. Whatever the words on the monument say, we will never hear the last of the Stewarts. Irrepressible in life, long after their mortal remains have crumbled to dust the remarkable family lives on in the imaginations of all who are fascinated by the extraordinary piece of work that is man.

The Stewart Dynasty

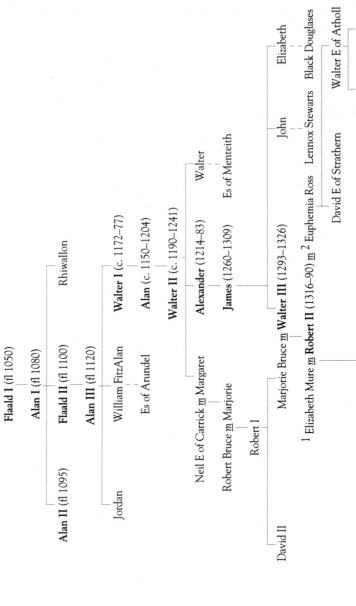

Flaald I (fl 1050)

Alan I (fl 1080)

Rhiwallon

Alan II (fl 1095)

Flaald II (fl 1100)

Alan III (fl 1120)

Jordan

William FitzAlan

Es of Arundel

Walter I (c. 1172–77)

Alan (c. 1150–1204)

Walter II (c. 1190–1241)

Neil E of Carrick m Margaret

Alexander (1214–83)

Walter

Robert Bruce m Marjorie

James (1260–1309)

Es of Menteith

Robert I

Marjorie Bruce m Walter III (1293–1326)

John

Elizabeth

David II

1 Elizabeth Mure m Robert II (1316–90) m 2 Euphemia Ross

Lennox Stewarts

Black Douglases

David E of Strathern

Walter E of Atholl

David   Alexander

Robert D of Albany

John E of Buchan

Alexander E of Buchan

David D of Rothesay

Robert III (John) (1337–1406)

Margaret m Archibald 4th E of Douglas

Euphemia m Sir Patrick Graham

Malise Graham

Archibald 5th E of Douglas m Euphemia Graham

Euphemia

Es of Douglas

James I (1394–1437)

James II (1430–60)

Mary m Ld Hamilton

James E of Arran

John E of Mar

Elizabeth

John E of Lennox

James E of Arran

Murdoch D of Albany

Robert

James

Walter

Alexander

James D of Ross

John E of Mar

James V (1512–42)

James III (1452–88)

Alexander D of Albany

John D of Albany

Margaret Douglas m Matthew E of Lennox

Charles E of Lennox

Arabella

James E of Arran

John M of Hamilton

Elizabeth m Elector Palatine

Sophia m Elector of Hanover

George I

Hanoverians

James IV (1473–1513) m Margaret Tudor m Archibald E of Angus

Mary Q of Scots (1542–87) m Henry Ld Darnley

James VI & I (1566–1625)

Anne Hyde m **James VII & II** (1633–1701) m Mary of Modena

Anne (1665–1714)

James Old Pretender (1688–1766)

Cardinal Henry (1725–1807)

Charles I (1600–49)

Charles II (1630–85)

William II & II (1650–1702) m **Mary** (1662–94)

Charles Young Pretender (1720–88)

William of Orange m Mary

A Brief Stewart Gazetteer

Continental Europe
> Dol-de-Bretagne
> Palazzo Muti, Rome
> St Germain, Castle
> Stewart Memorial, St Peter's, Rome

Scotland
> Bannockburn Battlefield
> Culloden Battlefield
> Doune Castle
> Dundonald Castle
> Edinburgh Castle
> Falkland Palace
> Holyroodhouse, Edinburgh
> Huntingtower Castle
> Largs
> Linlithgow Palace
> Loch Leven Castle
> Paisley Abbey
> Rothesay Castle
> St Andrews, Castle and Cathedral
> Scottish National Portrait Gallery, Edinburgh
> Stirling Castle

England
> Berwick
> Boscobel House
> Carisbrook Castle
> Clun
> Edgehill Battlefield
> Flodden Battlefield
> Fotheringay Castle
> Hampton Court
> Naseby Battlefield
> National Portrait Gallery, London
> Westminster Hall
> Whitehall, Banqueting House

The Stewart Dynasty

DAPIFERS OF DOL

Flaald I

fl. 1050 Dapifer (cup-bearer) of Dol, Brittany; earliest known member of the dynasty.

Alan I

fl. 1080

Alan II

fl. 1095 Died on 1st crusade.

Flaald II

fl. 1100 Follower of Henry I; first member of the dynasty known to have travelled to Britain.

Alan III

fl. 1120 m Avelina de Hesdin. Lord of Clun & Oswestry; favoured by Henry I; substantial English landowner.

STEWARDS OF SCOTLAND

Walter I

c. 1112–77 m Eschina. 3rd son of Alan III; c. 1136 settled in Scotland of David I; first hereditary steward of Scotland; given extensive lands around Renfrew (on which founded Paisley Abbey), in Lothian & Berwickshire.

Alan

c. 1150–1204 m (i) Eva (ii) Alesta. 2nd steward; crusader; acquired Rothesay Castle; built up Stewart connection in western Scotland.

Walter II

c. 1190–1241 m Beatrice of Mar. 3rd steward; during lifetime surname Stewart first used; Justiciar of Scotia.

Alexander

1214–83 m Jean of Bute. 'Alexander of Dundonald'; 4th steward; commanded victorious Scottish forces at Battle of Largs, 1263.

James

c. 1260–1309 m Egida de Burgh. 5th steward; steered cautious path through turmoil of Edward I's attempt to seize Scotland.

Walter III

c. 1293–1326 m (i) Marjory Bruce. 6th steward; military hero; auspicious marriage to daughter of Robert I; defended Berwick for father-in-law against Edward II.

MONARCHS OF SCOTLAND

Robert II
1316–90 m (i) Elizabeth Mure (ii) Euphemia Ross. 7th steward; regent during absences of David II; king of Scotland 1371; too infirm in body & mind to rule with much success.

Robert III
c. 1337–1406 m Annabella Drummond. Baptised John but adopted name Robert on accession; capacity to rule severely marred by depression & debilitating injury; latterly power passed to eldest son & brother.

James I
1394–1437 m Joan Beaufort. Captured on way to France, 1406; held in England until 1424; returned to rule Scotland with severity & acquisitiveness until assassinated at Perth.

James II
1430–60 m Mary of Gueldres. 'James of the Fiery Face'; stormy minority; ruthless; overthrew Black Douglases by 1455; killed by exploding canon at siege of Roxburgh Castle.

James III
1452–88 m Margaret of Denmark. Another stormy minority; reign of civil disquiet (imprisoned 1482); killed by unknown hand after Battle of Sauchieburn.

James IV
1473–1513 m Margaret Tudor. 'James of the Iron Belt'; vigorous & competent; spectacular reign marked by advances in education, arts & enforcement of law & order; ended in Scottish tragedy of Flodden Field after king had joined France in war with England.

James V
1512–42 m (i) Madeleine of France (ii) Mary of Guise. Long minority; intelligent, capricious, depressive; reign marked by Scotland's adherence to Roman Catholicism & ruthless repression of troublemakers.

Mary Queen of Scots
1542–87 m (i) Francis II of France (ii) Henry, Lord Darnley (iii) James, Earl of Bothwell. Raised & educated in France, 1548–61; disastrous 6-year reign ended with rebellion & imprisonment; fled to England & eventual execution.

MONARCHS OF SCOTLAND AND ENGLAND

James VI & I
1566–1625 m Anne of Denmark. 'Rex Pacificus'; intelligent & politi-

cally astute; growing influence on government after 1585 led to healing of religious divides & extension of royal authority. Acceded to English throne, 1603; spent most time there & managed different political system with some skill.

Charles I

1600–49 m Henrietta Maria. Brave, narrow-minded & politically inept; heavy responsibility for anti-government violence in Scotland & England which led to rebellion & civil war; defeated & executed.

Charles II

1630–85 m Catherine of Braganza. 'The Merry Monarch'; intelligent, idle, self-centred; exile and military failure in early life; restored to throne 1660; pragmatic survival policy followed with questionable competence; no legitimate offspring.

James VII & II

1633–1701 m (i) Anne Hyde (ii) Mary of Modena. Brother of Charles II; passionate convert to Roman Catholicism; tactless policies cost him thrones after a 3-year reign (1688/9); final years in French exile.

Mary II and William II & III

Mary (1662–94) dull Protestant elder daughter of James VII & II; 1677 married humourless cousin William of Orange (1650–1702); childless; 1688 William invited to England by opponents of father-in-law – Glorious Revolution; joint monarchs of England and Scotland; civil list & war with France.

Anne

1665–1714 m George of Denmark. Last Stewart monarch; second daughter of James VII & II; deceptively close grasp on political reality; instrumental in securing succession for German Protestant descendants of James VI & I rather than exiled Catholic Old Pretender.

PRETENDERS

'James VIII', The Old Pretender

1688–1766 m Clementina Sobieski. 'Warming pan baby' born to Mary of Modena & James VII & II; exiled, depressive, lugubrious; uninspiring Jacobite leader; after failure of 1715 rebellion lived mostly in Rome.

'Charles III', The Young Pretender

1720–88 m Louise of Stolberg. 'Bonnie Prince Charlie'; few months of glory during & after the 1745 Jacobite rebellion; thereafter declined from European hero to depressed alcoholic & left political stage.

'Henry IX', Cardinal

1725–1807 Last of direct Stewart line; bishop of Frascati; no serious claim to the British thrones; spent most of life in Italy; died in receipt of Hanovarian charity.

Bibliography

Akrigg, G.P.V., (ed.), *The Letters of King James VI and I*, 1984.

Amours, F.J., (ed.), A. *Wyntoun, 'Orygynale Cronykil of Scotland'*, 1903-14.

Anderson, A.O., (ed.), *Early Sources of Scottish History 500-1286*, 1922.

——, (ed.), *Scottish Annals from English Chroniclers*, 1908.

——, and Anderson, M.O., (eds), *The Chronicle of Melrose*,1936.

Anderson, M.O., *A Scottish Chronicle Known as the Chronicle of Holyrood*, 1938.

Ashley, M., *Charles II*, 1971.

Aylmer, G., *The King's Servants*, 1961.

Balfour Paul, J., *Scots Peerage*, 1904-14.

Balfour-Melville, E.M.W., *James I, King of Scots*, 1936.

Barrow, G.W.S., *The Acts of Malcolm IV*, 1960.

——, *The Anglo-Norman Era in Scottish History*, 1980.

——, *David I of Scotland (1124-1153): The Balance of New and Old*, 1984.

——, *Feudal Britain: The Completion of the Medieval Kingdoms, 1066-1314*, 1956.

——, *The Kingdom of the Scots*, 1973.

——, *Kingship and Unity: Scotland 1000-1306*, 1981.

——, *Robert Bruce and the Community of the Realm of Scotland*, 1988.

——, and Scott, W.W., *Acts of William I, King of Scots 1165-1214*, 1971.

Batho, E.C., and Husbands, H.W., (eds), *Hector Boece, 'History'*, 1905.

Baxter, S., *William III*, 1966.

Bingham, C., *James V, King of Scots*, 1971.

——, *The Making of a King: The Early Years of James VI and I*, 1968.

——, *The Stewart Kingdom of Scotland 1371-1603*, 1974.

Brown, K.M., *Blood Feud in Scotland 1573-1625*, 1986.

Bruce, J., *The Letters of Queen Elizabeth and James VI of Scotland*, 1849.

Bryant, A., *The Letters, Speeches and Declarations of King Charles II*, 1935.

Buchanan, P., *Margaret Tudor, Queen of Scots*, 1985.

Burnet, G., *A History of My Own Time*, 1897.

Calendar of State Papers Relating to Scotland and Mary, Queen of Scots, 1898-1965.

Carlton, C., *Charles the First: The Personal Monarch*, 1984.

Chambers, R., *Biographical Dictionary of Eminent Scotsmen*, 1868-70.

——, *Domestic Annals of Scotland from the Reformation to the Revolution*, 1859.

Childs, J., *The Army, James II and the Glorious Revolution*, 1980.

Clarendon, Hyde, E., Earl of, *History of the Rebellion*, 1888.

Collinson, P., *The English Captivity of Mary Queen of Scots*, 1987.

Cope, E.S., *Politics Without Parliaments 1629-1640*, 1987.

Coward, B., *The Stuart Age*, 1978.

Cust, R., *The Forced Loan and English Politics, 1626-1628*, 1987.

Daiches, D., *Charles Edward Stuart*, 1973.

Dickinson, W.C., Donaldson, G., and Milne, I.A., (eds), *Source Book of Scottish History*, 1958.

Donaldson, A., *Who's Who in Scottish History*, 1973.

Donaldson, G., *All the Queen's Men: Power and Politics in Mary Stewart's Scotland*, 1983.

——, *Scotland: James V to James VII*, 1989.

——, *Scottish Kings*, 1967.

——, and Morpeth, R., *Dictionary of Scottish History*, 1977.

Donnachie, I., and Hewitt, G., *Companion to Scottish* History, 1989.

Douglas, A.A.H. (ed.) *John Barbour, 'The Bruce'*, 1964.

Dunbar, A.H., *Scottish Kings: A Revised Chronology of Scottish History 1005-1625*, 1906.

Duncan, A.A.M., *Acts of Robert I, King of Scots 1306-1329*, 1988.

——, *James I: King of Scots, 1424-1437*, 1984.

——, *Scotland: The Making of the Kingdom*, 1989.

Dunlop, I., *Life and Times of James Kennedy, Bishop of St Andrews*, 1950.

Ferguson, J.P.S., *Scottish Family Histories*, 1960.

Ferguson, W., *Scotland's Relations with England*, 1977.

Fergusson, J., *Alexander III, King of Scotland*, 1937.

Fletcher, A., *The Outbreak of the English Civil War*, 1979.

Fothergill, B., *The Cardinal King*, 1958.

Fraser, A., *King Charles II*, 1979.

——, *Mary Queen of Scots*, 1969.

Gardiner, S.R., *History of England...1603-42*, 1883-4.

——, *History of the Great Civil War*, 1893.

Gibson, J.S., *Playing the Scottish Card: The Franco-Jacobite Invasion of 1708*, 1988.

Goodall, W., (ed.) *'Scotichronicon', The Works of John of Fordun and Walter Bower*, 1759.

Grant, A., *Independence and Nationhood, Scotland 1306-1469*, 1984.

Green, M.A.E., *The Letters of Henrietta Maria*, 1853.

Gregg, P., *King Charles I*, 1981.

——, *Queen Anne*, 1980.

Handover, P.M., *Arabella Stuart*, 1957.

Hannay, R.K., (ed.), *Letters of James IV*, 1953.

——, and Hay, D., (eds), *Letters of James V*, 1954.

Henderson, T.F., *The Royal Stewarts*, 1914.

Hibbard, C.M., *Charles I and the Popish Plot*, 1983.

Hirst, D., *Authority and Conflict England 1603-1658*, 1986.

Hulme Brown, P., (ed.), *Early Travellers in Scotland*, 1891.

Hutton, R., *Charles II*, 1989.

——, *The Restoration*, 1985.

Jones, J.R., *Charles II, Royal Politician*, 1987.

——, (ed.), *The Restored Monarchy, 1660-88*, 1979.

Kenyon, J.P., *The Stuarts*, 1986.

Kybett, S.M., *Bonnie Prince Charlie*, 1988.

Labunoff, Prince, (ed.), *Lettres et Memoires de Marie Reine d'Ecosse*, 1844.

Lee, M., *Government by Pen: Scotland Under James VI and I*, 1980.

——, *Great Britain's Solomon; James VI and I in His Three Kingdoms*, 1990.

——, *The Road to Revolution: Scotland Under Charles I, 1625-37*, 1985.

Lenman, B., *The Jacobite Risings in Britain 1687-1746*, 1980.

Levack, B.P., *The Formation of the British State: England, Scotland and the Union 1603-1707*, 1987.

Lockyer, R., *Buckingham*, 1981.

Lynch, M., (ed.), *Mary Stewart Queen in Three Kingdoms*, 1988.

Macdougall, N., *James III, A Political Study*, 1982.

——, *James IV*, 1989.

Mackay, A.J.G., (ed.), *John Major, 'History of Greater Britain'*, 1892.

——, (ed.) *Robert Lindsay of Pitscottie, 'Historie and Cronicles of Scotland, 1437-1575'*, 1899-1911.

Mackenzie, A.M., *The Rise of the Stewarts*, 1935.

Mackie, R.L., *James IV of Scotland*, 1958.

Madan, F., (ed.), *The Stuart Papers*, 1889.

Marshall, R.K., *Mary of Guise*, 1977.

Mason, R.A., (ed.), *Scotland and England 1286-1815*, 1987.

Mathew, D., *James I*, 1967.

McGladdery, C., *James II*, 1990.

McIlwain, C.H., *Political Works of James I*, 1918.

McLynn, F., *Charles Edward Stuart*, 1988.

——, *France and the Jacobite Rising of 1745*, 1981.

——, *The Jacobite Army in England*, 1983.

——, *The Jacobites*, 1985.

McNeill, P., and Nicholson, R., (eds), *Historical Atlas of Scotland c.400 - c.1600*, 1975.

Miller, J., *James II*, 1978.

Miller, P., *James [The Old Pretender]*, 1971.

Mitchison, R., *Lordship to Patronage: Scotland 1603-1746*, 1984.

Monod, P.K., *Jacobitism and the English People, 1688-1788*, 1989.

Moysie, D., *Memoirs of the Affairs of Scotland, 1577-1603*, 1830.

Nicholson, R., *Edward III and the Scots*, 1965.

——, *Scotland in the Later Middle Ages*, 1989.

Ogg, D., *England in the reign of Charles II*, 1956.

——, *England in the Reigns of James II and William III*, 1955.

Ollard, R., *The Escape of Charles II*, 1986.

——, *The Image of the King: Charles I and Charles II*, 1979.

Parry, G., *The Golden Age Restor'd: The Culture of the Stuart Court*, 1981.

Petrie, C., *The Letters, Speeches and Proclamations of King Charles I*, 1935.

Reeve, J.L., *Charles I and the Road to Personal Rule*, 1989.

Reid, N.H., (ed.), *Scotland in the Reign of Alexander III 1249-1286*, 1990.

Riley, J.P.W., *King William and the Scottish Politicians*, 1979.

——, *The Union of England and Scotland*, 1978.

Ritchie, R.I.G., *The Normans in Scotland*, 1954.

Round, J.H., *Studies in Peerage and Family History*, 1901.

Russell, C., (ed.), *The Origins of the English Civil War*, 1973.

Sanderson, M., *Cardinal of Scotland*, 1986.

Scott, R.McN., *Robert the Bruce*, 1982.

Seton, W.W., *Relations of Henry, Cardinal of York, with the British Government*, 1920.

——, *Some Unpublished Letters of Henry, Cardinal of York*, 1919.

Shire, M., *Song, Dance and Poetry of the Court of Scotland Under James VI*, 1969.

Skeet, F.A.J., *Charlotte Stuart, Duchess of Albany*, 1932.

Skene, W.F., (ed.), *John Fordun, 'Chronica Gentis Scotorum'*, trans. F.J.H. Skene, 1872-9.

Smith, A.G.R., (ed.), *The Reign of James VI and I*, 1973.

Smuts, R.M., *Court Culture and the Origins of a Royalist Tradition in Early Stuart England*, 1987.

Sommerville, J.P., *Politics and Ideology in England, 1603-40*, 1986.

Speck, W.A., *Reluctant Revolutionaries: Englishmen and the Revolution of 1688*, 1988.

Starkey, D., (ed.), *The English Court*, 1987.

Stenton, F., *The First Century of English Feudalism 1066-1166*, 1961.

Stevenson, D., *Revolution and Counter-revolution in Scotland 1644-1651*, 1977.

——, *The Scottish Revolution*, 1973.

Stevenson, J., (ed.), *Chronicles of John and Richard of Hexham*, 1856.

——, (ed.), *Chronicle of Lannercost*, trans. Sir H.E. Maxwell, 1839.

——, (ed.), *Life and Death of King James I of Scotland*, 1838.

——, (ed.), *William of Malmsbury, 'History of the Kings of England and His Own Times'*, trans. J. Sharpe, 1854.

Strickland, A., *Lives of the Queens of Scotland*, 1850-8.

Stringer, K.J., *Earl David of Huntingdon*, 1985.

——, (ed.), *Essays on the Nobility of Medieval Scotland*, 1985.

——, *Story of the Stewarts*, The Stewart Society, 1901.

Strong, R., *Van Dyck: Charles I on Horseback*, 1972.

Stuart, A., *A Genealogical History of the Stuarts*, 1790.

Stuart, M., and Paul, J.B., *Scottish Family History*, 1929.

Stuart, M.W., *The Scot Who Was a Frenchman*, 1940.

Tayler, A., and H., (eds), *The Stuart Papers at Windsor*, 1939.

Tayler, H., *Jacobite Epilogue*, 1941.

Thomson, T., (ed.), *John Lesley, 'History of Scotland, 1437-1561'*, 1918.

Thornton, P.M., *The Stuart Dynasty*, 1890.

Tomlinson, H., (ed.), *Before the English Civil War*, 1983.

Turner, F.C., *James II*, 1948.

Vaughan, H.M., *The Last of the Royal Stuarts*, 1906.

——, *The Last Stuart Queen*, 1910.

Watt, D.E.R., (ed.), *Walter Bower, 'Scotichronicon'*, 1987 onward.

Webster, B., (ed.), *Acts of David II, King of Scots*, 1982.

Wedgewood, C.V., *The King's Peace*, 1955.

——, *The King's War*, 1959.

——, *The Trial of Charles I*, 1964.

Williams, R.F., *The Court and Times of James I*, 1849.

——, *The Court and Times of Charles I*, 1849.

Willson, D.H., *King James VI and I*, 1956.

Wood, M., (ed.), *The Flodden Papers*, 1933.

Wooton, D., (ed.), *Divine Right and Democracy*, 1986.

Wormald, J., *Court, Kirk, and Community: Scotland 1470-1625*, 1981.

——, *Lords and Men in Scotland: Bonds of Manurent, 1442-1603*, 1985.

——, *Mary Queen of Scots. A Study in Failure*, 1988.

Index

Other Titles by Stewart Ross

MONARCHS OF SCOTLAND

The intriguing story of the Kings and Queens of the independent nation of Scotland, from Kenneth McAlpin to Queen Anne, and the Key role they played in the creation and preservation of the scottish Kingdom. Accessible, comprehensive and entertaining, this is an indispensable companion for lovers of Scottish Heritage.

£14.95 hb   ISBN 0 948403 22 5   192pp
£7.95 pb   ISBN 0 948403 38 1   192pp

SCOTTISH CASTLES

The grandeur and beauty of Scotland's castles, which number over a thousand, is reflected in this authoritive selection based on a variety of themes. Romantic retreats, lochside castles and baronial strongholds, all of which are open to the public, form part of the definitive and lively companion which illuminates the turbulent history of both the structures and their inhabitants. Also including practical information on opening times, access and entrance charges.

£14.95 hb   ISBN 0 948403 36 5   192pp
£7.95 pb   ISBN 0 948403 37 3   192pp

ANCIENT SCOTLAND

Highly illustrated, thematic chapters present the history of Scotland's ancient races and that of the relics of their civilisations. In its sweeping and broadly chronological survey, this invaluable reference book provides detailed descriptions of distant landscapes and their inhabitants.

£16.00 hb   ISBN 0 948403 54 3   192pp